Exploring a Heritage

CHURCH OF SWEDEN
Research Series

Göran Gunner, editor
Vulnerability, Churches, and HIV (2009)

Kajsa Ahlstrand and Göran Gunner, editors
Non-Muslims in Muslim Majority Societies (2009)

Jonas Ideström, editor
For the Sake of the World (2010)

Göran Gunner and Kjell-Åke Nordquist
An Unlikely Dilemma (2011)

Anne-Louise Eriksson, Göran Gunner,
and Niclas Blåder, editors
Exploring a Heritage (2012)

Exploring a Heritage

Evangelical Lutheran Churches in the North

Anne-Louise Eriksson, Göran Gunner,
and Niclas Blåder,
editors

Church of Sweden Research Series 5

☙PICKWICK *Publications* · Eugene, Oregon

EXPLORING A HERITAGE
Evangelical Lutheran Churches in the North

Church of Sweden Research Series 5

Copyright © 2012 Trossamfundet Svenska Kyrkan (Church of Sweden). All rights reserved. Except for brief quotations in critical publications or reviews, no part of this book may be reproduced in any manner without prior written permission from the publisher. Write: Permissions, Wipf and Stock Publishers, 199 W. 8th Ave., Suite 3, Eugene, OR 97401.

Pickwick Publications
An Imprint of Wipf and Stock Publishers
199 W. 8th Ave., Suite 3
Eugene, OR 97401

www.wipfandstock.com

ISBN 13: 978-1-62032-102-7

Cataloguing-in-Publication data:

Exploring a heritage : evangelical Lutheran churches in the North / edited by Anne-Louise Eriksson, Göran Gunner, and Niclas Blåder.

viii + 320 pp. ; 23 cm. Includes bibliographical references.

Church of Sweden Research Series 5

ISBN 13: 978-1-62032-102-7

1. Europe, Northern—Church history. 2. Evangelicalism—Lutheran Church. I. Title. II. Series.

BX8039 E85 2012

Manufactured in the U.S.A.

Scripture quotations are from the New Revised Standard Version Bible, copyright © 1989, Division of Christian Education of the National Council of the Churches of Christ in the United States of America. Used by permission. All rights reserved.

Contents

Contributors / vii

1 Exploring a Heritage: An Introduction—*Anne-Louise Eriksson and Göran Gunner, with contributions by Niclas Blåder, Hjalti Hugason, Roger Jensen, Marie Vejrup Nielsen, and Else Marie Wiberg Pedersen* / 1

PART ONE: Exploring a Heritage—Burning Issues

2 The Formation and Identity of the Church as a Present Challenge in Norway—*Roger Jensen* / 49

3 Burning Issues in the Evangelical Lutheran Church in Denmark—*Peter Lodberg* / 67

4 Ethics and Ecclesiology: Burning Issues for Church of Sweden—and Beyond—*Carl Reinhold Bråkenhielm* / 79

5 Same-Sex Marriage: A Burning Issue in the Evangelical Lutheran Church of Iceland—*Sólveig Anna Bóasdóttir* / 97

PART TWO: Exploring a Heritage—Influences from Growing Global Christianity

6 Building Church on Freedom from Within: Contemporary Congregational Life in the Evangelical Lutheran Church in Denmark—*Marie Thomsen* / 119

7 Church Development in Church of Norway—*Halvard Johannessen* / 137

8 Charismatic Movements within Church of Sweden —*Ulrika Svalfors* / 156

PART THREE: **Exploring a Heritage—The Role of Women**

9   Women's Situation in Church of Sweden—*Karin Sarja* / 177

10 Constructions of Gender, Liturgies, and Dichotomies from a Norwegian Perspective—*Merete Thomassen* / 191

11 Gender Issues and the Status of Women within the Evangelical Lutheran Church of Iceland —*Arnfríður Guðmundsdóttir* / 207

12 The Situation for Women in the Evangelical Lutheran Church in Denmark and Its Theological Underpinning: The Oestrogenic Church?—*Else Marie Wiberg Pedersen and Benedicte Præstholm* / 226

PART FOUR: **Exploring a Heritage—Lutheran Identity**

13 The Construction of Lutheran Identity in Church of Sweden—*Thomas Ekstrand* / 249

14 How Lutheran? An Icelandic Perspective —*Steinunn Arnþrúður Björnsdóttir* / 265

15 How Is Lutheran Identity Constructed in the Evangelical Lutheran Church in Denmark?—*Marie Vejrup Nielsen* / 288

16 The Lutheran and Ecumenical Identity of Church of Norway—*Harald Hegstad* / 305

Contributors

STEINUNN ARNÞRÚÐUR BJÖRNSDÓTTIR is the secretary for Ecumenical Affairs and Interfaith in the Evangelical Lutheran Church of Iceland and a doctoral student at the University of Iceland. Her research focuses on what effects the changes in Icelandic society 1980–2010 has on the Evangelical Lutheran Church of Iceland and especially on the role of the pastor.

SÓLVEIG ANNA BÓASDÓTTIR is Associate Professor in Theological Ethics, Faculty of Theology and Religious Studies, University of Iceland. Dr. Bóasdóttir has conducted research and published especially in the areas of gender studies, sexology and feminist ethics. She is currently Head of the Faculty of Theology and Religious Studies, University of Iceland.

NICLAS BLÅDER has a PhD in Systematic Theology at Linköping University, Sweden. Dr. Blåder is a fulltime researcher at Church of Sweden Research Unit. His research focus is on ecclesiology. He is presently working on a book about how Lutheran identity is constructed in different Lutheran churches worldwide.

CARL REINHOLD BRÅKENHIELM is active at the Department of Theology, Uppsala University, Sweden as professor in Empirical Worldview Studies since 1990. His research concerns worldviews and values in contemporary society and philosophical problem related to the relationship between science and religion. Professor Bråkenhielm has been the chairman of the Theology Committee of Church of Sweden since 2002.

THOMAS EKSTRAND is Associate Professor in Systematic theology, Uppsala University, Sweden and Faculty Director of Studies at the Faculty of Social Sciences, Uppsala University.

Exploring a Heritage

ANNE-LOUISE ERIKSSON is Associate Professor in Systematic Theology and Studies in World Views at Uppsala University, Sweden and Head of the Church of Sweden Research Unit. Dr. Eriksson has been working in the field of feminist theology, but also church and democracy, and theological literacy. She is a member of the Standing Commission of Faith and Order.

ARNFRÍÐUR GUÐMUNDSDÓTTIR is Professor of Systematic Theology with emphasis on Feminist Theology at the Faculty of Theology and Religious Studies, University of Iceland. Professor Guðmundsdóttir is an ordained pastor within the Evangelical Lutheran Church of Iceland, and a chair person of the Association of Ordained Women. She was an elected member of the Constitutional Assembly, which had the task of rewriting the Icelandic Constitution in 2011.

GÖRAN GUNNER is Associate Professor in Mission Studies, Uppsala University, and Researcher at Church of Sweden Research Unit, Uppsala. Dr. Gunner is also Senior Lecturer at Stockholm School of Theology, Stockholm, Sweden. He is also the main editor of Church of Sweden Research Series.

BENEDICTE HAMMER PRÆSTHOLM holds a Master in Theology and is a PhD Student in Systematic Theology at Faculty of Arts, University of Aarhus, Denmark. Præstholm's research area is gender, sexuality and changeability primarily in a Danish Lutheran context. She is an ordained pastor, and serves in a Grundtvigian electoral congregation. In 2010, she was an elected member of the committee appointed by the Ministry of Ecclesiastical Affairs that discussed the possibility of same sex blessings and marriages in The Evangelical Lutheran Church in Denmark. She is attached to the Centre for Contemporary Religion.

HARALD HEGSTAD is Professor in Systematic Theology at MF Norwegian School of Theology, Oslo, Norway. Professor Hegstad has conducted research and published especially in the areas of congregational studies, congregational development, and ecclesiology. He is presently a member of the General Synod of the Church of Norway.

HJALTI HUGASON is Professor in Church History at the Faculty of Theology and Religious Studies, University of Iceland, and is doctor in theology

Contributors

at Uppsala University, Sweden. Hugason has published books and articles in the field of church history of Iceland, on the church and state relations, freedom of religion, and religious motives in literature.

ROGER JENSEN is Senior Researcher in Systematic Theology at the Faculty of Theology, University of Oslo, Norway. Dr. Jensen has conducted research and published in the area of Luther research, in particular related to ethics, anthropology and ecclesiology, from both a historical and a contemporary perspective. He also serves as Director of The Pilgrim Center of Oslo.

HALVARD JOHANNESSEN is Lecturer in Pastoral Theology, at the Practical Theological Seminary, and PhD-student at The Faculty of Theology, University of Oslo, Norway. Johannessen's research area is spirituality and secularization, primarily within the current Norwegian folk church context. He is an ordained pastor in Church of Norway.

PETER LODBERG is Associate Professor in Missions Studies and Ecumenism, Aarhus University, Denmark. Dr. Lodberg is also Dean of Studies and Head of the Department of Systematic Theology, Aarhus University. He is an ordained pastor in the Evangelical Lutheran Church in Denmark and has served as General Secretary of Danchurchaid and the National Council of Churches in Denmark.

KARIN SARJA is Associate Professor in Church History, Åbo Akademi University, Finland, Doctor in Mission Studies, Uppsala University, Sweden, and Minister in Church of Sweden. Dr. Sarja has taught at Uppsala University, University of Gävle, and Stockholm School of Theology, and was previous research fellow at the Centre for Gender Research, Uppsala University. She is currently Liturgical Adviser at the Secretariat for Theology and Ecumenism, Church of Sweden.

ULRIKA SVALFORS is Postdoctoral Fellow and Senior Lecturer in Systematic Theology and Studies in World Views, Uppsala University, Sweden, and minister in Mission Covenant Church of Sweden. Dr. Svalfors has taught at Stockholm School of Theology in Systematic Theology and Pastoral Theology. She is currently part of the interdisciplinary project "Preconditions of environmental moral learning within education for sustainable development: a multidisciplinary study of young Swedes' attitudes, commitments and actions".

Exploring a Heritage

MERETE THOMASSEN is Dr. Theol. and Lecturer in Liturgical Studies at the Practical Theological Seminar, University of Oslo, Norway. Her research concerns feminist theology, liturgy, gender inclusive language and liturgical language in general. Dr. Thomassen is Minister in Church of Norway and an elected member of the Committee of Worship in Church of Norway and was until 2010 leader of the Committee of Gender and Gender equality in Church of Norway.

MARIE THOMSEN holds a Master in Theology and is currently a PhD fellow in Systematic Theology at the Department for Culture and Society, Aarhus University, Denmark. Her research focuses on congregational studies within the Evangelical Lutheran Church in Denmark and offers theologically informed empirical studies. Her work is carried out in close connection to the Centre for Contemporary Religion, which is an interdisciplinary research unit consisting of researchers from both systematic theology, sociology of religion and the science of religion.

MARIE VEJRUP NIELSEN, PhD, is assistant professor at the Institute for Culture and Society, Faculty of Arts, Aarhus University, Denmark. She is connected to the Center for Contemporary Religion, and her primary area of research is contemporary Christianity in Denmark.

ELSE MARIE WIBERG PEDERSEN is Associate Professor in Systematic Theology with an emphasis on Dogmatic, Faculty of Arts, University of Aarhus, Denmark. Dr. Wiberg Pedersen has among her research areas Ecclesiology and the understanding of ministry, often from the perspective of feminist theology. She has served as chair person of the Association of Women Pastors and Theologians (KVINT) and of the former Danish Ecumenical Council's ecclesiology group, as well as of The Equal Opportunities Committee at the University of Aarhus. She is currently attached to both the Centre for Contemporary Religion and the project Reformation Theology—Reception and Transformation at the Department for Theology.

1

Exploring a Heritage: An Introduction

ANNE-LOUISE ERIKSSON AND GÖRAN GUNNER

With contributions by
Niclas Blåder, Hjalti Hugason,
Roger Jensen, Marie Vejrup Nielsen,
and Else Marie Wiberg Pedersen

It belongs to the key characteristic of Protestant churches to be in transition, to reflect the pilgrim nature of the community of faith.[1]

FROM A HISTORICAL PERSPECTIVE, changes and decisive moments possess explanatory force for trying to understand why a certain church comes into view in a certain way. The aim of this volume, however, is not to explain how or why Evangelical Lutheran churches in the North have developed in a particular way. Nor is it to provide a comprehensive description of the four churches in the study. The goal is rather to explore how Lutheran church identity shapes itself today in Denmark, Iceland, Norway, and Sweden. What are the burning issues that engage the folk

1. Bishop emeritus Gunnar Stålsett, Church of Norway, in Ryman et al., *Nordic Folk Churches*, vii.

Exploring a Heritage

churches in Northern Europe in the beginning of the second millennium? Are there signs that also these churches are affected by the global emergence of a theology and practice commonly referred to as Neo-Pentecostal and/or Charismatic? What is the situation for women in churches embedded in societies that are ranked among the world's most egalitarian? And in what way does a Lutheran heritage have a say in how these churches shape themselves today?

In a historical perspective, similarities between the Lutheran churches in the North are easily understood. The borders between the Nordic and/or Scandinavian countries have fluctuated over time. Denmark, Norway, and Sweden constituted a union from 1397 to 1523. Seeing that most of today's Finland was then a part of Sweden, while Iceland was united with Norway, this Kalmar Union covered a vast area. Sweden's southern region today belonged to Denmark most of the time until 1658. Sweden and the most of what we today call Finland was actually a single country until 1809. As recently as 1905, Norway withdrew from the union with Sweden that had resulted from a peace treaty between Denmark and Sweden in 1814 when Sweden "received" Norway as compensation for the loss of Swedish Pomerania. Iceland was under Danish rule until 1904, when a process of growing independence started; the formal union treaty with Denmark expired as recently as 1944 and Iceland, in order to avoid the German occupation of the Danish kingdom, proclaimed itself a free republic. These examples from the political history of the Nordic countries should suffice to indicate the ties that bind the Nordic countries together. Furthermore, the Reformation in the sixteenth century turned the church in each of these countries into a state institution under the monarch and/or the government, sharing not just a Lutheran heritage but also a similar political context.

But as already mentioned, explanation is not the purpose of this work. As part of a larger research project conducted by the Church of Sweden Research Unit to examine how Lutheran identity shapes itself around the world today, the underlying assumption of this Nordic study is that the Nordic folk churches *de facto* form a separate entity from the rest of Protestant Europe, not to speak of from the rest of the world. What we from the Church of Sweden Research Unit hope to achieve with this volume is a picture of what Lutheran folk church identity has become in the far north of Europe. Where has our pilgrim nature brought us?

To accomplish this, we contacted some researchers in Denmark, Finland, Iceland, Norway, and Sweden and asked them to participate by looking at the Evangelical Lutheran church in their own country in the light of four specific questions. Unfortunately we were not able to find researchers in Finland who, at that time, could participate in the project. In that Finland has for a long time hosted two "state" or "folk" churches, i.e., the Evangelical Lutheran Church of Finland and the Orthodox Church of Finland, with an approximate membership of 80 percent and 1 percent of the population, respectively, the Lutheran church's context in Finland is somewhat different from that in the other Nordic countries.[2] Although it is much the larger of the two churches, the Evangelical Lutheran Church of Finland differs from the other Nordic Evangelical Lutheran churches in that it is not its country's one-and-only state-regulated—some would say privileged and/or protected—church. Whether or not Finland's Lutheran and Orthodox churches should be labeled as state churches depends on how one chooses to define a state church. While they both define themselves today as folk churches, their relationship with the state, regulated in Finnish law, sets them apart from other religious movements in the country.[3]

However, without Finland we cannot claim to present all the Nordic folk churches; neither can we, seeing that Iceland is included, pretend to a narrow Scandinavian approach. Instead we will work with material from four Evangelical Lutheran churches in the North, i.e., those in Denmark, Iceland, Norway, and Sweden. The articles that follow discuss the same four questions that have been asked in countries in Africa, Latin America, and Asia.[4] The task for the participants in the study was to write on the following topics:

1. How is Lutheran identity constructed today?

2. How are churches affected by the globally growing (Neo-)Pentecostal and/or Charismatic influences and/or fundamentalist movement today?

3. What is the situation for women? And what theology underpins the situation for women within the churches?

4. What can be said to be present-day "burning issues" and how are these issues part of the formation and identity of the church?

2. Until 1809 the dioceses of Åbo and Viborg, the Lutheran church in Finland was part of Church of Sweden.

3. The question of how to define the concepts of state church and folk church will recur in this volume.

4. A presentation of this wider study will be published in 2014.

State Churches and Folk Churches

There are many, diverse theological opinions about what it is to be a church. Ecclesiology has been, and still is, one of the church-dividing issues that challenge ecumenical aspirations.[5] Whatever ecclesiology one wants to represent, it must be said that churches like the Nordic folk churches are always more (some might claim less) than what is usually discussed under the heading of ecclesiology, i.e., they are more (or less) than "the congregation of saints, in which the Gospel is rightly taught and the Sacraments are rightly administered."[6] They are huge organizations, historically entwined with the state and embedded in the nation.

When studying identity in corporations, it is common to consider at least some of the following traits: working conditions, production technologies, production qualities, profits, public responsibilities, credibility, service, public relations, logotypes, buildings, and the behavior of employees. From an ecclesiological perspective, one might say that nothing of this has to do with what it means to be a church. But seeing that the folk churches are also organizations with many employees, that they perform tasks that make it necessary for the public to use their services, that they own buildings and property and so on, from certain perspectives they appear to be service organizations that are identified and recognized by, e.g., their logotypes, public relations, buildings, public responsibility and the behavior of their employees. And not only is it the case that what can be seen from outside, and what is measured by the public, are traits like the above; the churches themselves also seem to be concerned about their trademark and spend money and time working on how to present themselves to the public.[7]

At the same time, it is equally true that neither, e.g., the Evangelical Lutheran Church in Denmark, the one church of the four presented in this volume that is in the closest relationship with the state, nor Church of Sweden, the one that has gone through a formal disestablishment process, can be described as just a service organization. It would be more correct to see them as interest organizations, but for the believers and representatives of the churches that would probably not be a sufficient description. From inside the churches, the question of what it is to be a church is one

---

5. Cf. *The Nature and Mission of the Church*. Not only the document itself, but also the responses from different member churches of Faith and Order, prove this.

6. Augsburg Confession, VII.

7. Church of Sweden, for example, advertises in Stockholm's subways as well as on public television.

of self-understanding and self-image, i.e., the mental picture of oneself. When talking about persons, self-image has to do with how one is perceived by others (from the outside) but also an inner awareness of vitality (I am alive), continuity (I am the same throughout the years), activity (I am free to act as I want), integrity (there is only one of me), and demarcation (I am something apart from others).

Comparing churches with corporations and persons is of course inadequate if one wants to capture a church's soul and identity from an ecclesiological perspective, but such comparisons nevertheless seem to bring out something of importance. When examining and appraising a church, people are faced with an outer appearance made up of things like websites, logotypes, how the priest/pastor behaves at the funeral, the beauty of the buildings (or not), rumors and news concerning how "church people" are and so on. And out of these experiences people form an impression of whether or not the church at hand is alive, how it develops and how it differs from other churches or religious organizations; in other words, an impression concerning vitality, activity, continuity, integrity, and demarcation.

The four churches that are the focus of this study all name themselves "folk church." Part of their heritage is a strong, profound connection with the state and the nation. Since the Reformation and up to recent times they have been the hegemonic religious discourse in each country. Today this hegemonic position is contested on at least two points. First, Denmark, Iceland, Norway, and Sweden are judged to be among the most secular countries in the world. All four are in the upper right-hand corner on Inglehart and Welzel's *WVS Cultural Map of the World*, which plots traditional values versus secular-rational values on one axis against survival values versus self-expression values on the other.[8] Notwithstanding each of these four churches' high membership, their relation with the state is therefore no longer unproblematic. A vast majority of the population seems to be governed by secular and individualistic values that collide with some traditional Christian values. Secondly, immigration is adding new religious praxis to the culture. Immigrants represent religions and confessions that are entitled to the same treatment and rights as the old folk churches. This process of increasing secularization and a growing presence of other religions challenges the churches when it comes to relating to the state and constituting themselves as folk churches.

---

8. Inglehart and Welzel, "WVS Cultural Map of the World."

Exploring a Heritage

As mentioned earlier, the notion of state and/or folk church is by no means clearcut. It will become evident already from the brief introduction of each church that the authors in this volume do not have a shared understanding of what constitutes a state church or a folk church. This is a reflection of the situation in the different churches and countries. It is nevertheless a fact that all four churches have a history of being inseparable from the state, with a clergy who represented the state as much as the church. However, it is clear from the articles that the degree to which this must still be said to be the case does not necessarily have to do with an official separation of church from state. One can claim, as above, that the Evangelical Lutheran Church in Denmark is the one with the closest relation to the state, seeing that it lacks a clear *national* level of its own and is governed by the parliament. At the same time, at the parish level this church has a great deal of independence and self-government, perhaps more so than some of the other churches.

Defining folk church is even more complicated. On the one hand the term seems to suggest a strong connection between the church and the people and nation. There is a general understanding that a church is a folk church when its members include most of the people in a given country. However, the concept's theological underpinning does not necessarily have anything to do with how many or how few members there are in a church. The idea is rather that a folk church is a church not *of*, but *for* the people; a church that offers the gospel to all and everyone independently of faith and convictions, for instance as the Church Ordinance of Church of Sweden has it:

> Church of Sweden is an open folk church with the mission to communicate the Gospel in word and deed. The church has room for everyone, for the seeker and the one who doubts, as well as for those who are strong in faith, for the one who has not reached far, as well as for those who have advanced further on the path of faith.[9]

How to Read This Book

This book can be read in two ways. One involves constructing a picture of each country's folk church in turn by reading the chapter on that church in each of the four sections. Such a reading invites comparisons between

---

9. *Kyrkoordningen*, part VI. Introduction (translation by Niclas Blåder).

the countries, but one should be aware that one is then comparing "snapshots." What such a reading can give is a comparison of photographs that admittedly present similar motives, i.e., the four questions above, but where each photographer has had great freedom in the choice of perspective, lighting, etc.

The other way is to follow our thematic presentation. Our concern has not been to compare the churches but to explore Lutheran folk church distinctiveness in the North. While there are, of course, differences in how these four churches shape themselves, it is also the case that a shared faith tradition and culture, as well as our shared history, have generated a type of folk church that seems emblematic for the Nordic countries. Our point of departure is thus not a predetermined normative understanding of what a Lutheran church is or should be, but the fact that the four folk churches presented here are Lutheran churches and represent what Lutheranism is today in this part of the world. Therefore, we are more interested in the overall picture than in comparing the churches.

Even so, we believe each chapter needs to be placed in its particular context. We shall therefore conclude this introduction with a brief presentation of each church. This starts with general statistical information about each church, followed by an organizational chart. In order to locate each country's Lutheran church in its religious landscape, we include some statistics about other churches and religions. We then highlight some matters that we believe are typical for the present situation in each church. Presenting the Evangelical Lutheran Church in Denmark, Marie Vejrup Nielsen and Else Marie Wiberg Pedersen focus on the fact that the church's official English name might imply something different from what the Danish name, *Den danske Folkekirke* (lit. "the Danish folk church") connotes. Presenting Iceland, Hjalti Hugason describes the historical development of the Evangelical Lutheran Church of Iceland. And the presentation of Church of Norway by Roger Jensen cannot avoid focusing on the ongoing separation of church and state. In the Swedish presentation, finally, Niclas Blåder highlights the fact that the newly disestablished Church of Sweden faces the task of being one faith community among others. These nationally organized presentations are followed by some general remarks on the overall picture.

Exploring a Heritage

Denmark and the Evangelical Lutheran Church in Denmark

Statistics and Organization[10]

The Evangelical Lutheran Church in Denmark	2010	2000
Denmark's population	5,560,628	5,330,000
Members of the Evangelical Lutheran Church in Denmark	4,469,109	4,533,000
Parishes	2,123	2,125
Baptisms	49,432	Not available
Confirmations	49,366	45,683
Marriages	11,077[11]	18,149
Funerals	48,079	53,515

Members in other Christian denominations	
The Roman Catholic Church	39,067
The Pentecostal Movement	5,251
Orthodox and Eastern Orthodox Churches	approx. 2,000
The Baptist Church	5,152

Members in other major faiths and beliefs	
Islamic/Muslim communities	21,000
Buddhist communities	7,200
Jewish communities	2,220
Hindu/Hindu-inspired communities	approx. 500

Structure of the Evangelical Lutheran Church in Denmark[12]

The cornerstone of the structure of the Evangelical Lutheran Church in Denmark is the local congregation. All adult members (from eighteen years of age) of the church are eligible to vote in elections to the parish council and are entitled to stand for election to the parish council. The parish council is responsible for managing the economy and employing

---

10. Sources: "Danmarks statistik"; "Kirkestatistik"; "Religion i Danmark 2011."
11. Plus 1,670 church blessings of civil marriages.
12. Based on "Folkekirken og menighedsrådene"; "Folkekireken og Grundloven."

staff in the local church, not least for calling and selecting the pastor (who formally and administratively is then employed by the Minister of Ecclesiastical Affairs in the national government).

The pastor is responsible for the service and liturgy but shares this responsibility with the parish council, which decides whether or not to approve any changes in the liturgy. Thus, the management of the church is an expression of the priesthood of all believers.

There is only one office in the Evangelical Lutheran Church in Denmark. This office includes both pastors and bishops. Denmark is divided into ten dioceses; each presided over by a bishop. Bishops are elected by the members of parish councils and the pastors in the diocese. The bishop of Copenhagen holds a specific position of honor as *primus inter pares* but there is no office of archbishop.

Church income comes mainly from a membership fee collected by the national tax authorities, plus ear-marked grants from the state budget. This is how the state contributes to the administration of the church.

As part of a time-honored contract, the official register of people living in Denmark is still administered by the church on behalf of the national authorities, regardless of the citizen's religious affiliation. This includes registering the birth of citizens, naming and name changes, marital status and time of death, as well as church-related life events such as baptism, confirmation, marriage, and funeral. An exception is Southern Jutland, whose administration for historical reasons lies with the municipal authorities.

Exploring a Heritage

The Organization of the Evangelical Lutheran Church in Denmark

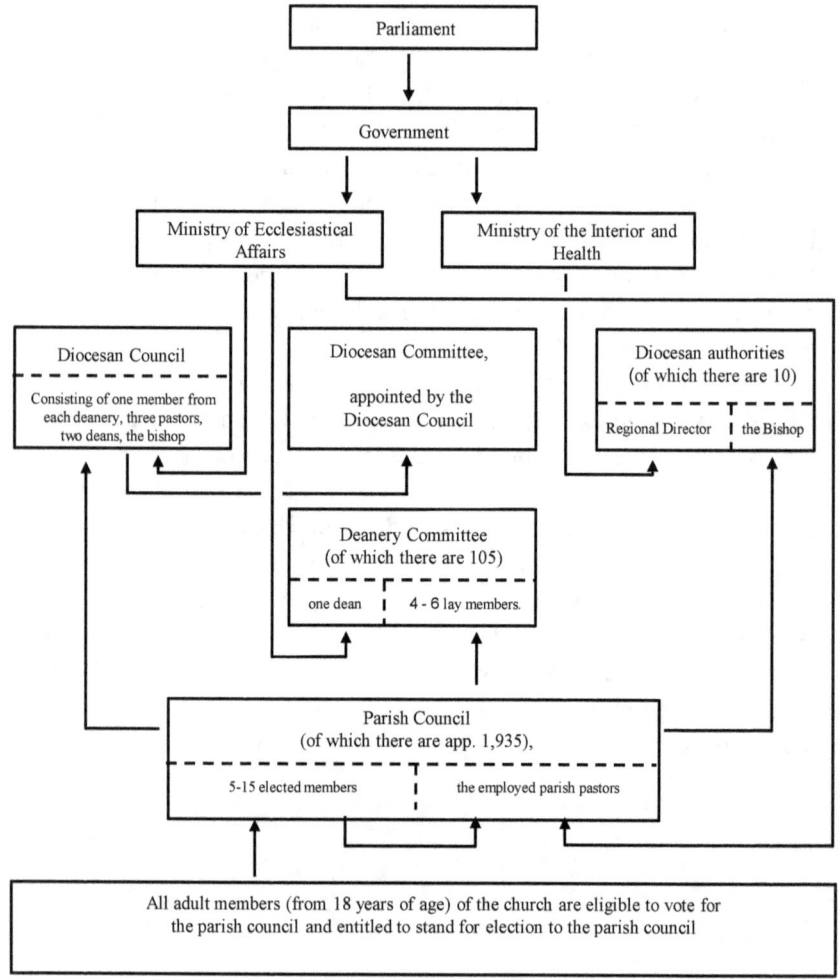

Official Home Page of the Evangelical Lutheran Church in Denmark:
In Danish: http://www.folkekirken.dk/; in English: http://www.lutheran-church.dk/

Exploring a Heritage: An Introduction

What's in a Name?[13]

The first issue confronting anyone writing about the Evangelical Lutheran Church in Denmark for an international audience is how to translate the church's name. In the initial invitation to take part in this project the church was described as the "Church of Denmark." This is in itself a somewhat controversial label, because it might be taken to denote a state church. Many within church and theology in Denmark would argue against such an understanding. They will maintain that the Evangelical Lutheran Church in Denmark is not a state church, because a state church is perceived as a church to which one's membership is directly tied to one's citizenship (compulsory membership), whereas in "the Danish church" membership is tied to baptism or, if you are already baptized, to an application for membership (voluntary membership). Since the latter is the definition of a folk church, the Evangelical Lutheran Church in Denmark is commonly defined and categorized as a folk church.

Something between a Free Church and a State Church

The category of folk church might surprise some people, such as sociologists, who often routinely categorize the church as a state church on account of the strong connection with the state, as can be seen from the formulation in the Danish constitution from 1849, § 4: "The Evangelical Lutheran Church is the Danish folk church, and is supported as such by the state." Another central connection is the church's administrative duties on behalf of the state, such as civil registration. This means that apart from some parts of Southern Denmark, all newborns, regardless of the family's religious affiliations, or lack of the same, are enrolled through the church office in the general public registration system. Moreover, the church's supreme ruling body is the monarch and parliament, and its administration goes through the Ministry for Ecclesiastical Affairs. The church does not have an independent supreme level of official administration or representation, such as a synod or an archbishop. The church is funded from church taxes paid only by members but administered through the public tax system and supplemented by a state contribution (12 percent). Thus, the church's finances are embedded in the state budget. To add to the complexity, part of a pastor's salary, as well as the whole of all bishops' salaries, are funded by the state.

13. Written by Marie Vejrup Nielsen and Else Marie Wiberg Pedersen.

At the same time, the church is governed at regional and local level through local democratic systems, such as the election of parish councils and the election of bishops. Also, the church is the framework for a large number of volunteer organizations and activities, such as scout movements, charity work, etc. This tension between a high degree of state regulation and a high degree of self-regulation has led to the description of a folk church as a church form somewhere between a state church model and a free church model.[14] And as indicated by both the name and the structure of the church, this church form exists in an intersection of at least three dimensions: church–state–nation/people.

The specific Danish church form with all its tensions has its historical background in the development of the constitution, as indicated above. From the Reformation in 1536 up to the Danish constitution of 1849, the church was completely under the control of the monarch. When the democratic constitution with its freedom rights had been formulated, the overriding question was the church's situation in a society that was moving towards modern parliamentary rule. The organizational model—the final outcome of the tumultuous times in the middle and late nineteenth century—has largely survived to this day, albeit with a few changes. Whereas in some ways the constitution is a continuation of the situation prior to 1849—a church closely tied to state power—the church is now related to a modern, parliamentary state and exists in a situation with a much greater degree of voluntarism, both within the church as such and within society as a whole, for instance through religious freedom.

One very important development within the church is the profound democratization of its structure on two levels: firstly through the political system, and secondly through the development of local parish church councils from the beginning of the twentieth century. At the same time, the church was constituted in such a way that it has no independent, official voice. Or, put differently, ideally all members have an equal share in the position of being the voice of the church.

An Inclusive Church—Encompassing Tensions

The formation of a church in this way should be seen in relation to the formation of the church as a common framework encompassing two levels of tension: the incorporation of opposing church movements and the

---

14. Lodberg, "Evangelical Lutheran Church in Denmark."

incorporation of an understanding of membership which includes both active and passive members.

The opposing church movements, which all originated in nineteenth-century revivals, have two major branches (with a variety of subgroups): The Inner Mission and the Grundtvigians. The Inner Mission is a conservative, pietistic church movement with an emphasis on a Christian lifestyle based on biblical teachings (often referred to as "the gloomy Danes"), whereas the Grundtvigian movements are more liberal (often referred to as "the happy Danes"). Both branches were incorporated in single church structure, that of the folk church within a common confessional framework, which is still the situation today. As at the time of its constitution, the folk church is generally dominated by a Grundtvigian or Grundtvigian-affiliated majority's liberal understanding of church (specific groups identifying strongly with a Grundtvigian stance). At the same time, Inner Mission and other movements of more conservative observance still play a significant part in Danish church life. The tensions which such very different stances within the same body clearly cause are resolved in the church constitution. One example is the appearance of electoral congregations, whereby a congregation can stay within the church to some degree, while having a greater degree of independence, such as the right to choose their pastor.[15] Especially the tension between the church parties that is instrumental in the formation of the church plays a part in the structure of the church in relation to the lack of an official voice. All parties were concerned that no one group should gain control over the church, and that it might therefore be a better option to let the church be run through the democratic, political system.

The formation of the church included another level of intergroup tension, namely the incorporation of both active and passive members in the focus on the parish as the basic unit of membership. Persons who live within the parish and have joined the church, primarily through infant baptism, are members. No distinction should be made between those who go to church regularly and those who may never show up. This of course was a provocation for some of the more active groups but it was part of the reconciliation of different tendencies that still makes up the landscape of the church.

At present, 80.9 percent of Denmark's population are members of the Danish folk church. But the main pattern of activity is for members to have a high level of activity in relation to major life rituals such

---

15. See the chapter by Marie Thomsen.

as baptisms, confirmations, weddings, and funerals, and a much lower level in relation to Sunday service. This should be qualified by taking into account the many other types of church service that have developed over the last ten to twenty years and become increasingly popular, such as family services, hymn singing for babies, and pre-confirmation teaching for ten-year-olds. Still, the overall pattern is one of high membership and low activity among members, as well as a gradual but steady decline in membership.

This situation of tension between specific church parties as well as between different types of members is summed up in the term "a spacious church." The church embraces diverse theological opinions, for example contrary views about the ordination of women, and a diversity of members that ranges from those who are very engaged in church life to those who show up only three or four times in their lives.[16]

A Church with Many Voices

There are also other areas of tension, such as the church's ecumenical involvement. On the one hand, the folk church is weak in ecumenical relations, particularly because the lack of an official representative makes it difficult to sign official documents. On the other hand, many Danish pastors and theologians have been instrumental in ecumenical work both in Europe and globally, and the church has an official ecumenical office, the Council on International Relations of the Evangelical Lutheran Church in Denmark. Again, the church is a spacious, common framework for a wide range of opinions and involvements and could be said to be an ecumenical project in itself.[17]

It should therefore be stressed that the lack of an official voice does not mean that this is a silent church. On the contrary, it might seem that the church with no voice is actually a church of many voices, since the floor is open.[18]

Of course, any attempt to speak on behalf of the church will tend to arouse controversy and debate. A good example is the debate concerning the signing of the Porvoo Agreement in December 2009 through the Council on International Relations. Furthermore, pastors frequently take part in public debates on a broad array of societal issues. This is another

---

16. See the chapter by Else Marie Wiberg Pedersen and Benedicte Præstholm.
17. Wiberg Pedersen, "Hvorfor er økumeni så svær i Danmark."
18. See the chapter by Peter Lodberg.

indication that the church is spacious with regard to significant tensions on theological and political issues, as well as with regard to the various levels of members' involvement.

The church has therefore been described as "a well-ordered anarchy," both in relation to its structure and in relation to the behavior of church members, pastors, and bishops.

A Church with Many Names

The various levels of tension are connected to the question of how the church should be termed. Those who wish to emphasize specific aspects of the church's development, such as the high degree of voluntarism and democracy, will most likely choose the term "folk church." In contrast, the term "Church of Denmark" indicates a continuation of the pre-constitutional church model, and will be chosen by those who wish to emphasize a church with close links to the political level of the official nation state and the monarch. As a third option, some might choose the term "the Danish national church," thereby pointing both to the church's official status and to its connection with national history and cultural identity. The official English term used in Denmark today is "the Evangelical Lutheran Church in Denmark," thus stressing that it is not *the* (only) church "of" Denmark, but *a* church "in" Denmark. In addition, this official name ties the local church to the universal, pointing to the fact that this church is part of an organization that transcends Denmark's national borders.

So, what's in a name? Quite a lot. In fact, going, as it does, straight to the heart of the church's identity, this is more than a theoretical discussion.[19] The many levels of tension within a model such as the Danish, emphasizing spaciousness, are not just a part of the church's history. They constitute the framework for the church today. It is therefore a part of the very framework that is being discussed in the light of the numerous changes in Danish society in recent decades.

Of course one cannot predict the future for this model. Still, some of the important issues that are already up for serious discussion are bound to influence the future of the Evangelical Lutheran Church in Denmark: the church and state relationship, changes in Denmark's religious landscape (for example multi-religiosity), and internal debates in the church (for example on homosexuality), as well as the changes already taking place in the other countries in the North.

19. See the chapter by Marie Vejrup Nielsen.

Exploring a Heritage

Iceland and the Evangelical Lutheran Church of Iceland

Statistics and Organization

The Evangelical Lutheran Church of Iceland	2010	2000
Iceland's population	318,452	283,361
Members of the Evangelical Lutheran Church of Iceland	251,487	247,420
Parishes	272	278
Baptisms	3,274	3,595
Confirmations	Not available	3,540
Marriages	1,201	1,518
Funerals	Not available	1,491

Members in other Christian denominations	
Evangelical Lutheran Free Churches	approx. 15,000
The Roman Catholic Church	9,672
The Pentecostal Movement	2,109
Orthodox and Eastern Orthodox Churches	535

Members in other major faiths and beliefs	
Islamic/Muslim communities	591
Buddhist communities	approx. 650

Structure of the Evangelical Lutheran Church of Iceland[20]

Þjóðkirkjan—the Evangelical Lutheran Church of Iceland—has a fivefold vision: it is a vital and powerful movement of people who journey together in the faith in God through Jesus Christ. It is a visible, colorful, and growing communion that awakens and nourishes Christian worship and spirituality. The church meets everyone on his/her journey, and renders service and shelter. The Evangelical Lutheran Church of Iceland is a forum for social dialogue in the light of the Christian faith, and it empowers people to serve God and neighbor.

There are close to 280 parishes in Iceland and about 150 priests and 30 ordained deacons. That means that in many cases a vicar leads more

---

20. Source: "Organization."

than one parish. Most parishes are very small; almost half of them have less than 100 members. Each parish is a financially independent unit, responsible for the construction and upkeep of its church buildings and all the work done in the congregation. Such work often consists of work with children and youth, pastoral care, counseling, and teaching.

The church is divided into 9 deaneries. Together they form one diocese led by the bishop of Island. There are also 2 suffragan bishops, one in Skálholt the other in Hólar. Together, these three form the bishops' meeting. The highest legislative body in the church is the General Synod. It meets once a year and has 29 elected representatives, 12 ordained and 17 lay-persons. The Church Council is the highest executive authority, with two clergy and two lay-persons elected by the General Synod and presided over by the bishop of Iceland. There is also a Pastoral Synod that meets annually for discussions on matters of theology and liturgy that are to be decided by the General Synod. The Bishop summons all the pastors, deacons, and theologians in the church to the Pastoral Synod.

Exploring a Heritage

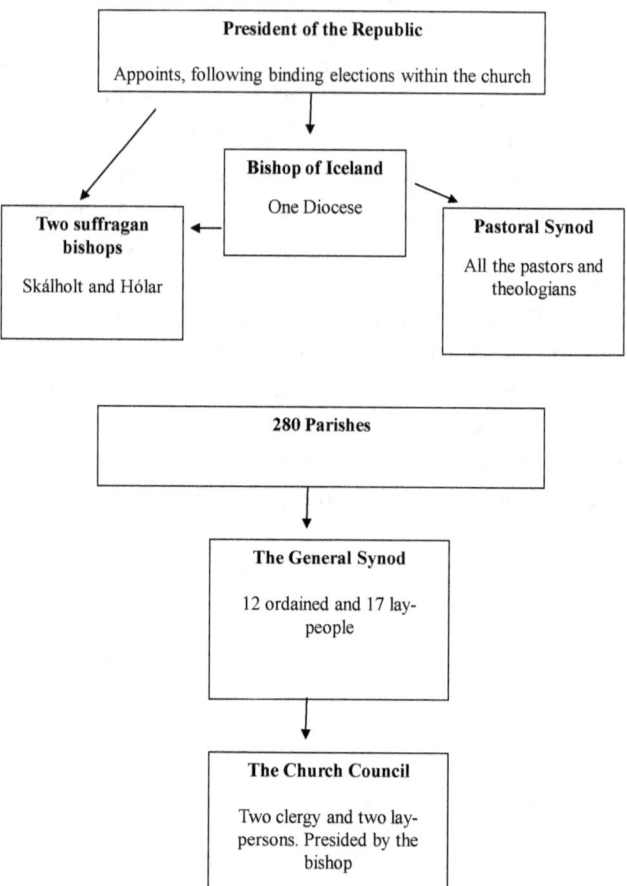

Official Home Page of the Evangelical Lutheran Church of Iceland: In Icelandic: http://kirkjan.is/; in English: http://www2.kirkjan.is/node/8313

Iceland—Historical Background[21]

As Iceland was part of the Danish-Norwegian state in the sixteenth century, during and after the Reformation the Icelandic church evolved along the same paths as its sister churches in Denmark and Norway. In practice,

21. Written by Hjalti Hugason.

Exploring a Heritage: An Introduction

therefore, the church became part of the state, whose power, during the period of autocracy, was solely in the hands of the monarch. In the mid-nineteenth century Denmark acquired constitutional government; there was a growing emphasis on rights (including religious freedom) and the church began to separate from the state on the basis of the constitution of 1849. At the same time, Icelanders had begun to campaign for independence. This led to a sovereign state under the Danish Crown in 1918. A republic was established in Iceland in 1944.

The constitution that Iceland was granted by the Danish king in 1874—a turning point in the campaign for independence—gave Icelanders greater autonomy in internal affairs, including the affairs of the church: chapter V (now VI) of the constitution contained a stipulation that the Evangelical Lutheran Church should be Iceland's national or state church and confirmed the principle of religious freedom. These stipulations—a somewhat simplified version of those in the Danish constitution—aimed for the same religious rights to apply in Iceland as in Denmark, as the Danes considered Iceland to be a province of their realm. This part of the constitution was transferred unchanged into the constitution of the kingdom of Iceland, and later that of the republic. Today, therefore, the treatment of religious rights within the constitution corresponds with the situation in Denmark. In 1995 the paragraphs on religious rights were brought up to date, while the chapter on human rights was under review and the principle of equality was being established in the constitution.

Relationship between Church and State

The constitutional provision on the Evangelical Lutheran Church of Iceland (Art. 62) is as follows: "The Evangelical Lutheran Church shall be the State Church in Iceland and, as such, it shall be supported and protected by the State. This may be altered by law."[22]

At first, legislation on the position and administration of the Icelandic state church developed along the same lines as in Denmark. Laws were passed on parish councils and the authorization of congregations to administer their churches, on the selection of parish pastors, elections of bishops, and various other matters intended to increase democracy within the church and decrease direct state intervention in its internal affairs. These laws were intended as a basis for a state church, i.e., a church where

22. *Constitution of the Republic of Iceland.*

parishes managed their own affairs and the church was equipped to gain increased freedom.[23]

In the twentieth century, multiple changes took place in Iceland, which resulted in a deep split between the Danish and Icelandic churches. It could in fact be said that the Icelandic church has been transformed from a typical Western Scandinavian church, similar to the Danish church, into an Eastern Scandinavian one. One of the explanations for this is that precedents were increasingly sought from Sweden, where Dr. Sigurbjörn Einarsson, one of Iceland's most influential church leaders in the latter half of the twentieth century and bishop of Iceland from 1959 to 1981, had studied.

In the early twentieth century a movement had arisen within the Evangelical Lutheran Church of Iceland to increase its freedom and establish a General Synod that would have decision-making powers over the church's internal affairs, as well as the right of recommendation and comment on its external affairs.[24] Progress on this was slow. A Church Council was established towards the middle of the century and, later, a General Synod whose roles were limited to policy making in various ecclesiastical matters and advising the government in relation to such matters concerning the church as came within the remit of Parliament or the executive. Towards the end of the century things started moving again; on January 1, 1998 the Established Church Act (Act on the Status, Management and Procedures of the State Church) came into force.[25] The laws from 1997 to 1998 may be regarded as the constitution or internal organization of the Evangelical Lutheran Church of Iceland.

According to Article 1 of the Act, the Evangelical Lutheran Church of Iceland is defined as an "independent religious community" based on Evangelical Lutheran confessions. It is stipulated that the state shall support and protect the state church, as is also stated in the Constitution. According to Article 2, the state church enjoys freedom in relation to the state, within legally defined limits. It also stipulates that the church, its individual parishes, and its establishments shall enjoy independent property rights, and act as independent parties in relation to the state where appropriate. As defined in Article 5, the church has authority over its administration within legally defined limits. This demonstrates that the

---

23. Sigurðsson, *Geschichte und Gegenwartsgestalt*, 83–91.
24. Hugason, "Þróun sjálfstæðrar þjóðkirkju á öndveðri 20," 73–104.
25. "Lög um stöðu, stjórn og starfshætti þjóðkirkjunnar."

Evangelical Lutheran Church of Iceland has gained much more freedom than its Danish sister church.[26]

As a result of the Act, the administration of ecclesiastical affairs has to a large extent been transferred from ministerial hands into the hands of the church itself, i.e., to *Biskupstofa*, the established Episcopal office. This is where the day-to-day administration of ecclesiastical affairs is carried out. For some time there was a specific Ministry of Justice and Church Affairs. Today, dealings between church and state are handled by the more recently established Ministry of the Interior; they consist mainly of legal amendments and matters pertaining to financial relations between church and state.

It is important for the relationship between church and state that the President of the Republic appoints the Bishop of Iceland and the two Suffragan Bishops, following binding elections within the church, with no ministerial interference.[27] The President is not obliged to be a member of the church, since limiting eligibility to the office of President to Evangelical Lutheran faith would contravene the constitution's stipulations on religious freedom and equality.

Financial Base for Church Activities

In previous times, the church owned a considerable quota of tenant farms in Iceland, assets that served as the financial basis for its activities. Adverse conditions for agriculture in the early twentieth century resulted in operational difficulties for the church. At the same time there was marked interest in boosting farm ownership by selling off state-owned land. The response to this situation was to make considerable cutbacks on incumbencies and streamline the church's activities. Meanwhile, the state took custodianship of church-owned land in return for guaranteeing episcopal and clerical remuneration. The land was disposed of in various ways, and the arrangement created friction between church and state. This problem was resolved in 1997 when the Evangelical Lutheran Church of Iceland relinquished ownership of all its land, apart from rectories, on condition that the state pledged itself to pay the salaries of the Bishop and the Suffragan Bishops, a certain number of pastors, and the staff at the episcopal office.[28]

26. Ibid.
27. Ibid.
28. "Grundvöllur fjármála þjóðkirkjunnar"; "Samningur íslenska ríkisins og þjóðkirkjunnar um fjárframlög."

Exploring a Heritage

The activities of the Evangelical Lutheran Church of Iceland also rely heavily on parish dues collected on its behalf by the state; the same applies to other registered religious communities.[29]

Membership and Ecclesiastical Activity

People become members of the Evangelical Lutheran Church of Iceland by being baptized or registered.[30] At the end of 2010 just under 80 percent of the population belonged to the church. Recently there has been a tendency to relinquish church membership. The nation's ecclesiastical behavior is typified by a high proportion of infants who are baptized in their first year (68 percent), a large proportion of teenagers who are confirmed, and an overwhelming majority of couples who undergo church marriage ceremonies (80 percent).[31] While civil burials are almost unheard of, the law stipulates that unconsecrated ground shall be available wherever needed.[32] On the other hand, only a small proportion of the nation attends church services on a regular basis apart from the main festivals, such as Christmas. The behavior can thus be typified as "belonging without believing."

Administration

Each parish has a parish council which deals with its administration. The country is divided into deaneries, in each of which local church councils operate, dealing with matters common to the parishes in the area. The Evangelical Lutheran Church of Iceland consists of one diocese, with the Bishop of Iceland assisted by two Suffragan Bishops; their roles are vague and in need of further clarification. Bishops are elected by the pastors together with denominated lay representatives who are, however, a small minority of the electorate. The Bishop deals with the overall administration of the church together with other ecclesiastical authorities. He has oversight of Christianity, doctrine, the administration of the Evangelical Lutheran Church of Iceland and ecclesiastical discipline, as well as more traditional episcopal duties such as ordination of pastors and consecration

---

29. "Lög um sóknargjöld o.fl."
30. "Lög um stöðu, stjórn og starfshætti þjóðkirkjunnar."
31. *Óútgefnar tölur frá Hagstofu Íslands fengnar.*
32. "Lög um kirkjugarða, greftrun og líkbrennslu."

Exploring a Heritage: An Introduction

of churches. He also nominates pastors selected by parish selection committees.[33]

The General Synod has supreme power in the affairs of the Evangelical Lutheran Church of Iceland, within legally defined limits. Its decisions regarding ritual and matters of doctrine are subject to discussion in the annual Pastoral Synod and the approval of the Bishop before final ratification. The General Synod is attended by twelve pastors and seventeen laypersons.[34] The Bishop is the church's external representative. He and, at times, the Pastoral Synod or the General Synod represent the church's voice in the community. The Evangelical Lutheran Church of Iceland has experienced certain difficulties in bringing its influence to bear in the modern, pluralistic society. Its work is rather traditional and its voice not very strong in society at large, not even after the financial and social stirrings the country has suffered since the autumn of 2008.

Trends and Currents

Iceland did not have any revivalist movements in the nineteenth century, possibly because the nationalist movement and the fight for independence played the part in Iceland that religious revivalism played elsewhere in the Nordic countries. The Icelandic community was very small: less than 80,000 in 1900 (currently just under 320,000). Furthermore, the population was overwhelmingly rural, with only 6,500 living in Reykjavík.[35] Revivalist movements do not thrive in communities of this kind. During the first decades of the twentieth century a liberal theological tradition was prevalent amongst the clergy of the Evangelical Lutheran Church of Iceland, also later spiritualism, which for a while was a very vigorous movement within the church.[36] Around the middle of the century a more traditional and ecclesiastical theology began to emerge, along with a reversion to high church rituals; to a certain extent it could be called a liturgical movement.[37] This was concurrent with the above-mentioned increase in an eastern Scandinavian influence within the church. More recently there has been some criticism that the liturgical and theological changes since the middle of the century have isolated the church from

33. "Lög um stöðu, stjórn og starfshætti þjóðkirkjunnar."
34. Ibid.
35. Jónsson and Magnússon, *Icelandic Historical Statistics*, 49, 67.
36. Pétursson, "Þjóðkirkja, frelsi og fjölbreytni," 226–29, 280–81.
37. Ibid, 366–68.

society as a whole.[38] Controversies over the permission—granted last year—for same-sex couples to get married in church[39] and over the contest in 2011 between a woman and a man for the office of Suffragan Bishop, with the man finally elected, demonstrate tension between liberal and conservative arms of the church. It is, however, difficult to detect well-defined theological trends.

The Icelandic Church has long been active in the ecumenical context. It is a long-time member of the Lutheran World Federation, the Conference of European Churches, and the World Council of Churches. It has also taken part in the Porvoo Communion from the outset.

What Lies Ahead?

In the early twentieth century, separation of church and state was a much-debated subject. Many felt that separation was imminent and wanted to do their utmost to facilitate it.[40] This was a time when many people left the Evangelical Lutheran Church of Iceland and used their constitutional rights to establish free churches of other denominations or Evangelical Lutheran congregations outside the church. Such congregations were established in many places in Iceland, though only three are still operating, all of them in the capital area. As the laws about the Evangelical Lutheran Church of Iceland do not cover independent congregations like the Danish electoral congregations, these Lutheran free churches have no formal links with the Evangelical Lutheran Church of Iceland, even if their pastors are ordained by the latter's Bishop. The relationship between church and state has lain dormant for a long time, although a few proposals have been put forward. In recent years, around two-thirds of respondents to public surveys have declared themselves in favor of changes to the relationship between church and state, generally implying separation.

In the autumn of 2008, Iceland's financial system crashed, with extensive economic and sociological repercussions for a large section of Icelanders. Unemployment, for example, rose sharply. People flooded the streets to protest, with the result that the sitting government had to resign. In the wake of this "Saucepan Revolution," Parliament established a Special Investigation Commission to identify the causes of the crash.

---

38. Kristjánsson, "Kirkjan í keng," 69–80.
39. See the chapter by Sólveig Anna Bóasdóttir.
40. Hugason, "Þróun sjálfstæðrar þjóðkirkju á öndverði 20," 20–47.

Exploring a Heritage: An Introduction

It produced a remarkable report, published in nine large volumes.[41] The office of Special Prosecutor was established with the remit to examine whether there had been illegal activities. Finally a committee was set up, known as the Constitutional Council, to completely review the constitution of the Republic.[42] In the autumn of 2011, the Council presented its proposal for a new constitution, where Article 19 concerns the position of the church:

> The status of the State Church may be determined by law. In cases where Althingi amends the status of the State Church the matter shall be referred to a referendum of all qualified voters in the country for approval or rejection.[43]

Should this proposal reach the statute book, the Constitution will contain no provision relating to a state church, nor any special state support or protection for the Evangelical Lutheran Church. However, this does not necessarily imply absolute separation of church and state. It is clear from the above that the Evangelical Lutheran Church in Iceland has evolved beyond the frame in which it can be seen as a state church. But it has to be asked whether the church is about to break out of the traditional frame of a "national" church organization in the Nordic model. If that is the case, it could be regarded as a church that has become autonomous and operates within a contractual relationship with the state, especially concerning financial matters.

---

41. "Skýrsla rannsóknarnefndar Alþingis."
42. "Upplýsingar."
43. *Frumvarp til stjórnarskipunarlaga ásamt skýringum.*

Norway and Church of Norway

Statistics and Organization

Church of Norway	2010	2000
Norway's population	4,858,200	4,478,497
Members of Church of Norway	3,835,477	3,869,147
Parishes	1,285	Not available
Baptisms	41,100	48,023
Confirmations	41,981	37,330
Marriages	9,549	14,041
Funerals	38,290	31,531

Members in other Christian denominations	
The Roman Catholic Church	57,348
The Pentecostal Movement	39,590
Orthodox and Eastern Orthodox Churches	7,664

Members in other major faiths and beliefs	
Islamic/Muslim communities	98,953
Jewish communities	818
Humanist Society	78,000

Structure of Church of Norway[44]

Church of Norway understands itself as a confessing, missionary, serving, and open folk church. There are 1,285 parishes and 1,600 churches and chapels that belong to Church of Norway. Parish work is led by a vicar together with an elected parish council. Elections are carried out every fourth year. All in all there are about 9,000 elected lay persons in the parish councils.

There are 11 dioceses and as many bishops. Church of Norway has no archbishop but the bishop in Nidaros (Trondheim) is *primus inter pares*. Collectively the bishops have a responsibility to coordinate what is happening in the church. They also comment on issues concerning doctrines for the General Synod and the ministry.

44. Source: Church of Norway's website, http://www.kirken.no.

Exploring a Heritage: An Introduction

The Church of Norway General Synod meets annually. Of the 115 delegates, 77 are lay people. The Church of Norway National Council, led by a lay-person, is the Synod's executive body. Central administrative functions are carried out by the Ministry of Government Administration, Reform, and Church Affairs. Financial responsibility for salaries and the maintenance of buildings is shared by state and municipal authorities. Additional parish activity largely depends on offertory money and voluntary activities.

The Organization of Church of Norway

```
                                    ┌──────────────────────┐
                                    │ The King in Council  │
                ┌──────────────┐    ├──────────────────────┤
                │  Parliament  │    │ Ministry of Government│
                │              │    │ administration, Reform│
                └──────────────┘    │ and Church affairs    │
                                    └──────────────────────┘

                        ┌──────────────────┐
                        │  General Synod   │
                        └──────────────────┘

                        ┌──────────────────────────┐
                        │     National Council     │
                        ├──────────────────────────┤
                        │   Sami Church Council    │
                        ├──────────────────────────┤
                        │ Council on Ecumenical and│
                        │ International Relations  │
                        └──────────────────────────┘
```

Council structure	Voluntary council and meetings	Ecclesial structure
Diocesan Council	Diocesan Synod	Bishops' Conference
Joint Parish Council in the municipality	Deanery Council	Bishop
Parish Council	Parish Meeting	Rural Dean
		Parish pastor/ Parish priest/Parson/Vicar/Rector

Official Home Page of Church of Norway:
In Norwegian: www.kirken.no; in English: http://www.kirken.no/english/

Exploring a Heritage

A Nation Trembling[45]

On July 22, 2011, Norway was the target of a terrorist attack. Experts and people in general assumed that the attack was carried out by radical Muslims fighting jihad, holy war, in the name of Allah. There was speculation as to whether Norway's participation in the war in Afghanistan, or the publication of the Danish Mohammed cartoons in Norway, could be the underlying reason. There were reports of Muslims being attacked in Oslo in the following hours.

In the first attack, a car bomb exploded in the executive government quarter in Oslo, killing eight people. Several others were wounded, many critically. Two hours later, a second attack took place on the island of Utøya at the summer camp of the youth division of the Norwegian Labour Party, currently the governing party; a gunman opened fire on the participants, killing sixty-nine of them.

Later that day the gunman was arrested, and there were reports that the same person was assumed to have been responsible for both attacks. The gunman, Anders Behring Breivik, was subsequently charged with terrorism for both attacks. At the time of writing, November 2011, the proceedings against Breivik have not yet started. Breivik has acknowledged that he is responsible for both the bomb and the shooting.

Oslo Cathedral came to be the place of mourning and remembrance following the terrorist attacks. As soon as central Oslo was opened for the public after the bomb explosion, people gathered in front of, around, and in the cathedral, laying down flowers and lighting candles. The floral tributes grew rapidly and came to cover every open space around the cathedral. In the following weeks, more than 100,000 candles were lit in the cathedral. People gathered from all over Oslo and many travelled from different parts of Norway to lay down flowers and take part in the mourning and remembrance in and around the cathedral. There were many other smaller spontaneous shrines all over Oslo, but the cathedral came to be the central place where people gathered.

The subsequent memorial services and concerts in the cathedral were attended by royalty, politicians, prominent persons in Norwegian public and cultural life, as well as ordinary people. The terrorist's terrible actions united Norway and Oslo Cathedral was the main meeting place. Even the Norwegian Humanist organization, although critical of the cathedral

---

45. Written by Roger Jensen.

being used in this way, acknowledged that Church of Norway had handled the situation in a good, inclusive way.

One thing that the events following the tragedies in Oslo and Utøya do illustrate is the close relation between the people of Norway and Church of Norway, a church whose members make up 79 percent of Norway's population.

Comparative Perspectives: Church–State–People

What sort of church is it that has such strong relations to the people? That Church of Norway is Evangelical Lutheran, that it is a folk church or that it is a state church, is only an initial answer. To comprehend the situation in Norway, one needs to understand the history of the state, the church and the people. Within and between each of these there are both historical and contemporary intersecting tensions and developments. Space does not permit an exploration of these interconnections but some central areas of interest can be mentioned.

Although all the Nordic countries have a common tradition, since the sixteenth century, of state churches with a Lutheran confession, the churches now differ in important respects as regards their relation to the state. Today, the process of reforming the church-state relationship, in which the church to a larger degree seeks and is given independence from the state and seeks self-government, is well under way in Norway. However, Norway is ten to fifteen years behind Sweden in this question, but many years ahead of Denmark, where the process of independence has not, and perhaps will not be, developed to the same extent as in either Norway or Sweden.

A comparison of church-state relations in Norway, Sweden, and Denmark is interesting from several perspectives. A look at each country's religious and political history reveals that tensions and conflicts have been treated differently, and thus have come to shape the churches in different ways. In Denmark-Norway, pietism obtained royal support, whereas the opposite applied in Sweden. During the nineteenth century, the tension between the official church and popular pietistic religiosity led to the establishment of free churches in Sweden, whereas in Denmark-Norway the pietistic lay movements were integrated to a greater extent in the official church and were gradually allowed to establish associations or societies within it.

Exploring a Heritage

In Norway, the integration of the pietistic lay and revival movements in the state church gradually made them a strong force within that church. In Denmark, the pietistic movements had less of an impact on religious life in the state church, mainly due to N. F. S. Grundtvig (1783–1872) and subsequent "Grundtvigianism." In Sweden, the pietistic movements were suppressed by the official church and established mainly outside it.

These historical developments help to explain both central differences between the Nordic state churches and the present situation regarding the relationship between church and state. They also contribute to our understanding of the interests at stake, and indicate that changing state-church relations can have different implications in each of the Scandinavian countries regarding church life and people's feeling of belonging to the church.

The history of the state church as a regional and local organization in Norway has bound people and church together. Oslo Cathedral's role following the tragic events on July 22, 2011, is an expression of this strong relation. It is not self-evident that this strong link will last as the relation between church and state is altered.

Identity as a Challenge Today

In the manifest that he published immediately prior to the terrorist actions, the terrorist Anders Behren Breivik promotes himself as both Christian and pagan. More precisely, he calls himself a cultural Christian and ethnic pagan, adding that he is neither religious nor a believer. He relates cultural Christianity to Western culture, i.e., non-Islamic culture, and ethnic paganism to Norse mythology, with a focus on hierarchic order, traditionalist mythology, nationalistic pride, masculine honor, etc.

Breivik's position and actions are of course so extreme that they hardly serve for comparisons. However, they do raise the principal question of identity. In recent decades, Norway's religious landscape has rapidly become multifaceted. How should Church of Norway understand and express its identity in a situation where it is about to become one faith community among others, one church among other churches? How inclusive or exclusive should it be regarding different cultural and religious expressions in general and different Christian confessional expressions in particular? To what degree or in what way is the Lutheran identity of Church of Norway a positive resource in expressing this identity? This overall question of inclusiveness versus exclusiveness also relates to one

Exploring a Heritage: An Introduction

of the most important gains of modernity: the equal right of women and men, i.e., the question of gender equality within the church. The question of identity is at present Church of Norway's most pressing issue. It is not easy to tell in which direction the church is moving.

Major reforms are in progress in Church of Norway. One of them, due to be undertaken in the coming years, is a worship/liturgy reform, in which contextuality and local variations in worship and liturgy are seen as an asset. This is a positive development in so far as it seeks to meet a constantly more fragmentized and diversified society. Still, a lack of awareness of the church's historical and theological identity makes the question of direction and end result both interesting and challenging.

In the summer and early autumn of 2011, Oslo Cathedral became a place where people could come and express grief and sorrow on their own terms. The common yet differentiated practice of sorrow and grief that took place in and around the cathedral was a vivid expression of an openness and inclusiveness that transcended traditional cultural and to some extent even religious barriers. The cathedral's sacral space was extended to include the surrounding area. The degree to which Church of Norway will be able to maintain the close relationship to the people of Norway in the future, as Norwegian society gradually evolves into a multicultural society, is an open question.

Exploring a Heritage

Sweden and Church of Sweden

Statistics and Organization[46]

Church of Sweden	2010	2000
Sweden's population	9,415,570	8,882,792
Members of Church of Sweden	6,589,769	7,360,825
Parishes	1,467	2,517
Baptisms	62,122	65,832
Confirmations	35,796	45,673
Marriages	20,337	24,386
Funerals	73,162	81,839

Members in other Christian denominations	
The Pentecostal movement	118,266
Orthodox and Eastern Orthodox Churches	117,228
Mission Covenant Church of Sweden[46]	109,418
Catholic diocese of Stockholm	93,642
Baptist Union of Sweden	29,910
Evangelical Free Church	49,030
The Swedish Alliance Mission	22,427
Salvation Army	14,826

Members in other major faiths and beliefs	
Islamic/Muslim communities	110,000
The Official Council of Swedish Jewish Communities	8,673
Swedish Buddhist Union	6,173

Structure of Church of Sweden[48]

According to Church of Sweden Church Ordinance, the parish is the church's fundamental unit. There are approximately 1,500 parishes in

---

46. Source: "Svenska kyrkans statistikdatabas"; *SST Årsbok 2011*.

47. Baptist Union of Sweden, Methodist Church, and Mission Covenant Church of Sweden are in a process of merging into a single uniting church.

48. *2010 Review and Financial Summary*.

Church of Sweden, 1,000 fewer than a decade ago. In the next few years the number will probably continue to fall as small parishes are merged into larger units. A parish is led by a vicar together with a parish council. The main task for the parish council is the parish's economy and its future direction. The parish council is also responsible for the employment of staff. Since the year 2000, priests, including vicars, are employed by the local parish, not by the diocese.

Church of Sweden has three orders: deacons, priests, and bishops. There are thirteen dioceses, each one headed by a bishop, except for the diocese of Uppsala, which has a bishop and the archbishop. The bishops are elected by the ordained in the diocese together with as many lay-persons. The Church Ordinance stipulates that the task for the diocese is to supervise and promote parish life in the diocese.

Church of Sweden has a national level, located in Uppsala, which focuses on questions and tasks of relevance for the entire church. Examples are international work, theology and research, finance, information, and laws and regulations. The work at national level is led by a General Secretary. The General Synod is the church's supreme decision-making body. It has 251 delegates, who meet annually.

Since 2000, Church of Sweden is a free church and its relations to the state have changed. The church now keeps records only of its own members. Its main financial base is a membership fee of approximately 1 percent of income; the fee is collected by the state together with state taxes. This service is also extended to other religions and Christian denominations.

Exploring a Heritage

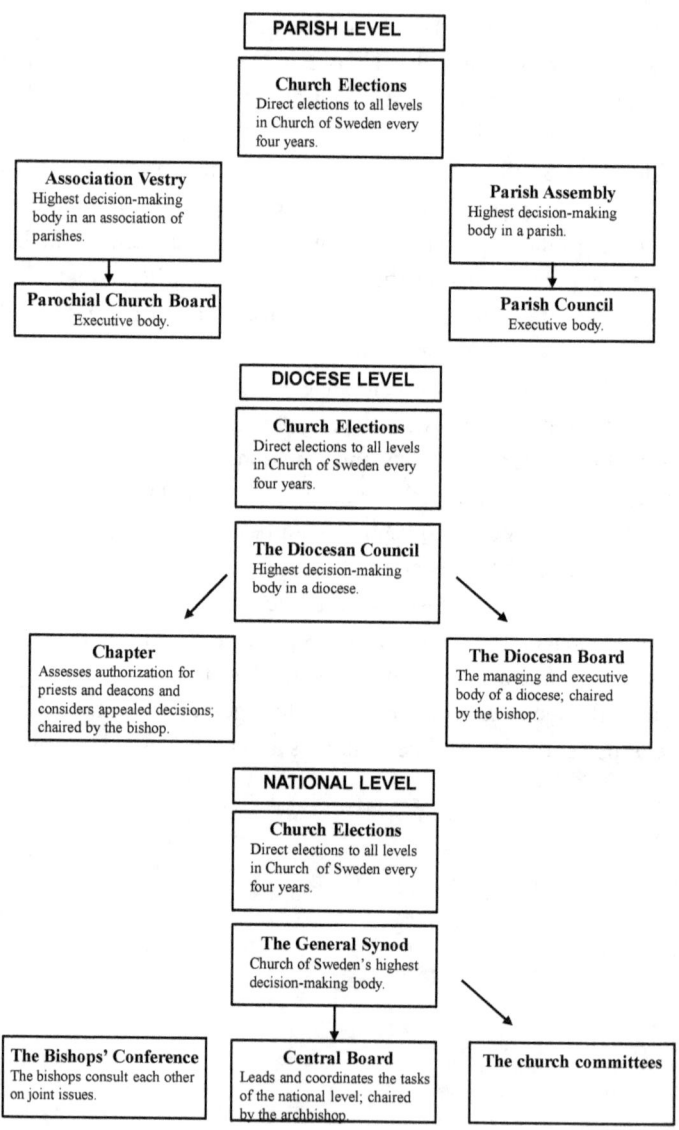

Official Home Page of Church of Sweden:
In Swedish: http://www.svenskakyrkan.se/; in English: http://www.svenskakyrkan.se/default.aspx?di=657804

Church of Sweden—Previously a State Church, Today . . . ?[49]

It is virtually impossible to draw a generally accepted picture of Church of Sweden. There are the perceptions of active parish members, elected officials and employees, as well as those of members who are never in touch with either the church organization or a local congregation, and those who are in touch from time to time. Then there are the views of non-members, society, and the media. There are highly positive and profoundly negative opinions, plus everything in between. Perhaps you could say that these pictures do not fit together because what they are seeking is impossible to capture in words. The church is neither its buildings, its members, nor its activities. At least not just that. The church is more—and in constant transition.

Over the past fifty years there have been numerous discussions in Sweden concerning issues about identity, how it is best understood and described. These discussions eventually led to a break in the five-hundred-year relation between church and state. Church of Sweden is now a free church, but what that means and its consequences remain to be seen.

Church of Sweden

Christianity reached Sweden more than a thousand years ago. Since then a church has existed in the geographic region we today call Sweden. Over the centuries, Church of Sweden has formed its specific identity. There have been developments and changes, and they will continue to occur. Some of them take time to become apparent; others are discussed and carefully planned, so that what is given by history can be made comprehensible in new situations and new contexts.

Since the Uppsala Synod in 1593, Church of Sweden is labeled Evangelical Lutheran. Today, Church of Sweden rests on its historical

---

49. Written by Niclas Blåder.

background; now, as before, people gather in congregations, and bishops consecrate for ecclesiastical service. Church of Sweden has over 6 million members, divided into 13 dioceses and almost 1,500 parishes. Its members make up over 70 percent of Sweden's population. This means that Church of Sweden is the world's largest Lutheran church in number of members. Even the name, Church of Sweden, shows that the church has, and above all has had, a profound impact on people and society in Sweden. This is the church to which the whole population was forced to belong until Baptists and other denominations were finally permitted in the second half of the nineteenth century. This is the church that has formed Swedish citizens for centuries, the church that until 1991 administered the civil registration of all Swedish citizens. In recent decades, however, changes have occurred at a rapid pace. Following disestablishment, approximately 50,000 people leave the church every year. Church of Sweden is not a religious authority for the individual in the way it used to be. Its importance for culture and society has diminished significantly. Some say that Church of Sweden is facing a crisis; others point out that this has been said of the church on numerous occasions in the past. Still others believe that religiosity has merely changed its form, and refer to surveys that show that people still put great trust in Church of Sweden, and that the decline in membership—albeit large—is not as great as was previously feared.

A Changing Society

Society is in a constant state of flux. It has always been that way but some changes are more rapid and extensive than others. The second half of the nineteenth century up to the present has been a time of great changes. An essentially agricultural Sweden, where the vast majority lived and worked in rural areas, has given way to industrialization and urbanization. The migratory flows to growing cities were accompanied by a process of democratization. Social movements grew, not least the trade union movement and the temperance movement. Universal suffrage was granted. Today, a majority of the population lives in urban areas. Industry is still important but other forms of economic activity have come to the fore. The collective is losing ground in favor of the individual.

Church of Sweden's situation changed considerably in this period, from being essentially the only Christian church in Sweden to being one of many Christian voices, although still by far the largest. Today the Christian Council of Sweden (CCS) has twenty-eight member churches. The ecumenical relations between Church of Sweden and the free churches have varied over the years, but today they are considered to be good, important, and stimulating. Regardless of this variation, the churches have lived side by side and have—more or less consciously—mutually influenced their development into what they are today. This development is also a reason for the current advance in cooperation and the agreements between many of the churches.

The changes in the social, political, and religious landscapes have been accompanied by trends towards secularization and individualization. In international surveys, Sweden—together with the other Nordic countries—stands out as a country where these concepts are highly ranked. However, secularization and individualization are not unambiguous concepts in everyday speech or in the scientific community. It is therefore difficult to pin down their importance in Sweden and Church of Sweden. A common interpretation of secularization and individualization points to the displacement of religion in society. Another interpretation focuses on how the "great stories," along with shared images and religious authorities, will lose their meaning in favor of individual perspectives. The latter seems to be the case in Sweden. But regardless of how the terms are interpreted, it is clear that Swedish society is undergoing a continuous change that greatly affects Church of Sweden, not least in that the knowledge of Christian faith and biblical stories that used to be passed on by families and taught in schools is now very weak.

In the past half-century, Sweden has become multicultural in a different way from before. Today, almost one and a half million out of Sweden's nine million inhabitants were born abroad. They have brought dreams and visions with them, their way of life, their stories and traditions. Sweden is in many ways a different country to what it was fifty years ago and, of course, this also affects the church. Partly as a consequence of society's changing ethnic makeup, partly because of the above-mentioned circumstances, voices began to advocate religion as something personal and therefore something that cannot be administered by a state church. At the turn of the twentieth century, Church of Sweden and the Swedish State completed a process that had started several decades earlier. A first step was taken 1951 when the laws changed so that Swedish citizens were no longer obliged to membership in a church or denomination; religious freedom had arrived. But the disestablishment of Church of Sweden took almost another fifty years. Today, Church of Sweden is—in most respects—a free church, with the General Synod, comprised of 251 elected representatives, as its supreme representative body.

Being a "Free" Church

Today, Church of Sweden decides its own internal affairs. This in many ways momentous transition from being a state church also means that the church's identity has changed to some extent. What is Church of Sweden today? Who makes up the church? What is its mission? There are many questions and they are being discussed at all levels within the church. Obviously the same questions could be discussed prior to the year 2000, but now that the church's identity is no longer tied to the Swedish State, they have acquired a new urgency. For example: What does the word *Sweden* in the name "Church of Sweden" mean, and what are the implications of how this question is answered?

These types of question are particularly relevant when, for example, reduced financial resources call for priorities that were less necessary before. The rate of baptisms is now falling towards 50 percent of all births and the name "Church of Sweden" causes some people to associate more to ethnicity than to a church. Of course, there are ways of dealing with such questions. Following the split from the state, the main text of Church of Sweden is the Church Ordinance. A central section presents a core view of the church's identity—it has to do with openness and inclusiveness:

> Church of Sweden is an open folk church with the mission to communicate the Gospel in word and deed. The church has room for everyone, for the seeker and the one who doubts, as well as for those who are strong in faith, for the one who has not reached far, as well as for those who have advanced further on the path of faith.[50]

Church of Sweden has seen and still sees itself as a folk church. Despite the concept's elusiveness, it aims to indicate that the church sees itself as a church not only, or predominantly, for those who are actively seeking access to church activities and worship services but to everyone in the country. How and in what ways people respond to the call of God is hidden to all but God. The central concept is therefore God's grace, not the human response. All that the church should and can do is to offer the Word and the sacraments. From this it follows that Church of Sweden

---

50. *Kyrkoordningen*, part VI. Introduction (translation by Niclas Blåder).

Exploring a Heritage: An Introduction

is a church whose congregations geographically cover the entire country and which thereby fulfills its mission of communicating God's grace to everyone. Church of Sweden is Church of *Sweden*, not least because its working field is the whole of Sweden. Every citizen has—if he or she so wishes—access to its churches and its activities. Open and with a non-demanding approach—that is how Church of Sweden wants to be comprehended. Another way to understand the church's identity—apart from its openness—is through the Church Ordinance's words about the basic task of the church:

> Church of Sweden appears locally as a parish. This is the primary unit within the church. The basic task of the parish is to celebrate service, to teach, practice diaconia and mission. The aim is that all people will come to faith in Christ and live by faith, a Christian community is created and deepened, the kingdom of God will spread and creation will be restored. Everything else that the parish does is support for and a consequence of this basic task.[51]

Jointly, the four dimensions build an entirety. Separately, none of them can fully express the nature of the church. Nor can the church be described fully by less than all four. The four dimensions point to Church of Sweden's double direction—inwards and outwards. Outwards the church tries, both nationally and internationally, through partners as well as in its own name, to live up to what the church considers to be its proper function, not least in social, environmental, peace and justice issues. Along with reaching "out," the church believes that no church can function without a core, without community, i.e., community can never be a "plus" that a church could lose and still be a church. Therefore, the Church Ordinance states that every parish is obligated to celebrate service every Sunday. Radical openness, but also social responsibility and attempts to build communities around the Word and the sacraments, are some of the ingredients that make up today's Church of Sweden.

Some Concluding Remarks

It might be a bit premature to draw conclusions in a book's introduction. After reading the four sections that follow, it is up to the reader to evaluate

---

51. Ibid., part II. Introduction (translation by Niclas Blåder).

the overall picture. Nevertheless, as editors of this book we want to point out a few things that might be relevant to a continued reading.

One conclusion that can be drawn already from the statistics is that the Lutheran churches in the North still—membership-wise—include the majority of the population in each country. Their national character is strong, although this is not always evident in the English names. It is worth noting that in the local language, none of the churches label themselves as Lutheran. They use names that point rather to being national or popular. In Icelandic the name is *Þjóðkirkjan*, which literally means the "national church." In Norway, the literal translation of the church's name is "the Norwegian church" (*Den Norske kirke*), just as *Svenska Kyrkan* literally means the "Swedish church." In Denmark the constitution talks about the church being Lutheran, but states that the Evangelical Lutheran Church is "the Danish folk church" (*Den danske Folkekirke*), indicating that the church is for the people of the country. All these names indicate a national or nationwide character of the church—it is *the* church in each country. And the countries are geographically divided into diocese and parishes that cover every square inch of the land. Of course, this does not imply a denial of the presence of other churches, but mirrors a historical situation.

Another thing that strikes the eye when reading the fifteen chapters that follow is a different use of language and concepts. Some of these differences may reveal dissimilar theological positions and self-understandings of the church as such. One difference with theological implications is that the churches use dissimilar words for naming the clergy in English. In their local languages, all four churches use the same word (albeit with different spellings, which is often the case between the Scandinavian languages): *prest* (Denmark and Norway), *prestur* (Iceland), and *präst* (Sweden). How should this be translated? Should the word be "priest," "minister," or "pastor" in English? The theologians from Denmark, Iceland, and Norway writing in this book have chosen to use "pastor," while those from Sweden use "priest." All the churches in the study ordain bishops and are members of the Porvoo Communion, with its Episcopal church structure. But of the four, only Church of Sweden claims an apostolic succession. This can be taken to indicate a more hierarchal ecclesial structure compared to the rest, as does the choice of preference for "priests" rather than "pastors." Nevertheless, Church of Sweden shares with the other four a synodal and democratic organization. And even if some formal decisions in Denmark and Iceland are still taken by the parliament, a strong defense of democracy within the organization must be seen as a characteristic feature of all these churches.

A glance at how the churches in Denmark[52] and Sweden[53] present their organization on their websites is also worth attention. The point of departure is the same in both cases, i.e., the local parish. But from parish level the Evangelical Lutheran Church in Denmark moves on to stress the members as the base of the organization. Church of Sweden's website similarly starts by writing about the local parish and its autonomy, although it is still a part of Church of Sweden as a whole. But unlike the Evangelical Lutheran Church in Denmark, the Swedish website continues by writing about the different categories of employee in the parish, such as priests, deacons, musicians, and others.

A shared characteristic is of course the idea of folk church, although the understanding of what that means, both practically and theologically, is far from clear. While the Danish authors, for example, seem to imply a church *of* the people, some of the Swedish texts seem to imply a church *for* the people. It is nevertheless safe to claim that being a democratic church is part of the folk church character, and seen as a consequence of a Lutheran heritage that stresses the priesthood of all believers. Being a folk church also means a nationwide presence with a geographical parish structure rather than faith-based congregations, even if the Evangelical Lutheran Church in Denmark accommodates such congregations within its parish structure. Such geographical presence reinforces an impression of these churches as national in character and may play a role in blurring what is really meant by being a folk church. It is worth noticing, however, that while the chapters from Denmark in particular but also Norway frequently use the term "fork church," the Swedish and Icelandic texts rarely do so.

The same two or three issues surface as being the most pressing in all the four churches. The first has to do with the relation between church and state. Church of Sweden has undergone a formal disestablishment, and Church of Norway is right now undergoing such a process and the question has been debated recently in Iceland. There appear to be no strong forces at work for a similar development in Denmark but the relation between church and state nevertheless seems to be constantly reformulated.

52. "Folkekirkens organisation."
53. "Organisation."

Exploring a Heritage

Another burning issue has to do with gender and homosexuality. Although the ordination of women to the priesthood has for a long time been a well-established fact in all four churches, there are still pockets of resistance. However, the new target for the more conservative and traditional groups (both high- and low-church theological positions), in their opposition to the liberal theology that on the whole characterizes the Lutheran folk churches in the North, is today the issues of gay marriages and the blessing of homosexual partnerships.

The debate on both these questions plays a role also for the debate concerning the relation between church and state. Denmark, Norway, Iceland, and Sweden are countries where views about women and sexuality have changed hugely over the past fifty years. This raises the question of the degree to which the churches have been able to formulate their own positions on these issues. Some would say that new church legislation, which allows women to officiate at the altar, the blessing of gay couples or, as in Church of Sweden, gay marriages performed by the church, is an expression of submissiveness to the state. Others would argue that it is an expression of the gospel, and that it is part of the Lutheran tradition to acknowledge that the will of God works also outside the church.

Seeing that the four churches portrayed in this study are more or less intertwined with societies that are among the seven which come out best in the *Global Gender Gap Report*,[54] it is not surprising that, generally speaking, the situation for women must be described as fairly good. However, that immediately raises the question of how such a thing can be measured. While many women now hold positions within the four churches' democratic systems, there is still an imbalance in the senior positions. The same is true of the clergy. Women bishops and deans are still far outnumbered by men.

It is also worth noting that, at first glance, the (Neo-)Pentecostal and/or Charismatic winds that are blowing through the churches in the Global South seem to be absent from the four churches in our study. One possible conclusion is that, membership-wise, these large church bodies seem to be affected only marginally, if at all. However, individual parishes and church members in Denmark, Norway, and Sweden are evidently combining traditional piety with global Charismatic influences to build new structures and theological emphasis. This is done differently in these three countries, with for example *electoral* and *free congregations* in Denmark,

---

54. In the WEF's 2010 *Global Gender Gap Report*, Iceland ranks most favorably, followed by Norway, Finland, Sweden, New Zealand, Ireland, and Denmark.

Exploring a Heritage: An Introduction

church development in Norway, and the *Oasis movement* and *Alpha courses* in Sweden.

It is obvious that the interest in claiming a Lutheran identity is stressed to different degrees. A Lutheran claim seems to be most important in the Danish chapters, followed by the Norwegian. At the same time it is hard to detect a shared understanding between and within the churches in the study on what it means to be Lutheran. There seems to be a tendency to use "folk church" and "Lutheran church" more or less synonymously. This lack of a normative consensus regarding what it means to be a Lutheran church confirms the overall assumption that is the point of departure for the whole of the research project concerning Lutheran formation today, launched by the Church of Sweden Research Unit. Seeing that three of the churches are among the largest in the Lutheran World Federation, such a non-normative understanding of Lutheran identity calls for further investigation.

Bibliography

2010 Review and Financial Summary for the Church of Sweden, National Level (*Årsredovisning 2010 för Svenska Kyrkans Nationella Nivå*). 2011. Online: http://www.svenskakyrkan.se/default.aspx?di=787172 (accessed 23/9/2011).

Constitution of the Republic of Iceland. No. 33, 17 June 1944, as amended 30 May 1984 and 31 May 1991. Constitutional Court of Armenia. Online: http://www.concourt.am/armenian/legal_resources/world_constitutions/constit/iceland/icelnd-e.htm (accessed 23/9/2011).

"Danmarks Statistik." Online: http://www.statistikbanken.dk/statbank5a/default.asp?w=1280 (accessed 10/10/2011).

"Folkekireken og Grundloven." Online: http://www.folkekirken.dk/om-folkekirken/folkekirken-og-grundloven/ (accessed 10/10/2011).

"Folkekirken og menighedsrådene." Online: http://menighedsraad.dk/menighedsraadene/folkekirken-og-menighedsraadene.html (accessed 30/10/2011).

"Folkekirkens organisation." Online: http://www.folkekirken.dk/om-folkekirken/ (accessed 30/10/2011).

Frumvarp til stjórnarskipunarlaga ásamt skýringum. Online: http://stjornlagarad.is/other_files/stjornlagarad/Frumvarp_med_skyringum.pdf (accessed 18/10/2011).

The Global Gender Gap Report. Geneva: WEF, 2010. Online: http://www3.weforum.org/docs/WEF_GenderGap_Report_2010.pdf (accessed 15/03/2011).

"Grundvöllur fjármála þjóðkirkjunnar." Online: http://www2.kirkjan.is/stjornsysla/fjarmal/grundvollur (accessed 18/10/2011).

Hugason, Hjalti. "Þróun sjálfstæðrar þjóðkirkju á öndverðri 20. öld. Fyrstu tilraunir til að koma á kirkjuþingi á Íslandi." *Ritröð Guðfræðistofnunar / Studia Theologica Islandica* 31 (2010).

Exploring a Heritage

Inglehart, Ronald and Chris Welzel. "The WVS Cultural Map of the World." World Values Survey. Online: http://www.worldvaluessurvey.org/wvs/articles/folder_published/article_base_54 (accessed 20/9/2011).

Jónsson, Guðmundur and Magnús S. Magnússon, editors. *Icelandic Historical Statistics*. Reykjavík: Hagstofa Íslands, 1997.

"Kirkestatistik." Online: http://www.km.dk/folkekirken/statistik-og-oekonomi/kirke statistik.html (accessed 10/10/2011).

Kristjánsson, Gunnar. "Kirkjan í keng. Hugleiðingar um þróun íslensku þjóðkirkjunnar á tuttugustu öld." In *Andvari*. Nýr flokkur XLII. 125 ár. Reykjavík, 2000.

Kyrkoordningen. Online: http://www.svenskakyrkan.se/default.aspx?id=637938 (accessed 20/03/2011).

Lodberg, Peter. "The Evangelical Lutheran Church in Denmark, 1940–2000." In *Nordic Folk Churches: A Contemporary Church History*. Grand Rapids: Eerdmans, 2005.

"Lög um kirkjugarða, greftrun og líkbrennslu." No. 36 4 1993. Online: http://www.althingi.is/lagas/139a/1993036.html (accessed 18/10/2011).

"Lög um sóknargjöld o.fl." No. 91 29 1987. Online: http://www.althingi.is/lagas/139a/1987091.html (accessed 18/10/2011).

"Lög um stöðu, stjórn og starfshætti þjóðkirkjunnar." No. 78 26 1997. Online: http://www.althingi.is/lagas/139a/1997078.html (accessed 18/10.2011).

The Nature and Mission of the Church: A Stage on the Way to a Common Statement. Faith and Order Paper 198. Geneva: WCC, 2005.

"Organisation." Online: http://www.svenskakyrkan.se/default.aspx?id=659322 (accessed 30/10/2011).

"Organization." Online: http://www2.kirkjan.is/node/10175 (accessed 18/10/2011).

Oútgefnar tölur frá Hagstofu Íslands fengnar. 26/9/2011.

Pétursson, Pétur. "Þjóðkirkja, frelsi og fjölbreytni." In *Til móts við nútímann*. Kristni á Íslandi 4. Reykjavík: Alþingi, 2000.

"Religion i Danmark 2011." Online: http://teo.au.dk/csr/rel-aarbog11/forside/ (accessed 10/10/2011).

Ryman, Björn, et al. *Nordic Folk Churches: A Contemporary Church History*. Forskning för Kyrkan 2. Grand Rapids: Eerdmans, 2005.

"Samningur íslenska ríkisins og þjóðkirkjunnar um fjárframlög." 10 January 1997. Online: http://www.innanrikisraduneyti.is/utgefid-efni/ymislegt/nr/674 (accessed 18/10/2011).

Sigurðsson, Bjarni. *Geschichte und Gegenwartsgestalt des isländischen Kirchenrechts*. Europäische Hochschulschriften / Publications Universitaires Européennes / European University Studies, series 2, 524. Frankfurt: P. Lang, 1986.

"Skýrsla rannsóknarnefndar Alþingis." Online: http://rna.althingi.is/ (accessed 18/10/2011).

SST Årsbok 2011. Sundbyberg: Nämnden för statligt stöd till trossamfund, 2011.

"Svenska kyrkans statistikdatabas." Online: http://statistik.svenskakyrkan.se (accessed 14/06/2011).

"Upplýsingar." Online: http://stjornlagarad.is/upplysingar/um-stjornlagarad/ (accessed 18/10/2011).

Wiberg Pedersen, Else Marie. "Hvorfor er økumeni så svær i Danmark—Brikker til en mosaik." In *En levende mangfoldighed: Brudstykker til en økumenisk historie i Danmark 1989–2005*. Købenavn: Aros Forlag, 2007.

PART ONE

Exploring a Heritage

Burning Issues

WHAT ARE THE BURNING issues in the church, and the most demanding problems? In this first section of the book we will look into central questions for each of the churches. What is considered to be a burning issue is of course a matter of interpretation and each writer has been free to decide what to highlight. Taken together, however, the four authors provide a snapshot of what is on the agenda for the Lutheran folk churches in the North today. The following chapters show that whether the issues have to do with ethical and theological questions, problems in the surrounding society, or decisions taken by legislative bodies, it is quite clear that what is currently a burning issue in one of the churches, has been, or soon will be, on the agenda also in the other churches.

Roger Jensen highlights the current debate on church-state relations in Norway in this section's first chapter, "The Formation and Identity of the Church as a Present Challenge in Norway." Specifically he discusses three important steps. The first, taken by Church of Norway (2002), uses religious freedom to argue that all churches and religious communities should be treated equally. The second step, taken by the Norwegian government (2006), argues for a "free state church" where Church of Norway should have its foundation in a special Church Act, adopted by the parliament. The third, taken by the parliament (2008), is a political agreement that Church of Norway shall continue to be a "folk church," implying that the church is a part of the state but not governed by the state. Jensen further discusses this new situation's ecclesiological implications and challenges for the church as a "free state church."

The second contribution, Peter Lodberg's "Burning Issues in the Evangelical Lutheran Church in Denmark," takes as a point of departure the church as a national folk church. The author argues that being a public church/actor in society is a challenge to the church and may even generate friction and splits. In his chapter, this challenge is considered in a discussion with four examples. The first is the church as an asylum for refugees, with a split between those defending human ideals and those arguing for strict laws. The second deals with the response to the call to bell ringing for environmental protection. The third is the discussion about the Evangelical Lutheran Church in Denmark's response to the Porvoo Declaration. The fourth example is same-sex marriage. Lodberg concludes that the church "is in the process of finding a new place in society and it serves as a battleground for different theological and political opinions."

Carl Reinhold Bråkenhielm discusses in the chapter "Ethics and Ecclesiology: Burning Issues for Church of Sweden—and Beyond" whether and, if so, how a theological justification can be found for Church of Sweden's endorsement of same-sex relationships. Two examples are discussed. The first deals with homosexuality and same-sex marriages. The second discusses how Church of Sweden takes authoritative decisions concerning bioethics, using historical tradition and contemporary context. The focus is on Christian ethics and the relationship to ecclesiology, as well as the tension between the identity of the church, the secular context, and social credibility. The author claims that, while wrestling with modernity, it is possible to preserve integrity and identity, besides being credible to the world. The conclusion states: "If God is at work in creation *and* through the gospel of God's grace, each of these perspectives is equally and perennially relevant. And thus they should be equally and perennially relevant for the church."

Same-sex marriage is also a burning issue in Iceland, as shown in the chapter "Same-Sex Marriage: A Burning Issue in the Evangelical Lutheran Church of Iceland," by Sólveig Anna Bóasdóttir. With a background in the Lutheran understanding of marriage and the relation between church and state, she analyzes the debate on same-sex relations in Iceland. She examines both the public debate preceding the amendment to marriage legislation in 2010 and the debate in the Evangelical Lutheran Church of Iceland in relation to the same-sex legislation, as well as the church's response to the law. The chapter concludes with a description of the necessary changes taken by the church, enabling the marriage liturgy to include two individuals of the same sex, with no distinction regarding the words "marriage" or "to marry."

2

The Formation and Identity of the Church as a Present Challenge in Norway

Roger Jensen

THE CHURCH AND STATE relation in Norway has been a topic of debate for centuries. It is a common tradition of the Nordic countries that the churches, since the sixteenth century, have been organized as state churches with a Lutheran confession. Confronted with the challenge of multiculturalism the church and state relation in Norway is presently changing in a paradigmatic way as both church and parliament await the year of 2012. In the year 2012 an agreement among all the political parties in the parliament of Norway made in 2008 is planned to be effectuated. The agreement will reform the church-state relationship. Nearly two hundred years after the Norwegian Constitution was written in 1814, the Norwegian parliament is preparing to rewrite the constitution regarding the place and role of the church. With all likelihood it will make Church of Norway into what is publicly called a "free state church." The background, the context, and the practical and theological challenges related to this process are the topic of what follows.

PART ONE: Exploring a Heritage—Burning Issues

Historical Background

In order to understand the situation in Norway, one cannot study Norway alone; one also has to look at the overall Nordic context that Norway belongs to and is part of. In the following, in order to understand both similarities and differences in how the church and state relationship has developed in Norway as compared to the other Nordic countries, I will initially focus on the complex and differentiated historical background. Based on this historical background I will discuss the formation and identity of the church as a present challenge in Norway.

Since the sixteenth century the governing of the church as an integrated part of the governing of the state has been a characteristic of the Nordic countries. The power and authority of the king and of the church came to be intertwined; the one came to lend authority to the other. Whereas Luther and the Reformation distinguished between the spiritual and temporal, as expressed in the teaching of the two realms, such a division is not characteristic of the Nordic countries. On the contrary, state and church came to be most tightly integrated.

In the Kingdom of Denmark-Norway the vicars were the main instruments in the local governing of the kingdom, as the most prominent representative of the king in the local communities. The Lutheran clergy represented both God and king seeing that not only gospel but also royal ordinances and new laws were preached from the pulpits. In the so-called *era of state pietism*[1] in Denmark-Norway, the knowledge by heart of the book commonly known as *Pontoppidan* was obligatory for confirmation. The book was an introduction to Christendom based on the *Small Catechism* of Martin Luther in the form of as many as 759 questions and answers, written by the Danish vicar Pontoppidan in 1737 and still in use in Norway at the beginning of the twentieth century. The confirmation, which came to be a precondition for obtaining civil rights such as right to marriage, right to property etc., was a vital instrument in establishing citizenship.

Religion gave legitimacy to the authorities. The king had his power and authority from God. The church was a central instrument in building the state and ensuring morals among the citizens, and religion also came to demarcate the territory of one state from another (cf. the Peace of

---

1. I.e., how legislation in Denmark-Norway was colored by the ideals of pietism in particular under the rule of King Frederik IV (1671-1730) and King Christian VI (1699-1746). Of special importance is the introduction of the confirmation (1736), the *Pontoppidan* (1737), and the establishment of public schools (1739).

Westphalia). Religious confession was an important part of the legislation of the state.

The West- and the East-Nordic Regions

Although there are many similarities in the development of the Nordic countries, scholars have lately also pointed to decisive differences.[2] This is especially related to the Reformation in general and the age of pietism in particular. In Denmark-Norway, the Faeroe Islands and Iceland, what has been entitled the West-Nordic Region, the church order quickly became Lutheran and the church became an integrated part of the state, as argued above. Former church property was taken over by the king and used in building the state, in a process similar to the dissolution of the monasteries in England. This did not happen in the same way in Sweden and Finland. In this so-called East-Nordic Region the situation came to be different. The churches in these countries came to have a larger continuity with the church of the Middle Ages, maintaining a larger part of the church property and having a larger degree of self-government compared to the West-Nordic Region.

The following attitudes with regard to pietism and the revivalist-movements in the eighteenth and nineteenth centuries came to enforce these differences. As pietism spread from Germany to the Nordic countries at the end of the seventeenth century, it was from the very beginning suppressed in the East-Nordic Region by strict legislation. In the West-Nordic Region pietism came to be supported by the king and spread through the clergy. During the nineteenth century the tension between official church and the popular pietistic religiosity in Sweden led to the establishment of free churches, i.e., churches *outside of* the official church, whereas in the West-Nordic Region the pietistic layman movements were integrated in the official church and gradually allowed to establish associations or societies *within* the official church. This happened also to a large extent in Finland, where religious and national revivalism coincided.

Pietism also came to represent a change in the relationship between the individual and God, revitalizing the Reformation concept of the "priesthood of all believers": a concept that in principle put all Christians on the same level facing God, at times causing tension between laity and

---

2. Cf. in particular the research of Dag Thorkildsen (Oslo, Norway) and Lisbet H. Christoffersen (Copenhagen, Denmark).

clergy, and that *de facto* had lost its function in the three hundred years following the Reformation as there was no room or possibility for criticizing clergy or doctrine without risking punishment. Radical pietism caused much disturbance in all of the Nordic countries in the first half of the eighteenth century, as many members of this movement were arrested or expelled as they were believed to be representing a type of social rebellion, hence a threat to the state. Nevertheless, the wing of pietism loyal to the state church in the West-Nordic Region continued in their loyalty to Lutheranism and the authorities and would work for both a spiritual religious revival within the official church and for improving the social welfare within society in general. Therefore pietism came to be accepted and promoted by the king of Denmark-Norway, although their religious assemblies were to be supervised by the local clergy. These assemblies in the second half of the nineteenth century developed into larger networks and associations.

As shown above, the Nordic countries confronted pietism and revivalism in the eighteenth and nineteenth century in different ways. Their different attempts to control or suppress these movements eventually resulted in freedom to assemble and freedom of religion, and as a result the clergy gradually lost their control over religious activity. This development in all the Nordic countries, at different stages, came to mean religious and ideological individualization, differentiation, and pluralization and a break with the religious unity of the pre-modern society. In this process of change Lutheran religion and church played a central role, representing both continuity and modernity. It was a process that went hand in hand with the process of breaking up the pre-modern agrarian society. While this process of religious and ideological individualization, differentiation and pluralization had already started in the middle of the nineteenth century in Denmark-Norway, it came much later in Sweden and Finland. The central issue in the nineteenth century in Sweden and Finland was on the freedom of the church, i.e., the question of self-government. This larger historical background explains common traits among the Nordic countries as well as differences—differences that can be fruitfully explained with the differentiation between the West- and East-Nordic Regions, such as: the particular high church characteristic of Church of Sweden compared to the other Nordic countries, and why Church of Sweden as of the year 2000 is no longer a state church.

Constitutional Basis for Church of Norway

The West-Nordic Region has a history of state churches stretching over five hundred years, a history where the state church as concrete regional and local organization has tied people and church together. With regards to Norway this long history has resulted in a constitutional basis for the relationship between church and state, as expressed in the 1814 Constitution of Norway. This is particularly evident from the second article of the Constitution of the Kingdom of Norway, which in its present revised and modernized form declares: "All inhabitants of the Realm shall have the right to free exercise of their religion. The Evangelical Lutheran religion shall remain the official religion of the State." Furthermore the king is the constitutional head of Church of Norway, exercising his authority through the Council of State, which appoints bishops and deans.[3] Legislation and finances concerning the church are passed by the parliament. The king's ministry, which is in charge of church affairs, provides the organizational and financial framework for Church of Norway, is responsible for the administration of comprehensive church legislation and regulations, and has administrative responsibility for the clergy and governing bodies within Church of Norway.

Through the twentieth century the king has delegated much authority to the church, i.e., authority linked to liturgy and the inner life of the church.

The Current Church and State Process in Norway

One decisive argument that has come to characterize the current debate in Norway regarding the church and state question is the argument over *freedom of religion*. This argument is by no means new to the debate. Through the twentieth century the argument of freedom of religion was promoted strongly by central voices within the church, both among laity and clergy (cf. the so-called Reform Movement), and was used in arguing in favor of freedom of the church and its independence from the state, i.e., the question of self-government. This argument was repeatedly rejected by politicians with support of the liberal part of the church through the century, as some feared that independence and self-government would

---

3. The Council of State decides on church matters in what is called "Kirkelig statsråd," i.e., a separate council constituted by those members of government who are baptized church members.

PART ONE: Exploring a Heritage—Burning Issues

make the church more conservative and alienate it to the vast majority of the church members. This position has to be understood in relation to the development of the church in Norway as described above: how the pietistic layman and the revival movements came to be integrated into the church and gradually became a strong force within the church. This was very different from Sweden, where the pietistic movements were suppressed and established outside of the official church, and very different from Denmark, where the pietistic movement did not have a strong impact on religious life—mainly due to Grundtvig (1783–1872) and the following "Grundtvigianism."

The Church Report of 2002

When the argument for freedom of religion was promoted at the end of the twentieth century, it was used differently. There have been two major reports on the state church issue: one church report from 2002 and one from the government in 2006. In the church report of 2002,[4] it was argued that all churches and religious communities in Norway should be treated equally. The privileged position of Church of Norway should cease and the present state church ought to be dismantled. It was further suggested that the Norwegian state should have a more active policy in supporting all churches and religious communities. In the church report, that was supported by the General Synod of the church, the argument for freedom of religion is not used in what had become the traditional way: as an argument in favor of self-government. The argument for freedom of religion is now used with regard to the multireligious and multicultural Norwegian society at the brink of a new century: the need for equal treatment of all religions and confessions. Hence the present church and state relationship should be changed and the constitution rewritten. This change in the use of the argument made it possible for both conservatives and liberals within the church to put the argument forth with equal strength—a *de facto* uniting of both the traditional want for self-government and the honest interest and care for the minority faiths.

There has also been an interesting aspect of the argumentation and the use of the argument for freedom of religion in the church report and in the subsequent argument, which is that it has hardly focused on the concrete negative implications of the present state church: actual

---

4. Bakkevig, *Samme kirke—ny ordning*.

concrete examples or cases of suppression of freedom of religion are not the starting point. The debate has been more ideological or political in character. Whether the role of Church of Norway as a state church *in praxis* has a marginalizing function with regard to other faith communities has only been discussed to a smaller extent, most likely because the Norwegian government traditionally[5] has had a supportive policy with regards to other faith communities outside of the official church, giving equal financial support *per capita*.

The Government's Report of 2006

The question whether it is possible to adjust the constitution in a way that simultaneously upholds the close relation between people and church, and gives the necessary attention and respect to minority faiths, came to be at the very center of the discussion following the government's report of 2006.[6] The report was intended to give a basis on which to decide whether Norway's state church system should be maintained, reformed, or abolished. The majority recommendation in the government's report argued in favor of a "free state church." A "free state church" would mean reforming the present state church arrangement so that Church of Norway should neither be established in the Constitution of Norway, as it is today, nor in the laws regulating all other churches and life philosophies, but be founded (by the parliament) in a brief separate Church Act for Church of Norway alone. Furthermore the General Synod of Church of Norway should define its own constitution. The following common principles were also underlined in the government report: that the state should be positive in supporting all churches and life philosophies; that the state should protect freedom of religion in an active way; that the state, alongside with the municipalities, has financial responsibility for the activity of the churches; and that religion and life philosophy are fundamental and good for the civil community and local societies. Furthermore it underlined that Church of Norway should continue as a folk church and that baptism is the only criterion for church membership.

The choice of terminology in the government's report, in arguing in favor of a "free state church," is both interesting and confusing. Giving an

---

5. Cf. the introduction of new legislation as of 1969: "Lov om trudomssamfunn og ymist anna."

6. *Staten og Den norske kirke* (NOU 2006:2).

PART ONE: Exploring a Heritage—Burning Issues

exact definition of the concept of a state church is not a simple task. One plausible way of defining the concept, as has been done in this paper, is to relate it to the question of power and authority. In a state church the authority of the state/king and of the church is intertwined, i.e., the governing authority of the state is also, to some extent, a governing authority of the church. According to such a definition the majority recommendation in the government's report would imply a disestablishment of the state church in Norway. Church of Sweden is no longer called a state church, although the process that took place in Sweden with regard to changing the state church relations, which was concluded in January 2000, to a large degree parallels what is suggested in the Norwegian government's report of 2006. In Denmark the introduction of freedom of religion in the constitution of 1849 resulted in a new definition of the church in the constitution, from being defined as a state church to becoming a folk church. In praxis the authority of the state and of the church has continued to be, and still is, intertwined in Denmark.

A positive way of characterizing the choice of terminology in the government's report of 2006 would be to say that it is intended to express the intention and hope of a continued close relationship between people and church. Critically, one could characterize the choice of terminology as disguising what is popularly thought of as possible negative implications of the fact that the church-state relation changes in a fundamental manner, i.e., that the changes can lead to a *weaker* folk church relation.

The following hearing among parish councils (1,085 responses) and from joint parish councils in the municipalities (222 responses) yielded an interesting result. About half of the respondents wanted a partial disconnection of the church and state relationship, but still a degree of connection to the Constitution of the Kingdom of Norway. The other half wanted the status quo concerning the church-state relationship, with minor reforms in the church's structure. The General Synod of Church of Norway endorsed the majority proposition of the government's report (75 percent of the synod).

There is an interesting difference in focus when comparing the two reports, differences that can be explained due to both their respective mandates and interests. The main focus and interest in the church report is on the religious and juridical rights of individuals and groups, as universal human rights—promoting and protecting these and arguing for changes in the present church and state relationship accordingly. Whereas the government report additionally has a strong interest and focus on the folk church, i.e., how the state church as a concrete regional and local organization of the church in Norway has tied people and church together. The report explicitly notes that the relationship between people and church as defined by the concept of folk church, which is argued for as both historically and presently being of great importance to the people of Norway both individually and collectively, is more important than the relationship between church and state.

The Parliament Agreement of 2008

Following the main lines of the church report with regards to observing basic human rights and the majority vote of the government report with regard to underlining the close relationship between church and people, there was in 2008 an agreement among all the political parties in the parliament on the question of reforming the church and state relationship.

The following aspects of the agreement were especially underlined and highlighted in the national media: a) that the church should appoint their own bishops and deans; b) that 50 percent of the members in government should no longer need to be members of Church of Norway; c) that bishops and vicars in general still should receive their pay from the state; d) that there should be no specific church tax; and, e) that the king of Norway should be a member of Church of Norway. The agreement also states that Church of Norway continues to be a folk church,[7] a new concept in the Constitution of Norway, yet similar to the definition of the Church in Denmark in the Danish Constitution of 1849.

This agreement between church and state implies that Church of Norway will continue to be a *part of* the state yet not *governed by* the state, hence a "free state church"—a concept that is used similarly to the concept of folk church. The condition for allowing this development, as underlined in the agreement, is that there is a sufficient democratic development within the church. The meaning of "sufficient" remained unclear. If this democratic development takes place, the overall vote of the parliament is planned to take place in June 2012. The agreement of 2008 was welcomed and hailed among bishops and church leaders. As this agreement implies a rewriting of the Constitution of Norway, it is the

---

7. The agreement of 2008 states a new § 16 in the brief new law only for Church of Norway (cf. the government's report of 2006, cited above).

successive parliament, the one that will be elected in 2013, that will make the agreement a constitutional and judicial reality.

Challenges and Open Questions

The history of the state church in Norway, stretching over five hundred years, is a history of tying people and church together. The state church has been the dominant supplier of conditions for religious identity and praxis in Norway, especially related to the rites of passage in the churches and the graveyards and through local church life: a religious identity and praxis that simultaneously is related to morals, to culture, tradition and local geographic places, the annual festivals, national festivals, national days of celebration and mourning, an identity that can be observed in art and cultural life, etc. Still almost 80 percent of the population of Norway are members of Church of Norway.

The state church has undeniably ensured religion a prominent place in the public sphere in Norway, related to national events and the life of the royal family. Until the beginning of the twentieth century the knowledge of *Pontoppidan* was decisive for obtaining central civil rights and the religious education in the public schools was conceived of as baptismal education until 1969. Gradually the baptismal education was conceived of as being the sole responsibility of the church, not the responsibility of the public school, resulting in an catechumenal program that has become known as "the faith nurturing reform program" of the church (*Trosopplæringsreformen*), which was decided upon and financed by the parliament in the year of 2003 granting similar financial support *pro capita* also to minority faiths.[8] The fact that the state finds it natural to finance the faith nurturing reform program is both a poignant expression of the tight bonds that exists between the people and the church after five hundred years of having a state church and is an explicit expression of the political agreement to maintain this relationship and, at the same time, a telling expression of how the state tries to maneuvers in a society that has become multireligious and multicultural.

The pressing question is: how will the changes and the gradual loosening of the bonds that takes place between state and church will affect the close relation between people and church? Will the openness and

---

8. In 2010 the government granted 130 million NoK (approximately € 16 million) to the faith-nurturing reform program of Church of Norway.

inclusiveness of the church that has come to characterize the state church change? Will the close relationship between church and people change? In the following I will discuss this question with regard to two central tenets in the Lutheran understanding of the church, i.e., the ecclesiology: *baptism* and the *priesthood of all believers*.

Ecclesiological Implications and Challenges

A unique radicalism and a sharp critique of the role and position of the ministry of the church came to mark the ecclesiology of the Lutheran reformation. The medieval division of the society between *two peoples*, clergy and people living in monastic orders on the one hand and laity on the other, came under radical critique as Luther argued that baptism is the sole sacrament of ordination. Hence, according to Luther, everyone who is baptized is already, through baptism, ordained a minister, bishop, or pope.[9] Not only were the *religiosi* (clergy, monks, and nuns) given direct responsibility for the life and the prosperity of the church, but such responsibility belonged to all baptized members of the church for ensuring the supremacy of Christ in his church. The role of the kings and princes in the lives of the Lutheran churches in the centuries following the Reformation exemplify this ecclesiological radicalism, a role they were given as baptized members of the church and as leaders of their people. The fact that others than the *religiosi* were given legitimate power in matters vital to the church was an expression of ecclesiological radicalism.

The critical question with regards to the ongoing state church process in Norway is whether, or to what extent, the radicalism of the Lutheran ecclesiology is institutionalized in new forms. The question is related to which way of organizing the church best preserves both the freedom and the authority of the baptized member of the church, and the special role and place of the ministry (the proclamation of the gospel and the administration of the sacraments). The government's report of 2006 goes further than the church report of 2002 in stressing the need for strengthening the *democratic structure* of the church through indirect and direct church elections, and the parliamentary agreement of 2008 makes the strengthening of the democratic structure a precondition for transforming the state church organization into a free state church organization. How does the question of democracy relate to Lutheran

9. Cf. Luther, *To the Christian Nobility of the German Nation*, WA 6:408, 11–13.

PART ONE: Exploring a Heritage—Burning Issues

ecclesiology? More concretely: how does the ideal of democracy relate to the understanding of Christ as head of the church as radically expressed in the Lutheran ecclesiology?

The church is in need of an organization in order to be and function as a church. The question at hand is a question of *criteria*: what criteria are vital for the shape and function of the organization of the church in order to maintain the radicalism of the ecclesiology of the Reformation? To ensure *openness* and *diversity*, the freedom and authority of the baptized member of the church must be among the core criteria for shaping the organization of the church. What is needed is a structure that ensures that the majority of church members allow the church to be and contain more people and more opinions than themselves; in other words, a structure that mirrors the role that the state church has traditionally had in Norway for ensuring openness and diversity (cf. the question of female ministry and homosexuality in Norway and in Church of Norway).

It is most interesting to observe that while the church report of 2002 almost one-sidedly describes the state church in a perspective of power, i.e., as a question of controlling and determining the development and future of the church,[10] the government's report of 2006 has a much wider perspective in describing the close and positive relationship between the church and the people in a way that corresponds to central tenets in Lutheran ecclesiology with regard to openness and diversity.

Yet, openness and diversity are not to be understood unconditionally—that would render the concept of church empty and hollow. Baptism is a central cornerstone in the Lutheran understanding of both the church and the ministry of the church. Baptism is understood as both something that once happened to the individual (*Taufe*) and as something that continuously takes place in the life of the individual, i.e., the Christian life (*Taufbrauch*). It is *the* theological criteria for belonging to the church as well as functioning as the sacrament of ordination. The word of promise (*Promissio*) given to the individual in the baptism also has the function of conveying authority to the individual with regard to church life and theology. This is understood explicitly as authority to express criticism regarding church life and clerics.[11] As long as the baptized person firmly holds on to the word of promise given in the baptism, no person or office has authority to challenge his or her relationship to God.

---

10. Bakkevig, *Samme kirke—ny ordning*; see chapter 6, cf. page 66.
11. Cf. Luther, *De libertate christiana*.

Hence, the church *as organization* was understood by the reformers as a necessary yet practical arrangement or organization for the baptized, in order for the proclamation of the gospel and the administration of the sacraments to take place. In this way baptism serves as the basis for the church and allows the church to be an open and inclusive church.

The Priesthood of All Believers and Western Democracy

However, this legitimate power and authority regarding church and clergy given to the laity by the reformers of the sixteenth century, i.e., the *priesthood of all believers*, was not unconditional in the sense of being a right in the modern sense of the word. The doctrine of the priesthood of all believers is an expression of recognition that all Christians are equal to God, hence also the recognition of the value of the individual. Yet, there is a vital conceptual difference when comparing this recognition to the recognition that is given the individual in modern democratic society with regards to participating in political decision making. According to fundamental democratic ideas, the value of the individual is by virtue of being human. According to Western legal theory, it is the individual who is the beneficiary of human rights.[12] The respect of the integrity of the other person becomes vital. When deciding on political questions in a representative democracy all citizens of society have an equal standing, each person has one vote. The government is elected; authority over society is given to individuals and can also be withdrawn from them. The extent of authority that is exercised by government is agreed upon and is the topic of debate. This is not the case regarding the authority of the priesthood of all believers.

Contrary to basic assumptions underlying Western democracy with regard to the integrity of the person, the Christian person according to Luther is not his or her own authority, but lives under the authority of Christ.[13] The Christian person is to serve Christ through serving the neighbor; hence the essence of the priesthood of all believers is *communio sanctorum*. Constitutionally and practically the priesthood of all believers is dependent on the special ministry, i.e., the proclamation of

---

12. Cf. Shiman, *Economic and Social Justice*. In this interesting book David Shiman discusses differences and similarities regarding economic and social justice comparing liberal to totalitarian regimes.

13. Luther, *De libertate Christiana*.

the gospel and the administration of the sacraments. In itself the special ministry of proclamation and administration does not have a higher standing with regard to the ministry of all believers, but only through fulfilling its church-constituting (and hence "priesthood of all believers"-constituting) function: "that the Gospel is rightly taught and the Sacraments are rightly administered."[14]

Being a Christian, thus belonging to the priesthood of all believers, is not by virtue of being human. Being a Christian is related to faith in Christ, faith in the promise (*promisso*) given in baptism (cf. *Taufe—Taufbrauch*). Being a Christian is a gift. The special ministry is the embodiment of the exteriority of the gospel. In being this embodiment the basic conditions of the Christian life become evident: the Christian does not live in himself or herself, but in Christ, i.e., outside of himself or herself. The priestly service of the Christian is to fulfill the service of reconciliation in the world. What follows is that the special ministry only has its authority with regard to the priesthood of all believers as long as it remains faithful to the word of Christ. What follows further is that the authority of the priesthood of all believers is in a fundamental and constituting way related to faith in Christ, to the promise given in baptism, and in living under the authority of Christ.

One central aspect of the modernization of Norway was the introduction of the parliamentary system and representative democracy in the second half of the nineteenth century. Questions related to the life of the church became a topic for politicians and to some degree a topic in the parliamentary elections. The king is the constitutional head of Church of Norway, yet exercises his authority through the Council of State (i.e., through those members of the council who are baptized church members), and appoints bishops and deans. Legislation and finances concerning the church are passed by the parliament. Hence questions relating to the church become a political question.

This praxis can be interpreted as a contextualized continuation of the radicalism characteristic of the ecclesiology of Luther and the Reformation. The critical question with regards to the state church structure concerns what happens when power and authority regarding church and clergy is practiced based on the modern notion of authority, as we know it from representative democracies, and not based on the notion of the priesthood of all believers, under the authority of Christ; i.e., when

---

14. Cf. the Augsburg Confession, VII.

questions regarding church and clergy become one of many elements in larger political strategies or controversies marked by an interplay between political ideology and pragmatic concerns, or when decisions being made are not for the best or for the welfare of the church. To what extent can such a system be characterized as being an expression of, or a modernization of, the priesthood of all believers, the radicalism of the Lutheran reformation?

In the representative democracy as we know it the highest authority is the human and the rules being obeyed are made by humans. Even though these rules express ethical standards that are based on a view of humanity that demands respect for the integrity of the individual, giving this view of humanity a normative character is principally open to debate. Within the church, humans are not the highest authority. The highest authority is Christ as witnessed in Scripture, institutionalized in the special ministry of the church.

These questions are related to modernization and secularization. One cannot argue that past or present political praxis in Norway violates the interests of the church. On the contrary, all the Nordic countries have a long state church history in which the interests of the church have been well looked after by the respective governments. As exemplified above, one can argue that the state report of 2006 shows greater concern for the well-being of the church, in giving emphasis to the question of maintaining a close relationship between church and people, than the church report of 2002. It is nevertheless a principal question and shows the recurring dilemma when two sets of authority are to be combined within one political system.

These reflections do not imply a rejection of democratic structures within the church. Quite the opposite, they instead imply a *framework* for democratic praxis within the church, relating decision making to the authority of Christ. Historically it is legitimate to argue that the priesthood of all believers and the following upheaval of the qualitative difference of two people, clergy and laity have been important in developing the idea of equality and democracy. One cannot say that democracy and the priesthood of all believers are contradictory to one another, or that democracy will undermine the priesthood of all believers if the two are combined. But one has to distinguish between the two, as the priesthood of all believers is an expression of the content of the church, whereas democracy is a form of governance. One cannot say that democracy is not a meaningful form of governing within the priesthood of all believers.

PART ONE: Exploring a Heritage—Burning Issues

The challenge is rather to find a form of democratic governing that best corresponds to the content or nature of the priesthood of all believers. One element in such a form is undeniably a widespread use of direct democracy, the possibility for all baptized members of the church to take part in church life and appointments through open democratic processes and elections. Another crucial element in such a form is to make sure to avoid the dictatorship of the majority over the minority, i.e., a form that gives minorities a legitimate voice. Yet another crucial element in such a form is to avoid a democratic system that undermines the church-constituting role of the special ministry. What is needed is a form and praxis that reflects the reality of the church, i.e., as given solely by the grace of God through word and sacrament, not through the acts and notions of man.

Concluding Remarks

Through the long history of the state church in Norway there have been different concepts or positions for the understanding of the church. Through the twentieth century the concept of folk church has been gradually embraced by almost all parties, from left to right, from the lay organizations to proponents of high church ideals. When discussing church-state relations all parties in the debate seek to continue the folk church tradition in Norway. To some extent this agreement disguises differences regarding ecclesiology, as the use and understanding of the concept of folk church has varied greatly through the twentieth century. To some, folk church is conceived of as the responsibility of the "true church" with regards to the people who are, as the surroundings of the church, an object of mission. To others, the folk church is related to ethnicity and nationality. And yet to others, the most critical groups that focus on the personal conversion of the individual as the criteria for belonging to the "true church," the folk church is often considered more as a threat.

Relating to Lutheran theology, a folk church in Norway is best understood as the church of the people, meaning a church for those in Norway, independently of offspring, heritage, and background, that through baptism and the holding on to the word of promise given in the baptism belong to the church that has contributed to shaping the Norwegian society over centuries.

The way the government's report of 2006 and the parliamentary agreement of 2008 both directly and indirectly underline and want to continue the close relationship between people and church is promising in relation to reforming the church-state relationship. What ecclesiological changes that gradually will occur as "the church becomes master in its own house," i.e., as authority is moved to the church organization and church bureaucracy in the development of a free state church and possibly a future state church separation, remain to be seen.[15]

One thing is for sure: the organization of the church, what is often called *applied ecclesiology*, is one of the most pressing *theological* issues in present day Norway.

Bibliography

Bakkevig, Trond. *Samme kirke—ny ordning*. Oslo: Den norske kirke, Kirkerådet, 2002.
Hegstad, Harald. *Den virkelige kirke: Bidrag til ekklesiologien*. KIFO perspektiv 19. Trondheim: Tapir Akademisk, 2009.
Jensen, Roger. "Salme ved reisens slutt—mellom religion og samfunn." *Minerva* 2009/2: 70–77.
———. "Sekulær fornuft vs. religiøse følelser?" *Minerva* 2008/2: 84–95.
———. "Trosrettferdighet og demokrati." In *Menneskeverd: Festskrift til Inge Lønning*, edited by Svein Aage Christoffersen, et al., 111–28. Oslo: Forlaget, 2008.
Jørgensen, Theodor. "Det almindelige præstedømme og det folkekirkelige demokrati." In *Det almindelige præstedømme og det folkekirkelige demokrati*, 42–66. Frederiksberg: ANIS, 1996.
———. "Kan kirken have flere meninger? Den rene lære i et pluralistisk samfund. Nogle dogmatiske og retsteologiske overvejelser." In *Gudsfolket i Danmark: Om kirkesyn og kirkeforståelse*, 95–108. Økumeniske studier 7. Frederiksberg: ANIS, 1999.
Kersbergen, Kees van, and Philip Manow, editors. *Religion, Class Coalitions, and Welfare States*. Cambridge Studies in Social Theory, Religion, and Politics. Cambridge: Cambridge University Press, 2009.
Knudsen, Tim. *Den danske stat i Europa*. København: Jurist- og Økonomforbundet 1993.
Luther, Martin. *To the Christian Nobility of the German Nation*. WA 6:408, 11–13.
Shiman, David. *Economic and Social Justice: A Human Rights Perspective*. Human Rights Education Series 1. Minneapolis: Human Rights Resource Center,

---

15. One interesting book recently published on ecclesiology is Hegstad, *Den virkelige kirke*. In this book Prof. Hegstad argues that the church is a social entity available to empirical study—similar to all other social entities. Hence Hegstad is critical of the tradition of talking about the "hiddenness of the church," an aspect of traditional ecclesiology that through the twentieth century has been vital among the liberal parts of the church in arguing in favor of an open and inclusive folk church.

PART ONE: Exploring a Heritage—Burning Issues

University of Minnesota, 1999. Online: http://www1.umn.edu/humanrts/ edumat/hreduseries/tb1b/index.html (accessed 28/03/11).
Staten og Den norske kirke. Norges offentlige utredninger 2006:2. Oslo: Departementenes servicesenter, Informasjonsforvaltning, 2006. Online: http:// www.regjeringen.no/nb/dep/kud/dok/nouer/2006/nou-2006-2.html?id=156177 (accessed 28/03/11).
Stenbæk, Jørgen. "Retsteologiske aspekter af den lutherske tolkning af det almindelige præstedømme." In *Det almindelige præstedømme og det folkekirkelige demokrati,* 67–102. Frederiksberg: ANIS, 1996.
Sørensen, Øystein, and Bo Stråth. *The Cultural Construction of Norden.* Oslo: Scandinavian University Press, 1997.
Thorkildsen, Dag. "Lutherdom, vekkelse og de nordiske velferdsstater." *TEMP: Tidsskrift for historie* 1 (2010) 131–44.
Thorkildsen, Dag, Hallgeir Elstad, and Øyvind Norderval. "The Limits of Ecclesiastical Reform in Norway." In *The Dynamics of Religious Reform in Church, State and Society in Northern Europe, 1780–1920,* vol. 2, *The Churches,* edited by Joris van Eijnatten and Paula Yates, 261–76. Leuven: Leuven University Press, 2010.
Wingren, Gustaf. "Begreppet lekman." Lecture at Oslo University, 1981. *Norsk Teologisk Tidsskrift* 83 (1982) 177–87.
Østergård, Uffe. *Europa: Identitet og identitetspolitikk.* København: Munksgaard/ Rosin-ante, 1998.

3

Burning Issues in the Evangelical Lutheran Church in Denmark

PETER LODBERG

THE EVANGELICAL LUTHERAN CHURCH in Denmark is theologically and politically understood as a national folk church as stated in the Danish Constitution § 4. It is supported by the Danish state as long as the church is Lutheran, and as long as more than fifty percent of the Danish population belongs to the church. A national folk church, thus, is placed in between a state church, where the state governs the church, and a free church, who is independent from the state in its governing structures. The folk church combines elements of both state church and free church, and the basic idea is that the people of Denmark govern their own church through the Parliament, *Folketinget*. Thus, in a folk church situation the state is secular, but the people, e.g., *Folketinget*, can decide that the state must support the church of the majority in different ways without compromising the idea of freedom of religion.

As a national church with a membership of approximately 80 percent one can expect that burning issues of an ethical and a political character in Danish society will have an impact on the life of the Evangelical Lutheran Church in Denmark. Moreover, the church is one of the few institutions you can find even in the smallest villages, where other institutions such as post offices, public schools, or hospitals have closed down and moved to other and more populated places. This gives the church a unique position in Danish society and a great responsibility, because it helps to establish a forum for public debate in areas which are deserted by political parties or public organizations. But, as we will see in the following, the role of being a public church in a society challenged by serious changes also has split the church into different factions and makes it very difficult to agree about the future of the church. As examples of this debate I will deal with the issue of refugees, bell ringing for the environment, the Porvoo Declaration, and same-sex marriages.

The Church between Church Asylum and Illegal Defense of Human Rights

One of the most burning ethical issues for the Evangelical Lutheran Church since the end of World War II has been that of refugees. It started already in 1945, when approximately 250,000 German refugees sought refuge in Denmark. Many of the refugees came from the Baltic states and East Prussia during the last months of the war. At the beginning they were protected by the German troops in Denmark, but after Germany was defeated in May 1945 it became an important and difficult question for the Danish government over what to do with the refugees, who made up approximately 5 percent of the total population of Denmark at that time.

The Danish government invited a group of ecumenically minded people like Professor Kristen. E. Skydsgaard and Rector Halfdan Høgsbro to establish the Danish Church Service for German Refugees. The idea was to gather a group of pastors from the Evangelical Lutheran Church in Denmark, who were supposed to conduct worship services in the camps in cooperation with those German pastors who themselves lived in the camps as refugees. All newborn babies were enrolled in an official church book organized by Ms. Bodil Sølling, who for many years served as Vice General Secretary in Danchurchaid and in the Executive Committee of the Lutheran World Federation.

The work of the Danish Church Service for German Refugees was heavily criticized by the Danish media—especially in Copenhagen. Halfdan Høgsbro and his colleagues were accused of treason, because they tried to establish a relationship with the German refugees. The editors wanted revenge over Germany's involvement in the war and not reconciliation. They were supported by public opinion and in several places leaflets were distributed in order to warn against any form of contact with the enemy, who was portrayed as being in Denmark to steal from hardworking Danes. Halfdan Høgsbro defended his position from a theological perspective and stressed the fact that all people are created by God, all people have sinned against God, and everybody is invited to receive the grace of Jesus Christ. Therefore, the Church Service was necessary and an obligation of the Evangelical Lutheran Church in Denmark. As a national church, it should be responsible for establishing church life in the camps. Høgsbro also stressed that reconciliation with Germany was a necessary requirement if the European machinery should start working again. According to Høgsbro, Europe had to help Germany back into the fellowship of European countries. His argument and position was supported by the Danish government.

After the last German refugee had left Denmark, attention of the public mind was drawn towards Eastern Europe. After 1956, Denmark took its share of refugees from Hungary. They were later followed by refugees from Czechoslovakia and Poland. In the 1970s, the military regimes in the southern part of Europe and Latin America produced a number of refugees and some of them found a home in Denmark. The Danish politicians and the Danish public welcomed the refugees and the Danes regarded their country as an important partner in the international humanitarian regime.

The Danish consensus started to break apart in the mid 1980s. Refugees from the civil war in Lebanon and the war between Iran and Iraq were met with increasing suspicion and even resistance from the Danish public and some politicians. In the summer of 1985, the Danish Refugee Council wanted to establish a camp for fifty (later thirty-five) refugees from Iran in a small village in the southern part of Jylland, close to the German border. The citizens protested and were supported by a small group of people. In 1987, this group organized themselves into a new organization named "The Danish Association," and among its ranks were former members of the resistance during the German occupation. They wanted to make the Danish public and politicians aware of the great threat to Danish culture, society, and economy coming from the countries in the Third World and especially from the Muslim countries in the Middle East—the so-called refugee-producing countries.

Also in 1987, the first church asylum took place in an Evangelical Lutheran Church in Denmark. During one of the Easter worship services, a group of Palestinian refugees participated in the service and refused to leave the Maria Church in Copenhagen after the service had ended.

PART ONE: Exploring a Heritage—Burning Issues

The local pastor and the congregation declared a church asylum inspired by the Sanctuary Movement in the United States, the Lutheran Church in the German Democratic Republic, and the role of some local pastors during the German occupation in 1940-1945 when Jews and resistance fighters were hid in certain vicarages. The church asylum lasted one week and ended when the Danish authorities promised to give the Palestinian refugees humanitarian residence permits.

The next church asylum took place in 1991-1992 in the church of Blågård in Copenhagen. During this church asylum a group of pastors protested against what was happening in the church. They called for the Minister of Justice to uphold the law in the country and act as the political and public authority that would expel the Palestinian refugees from Denmark, because they were not allowed to remain in the country after they have been denied residence permits. The group of pastors also maintained that the church is not allowed to establish itself as a state in the state as it was in the case of the ongoing church asylum.

The pastors supporting the church asylum, on the other hand, denied that they were creating a state in the state or misusing the gospel message about love for neighbors for political reasons. They maintained that they helped asylum seekers, who were legally in Denmark, and they called on the Minister of Justice to give the Palestinian refugees, who were stateless, humanitarian residence permits. The Minister of Justice and the Prime Minister refused to help the Palestinians, but the government was overruled by the majority in the Danish Parliament. The majority, which does not include the parties in the government, accepted the so-called "Law for Palestinians" and allowed for Palestinians who had been in Denmark for more than twelve months to get a humanitarian residence permit.

The third, and so far last, church asylum took place in the spring of 2009. More than sixty asylum seekers from Iraq took refuge in the Brorson Church in Copenhagen. Most of them fled Iraq in 2003 when the U.S.-led coalition invaded the country. As a member of the coalition, Denmark followed the situation in Iraq closely and it was important to the Danish government that Iraqi refugees should go back, because it would be a sign that the situation had improved after the invasion. The Danish authorities refused to give the Iraqi asylum seekers residence permit in Denmark, but the refugees feared for their lives and refused to return to Iraq. In August, the police entered the church and arrested the young men. Women, old persons, and children fled from the church. They disappeared, fled the country, or went underground. Quickly, the majority of the young men arrested by the police during the night raid were deported by plane to Iraq. About twenty of the remaining persons were later granted residence permits in Denmark, because their cases were reopened by their lawyers and the Danish refugee authorities.

A group of theologians and pastors reacted strongly against the decision of the police to raid the church. They saw it as a violation of the peace of the church and a sign of the growing brutality of the Danish administration and political majority against innocent people who had fled a war Denmark was taking part in. They called the church to be the *church*.

Another group of theologians and pastors supported the decision of the police, believing it to be the role of the authority to keep law and order. The church has no mandate of its own to enter into a conflict over refugees. The church shall preach the gospel and serve the sacraments every Sunday in worship services. The church should not be misused for political manifestations.

It is clear from Danish church law that there is no such thing as a church asylum. The asylum was self-declared by local pastors and congregations who had been challenged by refugees to help them. It is also clear that the political majority has shifted and that the present political majority does not regard the church as a safe haven for refugees. The church is part of the state administration and there is no free space that is respected by the state as belonging to the church itself. To be a national church is to be part of the public administration.

It is also clear from this historical overview that the interpretation of the Danish resistance during World War II still plays an important role for Danish identity and self-understanding. Pastors and local congregations who want to defend refugees from being expelled from Denmark see their opinion and practice in line with the Danish attitude towards the Jews during the German occupation, when groups and individuals helped save the Jews from being sent to concentration camps in Germany. The human rights ideal is "no more for the Jews," meaning today "no more for anybody," e.g., people under persecution and in hiding must be helped as human beings and not because of their nationality, religious, or ethnic belonging.

The group of pastors who argue that the law must be followed without any consideration about the human rights situation also understand its behavior and practice against the background of the experiences during World War II. This group wants to defend Denmark as present-day resistance fighters against a foreign presence in Denmark. The comparison between the 1940s and today is clear when old members of the Danish resistance movement call for a new defence of Danish culture, social life, and religion. Those who disagree with the old resistance fighters are regarded as the present-day collaborators with the enemy.

The debate about Danish policy towards refugees has reinvented the old discussion about the importance of World War II and has created a split in church and society between "us" and "them." At the same time the tense theological debate about church asylums has invited new interpretations of the meaning of the Lutheran understanding of the two kingdoms.

Bell Ringing for the Environment

In December 2009 Denmark hosted the UN Summit on Climate Change in Copenhagen. The expectations were high. All heads of state were to meet in order to set a new standard for protecting the environment. The Danish government and most political parties in the parliament encouraged everybody to take an active part in the summit. School classes prepared themselves, NGO's were organized, and in the National Council of Churches in Denmark the member churches were encouraged to mark the summit with special bell ringing for the environment. The plan was to have a global bell ringing, starting in the Pacific, in order to show that all churches are concerned about the environment and want to protect creation from pollution and damage.

In Denmark, the invitation to the bell ringing for the environment was met with strong political opposition from leading members of parliament. The argument was that bell ringing is only used for church services and at very special occasions in the country, for example when war is followed by peace. To use the bell ringing for advocating the protection of the environment was regarded as a political gesture and could have nothing to do with the church.

The debate exploded in the media and local congregations had to decide for themselves if they would follow the invitation to use the bells or decline it. The bishop of Roskilde, Peter Fischer-Møller, argued in favor of the bell ringing and saw it as an expression linked to the summit, which was hosted by the Danish people. He also pointed to the fact that some politicians tried to misuse the bell ringing for their own political benefit. Very close to holding the summit, an election for the local municipality councils was held and the bell ringing was an easy and a cheap way of making oneself known in the media prior to this election.

Thus the politicians were criticized by the bishop for politicizing the church by criticizing the church for politicizing. This interesting phenomenon has flourished during the last ten years, because the political majority in the parliament has left the old way of trying to reach a consensus in matters related to church politics. The majority uses its advantage in order to get its proposals through parliament. Especially after the cartoon crisis in 2005, religion has become a battleground in the "war on values" that has haunted Danish society. In this battle the politicians can use all targets, including the Evangelical Lutheran Church, because it has become a dominant political manifesto that too much religion (read Islam) will destroy the social cohesion of Danish society. This means that all new initiatives in public life that involves some sort of religious idea or manifestation are being criticized or even prohibited. The Danes have become afraid of public religion, because they have become afraid of Islam. The consequence is that all public religion, including the Evangelical Lutheran Church, is regarded with suspicion when it manifests itself in new ways.

The Porvoo Declaration

In 1992, representatives from the Anglican churches in England, Scotland, Wales, Ireland, and the Lutheran churches in the Nordic countries and the Baltic states formulated an ecumenical agreement called the Porvoo Declaration. They reached a common understanding of the nature and purpose of the church, a fundamental agreement on faith, and an agreement on episcopacy in the service of the apostolicity of the church. In the Porvoo Common Statement the churches have made the following acknowledgements:

i. we acknowledge one another's churches as churches belonging to the One, Holy, Catholic and Apostolic Church of Jesus Christ and truly participating in the apostolic mission of the whole people of God;

ii. we acknowledge that in all our churches the Word of God is authentically preached, and the sacraments of baptism and the eucharist are duly administered;

iii. we acknowledge that all our churches share in the common confession of the apostolic faith;

iv. we acknowledge that one another's ordained ministries are given by God as instruments of his grace and as possessing not only the inward call of the Spirit, but also Christ's commission through his Body, the Church;

PART ONE: Exploring a Heritage—Burning Issues

> v. we acknowledge that personal, collegial and communal oversight (*episcope*) is embodied and exercised in all our churches in a variety of forms, in continuity of apostolic life, mission and ministry;
>
> vi. we acknowledge that the episcopal office is valued and maintained in all our churches as a visible sign expressing and serving the Church's unity and continuity in apostolic life, mission and ministry.[1]

The bishops and the Interchurch Council of the Evangelical Lutheran Church in Denmark decided to ask all local congregations in Denmark if they supported the bishops in signing the Porvoo Common Declaration. The statement was translated and discussed in public meetings and by local congregation councils. The responses were sent to the bishops and approximately 70 percent of all responses were negative. It was clear from the many negative responses that most congregations and pastors did not understand the theological arguments used. It created mistrust and a hermeneutic of suspicion. The statement was regarded as too high church and too Anglican. The pastors were afraid that the office of the bishop would become too powerful, which was not in line with Danish tradition. Many of the responses did not want to see changes in the church and expressed a deep satisfaction with its actual position and work. Ecumenism was regarded as a threat to the confessional and national identity of the Evangelical Lutheran Church in Denmark.

Among the supporters of Porvoo the statement was welcomed, because it would open the Evangelical Lutheran Church in Denmark to the world. The universal and ecumenical dimension was stressed as part of being a modern church in the midst of a global world. Also the practical dimension of the Porvoo Common Statement was mentioned as a positive factor by the small minority who supported signing.

The bishops were in a difficult situation. They had supported the Porvoo process and the Danish representatives in the Porvoo working group. But the bishops were defeated by the majority of the local congregations. In 1995, the bishops decided not to sign Porvoo, but at the same time they stressed that there is no dividing issue between the faith of Anglicans and Lutherans. They hoped that the good relations could be enlarged and strengthened in the future.

The Evangelical Lutheran Church in Denmark was invited to be an observer in the Porvoo Fellowship and in 2009 the bishops asked the Interchurch Council to inform the Porvoo churches that the bishops were

1. *Together in Mission and Ministry*, 30–31.

ready to sign the Porvoo Common Statement. The signing took place after the worship service in the Cathedral of Copenhagen on October 3, 2010. As part of the signing an explanation was issued. It stressed the fact that the Porvoo Communion has not developed as some might have feared in 1995. There has been a general move towards the recognition of full admission for men and women to the ordained ministry. In some churches this has already been implemented, while others have initiated a process towards full equality between men and women. The Interchurch Council especially stressed that:

1. The Evangelical Lutheran Church in Denmark recognizes the admission on an equal basis of men and women to both the priesthood and the episcopate. In consequence of this, no distinction is made between priests ordained by a male or female bishop.

2. Within the understanding of the Evangelical Lutheran Church in Denmark there is only one ministry of the church (*ministerium ecclesiasticum*), to which both the priesthood and the episcopate belong. The episcopate is understood in a Lutheran context as a distinct form of the one pastoral office.[2]

The decision of the bishops and the Interchurch Council to sign the Porvoo Common Statement provoked critical reactions from people who wanted more time to discuss the matter again. Among critical politicians in political parties supporting the present government, the reaction to the signing was extremely negative. They regarded the Evangelical Lutheran Church in Denmark as a national church, which is not in a position to sign ecumenical statements or engage itself in binding ecumenical agreements with other churches. However, the political majority was not able to prevent the bishops from signing the Porvoo Common Statement, because the bishops considered the matter as an internal matter for the church to decide. But the discussion about Porvoo since 1994 shows that ecumenism is still an important issue that divides the church in two, because it touches upon the issues of the Evangelical Lutheran Church in Denmark having both a national and a confessional identity with a very close church-state relationship. Porvoo, however, also showed that the bishops, when agreeing among themselves, are in a position to defend their right to take their own decisions when it comes to the so-called internal matters in the church, such as signing ecumenical agreements.

2. *Signatory Declaration of the Evangelical Lutheran Church in Denmark.*

PART ONE: Exploring a Heritage—Burning Issues

Same-Sex Marriage

In 1989, the Danish Parliament passed a law that allowed two persons of the same sex to enter into a registered partnership. In many ways a registered partnership is equal to a marriage, but one of the differences is that a registered partnership is established through a ceremony in the town hall and not in the church. Since 1989, it has been debated in church and society whether the church should open up to allow people of the same sex to enter into registered partnerships in the church.

In 1997, the bishops in the Evangelical Lutheran Church in Denmark decided against church marriage, but pointed to the fact that a local pastor is free to hold a worship service where a couple in a registered partnership could be blessed. In 2005, six of the ten bishops and the bishop in Greenland issued an instruction to be followed when a couple in a registered partnership wanted the blessing of the church. It was stressed in the instruction that the blessing service did not bless the registered partnership itself, but the two persons who had chosen to live together in a registered partnership. It was also stressed that a local pastor was free to decide for him/herself if he/she would participate in this kind of worship service. The bishops were heavily criticized by people and institutions belonging to the pietistic tradition in the Evangelical Lutheran Church in Denmark. Thus the issue of registered partnerships in the church has become an issue for debate, particularly when new bishops and many local pastors are elected for office.

In 2009 and 2010, political parties in the parliament, mostly in opposition to the government, challenged the Evangelical Lutheran Church in Denmark to allow people of the same sex to enter into registered partnerships in the church. As a consequence of the political pressure and the ongoing discussion within the church, the then Minister of Ecclesiastical Affairs asked a committee of twelve members headed by the bishop of Copenhagen, Peter Skov-Jakobsen, to deal with a number of questions related to the issue of church and registered partnerships. The committee finalized its work in September 2010 and published its report to be discussed by all parties involved.[3] Three different questions divided the committee in diverse ways:

A majority (ten members) of the committee wanted to maintain the present order that marriage can still be established by a ceremony in the church in accordance to an authorized ritual. The minority (two members)

---

3. The report is titled *Folkekirken og registreret partnerskab: Rapport fra udvalg nedsat af kirkeministeren*.

wanted to split the legal part of entering into marriage, which should take place at the town hall, and the Christian part, that should take place in the church.

A majority (nine members) of the committee wanted to change the present situation so that registered partnership can be blessed in the church in accordance to an authorized ritual. Two members were against and wanted to uphold the position established in 1997 that allows a local pastor to bless the persons in a registered partnership in a worship service. One member opposed any form of ritual or the possibility of blessing persons in registered partnerships.

Half of the committee wanted to establish a new possibility for two persons of the same sex to enter into a registered partnership through a ceremony in the church. It was stressed that this is not the same as marriage or the introduction of a gender-neutral understanding of marriage. This group asked for two different rituals: one for marriage and one for registered partnerships.

The committee work did not bring new theological arguments into the discussion, but it shows the different opinions and highlights the changing climate within Danish society and church life in favor of a more open attitude to the life and reality of people of the same sex living together in a committed lifelong relationship. The question is, how should the church react to this new reality? Should it follow the changing attitude of the population or should it maintain old traditions? And how fast should it move to establish new rituals? Especially, when a national folk church who wants to encompass as many people as possible in the nation feels challenged by new political realities.

Conclusion

It is a blessing and a curse at the same time to be a national folk church like the Evangelical Lutheran Church in Denmark. The identification between people, nation, state, and church can be a blessing because it brings the church very close to its people: the people are the church, as implied in the name *Den danske Folkekirke* (the Danish folk church). But what happens when this old line of identification and tradition is changing or even breaking apart as it is in a globalized twenty-first century? How should the church adapt to new realities among people and in the state and nation when it comes to an influx of refugees, climate change, ecumenism, or new understandings of sex and gender? The church can choose to be the place

PART ONE: Exploring a Heritage—Burning Issues

where old virtues are protected and a museum for the ideals of the past. Or the church can decide to become a laboratory for discussion and new experiences to benefit an emerging society. In my analysis, the Evangelical Lutheran Church in Denmark is in the process of finding a new place in society and it serves as a battleground for different theological and political opinions about the future of church and Danish society. Many of the most important public debates over the last ten years in Denmark have been related to refugees (read: Islam), climate change, and same-sex marriages. Changes in religion, climate, and gender are concrete issues that have political and theological content and consequence. Perhaps the curse of being a national folk church in a postmodern society of never-ending changes is to be in a constant position of bewilderment and internal struggle, or, as bishop Wolfgang Huber is quoted to have said, "the church is an institutionalized conflict." Part of this conflict is also over how the relationship between church and state, and how free the church is to mind its own affairs. Being a national folk church in between a state church model and a free church model is an ongoing tension, because there will always be people who wants more state or less state in the governing of the church. But despite all the tensions and internal struggle the concept of national folk church has survived since its introduction in the first Danish constitution in 1849 and it seems it will continue to do so into the future.

Bibliography

Folkekirken og registreret partnerskab: Rapport fra udvalg nedsat af kirkeministeren. September 2010. Online: http://www.km.dk/fileadmin/share/publikationer/ betaenkninger/Rapport_om_folkekirken_og_registreret_partnerskab.pdf.

Signatory Declaration of the Evangelical Lutheran Church in Denmark regarding the Porvoo Declaration. October 2010. Online: http://www.interchurch.dk/fileadmin/ interfiles/Engelsk_hjemmeside_dokumenter/Signatory_Declaration.pdf.

Together in Mission and Ministry: The Porvoo Common Statement with Essays on Church and Ministry in Northern Europe. London: Church House Publishing, 1993.

4

Ethics and Ecclesiology
Burning Issues for Church of Sweden—and Beyond

CARL REINHOLD BRÅKENHIELM

THERE HAS BEEN A considerable disagreement between different Christian traditions when it comes to the authority of the church in moral issues. In theory the differences are obvious. Protestant churches emphasize individual conscience and the Roman Catholic Church the role of the Magisterium, brought to its peak in the claim to papal infallibility in matters dogmatic and moral. But in practice the difference is less obvious. Protestant churches have assumed the role of moral guidance teachers through episcopal letters or synodal decisions. And since the First Vatican Council (1869-1870), when the dogma of papal infallibility was declared, the Roman Catholic Church has issued no moral teaching under the specified conditions that make it infallible. It is also important to note that no moral teaching has been advanced on the basis of arbitrary authority and power, "but on bases which are open to rational scrutiny within both the Christian community as well as the larger human community."[1] One particularly clear example of this is in the ecclesial pronouncements on war and peace during the 1980s.[2] Even if subsequent

1. Gustafson, *Protestant and Roman Catholic Ethics*, 132.
2. See Bråkenhielm, *Power and Peace*.

PART ONE: Exploring a Heritage—Burning Issues

decades witness the phenomenon of an "ecumenical winter," no retreat from the openness to rational scrutiny in matters moral are visible. One may disagree with many of the papal pronouncements in the encyclicals *Veritatis Splendor* (1993) or *Evangelium Vitae* (1995) without denying their openness to rational scrutiny.[3] Contemporary ecclesial pronouncements on sexual and homosexual relationships are no exception to this rule—even if strong criticism is voiced against such statements.

Church of Sweden's endorsement of same-sex relationships has been heavily criticized from different churches—particularly in the Orthodox world and in the Southern hemisphere. It is not my intention to discuss this criticism in the present context. I will be focusing on the questions of if and how a theological justification for this decision can be found. I will (1) compare this decision to similar ecclesial decisions concerning new reproductive technologies, (2) seek the theological roots for pronouncements of this character (and thereby draw my inspiration from some theologians in Sweden or influenced by Swedish theology), and (3) spell out the ecclesiological consequences underlying this effort, wherein it is my conviction that ecclesiology is a dependent rather than an independent variable in theology. The understanding of the nature and purpose of the church is the outcome of other theological and empirical considerations—not the other way around. We should understand the church from ethics and practice rather than understanding ethics and practice from a particular conception of the church.

In sum, the focus in this chapter will be on Christian ethics and its relationship to ecclesiology. To what extent may Christian ethics *deviate* from traditional theological norms and values? Conversely, to what extent may Christian ethics still *retain* the form and content of traditional norms and values? And what are the consequences of the answers to these questions for our understanding of the identity of the church?

These are burning issues for the Christian community and the Christian theologian not only in Sweden but also worldwide. They require a renegotiation between Christian identity and social credibility. Christian identity is anchored in the biblical scriptures, but also in human reason and conscience. What interpretation of Christian ethics is consistent with its more general credibility? Common to contemporary forms of neo-atheism is the thesis that a credible interpretation of Christianity always violates the integrity of the Christian faith. In sharp contrast to this is Archbishop Nathan Söderblom's conviction that "the Christian believer

---

3. See Hüttner and Dieter, *Ecumenical Ventures in Ethics*.

has an ally in the heart of every human being."[4] The present chapter is written from the perspective of this conviction. Christian community can preserve its identity and integrity and be credible to the world at the same time.

Church of Sweden Wrestles with Modernity: Two Examples

Church of Sweden has entered into negotiation between Christian identity and social credibility at several moments in the last century and the decade after the millennium. I will limit myself to two examples. The first concerns sexual ethics, the second bioethics. But before the introduction of these examples, a few words about the procedure by which decisions in social and ethical matters are taken in Church of Sweden.

On the national level the church is led by the Archbishop of Uppsala, who represents Church of Sweden in international and ecumenical matters and speaks for the Bishops' Meeting, comprising all the bishops. But the decision-making body for Church of Sweden is the Church (of Sweden) Synod. The synod consists of 251 members, meets annually, and decides all matters concerning the regulation of church life. The Church Synod elects the Church Board, which is chaired by the Archbishop.

The Church Synod, the Bishops' Meeting, and the Church Board are assisted by the central administration of Church of Sweden (located in Uppsala). Many theological experts serve in this administration; some of them are linked to the Doctrine Commission, in which all the bishops are seated together with a number of theologians. Others are related to the Theology Committee, assisting the Church Board and consisting of some bishops, academic theologians, and lay experts. Statements of the church such as responses to government or parliamentary proposals (on, for example, family law or new reproductive technologies) are sometimes prepared by theological or other experts in the central administration, but sometimes channeled through the Doctrine Commission and/or the Theology Committee. All these actors—and particularly the Theology Committee—were involved in the final decision by the Church Assembly to open marriage for persons of the same gender.

It must be emphasized that this organization has been in place since Church of Sweden was disestablished and changed into a religious organization independent from the state of Sweden in 2000.

4. Söderblom, *Tal och skrifter*, 68.

PART ONE: Exploring a Heritage—Burning Issues

Example 1: Homosexuality and Same-Sex Marriages

After the Second World War the question of admitting women into the ministry emerged as one of the most pressing issues for Church of Sweden. The issue was resolved by a decision of the Church Synod in 1958.[5] Today preservative resistance has shifted to another issue, namely homosexual relationships and the introduction of same-sex marriages. One important milestone was a study made by a group appointed by the Bishops' Conference in 1972. This group, led by Holsten Fagerberg, submitted its report in 1974.[6] It covered exegetical as well as psychological and ethical issues. One of the most important conclusions was that Church of Sweden should work for stable and extended relationships between homosexuals and that homosexual relations should be recognized in the law. An act of blessing should be considered by the church.

The history from 1974 until 2008—when Church of Sweden Synod and the Bishops' Conference finally approved a parliamentary proposal on same-sex marriage and introduced a matrimonial liturgy for same-sex couples—has been long and cumbersome. This story is documented in other publications and will not be repeated in the present context.[7] Instead, let me turn to another example: bioethics.

Example 2: New Reproductive Technologies

In general, ecclesial attitudes to biotechnology have been perceived as preservative, if not rigidly negative. Christer Sturmark, chairperson of the Swedish Humanist Association, argues that Christian faith is against stem cell research and "the religious argument" against stem cell research is based on the idea that a fertilized embryo is a potential human being.[8] A closer scrutiny of pronouncements of Church of Sweden shows that this criticism is unfounded.

Problems of bioethics have been frequently addressed in Swedish legislation and a number of governmental studies have been published

---

5. Today approximately 40 percent of the ministers in Church of Sweden are women—and three of the thirteen bishops are women. The reform was questioned by a powerful and well-organized minority of minsters and laypersons, but today few oppose the reform.

6. Fagerberg, *De homosexuella och kyrkan*.

7. E.g., Lindfelt and Gustafsson Lundberg, *Kärlekens förändrade landskap*; Lindfelt and Gustafsson Lundberg, *Uppdrag samliv*.

8. Sturmark, *Tro och vetande 2.0*, 213, 218.

in recent decades. Church of Sweden has reacted to these proposals in various ways, mainly through formal responses in the form of statements by the Church Board. One example is the response to a government report in 2002 that concerned the legal framework for stem cell research.[9] The committee proposed that

- there should be no general prohibition against research on fertilized eggs
- research on fertilized eggs should be permitted under the current legislation from 1991
- the transfer of somatic cell nuclei (therapeutic cloning) should be permitted, but subject to the same restrictions as research on fertilized eggs
- reproductive cloning should be unequivocally forbidden
- donation of eggs for research purposes should not be forbidden, but subject to thorough scrutiny by the regional boards for research ethics.

In 2005 the parliament accepted these proposals. Thereby the parliament also endorsed the rules of the Swedish Research Council that (1) research on human embryos should be allowed up until fourteen days after fertilization, (2) therapeutic cloning should be allowed under the same conditions as research on human embryos, but (3) reproductive cloning should be prohibited. The law took effect July 1, 2006.[10]

One of the main reasons for this legislation was that medical research on stem cells and therapeutic cloning opened up possibilities for the cure of different kinds of diseases. In its response the Church Board was in fundamental agreement with this justification and argued that it is in line with the idea of human stewardship of creation.[11] But this stewardship should be exercised with respect for the dignity of human life. Basic to humanistic and Christian ethics is the principle that human beings should never be used only as instruments. The question is then whether stem cell research and therapeutic cloning violates this principle of human dignity. It is the conclusion of the Church Board that this is not case. The board argues for restrictions and caution but comes down on the positive side. This is also the case in the Church Board's response to pre-implantation

9. "Rättslig reglering av stamcellsforskning."
10. See *The Genetic Integrity Act*, especially chapter 5.
11. See "Yttrande Dnr Ks 2003:143."

genetic diagnostics (PGD), i.e., screening of embryos for genetic diseases before placement of healthy embryos in the female ovary.[12]

From these two examples, I will now proceed to a theological analysis. First, I will discuss a central argument by which ethical change has been resisted in Church of Sweden. It is the argument from God's orders of creation. Secondly, I will suggest an alternative conception of Christian ethics and suggest where such conception leads us concerning same-sex marriages and new reproductive technologies. And thirdly, I will try to spell out the ecclesiological conclusions from this analysis.

God's Orders of Creation

Let me first take a short look in the rearview mirror and consider what has been burning issues for Church of Sweden during the last century. Maria Södling's dissertation *Disorder in Creation* gives an insight into burning issues during the 1920s and 1930s. Södling's main thesis is that the central core of ecclesial social criticism was based on the establishment of boundaries between the feminine and the masculine. When the masculine and the feminine were "stirred up in the most distasteful way" the order of society and the church was disturbed. And she continues:

> The order was similarly threatened when women overstepped the boundaries that good taste and the order of creation had delineated for them. Such an overstepping could consist in using makeup and smoking cigarettes; a second way was in wanting to have control over one's own childbearing; a third was in striving to have a profession; and a fourth was in making demands for admission to the role of minister. The church critique of the era's moral disintegration, including women overstepping their boundaries, was certainly part of a broad moral-preservative tendency. But by framing women's demands for freedom as a threat against God's order of creation, the church argumentation represented a specific theological version of the period's general cultural criticism.[13]

During the 1930s and 1940s, ecclesial theology favored the idea of God's "orders of creation." This theology undergirded a preservative outlook on society in general and sexual relationship more specifically. Let us take a closer look at this influential line of thought!

12. See "Yttrande Dnr Ks 2004:406."
13. Södling, *Oreda i skapelsen*, 384; my translation.

The argument from the orders of creation has deep theological roots in Greek philosophy. The main idea is that as there is an order for nature through natural laws, there is also a law for society through the order of creation. In the late nineteenth century and the beginning of the twentieth, this idea was revived as a response to secularization, war, and social upheaval. This created a demand for theological guidance in the midst of social and political change. God's unique revelation in Christ was one response. Karl Barth was the most prominent representative of such a theology of revelation. Many theologians choose the alternative route of a theology of God's orders of creation. Paul Althaus (1888–1966) and Helmut Thielike (1908–1986) are two prominent examples. I will take my point of departure in a work by Emil Brunner (1889–1966). He published *Die Gebot und die Ordnungen* in 1932, but I will depart from a more mature work from 1943: *Gerechtigkeit. Eine Lehre von den Grundgesetzen der Gesellschaftsordnung*. It was translated into English under the title *Justice and Social Order* (1945) and into Swedish as *Rättvisa: En lära om rättsordningens grundlagar* (1945). God's orders were understood as fundamental structures for social life in general and necessary for the maintenance of human life. Marriage and family, work and economy, state, culture, and even the church are examples of such orders. An action is right in so far as it is in accordance with the will of God expressed in these orders of creation.[14]

One important aspect of Brunner's order theology concerned the relationship between men and women in marriage. Brunner argued that the institution of marriage is an order of creation. He affirmed that the nature of human beings are "embedded" in their sexual nature and that we cannot realize ourselves in any other relationship than in exclusive and permanent monogamy. Furthermore, this relationship must be just in the sense of being equal. Woman and man have the same value. They owe each other respect and love. Nevertheless, there is a hierarchy. Referring to St. Paul's letter to the Ephesians, Brunner claims that "man is the head of his woman" (Eph 5:23). The man should take the leading role in the marriage. Any other arrangement is degrading the woman and is "unnatural." "Patriarchy—neither matriarchy nor equality—accords with the order of creation."[15]

---

14. See further Bexell and Grenholm, *Teologisk etik*, chapters 9 and 3; "Schöpfungsordnung."

15. Brunner, *Rättvisa*, 186.

PART ONE: Exploring a Heritage—Burning Issues

The hierarchical structure of marriage is linked to a more general idea of a hierarchy in society in general. With unmistakable clarity, this comes to expression in St. Paul's letter to the Romans 13:1–10:

> Let every person be subject to the governing authorities; for there is no authority except from God, and those authorities that exist have been instituted by God.

And St. Paul generalizes his point in his concluding remarks:

> The commandments, "You shall not commit adultery; You shall not murder; You shall not steal; You shall not covet"; and any other commandment, are summed up in this word, "Love your neighbour as yourself."

To put it simply and crudely: the essence of love is submission. Justice is a distribution of power and goods according to the differences that exist between human beings with respect to their attributes and their social function.[16] Citizens should submit to their authorities, slaves to their masters, women to their men, children to their parents.

Emil Brunner did not identify these moral orders with the prevailing social order. Indeed all human realities are marked by sin and shortcomings. No existing social system is an accurate incarnation of the orders of creation as expressions of the will of God. Nevertheless, there is a tendency to single out certain hierarchical patterns of society and social behavior as exemplary—and other social arrangements as "distasteful."

The theological idea that there exists an order of creation finding expression in hierarchical social orders has had a deep grip on theological and religious imagination. It is clearly a line of thought found in the New Testament, promulgated by the church fathers (particularly St. Augustine), systematized and refined by Thomas Aquinas, modified by the reformers in the sixteenth century, inspiring the natural law theorists in the seventeenth and eighteenth centuries, and re-emerging in theology in the nineteenth and twentieth centuries. And even if it has been heavily criticized, it has kept re-emerging in the ecclesial opposition towards new reproductive technologies—but especially against homosexuality and same-sex relationships. One example is the recently deceased Archbishop Bertil Werkström in his response to a Swedish government's 1984 report on *Homosexuals and Society*,[17] which proposed a new law of partnership for gay and lesbians. Werkström opposed this proposal because homosex-

---

16. See further Bexell and Grenholm, *Teologisk etik*, 179, with references.
17. *Homosexuella och samhället*.

uality was seen as against the orders of creation.[18] Similarly, the majority of the Doctrinal Committee of the Norwegian church recently claimed that "there is broad agreement within the committee that marriage between woman and man is an expression of that order in creation which stems from the difference between gender."[19]

Challenges for Order of Creation Theology

One of the most serious objections to this theological idea of a system of orders of creation forming the objective criterion for ethical norms and behavior comes from postmodern philosophy. Postmodern philosophy is a heterogeneous phenomenon, but a common trait is a negation of the universal validity of moral norms. Order theology is incompatible with ethical relativism. And proponents of order theology are conscious of this. In 2003, a working group appointed by the House of Bishops of the Anglican Church of England stated the following in a "discussion document" on *Some Issues in Human Sexuality*:

> Most importantly, postmodernism fails to do justice to the fact that God has established an objective moral order through his creative and recreative activity in Jesus Christ. It is on the basis of this moral order that we recognize in God the source and standard of all that is beautiful, good and true and . . . it is only by living in conformity to this moral order that human beings can find the fullness of life for which God created them.[20]

Let me make two comments on this quotation. The first is that postmodern philosophy and order theology cannot both be true, but they can both be false. In other words, the moral relativism of postmodern theology might be untenable along with the kind of moral objectivism of order theology. One can argue that we need some kind of objectivism in ethics, but not the kind of objectivism argued by order theology. I will present such an alternative theology of creation in just a moment.

Secondly, the argument in the Anglican document has clear similarities to the position of Emil Brunner. The natural conclusion would seem to be that homosexual relationships are against the moral order established by God. Somewhat surprisingly, the Anglican document still argues that

---

18. See further Nilsson, *En fråga om kärlek*.
19. Austad, *Skriftforståelse og skriftbruk med særlig henblikk på homofilisaken*, 105.
20. House of Bishops, *Some Issues in Human Sexuality*.

there may be acceptable disagreements concerning same-sex relationships despite this general point of departure. How is this possible?

Emil Brunner has an argument about divorce that is instructive. He argues that divorce is against the moral order established by God. He refers to the teaching of Jesus according to Mark 10:1–12. Jesus is questioned by the Pharisees about divorce and Jesus response is that divorce is allowed because of their "hardness of heart." It was different in the beginning of the world. Brunner interprets these words in the following way: there is a difference between the absolute order of creation and the relative order of society. Divorce is against the absolute order of creation, but must be allowed according to the relative order of society which has to reckon with real human beings and their sinful nature. Human law is something other than divine law.

Brunner could have argued in the same way concerning same-sex relationships. With reference to Paul's letter to the Romans, Brunner argues that divorce is "unnatural" in the same way as homosexuality is "unnatural."[21] Would it not be possible to make a distinction between the absolute order of creation and the relative order of society also when it comes to same-sex relationships? Such relationships could be judged as against the moral order, but nevertheless be allowed in the relative law of society because of the human "hardness of heart." In this way an order theology could be reconciled with an openness to the introduction of same-sex relationships. But this is not Brunner's line of thought. Divorce is acceptable, but homosexuality is not.

An Alternative Theology of Creation

I shall return to this argument in a moment, but let me first consider another basic argument against the whole idea of moral orders established by God. This criticism has been voiced by the Swedish theologian Gustaf Wingren[22] and in a more systematic form by an American theologian, James M. Gustafson. Gustafson had a close relationship to many Swedish theologians. One of them was Gustaf Wingren. Neither Wingren nor Gustafson were particularly concerned with homosexuality and same-sex marriages. Wingren developed his argument on a more general level and Gustafson's main focus was medical ethics. But their ideas are highly relevant in the present context.

21. Brunner, *Das Gebot und die Ordnungen*, 106.
22. See Wingren, *Öppenhet och egenart*.

Wingren affirmed that God's will can be discerned in creation, i.e., in nature and society (without the help of God's revelation in Jesus Christ). But God's will is not expressed in certain immutable orders common to every age and every culture. "God's law is God's through being variable." God engages constantly in new actions, destruction appears constantly in new forms. God creates *now*. Therefore, God's will is discernible not primarily in fixed and immutable institutions or in hierarchical structures of dominion and submission, but in processes where life is renewed and flourishing.[23]

James Gustafson argues basically the same point in his *The Contribution of Theology to Medical Ethics* (1975)—with one crucial difference. Gustafson's main opponent is not classical order theology but the American theologian Paul Ramsey. Ramsey argued—incidentally, as did Emil Brunner—that love is "in-principled." Love follows certain rules and lives in accordance with certain orders. In the technical jargon of academic ethics, Ramey and Brunner's ethics are a kind of deontological ethics, i.e., an ethics of obligation and duty governed by principles and rules, rather than an ethics of value and ends.[24] Gustafson is not opposed to this version of Christian ethics, but he is in clear disagreement with Ramsey on another point:

> The crucial theological difference between Ramsey and me is in the emphasis that I give to God as the power that creates new possibilities for well-being in the events of nature and history, including the possibilities that emerge in the course of evolutionary development and the development of biological knowledge. *This emphasis opens ethically the possibilities for an alteration of some traditional principles, and an alteration of the ordering of certain traditional values in particular circumstances.*[25]

To put it in one sentence: God not only acts to sustain and preserve life; God also creates new possibilities for well-being to occur. What is right and good cannot only be identified in permanent and unchangeable rules; it must also be discerned in new rules and laws. Why is it necessary to have this openness for new rules and laws? One reason is, of course, that destruction always appears in new forms. But there is also another reason: new possibilities for good are constantly emerging. Psychology is one

---

23. Ibid., 111ff.

24. On "teleological ethics," see Gustafson, *The Contributions of Theology to Medical Ethics*, 40f.

25. Ibid., 44f.; my italics.

obvious example. Psychological knowledge about mental diseases gives new opportunities to limit human suffering, but such knowledge can also help human persons without such impediments to enrich their lives and realize a higher quality of life. One contemporary example is the cognitive therapy developed by the American psychiatrist Aaron T. Beck.

In sum, a tension between two ethical principles in Christian ethics is clearly discerned. On the one hand we have the principle of preservation and sustenance. Let us call this the *preservative principle*. On the other hand we have the principle of renewal and creativity, which we may term *the dynamic principle*. The theology of God's orders of creation clearly favors the preservative principle. The emphasis is on restriction, delimitation, and caution. The presumption is in favor of limits and "stop signs."[26] Gustafson and Wingren's theology on the other hand, can be understood as a plea for the dynamic principle in Christian moral theology.

Ethical Consequence of a Dynamic Theology of Creation

A dynamic theology of creation is highly relevant for the interpretation of human sexuality and new reproductive technologies. First, a few words about its relevance for sexual ethics.

Needless to say, human sexuality serves the constant renewal of the human species, but it has created new opportunities for expressing love and affection and the strengthening of human relationships. This is exactly what gay, lesbians, and transsexual persons have found. Sexual pleasure is a source for attaining a higher quality of life. For a Christian believer it is, ultimately, God who creates these new possibilities. We can take a trivial example from another area. Food satisfies our hunger, but our appetite can also be developed for increasing our delight in eating. We serve food with aesthetic sensitivity and use it to increase social bonds. Hunger and appetite create new possibilities for other goods to emerge beyond the mere satisfaction of biological needs. And this is also the case with human sexuality.

Two other issues need to be addressed. First, what is the place of the more restrictive perspective? Needless to say it is, and it has also been, repeatedly recognized in the discussion leading up to the Church Synod decision in 2009. The *form* of marriage is a permanent, loving, and faithful relationship between two individual human beings. This form is of central

26. Peters, "Proleptic Ethics vs. Stop Sign Ethics."

significance for the persons involved, the children that are raised in this relationship, and the network to which this family belongs.

Secondly, the discussion and decision of Church of Sweden in the area of same-sex marriage reflects an effort to strike a fair balance between the preservative and the dynamic principle. God is at work not only in order, but also in change. Wingren's theology was frequently highlighted in the process leading up to the Synod of Church of Sweden in 2009 and its decision to endorse the state proposal about same-sex marriages. The following quotation is one example:

> The fixed is represented by love in the sense of caring for others, while the movable is an expression of changes in cultural and social situations and institutions. Starting from love for one's fellow beings, existing laws, institutions and orders are criticised. This in turn leads to new laws, institutions and orders. In the area of relationships, one can today point to the widespread practice of living together in marriage-like relationship with no marriage ceremony. Registered partnerships could also be seen as an innovation in line with Wingren's model of social ethics.[27]

In sum, a dynamically interpreted theology of creation opens up to a more differentiated evaluation of homosexual and lesbian relationships.

Wingren and Gustafson's dynamic interpretation of God's orders of creation is also highly relevant for the interpretation of new reproductive technologies. In the beginning of my essay, I mentioned a couple of decisions by Church of Sweden Board concerning new reproductive technologies. I would now suggest that the board—and the theologians preparing the statements for the board—have tried to strike a similar balance in its response to biotechnological issues as has been done in response to governmental proposals on same-sex relationships. Of course, one may question whether the right balance has been struck. My main impression is that the accent has been on the dynamic rather than the preservative principle: new reproductive technologies have been understood in the perspective of new possibilities for human good and welfare rather than in perspective of the preservative principle—but without neglecting the need for sustenance and restrictions. Stem cell research, therapeutic cloning, and preimplantatory genetic diagnostics (PGD) do not as such violate this principle of human dignity. The board argues for restrictions and caution but comes down on the positive side.

---

27. "Samlevnadsfrågor," 63.

PART ONE: Exploring a Heritage—Burning Issues

My impression is further that the Magisterium of the Roman Catholic Church gives a more consistent priority to the preservative principle before the dynamic principle. It should, however, be noticed that several Catholic theologians from Karl Rahner onwards suggest another line of thought. Rahner makes a plea for the transcendental freedom of human beings. Human "nature" is not immutable. "In this lies the warrant for greater openness to experimentation than traditionalistic Catholics permit."[28] This plea for the dynamic principle is also endorsed by other Catholic theologians—even if it has not (as far as I know) been applied in the field of Catholic sexual ethics.[29]

Ecclesiological Conclusions

What then are the ecclesiological conclusions from such a dynamic theology of creation? More precisely, what understanding of the nature and purpose of the church emerges from a theology which sees God at work in history where Christians and non-Christians alike discern and endorse not only that which sustains and preserves life, but also that which gives rise to new possibilities for well-being? In short, what is the purpose and nature of the church if morality has to do with the presence of God?

It is frequently argued that the nature and purpose of the church is far wider than—and even different from—its moral authority. The churches of the Augsburg Confession believe that it is sufficient (*satis est*) that the gospel be rightly taught and the sacraments be administered in accord with the command of Christ.[30] Anywhere where men and women gather around the presence of Christ in Word and Sacrament we have a presence of the church. The gospel is the message of God's free forgiveness, God's grace. This is the core belief of the Lutheran churches. And they share the conviction that this is the central message of the New Testament.

If the nature and purpose of the church is the right proclamation of the gospel and the administration of the sacraments according to the command of Christ, it could be argued that morality is secondary and even irrelevant to the nature and purpose of the church. The nature and purpose of the church is not to strengthen morality and act as a moral supervisor in

---

28. See Gustafson, *Protestant and Roman Catholic Ethics*, 49ff., with references to the works of Rahner.

29. Ibid., esp. 144ff.

30. The Augsburg Confession, VII.

society. Such expectations—serious and well intended as they are—should not be the "burning issues" for the church.

But reducing morality by declaring it irrelevant for the central identity of the church goes against a long and powerful tradition where the church has been understood as a moral authority. The purpose of the church is not exhausted by its moral authority, but nor can its role as moral authority simply be discarded. Why not? The simple answer is: because moral action has to do with God's purpose for God's creation. "God is at work in history when men adopt a certain ethical attitude."[31]

This idea is closely linked to another thought. God is present not only in the Christian community and in other religious communities, but also in human realities outside religion and—needless to say—throughout the universe as a whole. This conviction is deeply rooted in the traditional creed of Christianity, but what is not universally acknowledged is that God's presence may also be discerned by men and women without a Christian belief—and even without any religious belief at all. Karl Barth is one example of a theologian who had serious misgivings about any real moral and religious insights beyond the revelation of God in Jesus Christ (even if some theologians have argued that he may be interpreted otherwise). But there are various reasons why such an exclusivist line of thought is untenable. Moral insights are not dependant on Christian belief, nor is Christian belief sufficient for such insights. This is also in line with the teachings of Jesus of Nazareth when he was approached by a devout Roman centurion who exclaimed that "[t]ruly I tell you, in no one in Israel have I found such faith" (Matt 8:10). In short, there are insufficient theological reasons for a Christian exclusivism in moral matters.

In other words: when Christians and non-Christians discern what sustains and preserves life and where new possibilities for well-being emerge, they discern God's action in the world. Therefore, moral discernment is a central purpose of the church. Needless to say, it is not the only purpose; proclaiming the grace of God and administering the sacraments are primary and essential. But if it is true that God is at work wherever life is sustained and preserved, where new possibilities for well-being emerge and where men and women discern and endorse these processes, then the church cannot simply retreat from its role as a moral authority.

What are the concrete consequences of this? What specific moral sensitivities should be evoked, sustained, and cultivated by Christian faith in the present situation? More specifically, what ecclesial explication of the

---

31. Jeffner, *Theology and Integration*, 65.

good ordering of society and of the right conduct of persons is required in the world at present? These are large issues that lay in the extension of the arguments in this essay, but they must be dealt with in another context.

Concluding Remark

Let me conclude with another quotation from the dissertation of Maria Södling. Toward the end of the dissertation she raises an important theological question about how theology is forged between historical tradition and contemporary context. She concludes with the following remark about Swedish ecclesial theology between the wars:

> ... the dissertation has shown that even if a theological conception of order dominated the church texts of the time, it was not all-prevailing. One also hears in the texts diverse voices that speak for the genders' similarity and freedom. Even if these voices had little impact on the church texts of the time, they raise the classic systematic-theological question about how theology is forged in the tension between tradition and context. Which theological thoughts were permitted in the church texts of the time, and which were not? Which theology was given space and which was pushed into the shadows? Discussion of the relationship between theology, tradition and context leads finally to the question of how an individual theologian chooses to form her theology in an intellectually and ethically responsible way.[32]

Burning issues from the perspective of the identity of the church and burning issues from the perspective of the secular context are often in tension with each other. If God is at work in creation *and* through the gospel of God's grace, each of these perspectives are equally and perennially relevant. And thus they should be equally and perennially relevant for the church.

---

32. Södling, *Oreda i skapelsen*, 385; my translation.

Bibliography

Austad, Torleiv, editor. *Skriftforståelse og skriftbruk med særlig henblikk på homofilisaken: Uttalelse fra Den norske kirkes lærememnd i sak reist av Møre biskop.* Oslo: Kirkens informatjonstjenste, 2006.
Bexell, Göran and Carl-Henric Grenholm. *Teologisk etik: En introduktion.* Stockholm: Verbum, 1997.
Brunner, Emil. *Das Gebot und die Ordnungen: Entwurf einer protestantisch-theologischen Ethik.* Tübingen: Mohr/Siebeck, 1932.
———. *Rättvisa: En lära om samhällsordningens grundlagar.* Stockholm: Svenska Kyrkans Diakonistyrelses Bokförlag, 1945.
Bråkenhielm, Carl Reinhold, editor. *Power and Peace: Statements on Peace and the Authority of the Churches.* Research Report 9. Uppsala: Life & Peace Institute, 1992.
Fagerberg, Holsten, editor. *De homosexuella och kyrkan.* Stockholm: Verbum, 1974.
The Genetic Integrity Act. Swedish Code of Statutes 2006:351. Online: http://www.smer.se/news/the-genetic-integrity-act-2006351/ (accessed 17/10/2010).
Grenholm, Carl-Henric, Jarl Hemberg, and Ragnar Holte, editors. *Etiska texter.* Stockholm: Verbum & Håkan Ohlssons, 1977.
Gustafson, James M. *The Contributions of Theology to Medical Ethics.* Pere Marquette Theology Lecture, 1975. Milwaukee, WI: Marquette University Press, 1975.
———. *Protestant and Roman Catholic Ethics: Prospects for Rapprochement.* Chicago: University of Chicago Press, 1978.
Homosexuella och samhället: Utredningen om homosexuellas situation i samhället. Statens offentliga utredningar 1984:63. Stockholm: Liber, 1984.
House of Bishops of the Church of England. *Some Issues in Human Sexuality: A Guide to the Debate: A Discussion Document from the House of Bishop's Group on Issues in Humans Sexuality.* London: Church House Publishing, 2003.
Hüttner, Reinhard and Theodor Dietner, editors. *Ecumenical Ventures in Ethics: Protestant Engage Pope Paul II's Moral Encyclicals.* A Project of the Institute for Ecumenical Research, Strasbourg. Grand Rapids: Eerdmans, 1998.
Jeffner, Anders. *Theology and Integration: Four Essays in Philosophical Theology.* Acta Universitatis Upsaliensis, Studia Doctrinae Christianae Upsaliensia 28. Uppsala: Uppsala University, 1987.
Lindfelt, Mikael and Johanna Gustafsson Lundberg. *Kärlekens förändrade landskap: Teologi om samlevnad.* Stockholm: Verbum, 2009.
———. *Uppdrag samliv: Om äktenskap och samlevnad.* Stockholm: Verbum, 2007.
Möller, Göran, editor. *Cohabitation and Life Together.* Uppsala: Theological Committee of the Church of Sweden, 2006.
Nilsson, Gert, editor. *En fråga om kärlek: Homosexuella i kyrkan: En bok från samtalsgruppen Kyrkan och de homosexuella.* Stockholm: Verbum, 1988.
Peters, Ted. "Proleptic Ethics vs. Stop Sign Ethics: Theology and the Future of Genetics." *Svensk teologisk kvartalskrift* 83/4 (2007) 146–68.
"Rättslig reglering av stamcellsforskning." Socialdepartementet. Statens offentliga utredningar 2002:119. Stockholm: Regeringskansliet, 2002. Online: http://www.regeringen.se/sb/d/108/a/2717 (accessed 17/10/2010).

PART ONE: Exploring a Heritage—Burning Issues

"Samlevnadsfrågor." Kyrkostyrelsens skrivelse till Kyrkomötet 2005:9. Online: http://www.svenskakyrkan.se/tcrot/km/2005/skrivelser/i_KsSkr_2005-9_ Samlevnadsfragor.shtml#P19_204 (accessed 17/10/2010).
"Schöpfungsordnung." In *Theologische Realenzyklopädie*, vol. 30. Berlin: de Gruyter, 1999.
Sturmark, Christer. *Tro och vetande 2.0: Om förnuft, humanism och varför människor tror på konstiga saker: En liten bok om stora frågor*. Nora: Nya Doxa, 2006.
Söderblom, Nathan. *Tal och skrifter*. Malmö: Världslitteraturens förlag, 1930.
Södling, Maria. *Oreda i skapelsen: Kvinnligt och manligt i Svenska kyrkan under 1920 och 30-talen*. Acta Universitatis Upsaliensia, Studies in Faiths and Ideologies 26. Uppsala: Uppsala University, 2010.
Wingren, Gustaf. *Öppenhet och egenart: Evangeliet i världen*. Lund: LiberLäromedel, 1979.
"Yttrande. Dnr Ks 2003:143." Svenska kyrkan. Online: http://www.svenskakyrkan.se/default.aspx?id=694328 (accessed 17/10/2010).
"Yttrande. Dnr Ks 2004:406." Svenska Kyrkan. Online: http://www.svenskakyrkan.se/default.aspx?id=694345 (accessed 17/10/2010).

5

Same-Sex Marriage

*A Burning Issue in the Evangelical
Lutheran Church of Iceland*

SÓLVEIG ANNA BÓASDÓTTIR

SAME-SEX MARRIAGE HAS BEEN a fiercely debated topic in many countries around the world during the last decade. In 2001, the Netherlands became the first country to recognize same-sex marriages as legally valid. This meant that according to legislation the marriage of a man and woman and the marriage of two men or two women were given equivalent status. Since then nine countries have followed the Netherlands in making same-sex marriage legal: Argentina, Belgium, Canada, Iceland, Norway, Portugal, South Africa, Spain, and Sweden. Several other countries currently have this issue under consideration.[1]

Same-sex marriage was legalized in Iceland in June 2010.[2] Therewith Iceland became the ninth country in the world to legalize same-sex

---

1. In the United States same-sex marriage is not recognized federally but same-sex couples can currently marry in six states. Mexico City also performs same-sex marriages, which are recognized in all thirty-one Mexican states.

2. Same-sex intercourse was decriminalized in 1940 when the Icelandic legislature adopted new *General Penal Code* (no. 19/1940) in accordance with legislative developments in Denmark. The decriminalization of same-sex intercourse was, however, not accompanied by a legal recognition of homosexuality; rather the legislation continued to regard homosexuality as inherently different from heterosexuality.

PART ONE: Exploring a Heritage—Burning Issues

marriage. Between 1996 and 2010 Iceland had legislation granting a *civil partnership* for gay and lesbian couples. It was substantially equivalent to the Nordic civil partnership legislations at that time in Denmark, Norway, and Sweden.[3] In Iceland, the status of civil partnership legislation and marriage legislation was almost identical but for one thing: a couple who entered into civil partnership was excluded from being adoptive parents. The same applied to fertility assistance: it was not available to women in civil partnerships. This was amended in 2006. That year the parliament passed an act ensuring full legal equality between same-sex couples in civil partnership and married couples. From 2006 to 2008 the only remaining difference between the marriage legislation and the civil partnership legislation was that the Evangelical Lutheran Church of Iceland, as well as other religious communities, was not allowed to conduct marriage ceremonies between same-sex couples. In June 2008, however, the Icelandic parliament changed this and granted all licensed religious communities in Iceland the right to conduct civil partnership ceremonies between gay and lesbian couples. From 2008, therefore, the only thing that differed between the civil partnership legislation and the marriage legislation were the appellations attributed to them. Gay and lesbian couples entered "civil partnership" but heterosexual couples entered "marriage." That arrangement existed until 2010. On March 23, 2010 the government presented a bill to repeal the civil partnership law and allow couples to *marry* regardless of gender. On June 11, 2010 the Parliament of Iceland approved the bill in a unanimous vote legalizing same-sex marriage. The law on *gender-neutral* marriage took effect on June 27, 2010.

My aims in this chapter will be twofold. First, by linking the theological debates on same-sex marriage to Protestant and Lutheran understanding of marriage in past and present, and by explaining the legal relations between church and state in Iceland, I intend to bring the debate on same-sex marriage into historical, political, and theological perspective. Second, I will account for the development of the theological and public debates in Iceland in 1996–2010 that led to the legislation on same-sex marriage in 2010. My argument throughout the chapter will likewise be twofold. On the one hand, I argue that the legislation in Iceland was greatly affected and even delayed by several years because of the way in which the Evangelical Lutheran Church of Iceland interfered with political intentions to legalize same-sex marriage. On the other hand, I contend that the strict,

---

3. Bråkenhielm's chapter in this volume gives some very interesting perspectives on the development in Church of Sweden regarding the issue I am discussing.

official, and conservative policy of the bishops of Iceland towards same-sex marriage was countered and challenged by a large group of progressive Evangelical Lutheran Church of Iceland pastors and theologians that gradually emerged in resistance to that policy.

Lutheran Understanding of Marriage

In his book *From Sacrament to Contract*, John Witte Jr. explores the many complex traditions of marriage in the West. According to him, the Western Christian church has from its apostolic beginnings presented four main perspectives on marriage: religious, social, contractual, and natural. Witte explains the four perspectives:

> A *religious perspective* regards marriage as a spiritual or sacramental association, subject to the creed, cult, and canons of the church community. A *social perspective* treats marriage as a social estate, subject to the expectations and exactions of the local community and to special state laws of contract, property, and inheritance. A *contractual perspective* describes marriage as a voluntary association, subject to the wills and preferences of the couple, their children, and their household. Hovering in the background is a *naturalist perspective* that treats marriage as a created institution, subject to the natural laws of reason, conscience, and the Bible.[4]

These perspectives on marriage, according to Witte, are both complementary and standing in substantial tension. The reason for the latter is that they are connected to rival claims of ultimate authority over the form and function of marriage. Which authority has the unconditional power over marriage?, asks Witte. Is it the church, the state, the marital couple, nature, or God? His answer is that it depends on the perspective; it depends on whether we belong to the Catholic tradition or the Protestant traditions. Lutherans, Calvinists, and Anglicans have developed three different Protestant models of marriage.[5] At the same time, all three Protestant models share important ingredients with the Catholic sacramental model of the mid-twelfth century. Like Catholics, Protestants view marriage as an association created for procreation and mutual protection. The same can be

---

4. Witte, *From Sacrament to Contract*, 2.

5. To be sure, Witte argues that each group is familiar with multiple perspectives on marriage, but holds that each group has also given precedence to one perspective in order to reach an integrated understanding.

said for the view that marriage is a voluntary association formed by the mutual consent of the couple. But, unlike Catholics, Protestants reject the subordination of marriage to celibacy and the celebration of marriage as a sacrament.[6] Let us look closer into these issues.

The Catholic sacramental model, Witte argues, holds firstly that marriage is a natural association created by God to allow men and women to be "fruitful and multiply." This positive point is, however, contradicted by a more negative one. Witte writes: "Since the fall into sin, marriage had also become a remedy for lust, a channel to direct one's natural passion to the service of the community and the church."[7] Secondly, Witte points out that marriage in the Catholic tradition is viewed as a contractual entity, formed by the mutual consent of the parties. "This contract prescribed for couples a lifelong relation of love, service, and devotion, to each other and proscribed unwarranted breach or relaxation of their connubial and parental duties."[8]

These two ingredients of marriage are, in Witte's view, shared by the Catholic and the Protestant traditions. The third Catholic view on marriage, however—that the temporal union of body, soul, and mind within marriage symbolizes the eternal union between Christ and his church, bringing sanctifying grace to the couple, the church, and the community—goes far beyond the Protestant view of marriage. To be sure, Witte argues, Protestants deny that celibate life has greater virtue over married life. To the contrary, according to them, it could easily lead to concubinage and homosexuality. Further, marriage in a Protestant view is not a real sacrament, but a free social institution ordained by God and equal in dignity and social responsibility with the church, the state, and other estates of society. Therefore, participation in marriage requires no prerequisite faith or purity and presents no sanctifying grace, as a true sacrament does.[9]

In a different way the Lutheran tradition developed a social model of marriage. That model does not conceive marriage to be a sacred estate of the heavenly kingdom of redemption but a social estate of the earthly kingdom of creation. Lutheran marriage was "the community of the couple in the present, not their sacramental union in the life to come."[10] Witte Writes:

6. Witte, *From Sacrament to Contract*, 5.
7. Ibid., 3.
8. Ibid., 3–4.
9. Ibid., 5.
10. Ibid., 6.

Though divinely ordained, marriage was directed primarily to human ends, to the fulfilling of "uses" in the lives of the individual and of society. Marriage revealed to persons their sin and their need for God's marital gift. It restricted prostitution, promiscuity, and other public sexual sins. It taught love, restraint, and other public virtues. All fit men and women were free to enter such unions, clerical and lay alike. Indeed, all persons were spiritually compelled to marry when they came of age, unless they had the rare gift of continence.[11]

A recent Lutheran view of marriage found in a 2003 Evangelical Lutheran Church in America document entitled *Journey Together Faithfully* confirms much in Witte's work.[12] *Journey Together Faithfully* interprets both Luther and the Reformation so that they affirm marriage as "natural and good, ordained by God in creation."[13] Further, the Lutheran tradition is said to set a high value on the personal relations between husband and wife and uphold the goodness of marriage—rejecting, however, the necessity of celibacy for priests. According to the document the creation stories "take for granted that sexual relations will be between a man and a woman. They assume that the male and the female, who complement each other biologically in other ways, are God's only given structure for human sexual relationships."[14] What is made very clear is that the Evangelical Lutheran Church in America still has no policy on the blessing of same-sex unions; rather it is the policy that "all single rostered people, including those who understand themselves to be homosexual, are expected to abstain from sexual relationships."[15] The 2003 document refers to an earlier document, *Message on Sexuality: Some Common Convictions* (1996), and its conception of human sexuality as "created good with the purposes of expressing love and generating life, for mutual companionship and pleasure."[16] *Journey Together Faithfully*, pointing out that in the *Message on Sexuality*

---

11. Ibid., 5.

12. The background for this document was a resolution from the 2001 Churchwide Assembly, comprising voting members from congregations across the ELCA, set up to study homosexuality with reference to two issues: 1) the blessing of same-sex unions and the ordination, consecration, and commissioning of people in committed same-sex unions; and 2) developing a social statement on sexuality. See *Journey Together Faithfully*, 3.

13. Ibid., 19.

14. Ibid., 12.

15. Ibid., 5.

16. Ibid., 19.

PART ONE: Exploring a Heritage—Burning Issues

homosexuality is still viewed as sinful, contests this view. Its conclusion is that this is not plausible anymore; people of homosexual orientation are "no more sinners than all other people" and should be welcomed into the life of the congregation of Lutheran churches.[17]

In the Lutheran tradition civil law administrates marriage. This means that the church has no legal authority over marriage. Luther taught that God's law should be administered by magistrates who were God's vice-regents in the earthly kingdom. He even taught that all church members should counsel those who considered marriage and caution those who sought annulment or divorce; these duties were part of the priesthood of believers.[18]

In the Lutheran social view of marriage, marriage is therefore the basis of society, and therefore churches, states, schools, and other institutions. The arguments for this can maybe best be understood in the context of the two-kingdoms theory. According to Lutheran teachings, God has ordained two kingdoms in which humanity is destined to live: the earthly or political kingdom and the heavenly or spiritual kingdom.

> The earthly kingdom is the realm of creation, of natural and civic life, where a person operates primarily by reason, law, and passion. The heavenly kingdom is the realm of redemption, of spiritual and eternal life, where a person operates primarily by faith, hope, and charity. These two kingdoms embrace parallel temporal and spiritual forms of justice and morality, truth and knowledge, order and law, but they remain separate and distinct. The earthly kingdom is fallen and distorted by sin. The heavenly kingdom is saved and renewed by grace—and foreshadows the perfect kingdom of Christ to come. A Christian is a citizen of both kingdoms at once and invariably comes under the structures and strictures of each.[19]

Based on Luther's own writing, Lutheran marriage is firmly placed within the earthly kingdom and not the heavenly kingdom. As part of the earthly kingdom, marriage can be argued to be a gift of God for all persons, Christians and non-Christians alike. Because marriage is a social estate of the earthly kingdom, it is subject to civil law and civil authority. Marriage is a civil institution as well as a religious one, according to a Lutheran view. This is a crucial point when it comes to the debate on same-sex marriage

17. Ibid.
18. Witte, *From Sacrament to Contract*, 6.
19. Ibid., 51.

in a country like Iceland. It is the state that empowers state officials, as well as pastors of the church and other recognized religious organizations, to confirm marriage. However, here it becomes interesting to reflect on the relationship between the Evangelical Lutheran Church of Iceland and the Icelandic state. In the next part I shall do just this.

The Relationship between the Evangelical Lutheran Church of Iceland and the Icelandic State

The Evangelical Lutheran Church of Iceland, to which over 80 percent of the Icelandic people belongs, is closely linked to the Icelandic state, enjoying its protection and support.[20] This situation has historical roots in the Icelandic constitution, which has remained largely unchanged since 1874. Articles 62 and 63 of the constitution read:

> The Evangelical Lutheran Church shall be the State Church in Iceland and, as such, it shall be supported and protected by the State.

> All persons have the right to form religious associations and to practice their religion in conformity with their individual convictions. Nothing may however be preached or practiced which is prejudicial to good morals or public order.[21]

Hjalti Hugason argues that the church-state relations in Iceland can generally be said to belong to a traditional Nordic model.[22] This means that

> the government supports the citizens' religious practices, primarily by maintaining a strong and formal relationship usually to a single denomination. The state/national church can be separate from the government to various degrees, and the relationship between church and state can be in various forms. Religious freedom can well be explicitly defined and it is not an aim of the government to achieve religious unity within the society. Inequality between denominations is, however, inevitably present.[23]

---

20. Hugason, "A Case Study of the Evolution of a Nordic Lutheran Majority Church," 107.
21. *Constitution of the Republic of Iceland.*
22. Hugason, "A Case Study," 111.
23. Ibid., 111, footnote 9.

PART ONE: Exploring a Heritage—Burning Issues

In addition to the constitutional relationship between the church and the state, Hugason argues there have also been legal, administrative, and financial connections between the state and the national church. However, this historical situation is undergoing change. In 1994–1995 the human rights part of the Icelandic constitution was altered. At that time, however, it was not considered essential to modify the historical position of the national church. The grounds for not doing so was the view that the Icelandic church system does not

> violate freedom of religion, as long as it does not limit the rights of those outside the Church of Iceland to pursue other religious practices, found their own religious organizations or remain outside all religious organizations, and people are not discriminated against on this basis.[24]

Since 1997, the relationship between church and state in Iceland has undergone change and developed outside the traditional borders of the state–national church model. Hugason suggests that the current situation can best be described according to the parameters of what he calls a *collaboration model*. The main characteristic of such a model is that the government

> supports the citizens' religious practices by working closely with one or more religious organizations. The collaboration is based on law, or co-operation and service agreements. Specific religious organizations can still be subject to special circumstances and those circumstances can even lead to some partiality. The citizens enjoy religious freedom and religious unity is not the government's goal.[25]

A good example of the historical collaboration between the church and state in Iceland is, as I have already mentioned, that pastors of churches and other registered religious associations that have the approval of the Ministry of the Interior are licensed by the civil authorities to conduct marriages. This means that couples can ask for marriage ceremonies to take place either with pastors (or leaders of religious associations) or in a registry office. Recent statistics show that church ceremonies are five times more popular in Iceland than civilian marriage ceremonies; over 80

---

24. Ibid., 110.
25. Ibid., 111–112, footnote 10.

percent of all marriages in Iceland are conducted by pastors of the Evangelical Lutheran Church of Iceland and other religious associations.[26]

Two recent examples of the close relations between the Evangelical Lutheran Church of Iceland and the Icelandic state can be taken from 1996 and 2005. In 1996, the Icelandic parliament passed the *Act on Civil Partnership* (no.87/1996). In the process of doing so the parliament asked the Evangelical Lutheran Church of Iceland about its position, in particular if it wished to be granted the authority to ratify civil partnerships. The answer, written by the bishop, made clear that the church was not ready to do that and did not wish for such a right.[27] One conclusion that can be drawn from this negative answer, which shows the close ties between the state and the church, is that this answer became a deciding factor in the state's decision at that time not to empower either the Evangelical Lutheran Church of Iceland or any other religious organizations to confirm civil partnerships. Ten years later, in 2005, the Evangelical Lutheran Church of Iceland received a similar request from a committee established by the Prime Minister. This time the question concerned same-sex marriage. The bishop's answer confirmed the same position as in 1995; the church did not wish to get the right to conduct civil partnership/same-sex marriage. As a response to that answer the Evangelical Lutheran Church of Iceland was encouraged by the state committee to change its position in order to be able to provide a church ceremony for same-sex couples as well as for heterosexual couples. In both above examples, however, the state decided not to go against the will of the church.

Public Debates on Same-Sex Relations

Debates about same-sex marriages, civil and religious, have been current in North America and Western Europe for some time, not least in countries where lesbian, bisexual, gay, and transgender (LBGT) people have gained sufficient visibility and legal standing to press for the right to marry. Before giving an account of the debate after 2000 on same-sex marriage, which is my main issue, I shall mention a few things concerning the development and reforms in the 1990s regarding same-sex couples in Iceland.

International pressure, as well as a growing visibility of homosexuality in Iceland in the 1980s, led to important steps taken by the Icelandic

---

26. These figures are from "Statistics Iceland" from 2004.
27. Parliament of Iceland, A-deild, bls. 564.

state towards legal equality for same-sex couples and heterosexual couples. The visibility of gay and lesbian issues can be related to the founding of an official gay and lesbian movement called Samtökin '78 as well as resolutions from the Council of Europe in 1981 and the Nordic Council in 1984 in which the governments of their member states were urged to put an end to discrimination against their gay and lesbian citizens.[28] In 1993, a committee was appointed by the Prime Minister to investigate the legal, the social, and the cultural situation of gay and lesbian people in Iceland.[29] In its report from 1994, which finally led to the 1996 legislation on civil partnership, the will to extend equal rights to gay and lesbian was emphasized as well as a clear intention that legislature should be used in fighting prejudice against this group.

In the context of legislation it is important to mention that in the field of family law there has been a formal Nordic co-operation for a very long time.[30] Iceland has participated in this co-operation the last few decades and revised its family law in accordance with Nordic proposals. To be sure, Nordic societies have much in common regarding human rights issues. The Nordic countries are in leading positions in the world when it comes to women's labor market participation, gender equality, and competitiveness. According to the World Economic Forum's 2010 *Global Gender Gap Report*, Iceland demonstrates the greatest equality between men and women, followed by the other Nordic countries, Norway, Finland, and Sweden.[31] In 1980 Vigdís Finnbogadóttir became the world's first democratically elected female head of state when she became the fourth president of Iceland. In 2009 Jóhanna Sigurðardóttir became the first openly lesbian head of government not only in Iceland but probably the world—at least in modern times.[32] These facts can serve as examples of the relatively liberal social environment when it comes to issues on gender and sexuality in Iceland.

When the Icelandic state changed its legislation on marriage in 2010, it followed two other Nordic countries; Norway and Sweden changed their laws on marriage a year before the Icelandic parliament chose to do so. To conclude this part and move on to the theological debate, a national survey from 2004 can serve as an example of the changing attitudes of

28. Council of Europe Parliamentary Assembly Recommendation 924 (1981) and Nordic Council Resolution 17 (1984).

29. Parliament of Iceland, A-deild, bls. 1706.

30. Snævarr, "Um sifjar og sifjarétt."

31. *Global Gender Gap Report 2010*.

32. Burns, "Iceland Names New Prime Minister."

Icelandic society toward same-sex marriage soon after 2000. In this survey people were asked if they considered that gay and lesbian couples should be able to marry a) at a civil ceremony, b) at a church ceremony, c) both civil and church ceremony, or d) not at all. The response rate was 63 percent. To question a) 18 percent answered positively. To question b) 3 percent answered in a positive way. To question c) 66 percent gave a positive answer. To question d) 13 percent answered yes. This means that already in 2004 the majority of the Icelandic population (87 percent) believed that gay and lesbian couples should be able to enter marriage and 69 percent of them thought that the marriage ceremony should take place within the church.[33]

To conclude, there is little doubt that the national poll from 2004 showing the will of the nation toward same-sex marriage influenced the final report of the Prime Minister's committee (2005) urging the Evangelical Lutheran Church of Iceland to change its negative attitudes to same-sex marriage. However, despite the pressure of the Icelandic administration towards the Evangelical Lutheran Church of Iceland to clear all possible obstacles for gay and lesbian couples, allowing them to be married in the church, this did not happen. When the Icelandic state changed the marriage legislation five years later (in 2010) the church still held the view from 2005 (based on its 1996 position).

Church Debates on Same-Sex Relations

It would be an exaggeration to contend that sexual issues generally have had much weight in the Evangelical Lutheran Church of Iceland. However, as in many other churches around the world, intimate relationships between lesbian and gay couples have received much attention the past ten to fifteen years. In this section I shall briefly account for the development from 1996, the year that the Icelandic state passed the civil partnership legislation, until the legislation of same-sex marriage in 2010.

The issue of how the Evangelical Lutheran Church of Iceland should deal with the new legislation of 1996 was on the agenda for several church meetings between 1996 and 1998. The Pastoral Synod, which is a yearly meeting of all pastors and deacons in service in the dioceses, as well as the General Synod, which is the decision-making body in the church and composed of lay and ordained representatives (one-third and two-thirds respectively), discussed the issue several times. Already in 1997, a year

33. "Meirihluti vill leyfa giftingar samkynhneigðra."

after the civil partnership law, the question of a prayer and blessing ceremony for civil partnerships arose. In 1999, the bishop of Iceland drafted a blessing ceremony for those pastors who had asked for it.

During 1999–2005 the Evangelical Lutheran Church of Iceland was relatively silent on the gay-lesbian issue. That silence, however, was broken in 2005 with the state committee's recommendations to the church recounted above. The Pastoral Synod in 2005 raised the issue and passed the following resolution:

> The Pastoral Synod of Iceland, held in Neskirkja June 22–24, 2005, asks the bishop to refer to a doctrinal committee the task of responding to the request for church involvement in contracting same-sex partnership, as when a man and a woman are concerned.[34]

This resolution led to the establishment of a doctrinal committee for the first time in the Evangelical Lutheran Church of Iceland's history. At the Pastoral Synod the following year (2006) the doctrinal committee presented a draft report: "The Evangelical Lutheran Church of Iceland and Civil Partnership."[35] The issue was approached by way of four themes: a) interpretation of Scripture, b) ethical questions, c) the church's diaconal mission, and d) ecclesiology.

Under the headline "Interpretation of Scripture" the committee asserted: first, the role of Scripture as the basis for the teaching of the church, according to Lutheran understanding; second, the saving act of Jesus Christ is said to be the key to this interpretation; and third, the task of theology and the church is to differentiate between matters of faith and salvation and issues of temporal order. Concerning the conflicting views on how to understand some biblical verses on homosexual intercourse, the doctrinal committee concluded that it did not consider them to be relevant to salvation. The negative biblical verses should not be used to condemn homosexuality as such nor the individuals who live in a compassionate relationship of love and dedication.

Under the headline "Ethical Questions" the doctrinal committee stressed the equality of all human beings as well as the moral responsibility of all people. The foundation of moral reflections and decisions should be the commandment to love God and neighbour (Luke 10:27) and the Golden Rule (Matt 7:12)—not least in disagreements. Next, the Lutheran

---

34. "The Evangelical Lutheran Church of Iceland and Civil Partnership."

35. Ibid. The content that follows is all included in this document. I do not refer to pages as this is an electronic document.

understanding of marriage was outlined: Martin Luther viewed marriage as God's order of creation, and the legislation regarding marriage in Lutheran countries is not a matter for the church to decide, but is rather for the civil authorities. Finally, it stressed that the church's participation in the legal establishment of marriage is based on a common cultural, legal, and religious understanding of what constitutes a marriage.

Under the headline "The Church's Diaconal Mission" the doctrinal committee emphasized that the Evangelical Lutheran Church of Iceland wants to bear witness to God's love and grace that cares for all, homosexual and heterosexual alike. Homosexuals and their families are in need of care and support from the Christian community and the church wants to support individuals in their wish and effort to live together in love and faithfulness. The doctrinal committee's suggestion was for the church to provide for those homosexual couples who desired a ceremony of prayer and blessing of their relationship by a pastor of the Evangelical Lutheran Church of Iceland. The committee argued that a blessing ceremony of this kind is an act of pastoral care, but should not be considered a ceremony with legal ramifications in the same way as a marriage ceremony.

Under the headline of "Ecclesiology" the doctrinal committee referred to the seventh paragraph of the Augsburg Confession, which states that for a true unity of the church "it is enough to agree concerning the doctrine of the gospel and the administration of the Sacraments. It is not necessary that human traditions, that is, rites or ceremonies, instituted by men should be everywhere alike." The Evangelical Lutheran Church of Iceland (ELCI) is in communion with other Lutheran churches and a founding member of the Porvoo Communion of churches, and this fact affects the way it forms its practice and liturgy.

The final conclusion of the doctrinal committee is that:

1. The ELCI calls people to follow Christ and in mission and practice point to his message of love, human dignity and shared responsibility. In accordance with Christ's indiscriminating love the ELCI considers all equal regardless of family status.

2. The ELCI advocates Biblical and Christian values, supporting life in abundance, promoting justice and safeguarding the wellbeing of all—especially those who are marginalized.

3. The ELCI acknowledges different sexual orientations and stresses that homosexuals are a part of the Church of Christ and receivers of his Gospel.

PART ONE: Exploring a Heritage—Burning Issues

4. The ELCI wants to support all Christians in their effort to have a responsible lifestyle and encourages everyone, heterosexual and homosexual alike, to heed the call of Christ and to love their neighbor. This should also apply to responsibility regarding sex, committed relationships and family life.
5. The ELCI supports marriage as a covenant between a man and a woman, based on Christian love. The ELCI also supports other forms of relationships based on the same premise.
6. The ELCI supports those individuals of the same-sex who commit themselves to a faithful loving relationship of shared obligations. The ELCI permits its pastors to perform a blessing of a civil partnership based on an authorized liturgy.

As can be seen in the doctrinal committee's final conclusion, the Evangelical Lutheran Church of Iceland is anxious not to discriminate people because of their sexual orientation and expresses support for all couples who want to live together in faithfulness and love, however, at the same time it underlines the important distinction between marriage and civil partnership. The proposal made by the doctrinal committee is that the proper church authorities—the Pastoral Synod, the Bishops' Meeting, and the General Synod—agree that pastors in the Evangelical Lutheran Church of Iceland will be allowed to bless civil partnerships of same-sex couples, using a blessing ceremony confirmed by the same authorities. During the 2006 Pastoral Synod the Evangelical Lutheran Church of Iceland's Liturgy Committee presented three blessing ceremonies, suggesting that they be tested in the church over the next few years. The doctrinal committee's final conclusion was to encourage an open debate within the church until the 2007 General Synod's meeting, where a final decision on the issue would be taken.

The doctrinal committee's proposal, however, was not the breakthrough some had hoped for. As mentioned earlier, the allowance to bless civil partnerships already existed in the church (since 1999). A formal blessing ceremony was not the issue any longer. The focus of the debate, both in society and church, had changed. More and more people had begun to question the distinction between marriage and civil partnership. The issue therefore was no longer if the Evangelical Lutheran Church of Iceland should offer a blessing ceremony to civil partnerships or not, but rather why the state should have two different cohabitation laws, one for heterosexuals and another for homosexuals. The focus had moved towards issues of discrimination.

Bóasdóttir—Same-Sex Marriage

Before the Pastoral Synod in 2007, over forty Evangelical Lutheran Church of Iceland pastors and theologians proposed that the Pastoral Synod should move beyond the formulation of the several rituals of blessing of civil partnerships. Instead, they wanted the synod to encourage the Icelandic parliament to change the marriage legislation and adopt a single legislation which included both heterosexual and homosexual couples. This should mean that the church's pastors would be licensed to conduct same-sex marriage as well as heterosexual marriage. The word "marriage" should apply to all couples without distinction. This proposal, however, was not voted on. Instead, a large majority of the Evangelical Lutheran Church of Iceland pastors in the Pastoral Synod in 2007 decided to refer the issue to the bishop and the doctrinal committee. The Pastoral Synod decided, however, to encourage the church to investigate the will of the pastors towards the issue, through a survey. Further, the Pastoral Synod asked the doctrinal committee to deliver a final proposal on the blessing ceremonies before the General Synod's yearly meeting later that year.[36]

Things can, however, happen fast. A few months after the Pastoral Synod in 2007, a new government was established in Iceland. This government's program expressed a clear will to give religious organizations, the Evangelical Lutheran Church of Iceland included, the right to conduct civil partnerships. During the same period a survey was made among all pastors of the Evangelical Lutheran Church of Iceland.[37] Two questions were posed: 1) "Are you positive or negative towards state intentions to give religious organizations the rights to conduct civil partnership?" 2) "How likely is it that you will use those rights?" The response rate was 75 percent, and 65 percent of the pastors were highly or somewhat positive toward getting those rights. Almost 65 percent thought they would use them. More than 20 percent were "very negative" and 6.5 percent were "slightly negative" to receiving those rights. Almost 80 percent of female pastors were highly or somewhat in favor of the state's intention to give the church those rights, while 59 percent of male pastors held the same position. Pastors who had worked for fifteen years or less in the church were both more positive and more likely to make use of those potential rights.[38]

Late in 2007, the General Synod concluded that if the Icelandic parliament decided to give the religious communities the right to conduct civil partnerships, the pastors would be free to do so. A conscience clause,

36. Björnsdóttir, "Hvað gerðist á Prestastefnu 2007?"
37. "Könnun meðal þjónandi presta um heimild til að staðfesta samvist."
38. Ibid.

PART ONE: Exploring a Heritage—Burning Issues

however, was included; no pastor would be forced to conduct civil partnership as it was an option not a command. Finally, the General Synod stressed its former decision that it was important not to change the name of civil partnerships to marriage.

Eight months after the General Synod's meeting, the parliament changed the law in June 2008 and gave the religious associations the rights to conduct civil partnerships. Ten days after the law took effect, an opinion poll that included all Evangelical Lutheran Church of Iceland pastors (123) was carried out by a newspaper.[39] The question now was whether the pastors intended to conduct civil partnerships under the new law. The response rate was over 90 percent, and 77 percent of the pastors answered positively to the question. Only nine pastors (7 percent) replied that they were not prepared to do so. About as many replied they were unsure. A few could not be reached. The bishop refused to answer.

As mentioned at the beginning of this chapter, the 2008 conclusion of the Icelandic parliament only stood for two years. During these two years the Evangelical Lutheran Church of Iceland was silent on the issue of same-sex marriage. In June 2010, the parliament legalized same-sex marriage. Two months before that, the Pastoral Synod gathered for its yearly meeting. Before that meeting, ninety pastors and theologians proposed that same-sex marriage should be discussed at the meeting, suggesting that the synod would sign the following declaration:

> The Pastoral Synod held in Vídalínskirkju the 27th–29th of April 2010 declares its support to the law proposal by the Minister of Justice and Human Rights on one marital law. The Pastoral Synod considers the Icelandic Evangelist Lutheran Church well prepared to take this step with the Government, against the background of the thorough theological discourse on the matter of the ELCI, sexual orientation and marriage, in the past years.[40]

A similar procedure to the 2008 Pastoral Synod recurred; voting on the proposal was avoided and the issue was referred to the Bishop and the doctrinal committee. This conclusion was a great disappointment to the group of pastors and theologians that had prepared the resolution cited above. Removing the resolution from the agenda of the Pastoral Synod meant that the synod, and thus the clergy of Iceland, lost the chance to demonstrate its commitment to and empathy for the gay and lesbian community. After the synod a group of pastors decided to start a campaign,

39. Jónsson, "Hýrnar yfir kirkjunni."
40. "Mannréttindaviðurkenning Samtakanna 78 2010."

writing articles in newspapers, opening a website, and using many different opportunities to make their voice heard. Less than two months after the Pastoral Synod refused to vote on their resolution supporting the upcoming law, the parliament legalized same-sex marriage. At that time, the Icelandic nation had definitely heard a clear message from the group of pastors regarding their great support for the new marriage law. Sunday June 27 became a day of great celebration around the country. Several churches arranged services that focused mainly on same-sex marriage. An article entitled "One Marriage Legislation" appeared in the Icelandic newspapers, signed by 111 pastors, deacons, and theologians, and stating:

> We, pastors, deacons and theologians working within the ELCI and other religious communities in Iceland, celebrate the new marriage legislation taking effect today. We celebrate that today both heterosexual couples and gay and lesbian couples can marry in their church.[41]

To conclude, on June 27 the gay and lesbian movement Samtökin '78 awarded the Evangelical Lutheran Church of Iceland group their yearly human rights prize for their "valuable contribution regarding same-sex marriage legislation in Iceland."[42]

Four months after the same-sex legislation took effect, in October 2010, the General Synod gathered for its yearly meeting, now making a resolution about some necessary changes concerning the church's internal issues in relation to marriage. A new definition of marriage and the marriage liturgy now contains terminology that includes two individuals of the same sex as well as a man and woman. No distinction is made between two women, two men, or a man and a woman regarding the word "marriage" or "to marry." Adapting to the new legislation, the doctrinal committee of the Evangelical Lutheran Church of Iceland approved a new liturgy of marriage, prepared by the Liturgical Committee, just weeks before the new legislation was passed. This is a common liturgy for both homosexual and heterosexual couples.

At the 2010 General Synod, however, the bishop made clear that no further theological discussion is needed on the issue of same-sex marriage,

---

41. The day before the new legislation (June 28) the Evangelical Lutheran Church of Iceland's bishop, Karl Sigurbjörnsson, asked gay and lesbian people for forgiveness over his words on marriage a few years before when he said that if marriage would not exclusively be defined as heterosexual, we could throw it away. See "Biskup biður samkynhneigt fólk um fyrirgefningu."

42. "Mannréttindaviðurkenning Samtakanna 78 2010."

PART ONE: Exploring a Heritage—Burning Issues

declaring that the issue is concluded on behalf of the Evangelical Lutheran Church of Iceland and that the confirmation of the marriage ceremony in 2011 is only a formality.

Bibliography

"Biskup biður samkynhneigt fólk um fyrirgefningu." *The Island*, 26 June 2010. Online: http://eyjan.is/2010/06/26/biskup-bidur-samkynhneigt-folk-um-fyrirgefningu/ (accessed 15/03/2011).

Björnsdóttir, Steinunn Arnþrúður. "Hvað gerðist á Prestastefnu 2007?" *Trúin og lífið*, 6 May 2007. Online: http://tru.is/pistlar/2007/05/hvad-gerdist-a-prestastefnu-2007/ (accessed 15/03/2011).

Burns, John F. "Iceland Names New Prime Minister." *New York Times*, Europe, 1 February 2009. Online: http://www.nytimes.com/2009/02/02/world/europe/02iceland.html (accessed 15/03/2011).

Constitution of the Republic of Iceland. Online: http://www.government.is/constitution/ (accessed 15/03/2011).

"The Evangelical Lutheran Church of Iceland and Civil Partnership." 2006. Online: http://www2.kirkjan.is/skjol/elci-and-registered-partnership.pdf (accessed 15/03/2011).

The Global Gender Gap Report 2010. Geneva: WEF, 2010. Online: http://www3.weforum.org/docs/WEF_GenderGap_Report_2010.pdf (accessed 15/03/2011).

Hugason, Hjalti. "A Case Study of the Evolution of a Nordic Lutheran Majority Church." In *Law & Religion in the 21st Century: Nordic Perspectives*, edited by Lisbet Christoffersen, Kjell Å. Modéer, and Svend Andersen, 107–22. Copenhagen: Djöf, 2010.

Jónsson, Andrés Ingi. "Hýrnar yfir kirkjunni: Þrír af hverjum fjórum þjóðkirkjuprestum myndu staðfesta samvist samkynhneigðra." *24 Stundir*, 5 July 2008, 22. Online: http://timarit.is/view_page_init.jsp?issId=259210&lang=is (accessed 15/03/2011).

Journey Together Faithfully, Part Two: The Church and Homosexuality. Chicago: Evangelical Lutheran Church in America, 2003.

"Könnun meðal þjónandi presta um heimild til að staðfesta samvist." Viðhorfskönnun - lagabreyting. Reykjavik: Outcome kannanir ehf., 2007. Online: http://www2.kirkjan.is/bskrar/skjol/konnun_sumar07.pdf.

"Mannréttindaviðurkenning Samtakanna 78 2010." Ein hjúskaparlög. Online: http://einhjuskaparlog.tumblr.com/ (accessed 15/03/2011).

"Meirihluti vill leyfa giftingar samkynhneig ðra." *Morgunblaðið*, 29 June, 2004. Online: http://mbl.is/mm/gagnasafn/grein.html?grein_id=806262 (accessed 15/03/2011).

Parliament of Iceland. A-deild, bls. 1706. *Alþingistíðindi*, 1991–1992.

———. A-deild, bls. 564. *Alþingistíðindi*, 1995–1996.

Snævarr, Ármann. "Um sifjar og sifjarétt." *Úlfljótur* 12/3 (1983) 3–20.

Statistics Iceland. Online: http://www.statice.is/ (accessed 15/03/2011).

Witte, John, Jr. *From Sacrament to Contract: Marriage, Religion, and Law in the Western Tradition*. Louisville: Westminster John Knox, 1997.

PART TWO

Exploring a Heritage

Influences from Growing Global Christianity

From the mid-nineteenth century, revival movements with pietistic influences spread in the Nordic countries, just as in many other parts of the world. In Norway and Denmark, the revival mainly took place inside the Lutheran churches and has continued to do so. In Sweden, on the other hand, it was mainly a growing movement outside Church of Sweden that led to the establishment of the traditional free churches. Interestingly enough, Iceland never had any influential revival movements at all.

Statistics show that many churches that are currently prosperous and growing around the world could be labeled Evangelical, Charismatic, Fundamentalist, or Neo-Pentecostal. Those movements are important actors in what is often referred to as a new and expanding "global Christianity." In many ways these movements are influencing not only newer but also older churches, both directly and indirectly. The main focus in this section concerns the extent to which such an influence is evident in the Lutheran churches in this study and how the situation can be described.

In the first chapter, "Building Church on Freedom from Within," Marie Thomsen writes about contemporary congregational life in the Evangelical Lutheran Church in Denmark. She discusses how the liberal laws from the mid-nineteenth century protect the unity of the church by providing room for many different forms of congregation inside the Evangelical Lutheran Church. She argues that the possibility of *electoral* and *free congregations* within the church makes way for new forms of piety. At the same time, regular parish life is left unaffected by, e.g., Charismatic and Evangelical influences. She ends with a discussion of Alpha courses as one common activity, mainly in these *electoral* and *free congregations*, as a way of fostering new members.

In his chapter "Church Development in the Church of Norway," Halvard Johannessen takes his point of departure in the catchword "church development." Using an analytical framework by Paul Heelas and Linda Woodhead that differentiates between various forms of religion, he discusses two books by Norwegian scholars. Johannessen argues that there are outside influences that include signs of a more Evangelical, Charismatic, Fundamentalist, or Neo-Pentecostal theology. He mentions worship, leadership, and ecclesiology as areas where this is to be seen. Those influences inspire future changes in beliefs and practices but while they could be labeled "new," they are also reinventing the old Norwegian pietistic tradition.

As in the chapter about the Evangelical Lutheran Church in Denmark, the Alpha courses play an important role also in Ulrika Svalfors's text, "Charismatic Movements within Church of Sweden." She focuses on two movements: the Oasis movement and the Alpha courses. She argues that in many ways these movements could be seen as peripheral in Church of Sweden today but they should also be seen in a wider network of religious organizations influencing Church of Sweden. She describes Alpha courses and the Oasis movement and discusses how they attract people and parishes in Church of Sweden by standing for a more conservative or evangelical theology.

In this section there is no contribution from Iceland, whose history does not include any revival movement of importance. Even today, Evangelical, Charismatic, Fundamentalist, and Neo-Pentecostal movements seem to be either absent or holding a low profile.

6

Building Church on Freedom from Within

Contemporary Congregational Life in the Evangelical Lutheran Church in Denmark

MARIE THOMSEN

Introduction

WE FIND OURSELVES IN a world where globalization is the dominating feature. This, generally speaking, means that everything is present everywhere at the same time. It also means that any individual, institution, or organization is facing a constant possible influence by global flows, trends, and movements. The reactions to this can vary being anything from very receptive to being remarkably unaffected. And so, the leading question for this chapter is where on that scale the Evangelical Lutheran Church in Denmark is placed when it comes to being influenced by global religious trends or movements. Depending on the situation, surely several elements can become decisive factors for the degree of receptiveness of any organization; in the case of the Evangelical Lutheran Church in Denmark, I will argue, these are: a unique structure, church history, and profound rootedness in its own tradition.

This chapter will illustrate the impact of these key factors when it comes to the question of how the Evangelical Lutheran Church in Denmark

119

PART TWO: Exploring a Heritage—Influences

is affected by three "players" in the global field of Christianity today: the Pentecostal, the Charismatic, and the Fundamentalist movements. The short answer to the question is: not much at all. But it would of course be neither fair nor accurate to leave it at that. Therefore, the first section will briefly describe the three global movements in question and how they do *not* directly influence the Evangelical Lutheran Church in Denmark. Secondly, a historical church background is necessary to explain both why the church as a whole is rather unaffected by these influences and how it, at the same time, shows clear signs of a "Charismatic turn" in specific areas. Thus, the second section will describe and explain some of the complex structures of the church: how liberal laws have become the protectors of church unity and how the unique concept of "electoral and free congregations" is now resulting in a new generation of congregations which are showing a strong influence from the Charismatic movement. The third section will treat Alpha courses in Denmark as a case study to discuss some of the challenges experienced with implementing (Charismatic) Holy Spirit theology in a Danish Lutheran context. Finally reflections on the current situation and future scenarios will be presented.

Three Global Movements

When it comes to religion it seems that the modernization of the world has brought out especially two visible responses: a return of religion, either in the shape of fundamentalism or as (individualized) experiential religious practice and spirituality.[1] Looking at Christianity in a global perspective, three actors have been very visible in the past century and still affect the contemporary scene with great conviction, namely: the Pentecostal, the Charismatic, and the Fundamentalist movements. These are all examples of the two types of response, and each carries one or both features in their theology and practice.[2]

The Pentecostal movement emerged in the USA in the early 1900s following a hundred years of primarily Pietistic awakenings. The origins are closely tied to the African-American pastor William Joseph Seymour and the "Azusa Street Revival." It includes a large number of denominations and independent churches that place great emphasis on the work of the Holy Spirit and gifts of grace such as speaking in tongues, healing, and

1. Mortensen, *Kristendommen under forvandling*, 178.

2. The following description is by no means thought to be exhaustive, but merely explaining the use of the terms for this chapter.

prophetic speech. Infant baptisms are substituted for adult baptisms and sometimes even re-baptisms for people who actively move to "accept Jesus as their Lord and Savior" late in life.[3]

Derived from classical Pentecostalism is the Charismatic movement(s).[4] The two terms "Pentecostal" and "Charismatic" are often used interchangeably, however, in this chapter they are used as two different aspects—the Pentecostal movement as a certain *type of church*, and the Charismatic movement as certain *ways of practice*. The latter points to the phenomenon whereby the strong emphasis on the Holy Spirit in both theology and practice, known from Pentecostalism, is being adopted into various denominations as diverse as Baptist and Catholic. And it is this "practical" sense of the term that will be used in the present chapter.

The Fundamentalist movement emerged as a Protestant movement in the USA in the early 1900s along with the series of books called *The Fundamentals: A Testimony to the Truth*, published from 1910 to 1915. The authors, formulating and describing the "fundamentals" of Christian theology, were several American and British theologians forming an opposition to the reigning theology at that time, which they found to be too liberal.[5] Today Fundamentalist movements play a significant role on the political scene in the USA—a feature not seen in Europe (yet?)—and they represent a radical emphasis on the Bible, which is also seen to some extent in the two other movements. What all three have in common is a claim to being advocates for an original conception of Christianity—it is a matter of truth and authenticity.[6]

How Are the Global Movements Influencing the Evangelical Lutheran Church in Denmark?

The three movements are still alive and growing both in numbers and geography. However, in order for this to happen they need to have a playing field. In Muslim, Hindu, or Buddhist-dominated countries the playing field is obviously narrowed down, but what about in a Christian dominated country as Denmark? If, for a moment, we were to disregard the

---

3. "Pentecostal Churches."

4. In the present chapter "Charismatic" is understood as referring to both second- and third-wave Charismatics. See Wagner, *The Third Wave of the Holy Spirit*.

5. The reason for the so-called liberal turn was in great part found in the historical-critical method of reading the Bible, occurring during the Enlightenment.

6. "Fundamentalisme (Kristen fundamentalisme)."

PART TWO: Exploring a Heritage—Influences

playing field populated by members of the Evangelical Lutheran Church in Denmark or people belonging to non-Christian religions, there would be roughly 17 percent left (approximately 770,000 people). It is here that both the Pentecostal and Charismatic movements are represented, but not in any overwhelming scale; fundamentalism even less so. There are about 5,000 members of Pentecostal churches in Denmark, which amounts to 0.65 percent of the leftover playing field and less than 0.1 percent of the Danish population. The Charismatic movement is harder to measure but an estimate is that around 15,000 people are members of other churches with Charismatic features, together not mounting up to all that much in comparison with the Evangelical Lutheran Church in Denmark's 4.5 million members. So let us instead take a look at the influences inside the Evangelical Lutheran Church in Denmark.

The Pentecostal movement has the least influence here. A handful of parish congregations within the Evangelical Lutheran Church in Denmark have Pentecostal features, but they make very little noise and do not have any direct influence as such. Fundamentalism is a practically unknown phenomenon. The Evangelical Lutheran Church in Denmark is based on theological broadness and this liberal approach makes it difficult for any fundamentalist wing to take up much space.[7] In addition, the Danish people have so far not proved very receptive to ideas of creationism or strict ethical demands for how to live their lives. And since the Danish people—or at least 80 percent of them—constitute the Evangelical Lutheran Church in Denmark, the church itself has not been very receptive to Fundamentalism at all. However, there is one exception in the periphery of the church, namely the recent founding of fourteen free congregations all rooted in the organization the Lutheran Mission (*Luthersk Mission*). These can be said to represent a somewhat Fundamentalist wing in the Danish landscape, which will be further discussed below in "Three Theological Types of the New Generation."

The Charismatic influence, in contrast, has become more and more visible within the past decades, and is often tied to activism. It seems that when a parish wishes to "do something," take action, or innovate, it is often carried out using activities with some kind of Charismatic inspiration. Whether activism or the Charismatic movement came first cannot be decided offhand, however, both are connected to the following two points:

1. The majority of electoral and free congregations in Denmark founded since 1989 have both Charismatic and activist features. These are

7. Cf. Introduction, under "What's in a Name?"

part of or closely connected to the Evangelical Lutheran Church in Denmark, which make them interesting in regard to how the church as such is affected by the three global movements.[8]

2. Along with this development, the program of Alpha (a teaching material with strong emphasis on "Holy Spirit theology") is widely used in the new electoral and free congregations, but only in a very few parish churches. The reason for the latter is a general skepticism in the parishes towards the Charismatic roots of the material.

These two cases will be treated later on in this chapter, but first we turn to an outline of the historical background for the electoral and free congregations along with a description of the two concepts.

Liberal Laws to Secure Church Unity

Going back to the ancient church, the worst-case scenario was division within the church. Schisms would mean breaking the body of Christ and therefore several synods were spent figuring out what to agree on in order to keep the body together as one united church in Christ. As history shows this project did not succeed and today there are various Christian churches with diverse theologies, practices, and structures. However, it seems that the Evangelical Lutheran Church in Denmark (along with many other Christian churches) still treasures the idea of protecting unity and therefore the question of how to avoid schisms is also central today (that is *within* the Evangelical Lutheran Church in Denmark).

As stated in the Introduction under "What's in a Name?," the solution for the Evangelical Lutheran Church in Denmark became the liberal path of "broadness" and "spaciousness." This path has among other things resulted in two specific laws that have shaped church life for the past 150 years. First, the law from 1855 on "parish optionality" (*loven om sognebåndsløsning*) and secondly the law on "electoral congregations" (*valgmenighedsloven*) from 1868. The Evangelical Lutheran Church in Denmark was and still is organized in parishes and membership is therefore geographically defined. This means that a person is baptized into the church as a whole but belongs to the local parish church where he/she lives. Membership provides access to certain services from the parish church, mainly carried out by the local minister, and prior to 1855 members were

---

8. The concept of "electoral" and "free" congregations will be explained below in the part "Electoral and Free Congregations Explained."

PART TWO: Exploring a Heritage—Influences

tied strictly to their parish minister. The law of 1855 entitled members to seek out another minister for any reason if that new minister would accept them (mostly it would be due to theological differences with the parish minister). In 1868 this was followed by the more radical law allowing members who were unsatisfied with the local conditions to establish a new congregation within the geographical borders of the parish and call their own minister, while still remaining within the Evangelical Lutheran Church in Denmark. This concept of electoral congregations (*valgmenigheder*) within the "mother church" is a unique phenomenon that has deeply affected the structure, self-understanding, and core values of the Evangelical Lutheran Church in Denmark.[9] Furthermore, according to the Danish Constitution the Evangelical Lutheran Church is the "Danish folk church" regardless of whether it is organized as parish, electoral, or free congregations.

Electoral and Free Congregations Explained[10]

In Denmark there are four official ways to organize Christian congregations:

1. Parish congregations (explained above)
2. Electoral congregations
3. Free congregations
4. Free churches

Electoral congregations define the unique concept of special congregations outside the parish structure, but still within the Evangelical Lutheran Church in Denmark. This means that the members are free to establish congregations if they for one reason or another are unsatisfied with the local church. The electoral congregations are not defined by geography like the parish congregations; they are, however, under supervision by the dean and bishop in the deaneries and dioceses in which they are geographically placed. The minister has to meet the same requirements for education as all other ministers which is neither the case for the ministers in free congregations or free churches (see below). The electoral congregation must apply for approval by the Ministry of Ecclesiastical Affairs in order for the members to remain members. These are exempt from paying church

---

9. A similar development has taken place in Norway, Iceland, and Sweden when it comes to allowing parish members to seek ministry from a minister outside one's own parish. Electoral congregations are, however, not part of church life in these churches.

10. See Thomsen, "Frie menigheder."

tax but instead have to cover all expenses for "running the congregation," including the salary of the minister whom they have called. The sometimes troubled task of being self-financed is something they share with the free congregations and free churches. In Denmark, church members (those of the Evangelical Lutheran Church in Denmark in particular) are not used to reaching for their pockets to support their local congregation. The church tax system has made a lot of people completely unaware that they pay anything to the Evangelical Lutheran Church in Denmark or for their membership. This mentality is difficult to change and therefore these self-financed congregations often struggle to make ends meet.

Free congregations have been founded since 1883. They are legally outside the Evangelical Lutheran Church in Denmark but share a Evangelical Lutheran confession. This means that there is no theological contradiction between these congregations and the Evangelical Lutheran Church in Denmark, but they are established by people who wish to have a greater extent of freedom (than, e.g., electoral congregations) in regard to organization and liturgy. This freedom is achieved since they are not under supervision by a dean or bishop. As mentioned, the ministers in these congregations do not have to meet the requirements of the ministers in the Evangelical Lutheran Church in Denmark, so they will often have unordained ministers with education from other theological seminaries than universities.

The concept of electoral and free congregations is rooted in Grundtvig's thoughts on freedom in the people and in the church.[11] This allows people to seek wider boundaries *within* the church, making it impossible to neglect internal differences because everybody is "under the same roof," but at the same time creating a church so spacious that it makes very little grounds for schisms.

Free churches are independent (Christian) churches with no connection to either the Evangelical Lutheran Church in Denmark or the state. The development of these churches contributes to the overall religious landscape in Denmark, but they are taking up very little space. In Denmark there are around 300 free churches with a total of 25,000 members, approximately the same number as the electoral and free congregations combined. In recent years several free churches, primarily Pentecostal with African background, have appeared, but the whole group mainly

---

11. N. F. S. Grundtvig (1783–1872), Danish theologian, politician, hymn writer, and more.

consists of (ethnic Danish) Apostolic, Baptist, Pentecostal, and Methodist churches.

A New Generation Breaking Through

The first generation of electoral and free congregations was founded from mid-nineteenth century in opposition to the reigning Pietism and Enlightenment ideas focusing on the individual at the expense of the community. These first electoral and free congregations were all Grundtvigian, meaning liberal and with a close connection between people, Christianity, culture, and nation. They later came in opposition to the other Danish awakening, namely the theological branch of Inner Mission (*Indre Mission*). Most of these congregations still exist, but since World War II no new Grundtvigian congregations have been established.

In 1989, something new happened. After decades of a complete standstill in founding new congregations, Aarhus Valgmenighed saw the light of day.[12] This electoral congregation, which is still striving and growing, became the starting point for a new generation of congregations, these being very different from the first. It seems that the only things the two generations have in common are: 1) that they are established due to dissatisfaction with certain contemporary issues in the Evangelical Lutheran Church in Denmark, and 2) that they are making use of the same law to create the congregational life they desire.

The approximately forty electoral and free congregations that constitute the new generation have four distinct features. First, they are characterized by *not* being Grundtvigian. Through the past 150 years Grundtvigianism has gained ground throughout the Evangelical Lutheran Church in Denmark, leaving no (or very little) need for creating new congregations with this theological character. Second, they are characterized by being *young*—not only because the congregations are relatively new but because of the age of the members. On average, 70 percent of the members are younger than 40, which is very different from the age composition of the first generation, with a predominance of members over 40. Third, these congregations are established due to an often flaming *discontent* with what they find to be a lack of meaningful and flourishing congregational life within the Evangelical Lutheran Church in Denmark. Fourth, there is a strong emphasis on both evangelism (mission) and religious fellowship

12. The terms "new congregations" and "new electoral and free congregations" are used interchangeably.

(between members), two features that the first generation is not emphasizing (strongly).

Now, it could seem that this new generation is very homogenous, but taking a closer look reveals theological and inspirational differences. With this we are back to how the three global movements—the Pentecostal, Charismatic, and Fundamentalist—influence the Evangelical Lutheran Church in Denmark, keeping in mind that the electoral and free congregations are a part thereof (however, the latter is not, legally speaking). In the following this new generation will be described as three different *congregational types*. The characterization is based on the "Electoral and Free Congregation Study 09,"[13] a survey study among the electoral and free congregations in Denmark. It focuses on theological self-identification, background for establishment, current activities (including the thoughts behind them), and reflection on challenges now and in the future. These four points combined draw the image of a new generation that might play an important part in shaping the future church life in Denmark.

Three Theological Types of the New Generation

The three congregational types of the new generation are defined by their theological self-identification and feature activities. As we will see, all three types can be defined as being inspired by the global movements. No matter how small the congregations and membership numbers might be compared to the rest of the Evangelical Lutheran Church in Denmark, they are still a part of it and therefore interesting in both contemporary and future perspectives. The three congregational types are:

1. Missionary-Charismatic-Conservative[14]

2. Missionary

3. Charismatic-Spiritual

The Missionary-Charismatic-Conservative type is, as indicated, characterized by being theologically conservative. Female ministers are not accepted and the Bible is used for giving practical guidelines for most issues in life, especially issues regarding sexuality and other moral and ethical matters. However, the rather conservative theology is accompanied by

13. Thomsen, *Danske valg- og frimenigheder*.

14. "Missionary" here is in line with "Inner Mission" and "Lutheran Mission" mentioned earlier. Here it refers to a theology with both conservative and evangelizing features.

PART TWO: Exploring a Heritage—Influences

very progressive modes of expression, especially in the work of finding new (and improved) ways of preaching the gospel. There is great focus on making the gospel known to and understood by the world of today. This type is very active and wishes to be visible in its local community, which is also reflected in the number of volunteers and congregational activities being above average compared to the other two types. The core activities besides the Sunday service are: *special services* during the week mainly based on certain themes or events, different life support groups carried out as pastoral care, prayer and/or intercession groups, and committed group communities often organized in so-called cell groups.[15]

The Missionary type consists solely of free congregations with affiliation to the Lutheran Mission. It is characterized by an even more conservative theology, and therefore it does not accept female ministers either.[16] This type is probably the closest one gets to Christian Fundamentalism in Denmark, and the conservative theology is not accompanied by progressive modes of expression. This type sticks to the traditional (Danish) Sunday service and does not conduct any special services at all. The emphasis is almost solely on the Bible and a literal reading of it, therefore the core activities, besides the Sunday service, are Bible study groups and different groups for children and young people centered on reading the Bible.

The Charismatic-Spiritual type is characterized by being theologically liberal. As opposed to the other two types, female ministers are fully accepted here. It has the most activities, but very little focus on being visible in the local community. The reason for the large number of activities may instead be found in the free-spirit mentality characterizing this type. The core activities are: special services with different spiritual elements, education in Christianity and spirituality, and groups defined by age or carried out as life support or self-help groups. In addition, this type also has a number of distinct activities such as Christian meditation, classes on gifts of grace, and prophecies.

The three congregational types are, as shown, different from each other, but all are in some way reflecting global movements. And as a whole they are even more different from the traditional parish congregations than from each other. Due the structure of the Evangelical Lutheran Church in

---

15. "Committed" here equals Z. Bauman's use of "ethical" communities as opposed to "aesthetical." See Bauman, *Community*, 72.

16. The "missionary" term is strongly emphasized and therefore this group was reluctant to stress any affiliation to the other theological terms. However, it is well known that the theology and practice of this group is traditionally defined as being conservative.

Denmark, the parish churches are obliged to serve a whole parish—often being more than 5,000 members. Therefore they are not as "profiled" as the new congregations, which only have between 20 and 700 members per congregation. The parish churches simply have a different task. They need to serve a large congregation of which only 1–2 percent attend Sunday services and less than 10 percent come into contact with the church during the week, mainly for funerals but also for different social activities and classes for children. Attendance in the new congregations is much higher (often 50 percent or more), probably because membership there is a conscious decision—far from the situation of being baptized into the Evangelical Lutheran Church in Denmark as an infant. In the parishes the work load is mainly carried by paid staff and the members do not shape the congregational life in the same "profiled" way as we see in the new congregations. This illustrates that the opportunity for creating new congregations within the Evangelical Lutheran Church in Denmark actually does result in structures and mentalities very different from the ordinary parish congregations. What effect this has on the "mother church" will be discussed in the following.

The New Congregational Types Shaping the Evangelical Lutheran Church in Denmark Now and in the Future?

Previous history has shown that what starts out as "rough edges" can over time become mainstream or even dominating (cf. Grundtvigianism). But how can we measure the effect of the new congregations on the rest of the Evangelical Lutheran Church in Denmark and thereby also get an idea of the influence of the global movements?

Theology is often conceived merely as dogmatic thoughts and reflections. However, it could be argued that change more than anything happens through doing rather than writing or saying. Activities are easy to try out, copy, incorporate, and shape for different settings—in short, they work well in an eve-changing, fast-moving world. Therefore, if we really want to know anything about the influence of the new congregations we need to take a close look at the activities throughout the Evangelical Lutheran Church in Denmark and the rest of the Christian landscape in Denmark.

Offhand, the Evangelical Lutheran Church in Denmark seems to be more inspired by the Roman Catholic traditions than anything else—candle light globes, icons, rosary beads, and confession services are appearing

PART TWO: Exploring a Heritage—Influences

in several ordinary parish churches. Being a Lutheran church, this is an interesting turn. However, rather than being an actual Roman Catholic turn it is probably connected to an experiential turn in contemporary religious life all together. Today we see an increased demand (also from members of the Evangelical Lutheran Church in Denmark) for religious experience. This demand is often met by offering different "event-based" activities: rock music services, a revival in the celebration of minor and/or almost forgotten holidays, meditation services, night church, etc. These activities tend to draw in a large number of people who would not attend the regular Sunday service. The new congregations are by now known for developing many such activities, some of which are then later adopted by parish churches. The dynamic seems to be that when something is a success in one place others take that particular activity and shape it into a good match for their own congregation.

Some activities, though, are easier to adopt than others, both because of content but also because of the different congregational structures and tasks. One example is that most of the new congregations have several groups or "committed communities," a phenomenon that is not very common in the Evangelical Lutheran Church in Denmark. But it is possible that it will be in the coming years, if the need for individual support increases. However, whereas the "committed communities" are the very backbone of most of the new congregations, this will probably never be the case in the Evangelical Lutheran Church in Denmark. The parish congregations are so big that each would consist of hundreds of groups, with the risk of losing the concept of unity along the way. In addition, it would require (or result in?) a massive growth in active members and there are no signs of that showing at present. However, more and more parishes are working on creating smaller communities within the big congregations, either based on age, gender, or social activities, or organized as support groups.[17] And even though "committed communities" are not a direct Charismatic influence, it does illustrate the dynamic exchange going on between parish churches and the new congregations.

An example of a common activity in the new congregations that has not gained a foothold in the Evangelical Lutheran Church in Denmark is Alpha courses. Here it is not a matter of organizational differences but of content. This is an interesting case because it shows that though the conditions may be the same—an increased need for general (theological) education mainly due to the widespread rejection of (institutionalized)

17. Thomsen, *Menighedsliv i Århus Stift*.

religion during the 1960s and 1970s, resulting in a generation with little or no knowledge of Christianity—the ways of meeting this need are very different. In the new congregations Alpha courses are widely used, whereas the concept is not by any means mainstream in the Evangelical Lutheran Church in Denmark. Looking at one of the neighboring countries, Sweden, the case is somewhat different. There Alpha is seen as an effective way to evangelize and educate, and is seemingly taken in without the hesitation or skepticism seen in Denmark.[18] The following part will take a closer look at Alpha in Denmark.

Holy Spirit Theology in a Danish Lutheran Context— Gains and Challenges

Alpha courses have spread to congregations in large parts of the world since the 1970s. It is a patented and structured concept with Charismatic roots and has been able to appeal to various denominations (Lutheran, Pentecostal, Presbyterian, Reformed, Roman Catholic, and many others). The reason for the wide appeal is probably that Alpha is a "beginner's course." This means that no particular dogmatic knowledge is required from the participants and it gives the different denominations a starting point from where they can afterwards teach their specific theology.[19]

In Denmark, Alpha has mainly spread from the free churches to the new electoral and free congregations, although some parish churches have also conducted Alpha courses with greater or lesser attendance and success. At present, approximately 25 parishes (of 2,200) are running Alpha courses, but more have tried it out once or twice over the years. According to the director of Alpha Denmark, Bess Serner, there are today more parish churches running Alpha than free churches. The reason, she adds, is probably that the free churches are more experimental and have already moved on to new concepts.

Alpha has been criticized (also outside the Danish context) for placing too much emphasis on the Holy Spirit, and several parish churches have contacted Alpha Denmark asking for permission to leave out the lectures on this specific topic. The ministers who contact Alpha Denmark seem to be very challenged by having to teach about healing and how to be "filled with the Holy Spirit." And since it is not allowed to alter the Alpha material, many parish churches have left the idea of using it all together.

18. Cf. Ulrika Svalfors in this volume.
19. For more information on Alpha see Ulrika Svalfors in this volume.

PART TWO: Exploring a Heritage—Influences

Bess Serner explains that she experiences a great awareness of the Charismatic roots of this material, and often even great skepticism towards it. Her response to the criticism is that there is not "too much" on the Holy Spirit in the Alpha material, just more than "nothing." Nevertheless, Bess Serner is in her daily work confronted with the difficulties in conveying Charismatic Holy Spirit theology in a Danish Lutheran context.[20]

Just how challenging it is to sell Charismatic Holy Spirit theology in a Danish Lutheran parish church context is illustrated by a document from 2004 titled *Guideline for Using Alpha in an Ordinary Lutheran Context*.[21] The mere fact that such a document has been produced indicates that there is something to be said on the matter. It was written by a representative from Inner Mission (*Indre Mission*) and the directors, at that time, for Alpha Denmark and the Dialogue Center (*Dialogcenteret*). The purpose was to help congregations adjust the material without altering it contrary to the Alpha concept.

As a beginner's course, most of the Alpha lectures can be accepted by various denominations without any problems. In the Danish context of the Evangelical Lutheran Church in Denmark, however, the lectures concerning healing, intercession, and speaking in tongues pose challenges for many ministers. These lectures all concern what one might call the "outer manifestations" of the Holy Spirit. And even though there may not be major doctrinal differences between traditional Lutheran theology and the content of the Alpha material, the lecture "How Can I Be Filled with the Holy Spirit?" stands out as a particular challenge. The challenge lies in the change of scope from a traditional Lutheran focus on the inner works of the Spirit in man (by the Word and sacraments) to a focus on the outer power by the Spirit and the personal experience and appropriation of this.

The document tries to respond to the reluctance and alienation concerning these lectures. Among other things the guideline describes what may be expected to happen during an intercession, e.g., physical reactions such as feeling hot or trembling. It also gives suggestions on how to conduct an intercession—reaching out the hands, closing the eyes, kneeling, or praying in complete silence. The document is characterized by a very pragmatic approach to the Alpha material and the authors try to build bridges where they are most needed. For example it is mentioned that in

---

20. Interview with Bess Serner, and a small survey among Alpha practicing parish congregations conducted by Marie Thomsen, April 9, 2010.

21. Linderoth et al., *Vejledning til at bruge Alpha i en almindelig luthersk sammenhæng*.

the case where none of the course leaders have experience with speaking in tongues, that the particular session should be kept very short. It is also stressed that no specific reaction should be forced out of any of the participants—it should always be left to God.[22]

It can definitely be discussed whether this guide is helping to a better understanding or rather giving hesitant ministers even more reason not to go through with an Alpha course. Physical reactions such as the ones described are not something often found at a regular Sunday service in the Evangelical Lutheran Church in Denmark. Therefore even reaching out hands in prayer (or intercession) can seem foreign to many ministers and even more so to a congregation. Even though Alpha is not thought to be a new way of conducting Sunday services, it is on one hand obvious that the Lutheran heritage, especially in the shape of the (Danish) Sunday services, leaves many members finding these concrete suggestions very foreign and may even be offensive to look at, not to mention participate in. On the other hand, as mentioned earlier, there are members seeking ways to make available church activities based more on experience and emotion. For this group the Charismatic movement might have a role to play and Alpha could perhaps be one of the tools for creating a more fulfilling spiritual life. A small survey among parishes having tried Alpha shows that what caused most hesitation to begin with—the Charismatic content—is the element that proves to be the biggest success. According to the parish churches contacted, the fact that Alpha drives the participants to formulate questions, reflect on theology, faith, and doubt, and then transform this into a religious practice is the biggest strength. They report that especially the "Holy Spirit Weekend" has created congregational fellowship in different ways than other church activities, in some cases resulting in a flourishing congregational life.

Alpha is by now a well-established concept—"old news" in some circles and just the breath of fresh air needed to make congregational life prosper in others. Once again it all comes down to doing. One can only guess about the future for Alpha in Denmark, but as a direct Charismatic influence it is the most tangible phenomenon right now. It is, however, very unlikely that the Evangelical Lutheran Church in Denmark will be influenced to such an extent that any fundamental changes in theology or organization are just around the corner. It seems that even for the most enthusiastic advocates for Alpha within the Evangelical Lutheran Church in Denmark the actual influence of Alpha is a Charismatic-light version

22. Ibid., 7–12.

PART TWO: Exploring a Heritage—Influences

and is by no means a path to drastic changes in the present shape of the Evangelical Lutheran Church in Denmark.[23]

History Repeating Itself—Same but Different . . .

Coming to the end of this chapter, it is time to go back to the beginning. There it was stated that the decisive factors for the degree to which the Evangelical Lutheran Church in Denmark is affected by the global movements were: a unique structure, the church history, and a profound rootedness in its own tradition. Through this chapter some of the complexities and unique structures of the Evangelical Lutheran Church in Denmark have been presented, leaving an image of a church that in a large scale is remarkably unaffected by the global movements, but does have elements, mostly connected to church renewal, inspired especially by the Charismatic movements. Paradoxically the reasons for the new congregations having a strong Charismatic—and in some cases somewhat Fundamentalist—inspiration are maybe to be found within the Evangelical Lutheran Church in Denmark itself. The church is not unaffected by the global movements, rather, the influence just plays out in a particular manner due to the structure and history of the church. The global movements have indeed affected some people and groups, but have not found a foothold in the parish structure, therefore they represent a minority. This minority, however, becomes very visible when it makes use of the law from 1868 and creates new (and "profiled") congregations. Members who find something to be missing, instead of leaving the Evangelical Lutheran Church in Denmark all together, reconstitute themselves inside it. This pattern has roots back to the first electoral and free congregations, which created dynamics within the church that made it what it is today—a church built on "freedom from within."

The argument that a sense of lack is also today driving the new congregations can be illustrated by the table below, which is based on a recent study of congregational life in the Diocese of Aarhus.[24] Aarhus is the second largest diocese in Denmark, consisting of a diversity of parishes in cities, villages, and everything in between (in quantitative studies this diocese is known to rate close to the national average). In total 56.4 percent of the ministers participated in the survey study. They were asked about their

---

23. Interview with Bess Serner, and a small survey among Alpha practicing parish congregations conducted by Marie Thomsen, April 9, 2010.

24. Thomsen, *Menighedsliv i Århus Stift*.

theological self-identification, and from their answers we clearly see that there are not too many places to go (in this diocese) if one wishes to seek out a self-proclaimed Charismatic or Spiritual minister. It also shows that today it is overall most likely to find one who is Grundtvigian, and very few ministers consider themselves to be Missionary.

Theological Self-Identification[25]

Q: To what degree do you associate yourself with the following theological terms?

Theological term	To a large degree	To some degree	Less so	Not at all	Do not know
Grundtvigian	29.1%	52.5%	15.2%	2.5%	0.6%
Missionary[26]	1.9%	4.4%	19.6%	72.8%	1.3%
Charismatic	0.0%	4.4%	8.9%	79.7%	7.0%
Spiritual	1.3%	13.9%	24.1%	57.0%	3.8%
Activist	7.0%	32.9%	29.1%	27.8%	3.2%

N: 158 (1 = 0.63 %)

And so history repeats itself—yet again congregations are established due to an experienced lack in the Evangelical Lutheran Church in Denmark. It was a lack of non-pietistic parish ministers 150 years ago, and today it is a lack of Charismatic and conservative theology. And whereas the opposition 150 years ago was generated in the wake of national political movements, today it is shaped by global movements. What the landscape will look like 150 years from now nobody knows. Maybe the (current) new congregations will be dominant, or maybe they will disappear as quickly as they were established. However, for now it seems that the old liberal laws protecting church unity by protecting minorities and diversity within the church are experiencing a revival—and the Evangelical Lutheran Church in Denmark is still united.

---

25. Ibid.

26. These numbers would be very different in the west coast of Denmark, where Inner Mission is dominating.

PART TWO: Exploring a Heritage—Influences

Bibliography

Bauman, Zygmunt. *Community: Seeking Safety in an Insecure World*. Cambridge, MA: Polity Press, 2001.
"Fundamentalisme (Kristen fundamentalisme)." *Den store danske*. Online: http://www.denstoredanske.dk/Samfund,_jura_og_politik/Religion_og_mystik/Reformationen_og_lutherske_kirke/fundamentalisme/fundamentalisme_(Kristen_fundamentalisme) (accessed 03/08/2011).
Linderoth, Jens, Helge Pahus, and Søren Skovenborg. *Vejledning til at bruge Alpha i en almindelig luthersk sammenhæng*. Karlslunde: Forlaget Mediecellen, 2004.
Mortensen, Viggo. *Kristendommen under forvandling: Pluralismen som udfordring til teologi og kirke i Danmark*. Højbjerg: Forlaget Univers, 2005.
"Pentecostal Churches." World Council of Churches. Online: http://www.oikoumene.org/en/handbook/church-families/pentecostal-churches.html (accessed 03/08/2011).
Thomsen, Marie. *Danske valg- og frimenigheder*. 2009. Not yet published.
———. "Frie menigheder—danske valg- og frimenigheder." In *Religion i Danmark 2010: En e-årbog fra Center for Samtidsreligion*, edited by Lene Kühle, 127–31. Aarhus: Aarhus Universitet, 2010. Online: http://teo.au.dk/fileadmin/www.teo.au.dk/samtidsreligion/religion_i_danmark_10/Religion-i-DK-2010-05-06.pdf (accessed 03/08/2011).
———. *Menighedsliv i Århus Stift*. 2010. Not yet published.
Wagner, C. Peter. *The Third Wave of the Holy Spirit: Encountering the Power of Signs and Wonders Today*. Ann Arbor, MI: Servant Publications, 1988.

7

Church Development in Church of Norway

HALVARD JOHANNESSEN

THE OVERARCHING AIM of the present chapter is to explore Charismatic, Pentecostal, and Fundamentalist influences on Church of Norway. These influences may reveal themselves as changes in beliefs, practices, new congregations, or divisions within the church. The scope is rather wide and I will narrow it down by choosing a delimited material and a single theoretical framework for exploring it. Influences from three distinct yet related forms of modern Christianity are mentioned: Charismatic, Pentecostal, and Fundamentalist. The interpretative anthology *Religion in Modern Times*[1] will contribute to clarify the three terms within a consistent theoretical framework or typology. As we shall see, the type of religion Woodhead and Heelas call "religions of difference" encompass important features of both Charismatic and Pentecostal Christianity as well as fundamentalism, which suggests that this concept is a promising category in my exploration. The typology itself shall be applied as an analytical tool and is also a resource for evaluating the material in light of the question: does the material represent symptoms of the aforementioned influences and how may it eventually challenge the identity of Church of Norway as a Lutheran folk church?

1. Woodhead and Heelas, *Religion in Modern Times*.

PART TWO: Exploring a Heritage—Influences

The chosen material is related to "church development," which is a popular catchword and phenomenon in the current Norwegian context. The material consist of two publications that present themselves as practical handbooks in church development from a Norwegian Lutheran perspective, primarily aimed at readers within Church of Norway. Both authors have served as theological teachers and pastors in Church of Norway. It should be clear that the material represents not only contextualized versions of church development from an inside perspective, it also represents a top-down perspective: this is how two authoritative voices in Church of Norway seek to reflect normatively on the phenomenon. My choice of material suggests that my findings will probably not be revolutionary; this is not the way to proceed if I want to find hardcore Pentecostal or Fundamentalist positions within Church of Norway. However, the material represents influential positions that relate to the mainstream. If it reveals influences from Charismatic Christianity and contemporary "religions of difference" that slightly challenge the identity of Church of Norway it may nevertheless prove its relevance.

After a brief introduction to church development as such, I will present Woodhead and Heelas's typology of religion in modern times. Using this as an analytical tool, my following exploration of the material will be focused on three key areas: 1) the concept of church, 2) the understanding of leadership, and 3) the concept of worship.

Church Development: Background and Current Influence

A forerunner of church development surfaced in the mid 1900s under the name "church growth." In the 1960s D. A. McGavran promoted numerical growth as the primary aim of mission. His strategy was the "homogenous unit principle": mission should address identifiable social units based on class, caste, ethnicity, or other bonds. From the 1970s this church growth ideology was transported from the field of cross-cultural mission to the domestic work of Evangelical churches in Europe and America. On the one hand, church growth ideology fostered new energy and new concepts of missiological thinking into conservative evangelical milieus. On the other hand, it was also criticized for its pragmatism, its dependence on the social sciences, its lack of an adequate theology, and especially on the differentiating and segregating consequences of the homogenous unit principle.[2]

2. Shenk, "Church Growth."

Much in line with the influence from church growth, the Institute for Natural Church Growth, now called Natural Church Development, was founded in Germany by Christian Schwarz in 1989. Natural Church Development claims to describe universal principles for growth and multiplication through a focus on the "health" of the local congregation. A core assumption is that healthy congregations grow automatically.[3] According to the Natural Church Development website, more than 40,000 congregations around the globe have applied their courses, tests, and coaching services. Natural Church Development has partner organizations in 70 countries, including Norway.[4] The website reports that close to 400 Norwegian congregations (Church of Norway and other) have used Natural Church Development methodology and pastors from Church of Norway currently make up the largest group of trained Norwegian Natural Church Development coaches.[5]

"Church development" in Church of Norway is, however, both a manifold phenomenon and a diffuse catchword. Natural Church Development is but one source of inspiration; the Nordic Oasis movement and American mega-churches such as Saddleback and Willow Creek are other sources. Since the 1990s a growing number Norwegian congregations have engaged in different concepts of Church development from below. During the last five years "church development" has become a catchword that has reached the top-level of the synodal structure of the church as well as vital parts of the theological milieu: the largest department of the secretariat of Church of Norway National Council is now called Department of Church Development. To engage in church development is part of Church of Norway vision document for the years 2009–2014.[6] The largest theological institution in the country, the MF Norwegian School of Theology, completes a three-year research program on church development in 2011 under the direction of professor of systematic theology Harald Hegstad, currently one of Norway's prolific writers on church development and a coauthor of this volume. Dissertations, handbooks, and several research articles have been published on the topic. The manifold movement related to church development is interesting in our context for many reasons: it is a source for new visions of the church, it influences the current praxis of the church, and it has given rise to new forms of congregations and divisions within

3. "The Essence of NCG."
4. "Structured for Unlimited Multiplication."
5. "K-vekst: Presentasjon."
6. "I Kristus, nær livet."

PART TWO: Exploring a Heritage—Influences

Church of Norway, analogous to tendencies Marie Ramsdal-Thomsen describes in her present chapter.[7] In addition to this, the theological roots of this movement have Evangelical and Charismatic leanings. This is the background and context of my chosen material, which will be presented below after presenting the topology I will use for my analysis.

Analytical Framework: A Typology of Religion in Modern Times

In their interpretative anthology *Religion in Modern Times*, Woodhead and Heelas argue that, broadly speaking, there are three main types of religions and theologies in modernity. They call them: a) religions of difference, b) religions of humanity, and, c) spiritualities of life. In addition there are: d) combination-types, of which experiential religions of difference and experiential religions of humanity are the most significant.

Religions of Difference

In their social aspect, the type called "religions of difference" is characterized by their maintenance of a different culture, ethos, and lifestyle than the surrounding society.[8] Moral and spiritual efforts, often following a personal conversion, are important among the members. Personal relationships within the group are given high priority. Due to the stress on the active subject, the objective works of the sacraments lose significance.[9] The divine, symptomatically understood in transcendent terms, is present in and through the religious group. The surrounding world, in contrast, has little religious value in itself.[10] Troeltsch's classic concept of the "sect" type is characteristic for the social aspect of "religions of difference."

The understanding of leadership is varied. Some religious groups are structured according to a formal hierarchy, others value personal piety and gifts of grace as main sources of authority, while there are also more egalitarian forms of leadership. Worship, understood in a general sense

---

7. By January 2010, twenty-two congregations were involved in the network for church development established by the Norwegian Mission Society. See Rønnestad, "Etablering av nye menigheter," 25.

8. Woodhead and Heelas, *Religion in Modern Times*, 28–29.

9. Ibid., 42.

10. Ibid., 34, 36.

as activities that draw human beings close to God while maintaining a proper distance, is a significant source of value and identity.

A strict representative for this religious category is Fundamentalism or what Woodhead and Heelas call "religions of heightened difference." Evangelical Christianity represents a mainstream example within this category. Charismatic Christianity also belongs under the umbrella of differentiated religion but is a combination type that also shows affinities with another important type of religion (see below).[11]

Religions of Humanity

The social aspect of "religions of humanity" is inclusion and tolerance. They do not set themselves clearly apart from the larger society, and rather than "congregation" or "church," the most common term they use in this context is "denomination." "Religions of humanity" emphasize the objective work of the sacraments rather than strong personal commitment.[12] Their members seldom seek new converts or members.[13] Commitment to a community of believers in which faith is nurtured is not emphasized. Ethical engagement is important and is often aimed at society or humanity as a whole.[14] The social aspect of "religions of humanity" has affinities with Troeltsch's concept of "church," where a formal belonging and an ethical lifestyle is more important than particular beliefs and active participation in particular religious groups.

Religious leadership in this category is often tolerant and well-educated. But given its stress on the freedom of the individual, leadership is exercised on a cultural and moral level rather than in a direct or social way.[15]

Worship gatherings are not necessarily unimportant, but a right living of everyday life that is emphasized over regular church attendance.[16] So-called liberal or modern Protestants belong to this category.[17]

---

11. Ibid., 28–31.
12. Ibid., 40–41.
13. Ibid., 80, 94, 102.
14. Ibid., 71, 100.
15. Ibid., 70–71, 75–76, 82–83.
16. Ibid., 71, 72, 81, 79.
17. Ibid., 73–74; Heelas and Woodhead, *The Spiritual Revolution*, 18.

PART TWO: Exploring a Heritage—Influences

Spiritualities of Life

The third main category, "spiritualities of life," have an individualistic, universalistic, and eclectic profile. Temporary workshops, events, and courses are preferred social forms. They are oriented towards the inner life of the subject in a way that resembles Troeltsch's third and last social form of historical Christianity, "mysticism." In their view on leadership, "spiritualities of life" are anti-authoritarian due to the stress on individual autonomy and on inner spiritual experience as the prime religious authority. As the divine is conceived of in immanent terms to which all can have equal access, there is a focus on techniques and exercises that enables the participant to experience their inner, true, or higher selves. Established religious traditions and institutions are often viewed with suspicion. This category is primarily associated with the ew Age movement and holistic spiritualities.[18]

Among these three types, the last has a tremendous impact on late-modern culture. Also "religions of difference" are on the rise, but generally, forms of "religions of difference" that incorporate traits of "spiritualities of life" may prove most successful in the future.[19]

Combinations

Combinations between "differentiated religion" and "spiritualities of life" are called "experiential religions of difference."[20] This combination type mixes a focus on community, commitment, and loyalty associated with religion of difference, with a stress on personal experience and life here and now akin to "spiritualities of life." The prime example of such a hybrid form is Charismatic Christianity, which has proved to be among the most rapidly growing forms of Christianity.[21] Woodhead and Heelas use Charismatic Christianity interchangeably with Pentecostalism, but in this text I will follow Marie Thomsen's distinction between Pentecostalism on the one hand, which is primarily an ecclesiological term pointing to certain kinds of free congregations, and Charismatic Christianity on the other

---

18. Woodhead and Heelas, *Religion in Modern Times*, 111–13.

19. Ibid., 153, 494–95. See also Heelas and Woodhead, *The Spiritual Revolution*, 147. Concerning the impact of spiritualities of life in Western settings, see Heelas, *Spiritualities of Life*, 5.

20. Woodhead and Heelas, *Religion in Modern Times*, 148–57.

21. Ibid., 29–30, 66, 148.

hand, which denotes certain kinds of practices and spirituality that are found in Pentecostal congregations but also influence traditional churches today. For this reason I stick to the term "Charismatic Christianity" in the following.

"Experiential religions of humanity" is the name of combinations between "religions of humanity" and "spiritualities of life." This combination shares the positive valuation of individual experience associated with "spiritualities of life." Moral strictness is replaced by an ethic of individual freedom and the emphasis on committing to community life is replaced by a focus on the fellowship of humanity as a whole.[22] The teachings of the Dalai Lama and of Paul Tillich are mentioned as two different examples of this combination.

Before I apply this typology, critical voices to Heelas and Woodhead's typologies should be mentioned. Charles Taylor has objected that this typology is too pessimistic regarding spirituality's relationship to transcendent religion. He claims that "spiritualities of life" are not wholly immanent as Woodhead and Heelas claim as they also have a genuine openness towards the transcendent. David Voas and Steve Bruce, on the contrary, have objected that the typology is too optimistic in the same respect. Voas and Bruce claim that "spiritualities of life" are a truly secular phenomenon, therefore they do not really have a place for the sacred and it may even be a fallacy to call them spirituality at all.[23] In other words, the validity of the typology is debated. That it is based on a wide range of varied material is probably one reason for this, making oversimplification a constant threat while applying it. With this precaution in mind, I will use it as an analytical tool that none the less points out some significant trends in modern religion.

Engaging the Material

Due to the church development movement's lack of a common concept or normative source, it is difficult to find a material that is fully representative. However, two books published within the context of Church of Norway can be related to church development in significant ways. The first is written by the associate professor emeritus in practical theology at the School of Mission and Theology in Stavanger, Ove Conrad Hanssen. His

22. Ibid., 149, 157–60.
23. Taylor, *A Secular Age*, 509; Voas and Bruce, "The Spritual Revolution," 43–44, 56–59.

book *Et godt tre bærer god frukt: Visjoner og strategier for utvikling og vekst i lokale menigheter*[24] seeks to present significant currents in the church development movement and to explore their relevance for Church of Norway.[25] The second is written by the pastor and former missionary Oddbjørn Stangeland, also affiliated with the School of Mission and Theology in Stavanger. His *Edderkopp og sjøstjerne: En fortelling om å krysse grenser i misjonal menighetsutvikling*[26] gives practical and theological reflections on his own experiences with church planting and church development. Both books are practical guides to church development in the Norwegian state church context, although with slightly different theological frameworks and approaches. Hanssen's book describes the main features of church development in general and then suggests how these insights can be adapted to a Norwegian context. Stangeland represents a different perspective; after planting a congregation and developing it for several years, he reflects on the outcome of such a process.

The Growing Church

When Hanssen speaks of the church, his objects are empirical assemblies that gather in worship of Jesus. Following Christian Schwartz he argues that a sound ecclesiology must balance the visible aspect (the assembly) and the hidden aspect (the body of Christ) of the church. Emphasizing the gathered assembly ensures this balance; if ecclesiological reflection only emphasizes formal membership, the result will be a spiritualizing ecclesiology that is found neither in the New Testament nor the Augsburg Confession.[27] This does not mean that the church should neglect the membership and faith of its average members, but it has to challenge them to become disciples: active members of the visible assembly.[28]

Following a claim made by George Lings, true churches have a certain "DNA" that can be decoded: 1) churches are missional assemblies,

24. "A good tree bears good fruit: Visions and strategies for development and growth in local congregations" (my translation). The book is published in cooperation with OASE. (For more on OASE in Scandinavia, see the chapter by Ulrika Svalfors).

25. Hanssen, *Et godt tre bærer god frukt*, 9.

26. "Spider and sea star: A story about crossing borders in missional church development" (my translation). The book is published in cooperation with the missionary organisations Areopagos and Norwegian Missionary Society, and with the ecumenical church development organisation DAWN Norway (Discipling a Whole Nation).

27. Hanssen, *Et godt tre bærer god frukt*, 79, 82–84.

28. Ibid., 68.

reaching out to their surroundings with the gospel; 2) they represent an inward fellowship characterized by reciprocal relations and unity; and 3) they seek to grow in holiness through worship. These features thereby gain a status as a kind of *notae ecclesiae*. To these three characteristics of the true church there are three corresponding, fundamental activities of the church: it stretches *outwards* in mission, *inwards* in fellowship, and *upwards* in worship.[29]

The true church gathers both in public worship services and in smaller cell groups. The cell group is the building block of the congregation.[30] They consist of small, personal fellowships that gather frequently. It does not gather for strictly spiritual purposes, and its members may also go on vacation together and support each other in everyday challenges. The point is to build committed relationships.[31] Due to the biological metaphor, the cell is not only tightly knit, it is also continuously growing. It divides and builds new cells as an inherent necessity.[32] If a congregation is not in a process of growth, it needs development. And the point of church development is not to make the congregation grow but to remove the obstacles that are stopping the growth that, according to the chosen metaphor, is natural.[33]

The concept of the church as a tightly related fellowship gains further support from Hanssen's cultural diagnosis. European societies are in need of mission. Even if the majority of the Norwegian population are formally church members, we are left with only a marginal group that regularly attends services. Society has discredited the traditional Christian values and lifestyle, and Christian knowledge has largely eroded during the last generation. The present situation jeopardizes the very future of the church in Europe, making church development and evangelization urgent. Resources in the movement outwards are tools such as Alpha courses and Natural Church Development, as well as materials developed by Saddleback Church and Willow Creek.[34]

Put in the context of Woodhead and Heelas, Hanssen's vision of church leaves only very few signs that point in the direction of "religions of humanity." He admits that the church must accept the membership

29. Ibid., 85–86.
30. Ibid., 100, 110.
31. Ibid., 114–15.
32. Ibid., 97, 109–11.
33. Ibid., 69–70.
34. Ibid., 61, 68, 104, 123–24, 128, 130.

and faith of all baptized, but most of his ecclesiology bears characteristic marks of "religions of difference": the church is an empirical social fellowship that demands an active personal commitment from its members. The group shall help the individual member grow as a disciple facilitating their spiritual life, ministry, and ethos. The congregation ought to show continuous growth in numbers as well as in spiritual life. That church and the surrounding society are different entities becomes clear by the emphasizing of evangelization, local mission, and the concept of a necessary growth itself. It also comes to the fore through a cultural diagnosis that underlines the threatening aspects of secularization and the marginalization of the church.

Equipping Leadership

Along these lines of differentiation, Hanssen suggest a vision of leadership established by Christian Schwarz. Here an equipping leadership is the first quality of a growing congregation. In order to be a sufficient leader, he or she needs not only sufficient knowledge but also a personal gift of grace. The role of the leader is to equip individual members so that they can discern their own gifts of grace, which is the main prerequisite for any kind of ministry. And the equipping for ministry is a central task for the leader. Further, church development needs leadership that is willing to make changes. The leader must be able to take leave of traditions and bureaucratic structures that hinder the work of the Holy Spirit. Strategies from Natural Church Development and the Oasis movement are recommended for leaders that need competence in building and maintaining personal relations in the group.[35]

All baptized members share a ministry and the questions of formal education, training, and ordination among the leaders are not of importance. The result is an egalitarian and democratic view on leadership that favors lay ministry, even if the content of ministry itself remains vague. Woodhead and Heelas point out that even if "religions of difference" can be authoritarian, they can also be egalitarian. In this case, the stress on lay ministry is supplied with a stress on individual gifts of grace as a necessary requirement, which points in the direction of what they call "experiential religions of difference." The external authority of the Bible is fused with inner sources of authority.

35. Ibid., 98–100, 122–24.

Worshipping Lifestyle

Hanssen states that the traditional Lutheran worship service does not represent a relevant spirituality in our contemporary culture. It needs inspiration from both contemporary youth culture and from biblical sources. It also needs variation and flexibility. It should let individuals contribute with their personal ministries and be more open for spontaneous acts. A larger space for feelings and spiritual experiences should be allowed.[36] Resources in this regard are of Charismatic origins, but Hanssen also draws on traditional Lutheran sources for inspiration.[37]

The main goal for Hanssen is more than increased attendance at the regular public worship services. It is to make disciples. There are many forms of worship and maybe fewer public services would help disciples to spend more time together with other Christian friends and build social fellowships.[38] This does not imply that worship services are of minor importance. It downplays public services, but emphasizes informal worship and more internal forms of spirituality and the whole life engagement that discipleship should be.

The evident importance of worship regardless of form is a sign of differentiated religion in itself. At the same time, the stress on flexibility and personal experience is once again a sign of influence from what Woodhead and Heelas call "spiritualities of life." All in all, Hanssen's visions of church, leadership, and worship do quite clearly suggest the category of "religions of difference." His understanding of leadership, and to some degree worship, also shows signs of the subcategory "experiential religions of difference" akin to Charismatic Christianity.

The Church as Missional Fellowships

The next contribution I shall explore is written by Oddbjørn Stangeland, church planter within Church of Norway. For this author, the basic definition of church is an assembly of two or three gathered in the name of Jesus (Matt 18:20).[39] It is the small and personal social entity, the "cell," that gains precedence in his ecclesiological vision. At the same time Stangeland points out that a living congregation should manage to sustain relation-

---

36. Ibid., 129.
37. Ibid., 126–27.
38. Ibid., 118–21.
39. Stangeland, *Edderkopp og sjøstjerne*, 80.

PART TWO: Exploring a Heritage—Influences

ships also on public and global levels. But on all levels the congregation is conceived of as relationships and Stangeland points at three equally important forms: "one-to-one fellowship," worship services, and cell groups.[40]

The cell group is presented as the biblical form of church and gains priority as such. Even if public services are important, cell groups can have their own worship services without partaking in a larger fellowship. Superficial, undemanding, and casual fellowships in the public services are worse than reducing the number of public services and such a reduction can be done in order to give priority to independent life of the cells. Different cells can foster different social and cultural preferences within the larger congregation. A healthy cell grows, divides, form new cell groups, and multiplies over time. This concept of cell-formed church has not only natural growth but also "church planting" integrated in its metaphorical essence.[41]

An urge for growth and church planting further goes hand in hand with a specific view for the majority of Church of Norway's members. Stangeland states that the purpose of the church is not to create Christians or believers, but to make disciples: people who have Jesus at the center of their life. Compared to this objective, most folk church members live as atheists. They might say they believe, but they do not partake in a congregational life and it is also claimed that their faith has no practical consequences.[42] "Discipling the whole nation" functions both as a vision and a slogan for this conception of church development.[43]

The concept of "discipling," implying a "disciplining" of individuals' lifestyles, spirituality, and morals, bears resemblance to what Woodhead and Heelas calls "religions of difference." The downplaying of the sacraments and the public role of the church on the one side, combined with the stress on small, tightly bounded fellowships on the other, support this observation. Demarcation lines between those inside (the disciples) and those outside (the practical atheists) give us further support.[44] The difference works on the one side as an argument for missional activities reaching out to the "undisciplined." But on the other side, as in Troeltsch's concept of "sect," social life and other activities should primarily be organized within the social group in order to foster and maintain the proper

40. Ibid., 83.
41. Ibid., 93–98.
42. Ibid., 65–72.
43. Ibid., 93.
44. Woodhead and Heelas, *Religion in Modern Times*, 28–29.

identity and difference of the group.[45] As I noted earlier, such a communal aspect is important both for "religions of difference" and for "experiential religions of difference."[46]

Gifted Leadership

Stangeland's egalitarian view on leadership might be captured by one of his dreams for Church of Norway: that 50 percent of its congregations in three to five years have volunteers that are confident enough to celebrate the whole Sunday service once a month, having the pastor and the organist as regular participants in the assembly. He states that church development should not only equip the congregation to survive without ordained pastors, but to be fully functional without them. In his missional concept of the pastoral function, the role of the pastor is to equip the congregation for ministry (Eph 4:12).[47] There is still need for educated and ordained ministry because of the demands of the current state church organization and the expectations in the folk church context, but essentially the whole congregation should share the pastoral tasks and ministry. In this shift, individual gifts of grace replace formal qualifications.

This vision of leadership primarily stresses the authority of religious experiences and personal abilities. In practice it will also be based on the local community's recognition of these individual judgments, as well as on the authority of the Bible. In other words, we have to do with a combination of values and criteria that belong partly to "spiritualities of life" and partly to "religions of difference."

Fluid Worship

Stangeland recognizes that his congregation has moved away from celebrating services each Sunday in order to spend more time building relationships. Cell church ecclesiology has in this way a direct influence on worship practice. But that does not mean that worship is neglected, rather it is reinterpreted. A biblical and genuine worship service only requires two or three persons gathered in the name of Jesus with an open Bible, bread, and wine, he argues. A cell group or family can celebrate biblical

45. Ibid., 42.
46. Ibid., 148.
47. Stangeland, *Edderkopp og sjøstjerne*, 102–4.

PART TWO: Exploring a Heritage—Influences

worship services where and when they find it suitable. Also larger public services should be prepared and carried out by the larger fellowship of the cell groups.[48] In addition to informal and public worship services, the concept of discipleship portrays the whole life of the individual as worship: the ideal life centered wholly on Jesus ought to be nourished in a range of different social settings.

In a way that resembles Hanssen's, these features point once again in the direction of "religions of difference" and "experiential religions of difference."

Summary

Our two contributions to church development have been treated independently, as they are not obliged to a common concept, theoretical framework, or methodology from their outset. Nevertheless, their concepts of church, leadership, and worship do share many of the same claims, visions, and agendas. In the following I will shortly summarize some of the traits they share.

First, social entities stand out as the main ecclesiological focal point. The church is primarily conceived of as local congregations that gather in groups as well as in public services, visible social fellowships that are bound together by personal relations and a shared commitment. The biological metaphor of the cell is applied as a definition of the true or biblical kind of church. The concept of the cell is used as what Lakoff and Johnson call an "ontological metaphor," which means that it essentially shapes the way of reasoning about the church.[49] The choice of metaphor enables the authors to postulate that the church is naturally programmed for continuous growth, divisions, and for planting of new cells. It makes "DNA" suitable as an ecclesiological term where one otherwise could expect the traditional term *notae ecclesiae*. Without the "cell" as their ontological metaphor for the church, these claims would seem less obvious and lose much of their force. For both authors, the DNA or marks of the true church consist of three basic activities: the movement inwards (a committing social life in the group), upwards (being a worshipping assembly), and outwards (reaching out in mission and evangelization, fostering growth, and multiplication).

---

48. Ibid., 83, 94–95.
49. Lakoff and Johnson, *Metaphors We Live By*, 25–29.

Second, the vision of leadership is egalitarian and emphasizes the gifts of grace. A central task of the leader is to equip each member for ministry. All have an obligation to contribute to the activities of the group through his or her ministry, based on gifts of grace. This vision of obligation supports an ideal of discipleship that is fostered and lived out in the context of fellowship. The leader may be an ordained pastor, but not necessarily so. The traditional concept of pastoral leadership through the preaching of the word and the administration of the sacraments are downplayed together with the traditional need for theological competence. This is done from the viewpoint of a functional understanding of the priesthood of all believers within the context of the group; its social life, missional activities, and, first and foremost, its worship gatherings.

Third, the understanding of worship goes in two directions: on the one hand it is emphasized as crucial because it is the main source for growth in holiness and commitment; while on the other hand the emphasis on tight personal relationships, combined with a wide understanding of worship as being together in the name of Jesus, is used as support for a multitude of forms and types of worship. This stress on worship that is combined with a stress on social activities results in a downplaying of the role of regular public services in favor of more frequent, informal spiritual gatherings.

Analysis

Throughout the exploration of the material I have applied the typology of Woodhead and Heelas to my findings. Generally the material shows most affinities with the category "religions of difference." I have shown that the ecclesiological visions fit most neatly into this category, but also that the view on worship, and to some degree the view on leadership, should be placed here. However, the concepts of worship and especially the understanding of leadership, reveal certain influences from "spiritualities of life" as well. We have seen this most clearly when it comes to the authoritative position of subjective experiences. The egalitarian attitude to leadership corresponds to this emphasis on individual experiences of the Holy Spirit as an important source for religious authority. And as worship is a privileged setting for experiencing the Spirit, worship is also a privileged place for contributing with one's different gifts and ministries. A focus on individual experience is combined with the differentiating and communitarian aspects. The result is a combination type akin to Charismatic Christianity,

PART TWO: Exploring a Heritage—Influences

symptomatic of "experiential religions of difference." As I have shown, some parts of the material also reveal direct influences from Charismatic Christianity. For the most part, however, it is most likely to consider these as corresponding tendencies. This conclusion further rules out the possibility for fundamentalism or religions of heightened difference. The differentiated influences are of an evangelical and more mainstream kind, and they are slightly mixed with influences from "spiritualities of life." At the same time, this evident influence suggests that the material cannot be called "Charismatic" as such, even though it shares some characteristics with Charismatic Christianity.

Woodhead and Heelas have argued that on a global level "experiential religions of difference" are currently successful, being one of the religious types that are growing most rapidly. From a growth perspective, which is so pivotal for church development, the choice of profile may be a sign that the present authors are moving in the right direction. But how may that profile affect the identity of Church of Norway from an ecclesiological perspective?

Some Ecclesiological Considerations

Many of the trends found in the material are not new in Church of Norway even though the phenomenon called "church development" is. For several hundred years, pietism has been an important force on Norwegian soil, shaping the spirituality of lay people and pastors alike in distinct ways. From this tradition we are acquainted with ecclesiological visions that favor smaller groups of converted people as the real church within the church; with an understanding of leadership that is egalitarian (and sometimes anticlerical) and that bases religious authority on personal experiences, gifts, and morals rather than on competence and formal criteria; and with an understanding of worship that favors informal spiritual gatherings outside, and not seldom instead of, public worship services in church. Similar to the present contributions to church development, these pietistic aspects of Norwegian church history may be categorized as "experiential religions of difference" with a stress on the differentiating aspect. Church development offers chances to reinvent this legacy for a new age.

But important parts of the identity of Church of Norway are at odds with this legacy and can also be categorized differently. As a Lutheran folk church, Church of Norway has a public and institutional aspect, developed into a well-established combination of synodal and episcopal structures with a corresponding bureaucracy. In the public sphere, church-related debates often deal with the church as an institution rather than a gathered assembly. Partly because of its regular public services, a well-educated clergy, established institution, and long traditions, it enjoys recognition and a folk church position in society. Most members seldom attend services but most still celebrate their rites of passage in church. Faith is a private matter and a sense of belonging seems to be more important than active engagement or beliefs. In light of the Augsburg Confession, Church of Norway is also a result of the preached gospel and the preaching of the gospel is the church's primary task.[50] The public ministry of the word and the sacraments is therefore crucial and this responsibility is mirrored in the traditional demand of a thorough academic training of those who shall be considered *rite vocatus* for the office.[51]

In the language of Woodhead and Heelas, these confessional and social characteristics show affinities with the "religions of humanity." The institutional aspect of the church, being still a part of the state, signifies that the church is not only of importance for the few, but for the Norwegian society in general. The Lutheran emphasis on the objective works of the sacraments rather than the subjective efforts of its members as being constitutive of the church, points also in the direction of the same religious category. The challenge from church development to the existing concepts of church, leadership, and worship can in each of those cases be described as a challenge to qualities that belong to "religions of humanity." When, for instance, the authors apply the metaphor of the cell that necessarily grows and multiplies on Church of Norway, they import a differentiating concept within the church which results in a confusing ecclesiology in a nation where the majority of the population are church members, and which has been predominantly Christian throughout most of its history. However, it could be argued that the material does address secularization and represents concrete efforts to deal with it. In an ever changing cultural landscape, the church needs to reinterpret its sources and calling if it is to communicate its continuing message. For this reason it needs critical theological reflection on its own traditions and institutions. Our material represents an important reminder that our society has changed drastically since the Reformation. But the authors' applying of concrete biblical imagery and church structures directly on a Norwegian

---

50. The Augsburg Confession, V, VII, VIII; Nørgaard-Højen, *Den danske kirkes bekendelsesskrifter*, 281.

51. The Augsburg Confession, V, XIV; Nørgaard-Højen, *Den danske kirkes bekendelsesskrifter*, 281.

late-Christian context is just another way of neglecting the inevitable forces of history. Other challenges arise when it comes to their views on leadership and worship. The visions expressed from church development contest especially the public and professional aspects that these have in Church of Norway today. The Sunday public service is challenged by the emphasis on informal social and spiritual gatherings. The public ministry of the word that presupposes theological qualifications and professional training is challenged by the emphasis on lay leadership based on divine gifts. In either case, the possible weakening of the institutional, public, and professional aspects of the church would also mean a weakening of cultural traditions as well as the church's confessional sources. These aspects belong to "religions of humanity" in general and to Church of Norway as folk church in particular. At the same time, these trends also represent a revitalization of the lay people that have been downplayed in our tradition. A clergy of "solo players" and a passive laity is not what the reformers aimed for. This must be kept in mind, but it should also be balanced by a reconsideration of the worldly character of Luther's sense of ministry, i.e., his ethics. Duties, work, and responsibilities in the secular realm are not inferior to the ministry of the church; they supply it. They may be called "worldly," but they are necessary and complementary ways of serving God and humanity. This aspect is absent in our material, which one-sidedly refers to engagement within the congregational domain through worship activities and missional efforts. This is arguably not what the reformers aimed for either.

Conclusion

The material analyzed in this chapter relates to church development. In the context of a Lutheran folk church, the contributions envision the church's nature, leadership, and worship afresh with numerical and qualitative growth as important objectives. They inspire changes in beliefs and practices, as well as new forms of congregations and divisions within the church. Considered in light of a typology of religion in modern times, the material can be said to represent the globally growing "experiential religions of difference" due to characteristics that it shares with Charismatic Christianity. While the views on ecclesiology, leadership, and worship have many historical precursors in Norwegian pietism, some positions, like the focus on continuous church growth, are rather new. As an exponent for a differentiated type of religion, church development seems to challenge especially those parts of Church of Norway identity that belong to "religions of humanity": the institutional, professional, and public aspects of the church. The engagement with church development in the Norwegian context in the time to come would profit from addressing these key areas from a theological perspective.

Bibliography

"The Essence of NCG." Online: http://www.ncd-international.org/public/essence.html (accessed 03/01/ 2011).

Hanssen, Ove Conrad. *Et godt tre bærer god frukt: Visjoner og strategier for utvikling og vekst i lokale menigheter.* Oslo: Luther Forlag, 2007.

Heelas, Paul. *Spiritualities of Life: New Age Romanticism and Consumptive Capitalism.* Oxford: Blackwell, 2008.

Heelas, Paul and Linda Woodhead. *The Spiritual Revolution: Why Religion Is Giving Way to Spirituality.* Oxford: Blackwell, 2005.

"I Kristus—nær livet. Visjonsdokument for Den norske kirke 2009–2014." Online: http://www.kirken.no/?event=doLink&famID=3200 (accessed 03/01/ 2011).

"K-vekst: Presentasjon." Online: http://www.k-vekst.no/kontakt/index.html (accessed 31/10/2010).

Lakoff, George and Mark Johnson. *Metaphors We Live By.* Chicago: University of Chicago Press, [1980] 2003.

Nørgaard-Højen, Peder. *Den danske kirkes bekendelsesskrifter: Kommentar.* København: Anis, 2004.

Rønnestad, Gunnar. "Etablering av nye menigheter i Den norske kirke." In *Halvårsskrift for praktisk teologi* 1–2010, 14–25. Oslo: Luther Forlag, 2010.

Shenk, Wilbert R. "Church Growth." In *Dictionary of the Ecumenical Movement*, edited by Nicolas Lossky et al., 202–3. Geneva: WCC Publications, 2002.

Stangeland, Oddbjørn. *Edderkopp og sjøstjerne: En fortelling om å krysse grenser i Misjonal menighetsutvikling.* Oslo: Luther Forlag, 2008.

"Structured for Unlimited Multiplication." Online: http://www.ncd-international.org/public/FAQ-Network.html (accessed 31/10/2010).

Taylor, Charles. *A Secular Age.* Cambridge, MA: Harvard University Press, 2007.

Voas, David and Steve Bruce. "The Spiritual Revolution: Another False Dawn for the Sacred." In *A Sociology of Spirituality*, edited by Kienan Flanagan and Peter C. Jupp, 43–62. Aldershot: Ashgate, [2007] 2010.

Woodhead, Linda and Paul Heelas, editors. *Religion in Modern Times: An Interpretative Anthology.* Oxford: Blackwell, 2000.

8

Charismatic Movements within Church of Sweden

ULRIKA SVALFORS

IN THIS CHAPTER I intend to investigate Charismatic influences in Church of Sweden today by studying two phenomena: the Oasis movement and the Alpha course. The Oasis movement is a revival movement within Church of Sweden and the Alpha course is a sort of revival teaching on Christian belief. Both relate to the global Charismatic movement, connected to Pentecostal and Fundamentalist movements.

In a way both are peripheral to Church of Sweden, but just as Marie Thomsen points out in her chapter it is not accurate to leave it at that. Thomsen analyzes how Pentecostal, Charismatic, and Fundamentalist movements have influenced separate parish congregations in the Evangelical Lutheran Church in Denmark. This study focuses on the ideas of the Alpha and the Oasis movements, taking it for a fact that they do exist *within* Church of Sweden and already influence it. The question is about what they teach and how that can be related to Pentecostal/Charismatic/Fundamentalist ideas as well as Church of Sweden with its Lutheran heritage.

My study will be a discourse analysis of texts collected from websites of the movements, their magazines, and books from the Alpha course. In this chapter, discourse is understood in a Foucauldian way: a discourse is a totality of ideas that, through a performative language, makes certain ways of thinking and acting normative, while excluding other thoughts and behavior.[1] Another way to put it is that a performative language exercises disciplinary power by the different normative ideas (verbal as well as others) of the discourse.[2] In my analysis the agents are downplayed and instead the content of the ideas are uncovered, as well as the discourse's disciplinary power. In this chapter the expression "the talk" is used interchangeable with "discourse" to emphasize that it is what is said, and not the practice of the discourse, that is analyzed.

In reading the material I have been searching for notions and ideas that are frequent. These ideas form the fundamentals of the talk. When these frequent notions are uncovered I turn to the disciplinary power of the talk to demonstrate how truth and normality is established by a normalization process. The analysis will of course not give a full picture of the movements, nor even a full picture of what is said by them, but instead show some central ideas in the movements and how knowledge and truth are shaped out of these. The study is also a way to get a grip of Christian understandings in Sweden today, seeing that these ideas are not only shared by the movements studied here.

Some definitions have to be established before proceeding. When it comes to "Pentecostal," "Charismatic," and "Fundamentalist," I follow the definitions made by Thomsen in her chapter.[3] "Evangelical" aims at "Evangelicalism," the result of the "Evangelical Revival" in nineteenth century with roots in pietistic movements in the sixteenth century and Wesley's preaching in the eighteenth century.[4]

But Evangelicalism has not stayed within Church of England; it has spread all over the world. Evangelical movements are transdenominational (just like the Charismatic movement) and they nurture biblicism (here: a softer variant of Fundamentalism where answers are sought first of all in the Bible, but not in a literal manner), emphasize salvation and evangelization, and are apologetic and exclusivist (Jesus is the only way to salvation).[5] Evangelicals can be charismatic, but this is not necessary. "Evangelical" should not be confused with the expression "Evangelical

---

1. Foucault, *Diskursens ordning*.
2. Foucault, *Övervakning och straff*, 21–24, 228–29.
3. Cf. Marie Thomsen in this book.
4. Bundy, "European Pietist Roots of Pentecostalism," 611; Synan, "Evangelicalism," 614.
5. Alvarsson, "Pentekostal, evangelikal och karismatisk," 43–44.

PART TWO: Exploring a Heritage—Influences

Lutheran," an expression that emphasizes the connection to the Lutheran reformation in sixteenth century, in contrast to later use of "Evangelical" that has been described above.

A Short History of the Oasis and the Alpha Movements

The name Oasis alludes to the oasis in the desert, a place to find fresh water. The movement defines its mission within a Church of Sweden context thus: "The Oasis movement has its foundation in Evangelical Lutheran faith and wants to serve Church of Sweden with an open mind towards other churches."[6] It started in 1983 and views itself to be an emanation of "the global Charismatic renewal" and to be part of the biggest ever revival movement in church history.[7] Its counterparts exist in Norway, Denmark, and Finland.

Oasis collaborates with the Word of Life, Kairos New Wine, the Friends of Israel, and with Pentecostal congregations.[8] They partake in the Evangelical Jesus manifestation (*Jesusmanifestationen*) held in Stockholm in May every year, and one of the "inspirers" of Oasis is part of the manifestation's steering committee.[9] Ulf Ekman, the leader of Word of Life, as well as Stanley Sjöberg, a well-known Pentecostal pastor, are frequently speakers at Oasis meetings.[10]

The Oasis movement has no registered membership. The organization consists of four employed so-called "inspirers," a board of ten people, twenty-four leaders working with adults, seven leaders working with youth, four "theological advisers," and two administrators.[11]

The movement arranges inspiration days and conferences in Sweden, for instance big summer meetings with several thousand visitors. These meetings cater for the whole family, with different activities for different ages. Oasis also publishes the Oasis paper (*Oasbladet*) four times a year.[12]

---

6. See "Om Oas-rörelsen." All translations in the chapter will be my own.
7. Ibid.
8. See for instance *Oasbladet* 2/2010, 21.
9. See "Ledningsgruppen."
10. See for instance "Höstoas, Rättvik 2008," "Sommaroas, Borås 2009," "Pingstoas, Stockholm 2010," and "Höstoas, Rättvik 2010," in "Föredrag och predikningar" in "Oasshopen."
11. See "Inspiratörer," "Styrelse," "Ledarskap," "UngdomsOas," "Teol rådgivare," and "Administration" in "Om Oas-rörelsen."
12. See "Om Oas-rörelsen."

The Oasis movement has a children and a youth section too: Children Oasis and Y-Oasis. These will not be studied in this chapter as the adult Oasis is in focus. Neither will preparation for confirmation, a new program from 2011, be examined.

Alpha has its beginning in an introductory course on Christian belief for new Christians in the Anglican congregation of Holy Trinity Brompton in London. It started as a four-week course in 1977 for "new Christians" and has grown to comprise fifteen topics worked through over ten weeks and a weekend, with approximately five hundred participants per course, which run three times per year.[13] Every occasion starts with a meal and continues with a lecture and ends with conversation and prayers in small groups. The near-required weekend away from home focuses on the Holy Spirit as a person and as a spiritual gift giver.[14] Since 1990 the director of Alpha International is Nicky Gumbel, who has written the texts for the Alpha course.

Alpha has connections to the Toronto Blessing of the mid-1990s, out of which Vineyard was born. Nicky Gumbel was deeply touched during a visit to Toronto where he participated in meetings. What is called the "Ministry Time" during the "Holy Spirit Weekend" in Alpha is associated to John Wimber, one of the founders of Vineyard.[15] Bill Hybels, the founder of the successful mega-church Willow Creek, in USA, and also creator of the Global Leadership Summit held all over the world (October 2010 in Gothenburg) is promoting the course: "Alpha is one of the best known evangelistic programs in the world. I don't think anybody rejoices more in its effectiveness than I do."[16]

One parish that as early as 1996 took the opportunity to start Alpha courses in Sweden was Sollentuna, a parish in Church of Sweden. It was the coworkers in this parish that were entrusted to translate and adapt the British course to the Swedish context.[17]

Like in the Oasis movement, you cannot be a member of Alpha Sweden. The organization has five persons on its staff.[18] In nearly all material that Alpha Sweden offers there are statistics that describe how many have participated in an Alpha course in Sweden and around the world. The

---

13. Gumbel, *Handboken om Alpha*, 11–12.
14. Hunt, "The Alpha Course and Its Critics," 5.
15. Ibid., 11.
16. "Other Leaders & Church Leadership."
17. "Alpha—grundkurs i kristen tro."
18. See "Kontakt."

figures are constantly growing. On their website it states that over 75,000 Swedes have participated in an Alpha course.[19]

The Talk of the Oasis Movement

The Oasis movement's vision is to "put forward the Charismatic life in church through pointing out the Truth of the Bible . . . [and] . . . the power of prayer . . . to build up the body of Christ."[20] When elaborating this vision three main words, or notions, become central for Oasis: renewal, evangelization, and unity.[21] I will here develop the two first notions to some extent to make clear what this talk is all about. The notion "unity" will be treated below in the section "Disciplinary Power in the Oasis Movement."

"Renewal" refers both to the renewal of the individual and the renewal of the church/parish. On an individual level the Oasis talk emphasizes the need of conversion. The idea of conversion is closely connected to being filled by the Spirit.[22] Educational and inspirational texts often deal with the Holy Spirit, and the individual's possibility to be filled with the Spirit and so get special spiritual gifts.[23] Seminars on the special gifts of the Holy Spirit and intercession are always part of national meetings, for example healing services.[24]

What is it to be converted in Oasis? It is to become authentic, or "a flourishing original."[25] It is to become something else than "the world" makes us, which is described as "a copy."[26] "The world" should here be understood ideologically as the non-Christian worldviews producing norms and ideas that are more or less "seduced by the devil."[27]

If the individual does not convert, she might be an "ordinary" Christian but she will not be able to see God.[28] This differentiation between

---

19. See "Material."
20. See "Att ordna ett oasmöte" in "Om Oas-rörelsen."
21. See "Om Oas-rörelsen."
22. Ljungman, "Vad är andedop?" 14.
23. See for instance "Vad är andedop?," 14; and Aro, "Värdefullare än guld," 4.
24. See for instance invitation to the Oasis meeting in Borås in July 2010, in Oasbladet 1/2010, 15.
25. Pleijel, "Behövs omvändelse?" 7.
26. Ibid., 10.
27. Ibid., 11.
28. Cf. Halvard Johannessen in this book.

"ordinary" and "authentic" Christians is important in the Oasis talk.[29] "Ordinary" Christians are part of the non-renewed church turning away from God, i.e., she is part of secularization. If, on the other hand, the individual converts she is able to see God and by that becomes "authentic."[30] The veil picture seems to imply something that happens once for all, but the Oasis talk describes the conversion more as a process that needs to be repeated many times.[31]

The renewal of the church is something that takes place on the organizational level in Oasis.[32] Here it is about the need for the church/parish to be converted in its spirituality so it becomes devoted, or authentic, as a community. This is mainly done through the leadership. The leaders need to train the community in discipleship in such a way that the individuals turn to God and so get filled with the Spirit.[33] This requires a renewed leadership, which reads the Bible as God's Word.[34] The use of "God's Word" is an indirect criticism of using the Bible as one of many sources for preaching and living.[35] The Bible should be *the* source, the one and only, and Oasis offers seminars and texts where this view is expounded.[36]

In a renewed parish the services are filled with praise through songs. The preaching is "Jesus centred and Biblical," as it is put in a description in *Oasbladet*.[37] Or, as a priest in Varberg writes, "services [are] characterized by sacramental consciousness with great openness to the Charismatic renewal."[38] The renewal will make parishes and people alive and authentic, as Börjesson concludes with retired Bishop Bertil Gärtner's words when looking back on the Oasis movement's work:

29. Pleijel, "Behövs omvändelse?" 7.
30. Ibid., 10.
31. Ibid., 11.
32. Andersson, "Omvändelse—för vilka?," 10.
33. Nordlander, "Förvandling av församlingar," 2; Sjöberg, "Angeläget om John Sung," 10–11.
34. See invitation to a weekend ("Mission Impossible") for youth leaders in *Oasbladet* 3/2010, 24.
35. See for instance Simonsson, "Kära alla Oasvänner!," 9: "Dare to believe that the Bible is God's Holy Word, even though voices both within and outside the church claim something else!"; Nordlander, "Guds rike är nu här," 2; Långström, "Jag kallar er vänner," 6.
36. See for instance the invitation text for the Oasis meeting in Piteå in July 2011, in *Oasbladet* 1/2011, 4, and all Oasis meetings offered through the website.
37. Frykman, "Kastalakyrkan. Kungälv," 6.
38. Jonsson, "Appelvikshöjds kyrka. Varberg," 3.

PART TWO: Exploring a Heritage—Influences

> Christians have been deepened in their faith. The Bible has been given new authority. The community in prayer both in small groups and in whole parishes have made people come together in a new way. The gifts of the Spirit have begun to work. Sick people have been healed. . . . The song of praise is heard in more and more parishes with a new force.[39]

The emphasis on conversion makes evangelization an urgent mission for Oasis.[40] In 2010 a motion in Church of Sweden Synod for "re-evangelization" of the country was dismissed. Nordlander (part of "the Leadership") finds this astonishing, since he agrees with the writer of the motion on the poor spiritual situation in Sweden.[41] Nordlander wants to "go back to the sources," *ad fontes*, which are "the Bible, the tradition, and renewal in the Spirit."[42] Evangelization is like this: often promoted as urgent, not least since today can be understood as nearing the end of time.[43]

The Oasis Talk as Charismatic and Lutheran

Oasis is an example of a Charismatic movement. The talk focuses on the necessity of conversion, i.e., becoming authentic through experience of the Holy Spirit. This makes evangelization central in Oasis. The emphasis on the truth of the Bible is a sort of biblicism, also found in Evangelical movements. Patterns and models of belief and behavior are fetched from the Bible, such as the idea of being a disciple, and directly applied to current situations.[44]

However, sometimes the tradition is of equal importance as the Bible in Oasis. This is not a Charismatic trait, but part of Oasis being Lutheran. Lutheran ideas are expressed for instance in the focus on the church and the parish, healing as an inner healing, and that speaking in tongues is not highlighted very much.[45] The importance of good services (liturgy) and

---

39. Börjesson, "Hur det började," 4.

40. This is also an effect of the declining of the church in West, as Halvard Johannessen writes in his chapter in this book.

41. "Återevangelisering av Sverige."

42. Nordlander, "Nu är det jul igen . . ," 2.

43. See for instance seminars held on the Summer meeting in Borås 2010, in *Oasbladet* 1/2010, 13.

44. In this Oasis resembles "the Missionary-Charismatic-Conservative" congregational type in Marie Thomsen's chapter.

45. Kärkkäinen, *Pneumatology*, 83–84.

leader training (priest education) are other ideas that are part of Church of Sweden.

Another Lutheran characteristic is that the sacraments, the Eucharist and baptism, are important for the self-identity of the movement. The expression "Spirit baptism" is for instance avoided, seeing that the movement does not want to give the impression that there exist two sorts of baptism.[46]

The Talk of the Alpha Movement

Alpha talk is focused on two topics at the same time. There is the talk about discipleship, and the talk about Alpha.

The main purpose of the Alpha course is to make disciples of the participants. Therefore the talk about discipleship has a significant place in Alpha. Individuals are turned into disciples through teaching the fundamentals of Christian belief.[47] The intention is to give explanations which are directed to the intellect, the heart, and the will.

Alpha, through its leaders, appeal to the intellect since the Christian faith, according to Alpha, is built on historical realties.[48] The intellectual part of making disciples therefore contains a presentation of these "facts." But it also contains argumentation for how reasonable it is to believe.[49] Explanations directed to the heart are also of a cognitive character. This is about how to experience God, through prayer as well as through the community with others.[50] Finally, explanations are directed to the will and consist of propositions that the participant has to decide on.[51] This is evangelization: to make disciples by making Jesus known, believed, and followed.

But the talk about discipleship is only one part of Alpha. The other part is about Alpha itself, or how Alpha makes disciples in practice. This is an interesting part of the Alpha talk, the how and when is just as important as the what. The talk about Alpha has four main areas: caring, small groups, lectures, and intercession.

---

46. Ljungman, "Vad är andedop?," 14.
47. Gumbel, *Handboken om Alpha*, 20.
48. Ibid., 21.
49. Ibid.
50. Ibid., 22.
51. Ibid., 21–23.

PART TWO: Exploring a Heritage—Influences

Caring for people, says Gumbel, has to be genuine and honest because relations that Christians build must come from the heart.[52] The goal is that participants shall meet Jesus Christ and become disciples, which in Alpha is the same as becoming spiritually mature.[53] The caring is what makes the explanations trustworthy. Crucial in this journey, or process, to discipleship is that the leaders express warmth and understanding, and that they listen to and cherish the participants.[54]

Alpha is mainly carried out in small groups. Not more than twelve, including four leaders, are recommended.[55] It is in the small group that caring comes through. Small groups stimulate discussions and all the questions that the participants have can be posed (the last "a" in "Alpha" stands for "all questions allowed"), according to Gumbel.[56] But there are questions which should be dismissed. Some should be dismissed because the participants are not ready for them, others because they are unfruitful.[57] Therefore it is important to create the warm and attentive milieu that the caring aims at.

It is also in the small group that participants are to learn how to read the Bible and to pray, when they are ready for it.[58] Imitation is the main form for learning about Christian belief and life in Alpha. All this makes way for a very special form of community characterized by intimacy and attention:[59] a community that is expected eventually to effect and permeate everything in the parish/congregation.[60]

Lectures are another important part of the talk about Alpha. There are fifteen lectures, all presented in a separate book: *Alpha. The Questions of Life. An opportunity to investigate the meaning of life.* These lectures consist of the explanations described above. But in the handbook of Alpha the leaders also are told how to perform these lectures. It is, for instance, important that the leaders are convincing, since the explanations in Alpha consist of arguments for the reasonableness of becoming a Christian. The

---

52. Ibid., 87.
53. Ibid., 89.
54. Ibid., 87–94.
55. Ibid., 104.
56. Ibid.
57. Ibid., 105.
58. Ibid., 105–6.
59. Ibid., 109.
60. *Alpha Nytt* 2010, 8, 11.

lectures need also to be carried out in a personal and practical way.[61] This is attained through the leader's sincerity and conviction.

Finally, intercession is a vital part of the talk about Alpha. All sorts of intercession must be performed under the authority of the Bible, which means that it is performed as described in the Bible.[62] The Bible founded patterns are important since they guarantee that what is said and done is blessed by God himself, according to the handbook on Alpha.[63]

The goal and culmination of the talk about discipleship and Alpha is: the participants will accept the explanations, say yes to following Jesus, and so be filled with the Holy Spirit. It is described in vivid language as a stirring experience: the body is shaken, tears pour, knees are shaken, and the person might fall.[64] One of the evidences of conversion is speaking in tongues. This is described as something that can happen, but not as something necessary.[65] Nevertheless, it is held forward as something to pray for and long after. The "Holy Spirit Weekend" is designed to make it happen. In this way speaking in tongues turns out to be the sign *per se*, even if the handbook of Alpha is a bit ambivalent on this point. It is, anyway, significant for Alpha to highlight outer manifestations of the Holy Spirit.[66]

The Alpha Talk as Evangelical and Charismatic

Gumbel places Alpha in a pietistic tradition.[67] One of the pietistic forms is Evangelicalism. Evangelical traits in the Alpha talk are the nearly literal understanding of the Bible (biblicism), the emphasis on conversion (becoming a disciple) and evangelization (getting people to Alpha courses), and the apologetic style (to convince about the reasonableness of belief).

The strong emphasis on the Holy Spirit makes the Alpha talk Charismatic. Both in theory (lectures) and in practice ("the Holy Spirit weekend") much time is given to explain and experience the Holy Spirit. The preoccupation with the special gift of speaking in tongues draws the movement a bit closer to Pentecostal movements than the Oasis movement. The talk of the Alpha movement can therefore be characterized as

61. Gumbel, *Handboken om Alpha*, 123–25.
62. Ibid., 139.
63. Ibid.
64. Ibid., 40, 46, 84, 101.
65. Ibid., 55.
66. Cf. Marie Thomsen in this book.
67. Gumbel, *Handboken om Alpha*, 24–25.

PART TWO: Exploring a Heritage—Influences

Charismatic Evangelical, with a Pentecostal trait. It seems like Alpha and "Church development" in Norway share the same roots.[68]

To sum up so far: fundamental ideas in the talk of the Oasis movement are renewal, conversion, evangelization, and unity (not yet treated in the chapter). In Alpha the fundamental ideas are discipleship, caring, small groups, lectures, and intercession. These ideas, or fundamentals of the talk, are part of normalizations processes that establish truth.

Disciplinary Power in the Oasis Movement

In Oasis the disciplinary power establishes the "true Church," through establishing a leadership in opposition to trendy Christians, churches, and church leaders that betray the truth by negotiating with the world and the Word. Polemical issues are, beside the severe condition of the church and Christians, for instance: the ordination of women, homosexuality, and same-sex marriage.[69] To all of this, a clear and definite "no" is expressed.

The notion "the Church" is at the center of this normalization process.[70] The Church is not Church of Sweden or any other established church in Sweden. The Church crosses confessional barriers at the same time as it is emerging *within* Church of Sweden, through the Oasis movement. One of the founders and theological advisers of Oasis expresses a longing for a-political and non-liberal places.[71] This can be apprehended as a vision in the Oasis movement, a vision seen as missing in Church of Sweden of today. While elaborating the vision, the question of truth is a frequent subject. The truth that Oasis establishes through its ideas is the truth about "the Church," or more accurately the *true Church*.

But what does it mean to be "true"? One part of it is to read and follow the Holy Scripture which Oasis states most churches in Sweden do not do today.[72] What differs seems to be the degree of biblicism. Oasis wants to apply biblical models more directly than what they think is mostly done in Church of Sweden.

---

68. Cf. Halvard Johannessen in this book.

69. "Oasrörelsen i Sverige uttalar sig om könsneutral vigselordning." See also Lindsten, "Hon är ledare men inte präst."

70. The word is spelled with a capital "C" and in definite form ("the Church"), which underscores that it is a holy institution and not of humans.

71. Gärtner, "Vara kvar eller inte?," 9–10.

72. Simonsson, "Kära alla Oasvänner!," 9.

The logic Oasis gives is that it is only through the renewal of the church that the truth ("God's Word") will become clear.[73] The idea seems to be that the Bible, in all its texts, has one and only one correct interpretation. This interpretation is the truth, even though the thought of *one* interpretation rules out interpretation as such and enforces biblicism.[74] Without renewal of the church, the truth will not be clear. And the renewal of the church depends on the renewal of the individuals.

By putting the Word, Holy Scripture, at the foundation of the church, the "true Church" will be characterized by "community in faith," says Oasis.[75] The "true Church" turns out to be the *unity* (the third notion important to Oasis) between renewed parts of different churches and renewed Christians, i.e., the Oasis movement. At the bottom of this unity rests an idea about a "true" community where participants share the same belief. The unity is in this way established by generating the homogenization of belief.

In the normalization process of Oasis, the idea of the necessary renewal becomes intelligible in relation to a secularized Church of Sweden. A surprising outcome of the ideas in Oasis is therefore that the evangelization is not directed to secularized people in Sweden, but to secularized Christians, especially in Church of Sweden.

"The Leadership," as well as the "inspirers" and the "theological advisers," plays a significant part of this normalization process. They are the ones that organize conferences, give lectures, write in *Oasbladet*, inspire parishes by their Oasis talk, and give theological explanations of the Oasis talk. Important statements from the movement, like on homosexual marriage, are signed with the label "the Leadership."[76] All these different persons share the Oasis talk, and this is the foundation of the disciplinary power that, through fundamental ideas, establish the "true Church" as normative.

---

73. See for instance advertise of a network in 2/2009, 3, and Långström's invitation to Oasis' summer meeting in 2011, in *Oasbladet* 4/2010, 15.

74. See for instance Nordlander's reasoning about living in accordance with God, as the Bible express it, in *Oasbladet* 4/2010, 2. Through the renewal, parishes as well as disciples will be filled with "grace and truth" (*Oasbladet* 4/2010, 13).

75. See for instance Gärtner, "Vara kvar eller inte?," 9–10.

76. "Oasrörelsen i Sverige uttalar sig om könsneutral vigselordning."

PART TWO: Exploring a Heritage—Influences

Disciplinary Power in the Alpha Movement

One way to describe how the disciplinary power works in the Alpha talk is as follows: in the ideas of discipleship the true Christian is established through construction of the truth of the Bible, in a careful formation of leaders and witnesses. All of these are constitutive parts of the normalization process where the idea of a "true Christian" becomes normality and other ways of thinking about being Christian are ruled out.

One of the prerequisites in Alpha is that people who come to the course are immature, not seldom also unhappy, lost, and in acute hunger for something real that they have not been able to find in life so far.[77] They are also often living a questionable moral and "un-Christian" lifestyle, such as living together without being married, being criminals, being alcoholics, or accepting abortion or homosexuality.[78] If someone leaves the course before it ends, it is interpreted as if the person has fallen way to the temptations in this world.[79] Participation in the course is the only way to become a *true Christian*. There are really no alternatives to Alpha's Christianity, what is presented is the true Christian belief.

Participants become disciples through personally held lectures, caring in small groups, and intercession: both by taking part of them and by being told about their significance. All this is made possible by establishing the truth of the Bible, which is referred to as universal and taken for granted.[80] Through many Bible citations (a big part of the lectures actually consists of Bible citations) and narratives, the message of the Alpha movement is formed as something objective and absolutely true.[81]

Leader training is a crucial part of the Alpha course. It is the leaders that make Alpha happen and by their presence ensure and convince the participants about the truth of Alpha. Every leader and help leader is supposed to go to a counseling education course three times, but new leaders mainly learn by observing "old" ones.[82] There are also three DVDs for leaders in which Gumbel lectures on the topic.

---

77. See witnesses in Gumbel, *Handboken om Alpha*, for instance 57–62, 79–83, 97–99.

78. Ibid., 15, 20.

79. See for instance ibid., 90.

80. Sjödin, "To the Reader," 10: "Alpha peels of the cultural layers and meets the human of the 1990s with her own questions . . . in a relaxed way."

81. Gumbel, *Handboken om Alpha*, 122.

82. Ibid., 110.

A vital part of Alpha is also the witness. Within the handbook on Alpha a chapter of testimony follows every "fact chapter." The peak, or kernel message, of the testimonies are the shift the testifiers felt in life when going to an Alpha course.[83] The witnesses become proofs for the truth of Alpha. They legitimize the message and ensure that the conversion will happen if the participants follow the course to the end.

The leaders and the witnesses share the Alpha talk and in so doing are part of the disciplinary power that through the fundamental ideas establish the "true Christian" as normative.

Oasis and Alpha as Interplaying and Conflicting Truth-Claiming Processes

As normalization processes the two movements Oasis and Alpha overlap each other. The truth of the Bible is used and established in both processes, just as passionate and caring leaders/witnesses.

An interesting thing with both movements is that they appeal to people without analyzing the contemporary society at any length. The story of the church is intact. To evangelize is to mediate a specific "language," to offer a cultural and linguistic phenomenon out of which individuals can interpret their life. Successful Christian evangelization, therefore, "is not primarily apologetics to those outside but catechesis to those who have joined."[84] This is what Alpha and Oasis do, although in different ways.

But even if the two movements share some characteristics, they also differ. The disciplinary power that the Alpha movement expresses could be understood as an innocent pedagogical mechanism: the movement forms individuals into disciples of Alpha's belief by stating what it is to be a "true Christian." But in a discursive power perspective the compulsion to evangelize, the desire to lead people to a "true" Christian belief is a violent force that excludes protests and criticism. In this way the openness to "all questions" is an illusionary openness, hiding that the truth that is enabled by the normalization process is not absolute but relative to the ideas.[85] This homogenization trait of Alpha is partly the reason why it has been called

---

83. Se for instance the witness of Martin Bennett in Gumbel, *Handboken om Alpha*, 57–65; and Gumbel, *Alpha: Livets frågor*, 123.

84. Tomlin and Millar, "Assessing Aspects of the Theology of Alpha Courses," 259.

85. See also Hunt, "The Alpha Course and Its Critics," 6.

"an evangelical McDonaldisation" by Stephen Hunt, professor of sociology in England."[86]

The Oasis movement on the other hand comes forth as a movement made possible by dissociation on an organizational level. It is therefore possible to describe the disciplinary power in Oasis as a demagogical mechanism: the movement forms individuals into renewed Christians of Oasis standard by stating what the "true Church" is. The Oasis talk makes the establishment of the "true Church" possible through the demagogical mechanism that is represented as necessary and inescapable. The inescapability is an effect of the hidden interpretation and the "true Church" is in this way a violent expression of the talk.

The violent expression of the two movements can be interpreted as emerging out of a conflict: a conflict of ideas, life, truth, and power. Oasis and Alpha are antagonistic discourses fighting over the correct interpretation. But they also, in different manners, fight with Church of Sweden at large. Oasis does this by separating on an organizational level, challenging the institutional leadership in Church of Sweden by establishing an alternative leadership, and by separating inspirers and theological advisers. Oasis exists because of an apprehended lack in Church of Sweden. Alpha challenge Church of Sweden on the same points, but do so in a different way. The emphasis on lay leadership based on divine gifts puts leadership based on theological education in question. The homogenization trait of both the movements challenges Church of Sweden's identity as a church with a "high degree of comprehensiveness."[87]

The Pressure to Become Truly Spiritual

In the beginning I said that Oasis and Alpha are two rather peripheral movements in Church of Sweden. Two conditions put that into question. First, many adherents become active members in Church of Sweden and some even leaders. Oasis is especially challenging Church of Sweden on an organizational level.

Second, the fact that Alpha comes in a convenient package attracts more and more parishes in Church of Sweden, not only the ones that are part of the Swedish Evangelical Mission (Swedish *EFS*, the Evangelical wing of Church of Sweden). This means that conservative evangelical theology may be the first interpretation of Christian belief a new arrival

---

86. Ibid., 7.
87. See "Identity of the Church."

in the church will meet. And they tend to come back, and stay. This is the experience of, for instance, the parish in Sollentuna and S:ta Clara in Stockholm, but also other parishes.[88] Alpha in particular is challenging Church of Sweden on the level of interpretation.[89]

But, as a final reflection, Oasis and Alpha do something more out of a discursive perspective. They infuse a sort of insecurity in established churches. Their conviction is that nothing less than everyone is at stake when it comes to spirituality, the restless feeling that we must give more of our heart, our time, our will, and our thoughts to the loving but righteous God. This is what these kinds of highly truth-claiming movements hope for, so also within Church of Sweden. Oasis and Alpha challenge the truth and authenticity of Church of Sweden's spiritual expressions, they emphasize that there is more to do and believe. The time will show what impact this interpretation of Christian belief will have on Church of Sweden in the long run.

Bibliography

"Alpha—grundkurs i kristen tro." Online: http://www.svenskakyrkansollentuna.com/templates/Page____2287.aspx (accessed 21/06/2010).

Alpha Nytt. Online: http://www.alphasverige.org/Alphanytt.html (accessed 21/06/2010).

Alvarsson, Jan-Åke. "Pentekostal, evangelikal och karismatisk: Definitioner av några viktiga begrepp." In *Pingströrelsen—rötter och identitet*, edited by Claes Waern and Jan-Åke Alvarsson, 40–49. Stockholm: Libris, 2007.

Andersson, Leif. "Omvändelse—för vilka?" *Oasbladet* 1/2011.

Aro, Stefan. "Värdefullare än guld." *Oasbladet* 1/2010.

Bundy, David D. "European Pietist Roots of Pentecostalism." In *The New International Dictionary of Pentecostal and Charismatic Movements*, edited by Stanley M. Burgess, 610–13. Grand Rapids: Zondervan, 2002.

Börjesson, Gustav. "Hur det började." *Oasbladet* 4/2009.

Foucault, Michael. *Diskursens ordning.* Translated by Mats Rosengren. Symposion bibliotek; Moderna franska tänkare 15. Stockholm: Brutus Östlings, [1971] 1993.

———. *Övervakning och straff: Fängelsets födelse.* Translated by C. G. Bjurström. 4th edition. Arkiv moderna klassiker. Lund: Arkiv förlag [1975] 2003.

Frykman, Peter. "Kastalakyrkan. Kungälv." *Oasbladet* 3/2010.

Gumbel, Nicky. *Alpha: Livets frågor: En möjlighet att utforska meningen med livet.* Sollentuna: Alpha Sverige, 2006.

———. *Handboken om Alpha.* Revised by Aili Lundmark. Sollentuna: Alpha Sverige, 2006.

Gärtner, Bertil. "Vara kvar eller inte?" *Oasbladet* 3/2009.

88. Stadell, "Lärande i smågrupp—Alpha," 7; and *Alpha Nytt* 2010, 10.
89. Cf. Marie Thomsen in this book.

PART TWO: Exploring a Heritage—Influences

Hunt, Stephen. "The Alpha Course and Its Critics: An Overview of the Debates." *Penteco Studies* 4 (2005) 1–22.
"Identity of the Church." Online: http://www.svenskakyrkan.se/default. aspx?id=657792 (accessed 17/04/2011).
Jonsson, Martin. "Appelvikshöjds kyrka. Varberg." *Oasbladet* 3/2010.
"Kontakt." Online: http://www.alphasverige.org/kontakt.html (accessed 18/04/2011).
Kärkkäinen, Veli-Matti. *Pneumatology: The Holy Spirit in Ecumenical, International, and Contextual Perspective.* Grand Rapids: Baker Academic, 2002.
"Ledningsgruppen." Online: http://www.jesusmanifestationen.se/viewNavMenu. do?menuID=35 (accessed 15/04/2011).
Lindsten, Jan. "Hon är ledare men inte präst: 'Kristendomen är i kris i Sverige.'" *Borås Tidning*, 23 July 2008.
Ljungman, Staffan. "Vad är andedop?" *Oasbladet* 4/2009.
Långström, Hakon. "Jag kallar er vänner." *Oasbladet* 3/2009.
"Material." Online: http://www.alphasverige.org/material.html (accessed 18/04/2011).
Milbank, John, Catherine Pickstock, and Graham Ward. *Radical Orthodoxy: A New Theology.* London/New York: Routledge, 1998.
Nordlander, Leif. "Förvandling av församlingar." *Oasbladet* 2/2010.
———. "Guds rike är nu här." *Oasbladet* 3/2010.
———. "Nu är det jul igen . . ." *Oasbladet* 4/2010.
———. "'Vägens människor'—hur ska vi hitta Guds väg?" *Oasbladet,* 3/2009.
Oasbladet. Online: http://www.oasrorelsen.se/oasbladet (accessed 21/06/2010).
"Oasrörelsen i Sverige uttalar sig om könsneutral vigselordning." Online: http://www .oasrorelsen.se/images/pdf/uttalar.pdf (accessed 21/09/2010).
"Oasshopen." Online: http://oasrorelsen.se/oasshopen. (accessed 21/06/2010).
"Om Oas-rörelsen." Online: http://oasrorelsen.se/om-oasroerelsen (accessed 21/06/2010).
"Other Leaders & Church Leadership." Online: http://www.alpha.org.nz/media-room/ leaders (accessed 05/11/2010).
Pleijel, Bengt. "Behövs omvändelse, när alla säger att jag duger som jag är?" *Oasbladet* 1/2010.
Simonsson, Berit. "Kära alla Oasvänner!" *Oasbladet* 4/2010.
Sjöberg, Stanley. "Angeläget om John Sung." *Oasbladet* 1/2009.
Sjödin, Anders-Petter. "To the Reader." In *Alpha: Livets frågor: En möjlighet att utforska meningen med livet.* Sollentuna: Alpha Sverige, 2006.
Stadell, Staffan. "Lärande i smågrupp—Alpha." *Religionspedagogisk tidskrift* 19 (2009) 613–16.
Synan, H. V. "Evangelicalism" and "Fundamentalism." In *The New International Dictionary of Pentecostal and Charismatic Movements,* edited by Stanley M. Burgess, 655–58. Grand Rapids: Zondervan, 2002.
Tomlin, Graham and Sandy Millar. "Assessing Aspects of the Theology of Alpha Courses." *International Review of Mission* 96/382–383 (July–October 2007) 256–62.
"Återevangelisering av Sverige." Online: http://www.svenskakyrkan.se/default .aspx?id=674576 (accessed 17/04/2011).

PART THREE

Exploring a Heritage

The Role of Women

THE FOUR CHAPTERS CONCERNING the situation of women seem to highlight two concerns in particular: the ordination of women and inclusive language. Although the number of women pastors and bishops is increasing, the ordination of women is still clearly an issue that generates tension. That is even more the case concerning inclusive language. A third factor that emerges in the texts is that the theological underpinnings for women's equal participation in church life in general, and for the ordination of women in particular, draw upon emancipator qualities in the theology of Martin Luther. It seems perfectly reasonable to talk about women's ordination as a Lutheran trait, found in all the four folk churches we have studied.

In the first chapter in this section, "Women's Situation in Church of Sweden," Karin Sarja's point of departure is the most recent Church of Sweden member survey; she discusses the proportion of female worshippers, the number of women employed by Church of Sweden, and the gender makeup of its leadership. Although the numbers are comparatively satisfactory, she goes on to discuss some of the obstacles women face and gives as an example the resistance that women pastors still encounter in some parts of Sweden. In her concluding remarks she reminds us that Lutheran churches claim that God can be at work in both spiritual and worldly domains and that the civil legislation protecting women's rights has been, and still is, an asset for women in Church of Sweden.

Being herself a leading voice within the feminist liturgical movement in Norway, it is hardly surprising that in her chapter, "Constructions of Gender, Liturgies, and Dichotomies," Merete Thomassen discusses women's role in Church of Norway mainly with reference to the debate on inclusive language. What becomes clear from Thomassen's account is that women are welcome in Church of Norway, but feminist theology is not. There is agreement about the importance of a more balanced representation of women and men on all levels, but a feminist critique of a masculine gendered God-talk and androcentric theology is considered to go against Christian theology.

Arnfríður Guðmundsdóttir traces the present-day situation for women in the Evangelical Lutheran Church of Iceland to both the Reformation and the first and second waves of the secular women's movement on Iceland. Although women's situation is becoming more and more equal to men's on most levels in the church, there is a clear difference if one compares the situation for women in the rural areas and Reykjavik. In the capital women are less represented whether as ordained or as members of parish councils. In contrast to the other three churches studied here, the Evangelical Lutheran Church of Iceland accommodates and supports The Women's

Exploring a Heritage

Church. This independent association, founded in 1993, organizes services and activities for women. Right from the start, The Women's Church has emphasized the need for inclusive language and female imagery when talking about God.

A quick glance at the situation in Denmark reveals that women in many ways seem to have achieved equality with men. Today, women pastors outnumber male pastors and almost half of all the members of church councils and other decision-making bodies are women. However, the Danish contribution by Else Marie Wiberg Pedersen and Benedicte Præstholm broadens the perspective from addressing only women to gender in general. While the ordination of women and equality between men and women are said to be *status confessions* in the Danish folk church, there is resistance based on a polarized essentialist understanding of gender, and so-called male activities are used to attract men. The question of whether "women's equality" has been a political issue enforced by the state rather than a theological one is quite often debated in all the four churches in this study. Pedersen and Præstholm strongly emphasize the awareness of Lutheran theology and ministry as the force behind what in Denmark today, in spite of gender-dichotomizing voices, must be described as an "institutional and theological success."

9

Women's Situation in Church of Sweden

KARIN SARJA

ON SEPTEMBER 23, 2008, Uppsala Cathedral was full when the sermon delivered by Bishop Antje Jackelén was interrupted by applause. This is not customary in Church of Sweden. In addition, this occurred during the opening service of Church of Sweden Synod, the supreme decision-making body of Church of Sweden. The Church Synod is inaugurated in the presence of the King and the Queen, the Archbishop, the thirteen diocesan bishops, and elected representatives. Bishop Jackelén's sermon was based on Acts 16:11–15, which depicts Paul, Silas, and Timothy at Philippi, a Roman colony and town in the "first Macedonian district." On the Sabbath, these men spoke with several women. The text continues:

> A certain woman named Lydia, a worshipper of God, was listening to us; she was from the city of Thyatira and a dealer in purple cloth. The Lord opened her heart to listen eagerly to what was said by Paul. When she and her household were baptized, she urged us, saying, 'If you have judged me to be faithful to the Lord, come and stay at my home.' And she prevailed upon us. (Acts 16:14–15)

In her sermon, Bishop Jackelén called the people's attention to the Acts account of the arrival of Christianity to Macedonia and Europe, and

PART THREE: Exploring a Heritage—The Role of Women

pointed out that, although Paul had envisaged something else, the first person to receive the Christian baptism on European soil was a woman. In a dream, he had heard a male voice summoning him to that part of the world. But instead of encountering a man, he meets Lydia and other women. The narrative continues from the baptism to a meal at which Lydia persuades Paul and his friends to stay in her house, and to establish a small "house church" in Philippi led by Lydia. In her sermon, Bishop Jackelén pointed out both the possibilities and the limitations for women as early as the time of the first Christian church. When Paul spoke with Lydia, he hardly used words indicating that "women should remain silent in the congregation." There is no mention of women's subordination in this passage from the Acts. A more egalitarian line of Christianity is evident here. When Antje Jackelén added the following about Lydia, Uppsala Cathedral was filled with warm applause:

> And considering that she is a dealer in purple cloth, I just cannot resist giving her a little business advice: Invest in episcopal shirts for women—that is an underdeveloped but growing market.[1]

The worshippers obviously sympathized with Antje Jackelén's words, which ultimately amounted to a desire for more women bishops in Church of Sweden. The sermon was given in 2008 during a service that was part of a fiftieth anniversary celebration in Church of Sweden, under the heading "A historic choice." It had been fifty years since the decision was made to ordain women. The anniversary attracted a great deal of attention and considerable financial support. This resulted, in particular, in the publication of two books: one anthology with contributions from researchers from different discipline, and one book in which women priests came forward with their stories about their calling, faith, and life.[2] There were those who claimed that the fifty-year-old decision was not worthy of celebration, but the reasons for this varied. Those who were against opening up the ministry to women regretted both the resolution in 1958 and the anniversary.[3] And women priests who had long lived and worked

---

1. Jackelén, "Apg 16: 11–15."

2. Hössjer Sundman, *Äntligen stod hon i predikstolen!*; *Du ska bli präst*. The decision to ordain women was made in 1958. In 1960, the first three women were ordained: Elisabeth Djurle, Ingegerd Persson, and Margit Sahlin. The book *Du ska bli präst* was written after a decision in the Church Synod.

3. For example, Dag Sandahl, a priest in Church of Sweden, continuously followed the jubilee year 2008 in his blog, commenting extensively on, and reviewing his reasons for, thinking that both the resolution and the celebration was a mistake. See "Dagblogg," e.g., September 2008.

among colleagues opposing to their ministry were not willing to take part in any celebration.[4] Conflicting feelings were provoked by celebrating a decision for which Church of Sweden had long neglected taking the full consequences necessary in supporting women priests, but had instead let them experience both opposition and harassment. At the same time, one can emphasize that Church of Sweden celebrated its fifty years with women priests joyfully, with festive services, book publications, and exhibitions. Gratitude for the women priests' services to Church of Sweden and wishes for greater equality between women and men were expressed. The celebratory slogan "A historic choice" can be said to have elucidated both the opportunities and limitations for women in the past and present in Church of Sweden.

Themes, Organization, and Material

In the present chapter, questions concerning opportunities and limitations for women in Church of Sweden will be a recurring theme. In my view, this is a fruitful way of analyzing and systematizing the body of information presented on an issue that is in itself far-reaching, namely, women's overall situation in Church of Sweden. The account will be primarily based on a statistical survey. Several aspects will be discussed, such as the proportion of female worshippers, the number of women employed by Church of Sweden, and the makeup of its leadership with regards to gender. The material for this part of the chapter has primarily been obtained from the most recent membership survey.[5] In the subsequent section, limitations affecting women in Church of Sweden will be elucidated through a concentrated case study of selected examples of resistance against women priests. This selection and focus are motivated by the fact that the complex problems related to women priests has long been central in the Swedish Church, and that the debate includes questions relevant to a chapter on the situation of women in the church. Moreover, as will be made clear below, the problems are still of immediate concern. The material for the section on limitations affecting women priests has been obtained from current sources, such as the press and the Internet, as well as from a study on the working environment in the Luleå Diocese. The concluding remarks comprise a kind of summary and a glance into the future. In other words, the present chapter will describe and discuss a number of aspects of the situation of women

4. Brandby-Cöster, "Dubbla budskap—vilket ska firas?," 162.
5. *2010 Membership Survey.*

PART THREE: Exploring a Heritage—The Role of Women

in Church of Sweden, thus providing an overall problem-oriented picture. Though the problems outlined here will be analyzed only to a limited extent, they are well worth looking at in more detail in future research.

Women in Church of Sweden Today: A Statistical Survey

With almost seven million members, Church of Sweden is the world's largest Lutheran church. It is present throughout Sweden, its organization being based on thirteen dioceses and almost 1,500 parishes. Providing a contemporary account of the situation of women in this church is thus not a trivial task, but can be partly accomplished using statistical data. Statistics on different aspects of the church can be reported, such as the proportion of female worshippers, voluntary workers, elected representatives, or employees. In many cases, the statistics may provide a perfectly satisfactory knowledge base. But it is sometimes difficult to learn about actual congregational life and how women and men, respectively, participate in the congregation.

In the most recent statistics available on participation in services in Church of Sweden, we find that just under half of the church's members had participated in services in connection with baptisms, confirmations, weddings, or funerals on some occasion in 2009, whereas slightly more than 20 percent had participated in Sunday services on a regular basis. The extent to which women and men participated in church services was largely equal. A certain statistical difference can be discerned concerning women's participation in Sunday services on a number of occasions during the year and in services in connection with confirmations, weddings, or funerals on a number of occasions throughout the year. Thus considered, the proportion of women is a few percentage points higher. For participation in connection with a baptism, confirmation, wedding, or funeral, the percentages were 29.8 percent women and 25.9 percent men. For Sunday services, the figures were 10.6 percent women and 8.5 percent men. More men than women declared that they had not been to church at all during the past year. Women are more likely to have visited Church of Sweden in connection with a service or concert.[6]

Women do different kinds of voluntary work within the church. It is known that traditionally they organize church coffee, attend to parish houses, engage in visitor groups, do needlework to provide church interiors with new textiles, and a great deal more. Knowledge is available on

6. Ibid.

important aspects of women's voluntary organizations within the church. This concerns organizations such as Women in Church of Sweden. The name of this organization dates from 1995, but its roots are in Church of Sweden's Women's Council, which was established in 1947. One of the initiators of this movement, and its chairperson for several years, was Margit Sahlin, one of the first three women to be ordained in Church of Sweden in 1960. Women in Church of Sweden had slightly more than 1,000 members in 2009. An additional example is the association Women for Mission (previously Swedish Women's Missionary Society), which was founded as early as 1903.[7] Women's commitment to and work in church sewing circles is well documented and have been important in the history of Church of Sweden. In 2003, 47,091 women participated in Church of Sweden sewing circles all over the country.[8] Over the years, sewing circles have collected considerable sums of money that have been donated to missionary work in other countries, Christian aid organizations, and parish work in the immediate area. What has been outlined here concerning women's voluntary work and organizations in the church are examples of women organizing themselves for special purposes. Women have formed organizations on the basis of their own or others' expectations that, as women, they have common interests and opportunities for identification and solidarity. In Church of Sweden, it may also have been strategically important for them to organize themselves as women in order to influence decisions, promote other women's opportunities, and demonstrate women's competence and qualifications.

From the age of sixteen, all baptized members of Church of Sweden can participate in electing members of decision-making bodies at various levels of the organization. The members of the Church Synod, the highest decision-making authority, are chosen in such elections. The Church Synod, which consists of 251 elected members, convenes once a year. According to the 2009 election results, 119 of its members are women. Thus far, no woman has served as chairperson of the Church Synod. In brief retrospect, it can be noted that the first women to participate in the Church Synod were Ester Lutteman and Gunni Hermelin. They were elected in 1938, whereas the first women priest to be elected was Christina Odenberg in 1979.[9] The Church Board, which is the board of Church of

---

7. "Kvinnor i Svenska kyrkan."
8. Wejryd, *Svenska kyrkans syföreningar 1844–2003*, 324.
9. Edqvist, *Kyrka, stat, samhälle*; Wejryd, "Inledning," 14. Odenberg was ordained 1997 as the first woman bishop in Church of Sweden.

PART THREE: Exploring a Heritage—The Role of Women

Sweden at the national level and the highest decision-making body when the Church Synod is not in session, has thirty members, including both members and deputy members, and is chaired by the Archbishop. Eleven of the thirty members are women.[10] The Church Synod appoints a number of committees for different areas of responsibility within Church of Sweden. These committees consist of approximately the same number of men and women. One exception is the Doctrinal Council, which counts the church's fourteen, predominantly male, bishops as its members and is thus obviously male dominated. Inquiring into the proportion of women and men among the elected representatives at the diocesan and congregational levels is beyond the scope of the present chapter.

Women are employed in several occupational groups in Church of Sweden. In 2009, 3,404 priests received monthly or hourly wages. Of these, 1,384 (41 percent) were women and 2,020 men. Priests can hold a number of offices. The most common position is that of assistant vicar, which can simply be described as a common parish priest. Women constitute 48 percent of this category, or 855 out of 1,795. A certain proportion of priests are vicars, which is a leading position in the church. Of the 936 vicars in Church of Sweden, only 234 (25 percent) are women. It has been pointed out that the existence of women priests is now an established fact, but that women priests in leading positions are not as widely accepted. It can also be noted that the proportion of women vicars varies greatly across dioceses. There is a considerable difference between the Dioceses of Gothenburg, for example, where the proportion of female vicars was 7 percent in 2007, and the Diocese of Visby, where that proportion amounted to 30 percent in the same year.[11]

Of the 1,180 deacons employed by Church of Sweden in 2009, as many as 1,029 (87 percent) were women. The position of deacon is, thus, largely dominated by women. Among church musicians, 1,536 of 2,452 (63 percent) are women. In Church of Sweden, there is also a large group of employees working as pedagogues, preschool teachers, youth leaders, and the like. In this group, 86 percent are women (4,277 women out of a total of 4,954). The great majority of women in the latter occupational groups are counterbalanced by male dominance in occupations such as verger and churchyard worker. In this group, the proportion of women is

---

10. "Kyrkomötet." For information in English on the General Synod, the Church Board, etc., see "Welcome to the Church of Sweden."

11. See, e.g., Engström, "Hur står det till idag då?," 34-35; *Statistics on the Proportion of Employees in Church of Sweden.*

33 percent, or 2,060 out of a total of 6,273.[12] Thus, the gendered division of labor seen on the Swedish labor market at large is also found in Church of Sweden. Women dominate in occupational groups responsible for care and the education of small children. In the church context, deacons and those working with children and youth can be considered to belong to this category. Men are, to a larger extent, employed in occupations that are technically oriented or that demand manual labor, such as churchyard work, or in leading executive positions. The impact of this general pattern is clearly demonstrated if we look at the proportion of men and women as vicars in Church of Sweden.

The Archbishop and the remaining thirteen bishops play a leading role in Church of Sweden. No woman has served as Archbishop thus far, but up to and including the year 2010, five women are currently, or have been, bishops. The first was Christina Odenberg, who held the office of bishop in the Diocese of Lund between 1997 and 2007. Later, Caroline Krook was bishop in the Diocese of Stockholm during the period 1998–2009. Today, Church of Sweden has three women bishops: Antje Jackelén, in Lund, who was ordained in 2007; Eva Brunne, in Stockholm; and Tuulikki Koivunen Bylund, in Härnösand. Both Brunne and Bylund were ordained in 2009. There are also three women among the thirteen cathedral deans. Another way of looking at the picture of women as leaders in Church of Sweden is to examine its organization at the national level, including the female leaders at that level. The divisions responsible for church law as well as cultural and educational affairs are headed by women; so is the secretariat in charge of theology and ecumenism as well as the secretariat serving the Archbishop and the Secretary General.

A revised edition of the Service Book, which contains the liturgies of Church of Sweden, is planned to appear in 2015. In the new version, the liturgical formulations are to be redrafted to offer more inclusive language in accordance with a decision of the Church Board. The fact that an inclusive liturgical language is now being considered from a gender perspective can be regarded as a consequence of increased gender awareness in the church, as well as of gender-oriented theological research into language and liturgy, among other things.[13]

---

12. All statistics obtained from the *Statistics on the Proportion of Employees in Church of Sweden.*

13. On the national secretariat of Church of Sweden, see "Vad är kyrkokansliet i Uppsala?" On the Church Service Book, see "Kyrkohandboken förnyas." For examples of research, see Edgardh, *Feminism och liturgi.*

PART THREE: Exploring a Heritage—The Role of Women

Today in Church of Sweden women have great opportunities to serve in elected bodies at the national level. The situation is probably similar at the diocesan and congregational levels, even though that has not been accounted for here. Women are also represented and, in many cases, form a majority in various occupational groups in Church of Sweden, as well as in their capacity as leaders at the national level. In addition, women constitute a considerable share of the volunteer force. On the other hand, there is a shortage of women priests in leading positions at the diocesan level, e.g., bishops and cathedral deans, and at the local level, e.g., vicars. The kind of leadership that entails a woman serving both as a leader and as a priest seems to be a rather far-off phenomenon in Church of Sweden.

Limited Opportunities for Women Priests

Within Church of Sweden, different piety traditions are represented. Among these, various opinions on roles and duties of women and men can be found. As an example we can mention the conservative Schartauan and Laestadian traditions found on the West Coast and in North Bothnia, respectively, both of which originated from revival movements in the church during the nineteenth century. In these traditions or movements, people have generally taken a conservative approach towards the role of women and there has been opposition to the ordination of women. It is even so that piety traditions that hold different opinions on questions like ecclesiology and sacramental theology still can be allied in their shared opposition against women becoming priests. Women priests in Church of Sweden are well aware of the situation and know which geographical areas dominated by a specific piety tradition might be difficult working in. These are factors that women priests have to relate too.[14] Whenever women are bold enough to apply for positions in parishes in which such a tradition predominates, it often attracts attention and causes debate. One such debate could be followed in Laestadian North Bothnia early in 2010. The local newspapers reported from the parish of Övertorneå, where the appointment of an assistant vicar had aroused heated emotions. The retiring priest was of the opinion that what was needed was "a scarred boar as assistant vicar," i.e., a thick-skinned, male clergyman. It was said that the parish was not ready for a woman priest. The parish council expressed the opinion that a woman's place in the parish was hardly that of an assistant

---

14. On the situation in the deanery of Falkenberg, Gothenburg Diocese, see "Bara 16 av 99 präster i Halland är kvinnor."

vicar. However, the council was not unanimous and a majority decided to appoint a woman.[15]

Women priests do not figure as celebrants or preachers in services of the Charismatic Oasis Movement, which is a revival movement within Church of Sweden.[16] It can further be noted that piety movements not welcoming the services of women priests have developed in certain geographical areas of Sweden. One example is the Bjärka-Säby, a mansion south of Linköping, southeastern Sweden, where a network surrounding the Christian periodical *Pilgrim* has emerged as a well-reputed center for retreats and meetings. At this location, as well as at one of the church's diocesan centers, an ecumenical clergy meeting organized in February 2011 on the initiative of *Pilgrim*, the Diocese of Linköping, and the Roman Catholic Diocese of Stockholm. Among the participants, several well known within Swedish Christianity could be found, but women priests from Church of Sweden and others serving as priests in churches in Sweden, due to the official program, were nearly invisible.[17] In the Oasis Movement, as well as in the movement surrounding *Pilgrim*, one can encounter women as leaders, but nearly no women priests.

Additional piety traditions discussed here could be mentioned. These traditions and movements are united in that they almost always advocate a way of thinking in terms of difference and distinctiveness with regard to women and men and their duties in the church as well as in society at large. Various arguments can be raised in favor of this way of perceiving gender. However, it usually leads to an opposition towards ordaining women. As is evident from the above examples, an opposition still exists in Church of Sweden of today. Yet another example can be found in a survey study commissioned by *Kyrkans Tidning* and carried out in 2008. Questions were put to 554 randomly selected acting women priests ordained between 1960 and 2007. The survey was answered by 72 percent of the group. Of these, almost 60 percent declared that they had been discriminated against on the basis of gender more than once while performing their official duties. Among the female vicars, 73 percent had experienced discrimination and/

---

15. "'Det behövs en ärrad galt'" was the headline of an article by Linda Danhall appearing in the online edition of the newspaper *Norrländska Socialdemokraten*. Additional articles were written on this Övertorneå debate as well as on the appointment of a vicar at Pajala, another North Bothnian town, in 2009.

16. See Svalfors's contribution in this volume.

17. See "Ekumeniskt präst- och pastorsmöte," an announcement in *Kyrkans Tidning*, the official periodical of Church of Sweden, For more about the periodical *Pilgrim*, see Svalfors, *Andlighetens ordning*

PART THREE: Exploring a Heritage—The Role of Women

or negative treatment. The same study further revealed that women priests in the Luleå Diocese were the most affected by discrimination: 86 percent of the women that answered the survey questions reported having been subjected to negative or discriminatory treatment while carrying out their duties as priests.[18]

The results reported on discrimination of women priests formed the basis of a study of the working environment and gender equality in the Luleå Diocese in 2008. They were also the incentive behind efforts to deal with these issues in the diocese through the project "'Att leva som vi lär'—med jämställdhet i fokus" ("'Practicing what we preach'—focusing on equal opportunities").[19] The project was carried out using a qualitative method in the form of a number of in-depth interviews with employees and elected representatives in parishes in the Luleå Diocese. It showed that a "culture of benevolence" and a "culture of conviction" built up the working environment problems that exist and that are particularly evident to women priests. In this northern diocese, there is a low church revival in the form of the Swedish Evangelical Mission (EFS) as well as the above-mentioned Laestadian revival. Both these movements have upheld the conviction that women are not meant to be priests, even though this belief is not common in the Swedish Evangelical Mission today. It is stated in the study that the culture of conviction can be utilized in a discriminatory fashion. Claiming that something is against one's theological beliefs is all it takes in order to gain acceptance for different kinds of discriminatory behavior. In this way, one does not have to argue even if the issue conflicts with the Working Environment Act or the regulations of Church of Sweden. Thus, on the basis of theological conviction, a person can be allowed to discriminate against other people without being challenged, as the culture of conviction itself contains a hierarchy in which a priest—preferably a male one—cannot be called into question. If the culture of conviction is moreover combined with the culture of benevolence, manifested as an exaggerated goodness and fear of conflict, the working environment problems become obvious and severe, not least for women priests.[20]

The 2008 study referred to in this chapter indicated that women priests are subjected to discrimination or negative treatment. The present

---

18. "Varannan kvinnlig präst utsatt för diskriminering."

19. *En kvalitativ undersökning av arbetsmiljön i Luleå stifts församlingar 2008*; "Att leva som vi lär."

20. *En kvalitativ undersökning av arbetsmiljön i Luleå stifts församlingar 2008*, 10–12.

chapter has provided additional examples of women priests' limited opportunities to practice the ministry. Their function as priests has been met with silence in the Oasis Movement and their capacity as potential officeholders has been debated, as was the case in Övertorneå. At the same time, the Luleå Diocese has expressed a readiness to change, with a view to following—in the spirit of the project "Att leva som vi lär"—civil and ecclesiastical regulations, laws, and gender equality plans that are already in place. It is thought that it is only in this way that the church can become credible and show that it does indeed practice what it preaches.[21] The legislation prohibiting gender discrimination also applies to Church of Sweden and its workplaces.[22]

Concluding Remarks

It can be difficult to foresee the future concerning the situation of women in Church of Sweden. However, note can be taken of the proportion of girls and boys among the children who are baptized and the teenagers who go through confirmation. In 2009, approximately the same number of boys and girls—slightly more than half of all children born in the Swedish population—were baptized. On the other hand, there are considerable differences among those who choose to be confirmed. Almost 15 percent more girls than boys are confirmed in Church of Sweden, irrespective of whether al fifteen-year-olds are counted or only those fifteen-year-olds who are members of the church. Of girls at age fifteen who were members in 2009, 47.5 percent were confirmed; the corresponding percentage for boys was 32.4 percent.[23] Whether these proportions will be reflected in future churchgoing congregations remains to be seen. It is, however, likely that more women than men will be sitting in the pews. These churchgoers will encounter a larger proportion of women priests, but probably not an equally large proportion of women vicars, cathedral deans, and bishops. Swedish society, as well as Church of Sweden, is marked in many ways

21. "Att leva som vi lär."
22. The Discrimination Ombudsman (DO) is a Swedish state authority working against discrimination and for all individuals' equal rights and opportunities. This function is performed principally through ensuring that the anti-discrimination legislation is followed. This legislation prohibits discrimination based on gender, gender identity or expression, ethnic affiliation, religious or other belief system, functional impairment, sexual orientation, or age. See Diskrimineringsombudsmannen.
23. *2010 Membership Survey*. Out of all fifteen-year-olds, 38.7 percent of the girls and 26.1 percent of the boys were confirmed.

PART THREE: Exploring a Heritage—The Role of Women

by equality between women and men. However, where leadership is concerned, women encounter more opposition than men do. In Church of Sweden, this seems to be particularly true of positions in which women serve as both leaders and priests. When writing this chapter four dioceses in Church of Sweden have quite recently chosen new bishops—all men. With this in mind, as well as the statistics on women vicars in the church, I think that Bishop Antje Jackelén's wish that more purple cloth should be made into episcopal shirts for women will not be fulfilled in the foreseeable future.

The situation of women in Church of Sweden today is a success story in many respects. However, it is not likely that the story will end with "... and they lived happily ever after." These doubts are based on what we know about the past and present of Church of Sweden, about the simultaneous existence of the principles of equality and gender-based super- and subordination, and about women's opportunities and obstacles. These two tendencies—which were outlined in Antje Jackalén's sermon on St. Paul's encounter with Lydia in Acts, and which researchers have astutely shown are evident in the history of Christianity—exist today and will continue to exist tomorrow. Women in Church of Sweden can rely on church history and theology that assert an egalitarian view of women and men's functions and on civil legislation prohibiting discrimination in working life and promoting gender equality.[24] As a Lutheran church, Church of Sweden may also claim that God can work in both the spiritual and worldly domains, and that therefore civil legislation protecting women's rights is an asset. However, women in Church of Sweden, particularly women priests, can also take for granted that they will confront, now and in the future, a gendered order that emphasizes men's superordination and women's subordination. This order is well documented and well known throughout the world. Even if it is defended in different ways and appears in different guises, it is still the same unequal system.

---

24. For research showing evidence of both subordination and egalitarian attitudes, see, e.g., Grenholm, "Genderisering och livsåskådningsreflexion," 83–84; Malone, *Women & Christianity*, volume 3, 299–301; Sarja, "'Jag ville vara prest,'" 76; Södling, *Oreda i skapelsen*, 378–79.

Bibliography

2010 Membership Survey. Unpublished. Analysenheten, Kyrkokansliet i Uppsala.
"Att leva som vi lär." Luleå stift. Online: http://perm.infodata.se/luleastift/projekt/
attleva/index.htm (accessed 15/11/2011).
"Bara 16 av 99 präster i Halland är kvinnor." *Hallands Nyheter*, 21 April 2010. Online:
http://hn.se/nyheter/halland/1.797658-bara-16-av-99-praster-i-halland-ar-
kvinnor?newUrl=null (accessed 15/11/2011).
Brandby-Cöster, Margareta. "Dubbla budskap—vilket skall firas?" In *Äntligen stod hon
i predikstolen!: Historiskt vägval* 1958, edited by Boel Hössjer Sundman, 162–80.
Stockholm: Verbum, 2008.
"Dagblogg." Online: http://www.ostran.se/bloggar/dagblogg (accessed 15/11/2011).
Danhall, Linda. "'Det behövs en ärrad galt.'" *Norrländska Socialdemokraten*, 11
January 2010. Online: http://www.nsd.se/nyheter/overtornea/artikel
.aspx?ArticleID=5107932 (accessed 15/11/2011).
Diskrimineringsombudsmannen. Online: http://www.do.se (accessed 15/11/2011).
Edgardh Beckman, Ninna. *Feminism och liturgi: En ecklesiologisk studie*. Stockholm:
Verbum, 2001.
Edqvist, Gunnar. *Kyrka, stat, samhälle: Hur var läget och hur är det nu?* Unpublished
manuscript. Uppsala: Kyrkorättsavdelningen, Kyrkokansliet i Uppsala, 2009.
"Ekumeniskt präst- och pastorsmöte. Jesus sade: 'Kom och ät!' 15–17 februari 2011."
Kyrkans Tidning, 7 October 2010. Online: http://www.tidskriftenpilgrim.se/
bokning_pdf/prast_pastorsmotet.pdf (accessed 15/11/2011).
Engström, Elin. "Hur står det till idag då? Från att få bli till att få vara präst." In
Äntligen stod hon i predikstolen!: Historiskt vägval 1958, edited by Boel Hössjer
Sundman, 23–42. Stockholm: Verbum, 2008.
En kvalitativ undersökning av arbetsmiljön i Luleå stifts församlingar 2008. Synovate.
Online: http://perm.infodata.se/luleastift/projekt/attleva/Synovates%20undersök
ning%20om%20arbetsmiljö%20i%20Luleå%20stifts%20församlingar%20variant
.pdf (accessed 15/11/2011).
Grenholm, Cristina. "Genderisering och livsåskådningsreflexion: Könsanalytiska
perspektiv på teologisk forskning." In *Var kan vi finna en nådig Gud?: Om
könsmaktsordning i kyrka och teologi*, edited by Anne-Louise Eriksson, 83–95.
Uppsala: Uppsala Universitet, 2002.
Hössjer Sundman, Boel. *Du ska bli präst: Livsberättelser 50 år efter kyrkomötets beslut*.
Stockholm: Verbum 2008.
―――, editor. *Äntligen stod hon i predikstolen!: Historiskt vägval* 1958. Stockholm:
Verbum, 2008.
Jackelén, Antje, "Apg 16: 11–15 (18:e Trefaldighet, I): Kyrkomötets öppnande." Online:
http://www.svenskakyrkan.se/default.aspx?id=2727&file=Sve%2fBin%c3%a4rfile
r%2fFiler%2fA83835A3-D0DA-43A7-86AB-AAF6D90A3259.pdf&filename=Bis
kop+Antje+Jackel%c3%a9ns+predikan+vid+kyrkom%c3%b6tets+%c3%b6ppna
nde%2c+23+september+2008 (accessed 15/11/2011).
"Kvinnor i Svenska kyrkan." Online: http://www.kvinnorisvenskakyrkan.se (accessed
15/11/2011).
"Kyrkohandboken förnyas." Online: http://www.svenskakyrkan.se/kyrkohandboken
(accessed 15/11/2011).

PART THREE: Exploring a Heritage—The Role of Women

"Kyrkomötet." Online: http://www.svenskakyrkan.se/kyrkomötet (accessed 15/11/2011).

Malone, Mary T. *Women and Christianity.* Volume 3: *From the Reformation to the 21st Century.* Maryknoll, NY: Orbis, 2003.

Sarja, Karin. "'Jag ville vara prest': Ida Granqvist i predikstolen 1916." In *Äntligen stod hon i predikstolen!: Historiskt vägval* 1958, edited by Boel Hössjer Sundman, 61–78. Stockholm: Verbum, 2008.

Statistics on the Proportion of Employees in Church of Sweden. Unpublished material. Svenska kyrkans Arbetsgivarorganisation, 2010.

Svalfors, Ulrika. *Andlighetens ordning: En diskursiv läsning av tidskriften Pilgrim.* Uppsala: Uppsala universitet, 2008.

Södling, Maria. *Oreda i skapelsen: Kvinnligt och manligt i Svenska kyrkan under 1920- och 30-talen.* Uppsala: Uppsala universitet, 2010.

"Vad är kyrkokansliet i Uppsala?" Online: http://www.svenskakyrkan.se/kyrkokansliet (accessed 15/11/2011).

"Varannan kvinnlig präst utsatt för diskriminering." *Dagen*, 6 March 2008. Online: http://www.dagen.se/dagen/article.aspx?id=150761 (accessed 15/11/2011).

Wejryd, Cecilia, "Inledning." In *12 kvinnor: I 1900-talets svenska kyrkohistoria*, edited by Göran Lundstedt, 9–22. Skellefteå: Artos & Norma bokförlag, 2010.

———. *Svenska kyrkans syföreningar 1844–2003.* Stockholm: Verbum 2005.

"Welcome to the Church of Sweden." Online: http://www.svenskakyrkan.se/default.aspx?di=657804 (accessed 15/11/2011).

10

Constructions of Gender, Liturgies, and Dichotomies from a Norwegian Perspective

MERETE THOMASSEN

IN 2008, A NEW Strategic Plan for gender equality in Church of Norway was adopted by Church of Norway General Synod, the highest democratic level of the church, for the period of 2009–2014.¹ The main objective of the Strategic Plan was formulated as a vision of a fellowship of "equal but different" and "gender equality between women and men, girls and boys." The Strategic Plan dealt with five areas: to gain gender equality at all hierarchical levels in Church of Norway among employees and elected representatives in church democracy; to ensure theological and political competence on gender equality; to ensure gender perspectives in worship, liturgy, deaconry and religious education; to strengthen gender equality in processes concerning democratic and structural reforms in the church; and to develop theological perspectives on physical and sexual abuse.²

Though this plan was adopted without any considerable debate, Church of Norway has decided not to use the gender-inclusive formulations that recently were suggested in a new liturgy proposal for the Sunday High Mass. The reason for this was that gender-inclusive language was

1. *Strategiplan for kjønn og likestilling.*
2. Ibid.

PART THREE: Exploring a Heritage—The Role of Women

considered as too problematic and "unclear" for common use in the main service liturgy.[3] The decision is made on the basis of a consultative hearing on the liturgy proposal. In some consultative statements, gender-inclusive language is characterized as "extreme feminist theology," "a break with our church's teaching and tradition," as a theology that "belongs to other religions than Christianity," and as "gender political activism."[4] Thus, in spite of the Strategic Plan addressing gender-inclusive language as an objective, when it comes to practical use in the Sunday service, gender-inclusive language is considered as extreme feminist theology. It is worth noting that the word "feminist" never is mentioned in the Strategic Plan, though the objectives corresponds fully with classical feminist theological objectives.

This twofold reaction seems to be typical for how questions concerning gender equality are considered in Church of Norway. The Strategic Plan shows that the church has obliged itself to be a gender-equal church. The basic rights are assured. But despite broad agreement, there are ongoing discussions on certain topics according to gender and gender equality in Church of Norway. These topics are at first glance theological, not structural. Most participants in the debates agree that women should be equally represented and partake in all discussions and decisions on every structural level. But gender topics that challenge traditional theology are considered as much more complicated than solely women's representation. When it comes to gender and power analysis of the existing theology and eventual demands for change, arguments like "extreme feminist theology" and "feminist, not Christian" are heard from voices in the church. To sum up the problem: women are welcomed in Church of Norway, but feminist theology is not, i.e., women are welcome as long as that does not challenge a masculine gendered God-talk and androcentric theology.

In the consultative statements that were written during 2009, several dichotomies occurred. Christian versus feminist is one of the most obvious. The use of gender-inclusive language awoke voices that had not been heard for several years. In 1993, a similar discussion was raised concerning liturgies that were celebrated during The Ecumenical Decade: Churches in Solidarity with Women 1988–1998.[5] But the consultative statements in 2009 showed several other dichotomies than what was pointed out 1993. One was "creation theology" versus a notion called "salvation theology."

---

3. *Gudstjenestereformen—hovedgudstjenesten*, 1.

4. *Summary of the Consultative Statements Question* 130a.

5. I analysed the argumentation in my doctoral thesis, Thomassen, *Kjønnsinkluderende liturgisk språk*.

This is not a common notion in church or in theology in Norway, but appears in the ongoing discussion of the liturgy reform. The preparatory document, which summons the consultative statements and recommends the changes in the liturgy, says: "Creation theological motifs are strengthened at the expense of salvation theological motifs."[6] The idea seems to be that creation theology does not include a soteriology. Feminist theology and creation theology are presented as radical and liberal ideas that are in conflict with Christian soteriology. A third dichotomy that appears in the consultative statements says that the proposed liturgy is anthropocentric instead of theocentric, seeing that the service is seen as a communion between people rather than a meeting with God.[7] The dichotomies of feminist versus Christian, creation theology versus salvation theology, and anthropocentric versus theocentric seem to be connected in several ways. Secularization might be a keyword in this connection. The theology and structures of Church of Norway are in agreement with a West-Nordic Lutheranism, influenced by a low church and pietistic theology, with strong resistance to so-called liberal or radical theology.[8] The dominant theological tradition is based on Lutheran Orthodoxy and religious revivalism developed from the pietistic heritage, and the lay movement is strong. Creation theology, anthropocentrism, and feminist theology seem to be dramatic moves towards liberal theology, and feminist theology is perceived as the extreme point of liberal theology. In other words, the theological foundation could be at risk in Church of Norway when God's masculinity is doubted. Gender-inclusive language is not only a question of making women visible as created in the image of God, but an attack on the last bulwark against secularization.

Discussions on Gender in Church of Norway

Since the discussion of women's rights in the late nineteenth century, women's liberation has been considered as something that was forced on the church from political and secular forces outside the church, not as a result of internal, theological processes. In the 1950s and 1960s, the debate was raging around the ordination of the first women pastor in Church of Norway, Ingrid Bjerkås. It was claimed that ordination of women was an expression of unfaithfulness to the Bible, the common Christian creed and

6. *Gudstjenestereformen—hovedgudstjenesten*, 1.
7. Ibid.
8. Thorkildsen, "Religious Identity and Nordic Identity."

tradition, and a break with the God given and universal order of creation.[9] The universal order of creation was a hierarchical conception of women subordinated to men as men were subordinated to Christ, according to Ephesians 5:21-24. The idea of the gendered spheres, which was developed in modernity and used to support the idea of the creational order, was still at play in the debate on women pastors and used to maintain dualistic and oppositional gender categories.[10] But on the other side, the arguments *for* ordination of women were also reflecting the idea of gender dualism and dichotomies. They argued that women's ability to be caring would strengthen the ministry as a whole. Women would be performing their ministry with compassion, tenderness, and caring, according to their female nature.[11] These arguments succeeded. Women's ministry was accepted in Church of Norway because women's entrance was perceived as something different from men: women would ensure gendered difference by bringing their female nature in to ministry.

These arguments are still valid in Church of Norway. An unspoken "feminism of difference" lies beneath the struggle for gender equality in the church. The Norwegian concepts *likeverd* and *likestilling* mark the difference between a feminism stressing that women and men are different but of the same value, and a feminism of gender equality. While *likeverd* expresses an acceptance of gender differences, but asks for a similar evaluation of both genders, *likestilling* demands equal rights for both genders and challenges gender dualism. In English there are no exact notions to distinguish *likeverd* from *likestilling*. "Equality" is used for both terms. To mark the distinction, in this chapter I use "equal but different" for *likeverd* and "equality" for *likestilling*. The Strategic Plan uses both concepts in its main objective: "A fellowship of "equal but different" and "equality between women and men, girls and boys." It seems to be easier to accept the thought of "equal but different" in Church of Norway, because it maintains the traditional gender dualism which is well known in church and theology. Gender equality on the other hand, is regarded as secular. The distinction between "equal but different" and "equality" can to a certain extent explain why some women are more desirable than others in Church of Norway. Women who accept the idea of "equal but different" and gender dualism fit into the oppositional gender structure. Women who want gender equality challenge the same structure and do not fit in.

9. Norderval, *Mot strømmen*.
10. Ibid., 55.
11. Elstad, ". . . om der kom kristne Kvinder paa Prækestolen."

Church of Norway has a democratic and hierarchical structure on the local, regional, and national level. The parish council corresponds to the local level, the diocese council to the regional level, and Church of Norway General Synod to the national level. These councils are obliged to the so-called 40–60 rule, according to Norwegian law, which means that every council shall have not less than 40 percent and not more than 60 percent representation of any gender.[12] At the regional and national level, this has proved to be quite possible to fulfill. But at local level, it has in small parishes proved to be difficult to reach this goal, although most parish councils manage it.

Gry Friis Eriksen made an investigation in 2004 on how gender equality was integrated at the national and regional levels in Church of Norway after the Ecumenical Decade 1988–1998. After the Ecumenical Decade, Church of Norway adopted a mainstreaming strategy to ensure gender equality, and Friis Eriksen's task was to explore whether the mainstreaming strategy was fruitful. By interviewing employees and council members at the two levels, she found a clear tendency: all the persons interviewed were clearly for gender equality. But among them, the youngest claimed that it was not necessary to make special efforts to gain gender equality, because they considered Norway to be a society with strongly integrated equality and egalitarian values.

Norway adopted The Gender Equality Act in 1978 and has in many ways been in the forefront concerning gender equality.[13] The youngest persons being interviewed were of the opinion that young people were brought up with a mentality that guaranteed the integration of gender equality. The need for special attention to gender issues was considered as unnecessary and gender equality was expected to be automatically implemented. But Friis Eriksen's investigation showed that gender equality definitely did not come automatically. By the mainstreaming strategy, gender perspectives were quickly forgotten at both the national and regional level in Church of Norway. Exceptions were found in dioceses and councils where individual employees or certain elected representatives paid special attention to gender topics. Friis Eriksen claimed the need for a double gender-equality strategy: both a mainstreaming strategy and an intentional strategy where gender equality was specially focused on in relation to each topic.

---

12. *Likestillingsloven* § 2.

13. In 2010 Norway ranked second best, after Iceland and followed by Finland and Sweden, in the World Economic Forum's *Global Gender Gap Report*.

PART THREE: Exploring a Heritage—The Role of Women

The Strategic Plan from 2008 is adopting such a double strategy. Church of Norway has to follow the Norwegian Gender Equality Act. But the Gender Equality Act contains an exception, § 2: "Exceptions for inner conditions in religious communities." These exceptions comprise religious leaders in communities where gender equality is in conflict with the religion's belief and theology. So far Church of Norway has made exceptions according to § 2, but the Gender Equality ombudsman claims that Church of Norway by its practice has demonstrated that gender equality is not in conflict with Christian belief and theology, since the religious community ordains women ministers and chooses women bishops. The consequences of leaving § 2 is under deliberation and the Norwegian Association of Women Theologians is pushing for Church of Norway to make itself fully responsible for adhering to the Gender Equality Act.

The numbers of women ministers are rapidly increasing. Church of Norway ordained the first women minister in 1961, Ingrid Bjerkås, and in 2011 a fifty-year celebration was arranged. The women studying theology now make up about 50 percent of all students. In 2008 and 2009, the total amount of ordinations counted more women than men. In 2008, 52 percent of the new ministers were women and in 2009 the proportion rose to 60 percent. Although the total number of women ministers in Church of Norway is far from dominating, this has led to a debate about the "feminization" of the church.[14] The Church Department statistics show that in 2006 the total proportion of women clergy was 19.2 percent, in 2009 25.7 percent. The number is obviously increasing, but the regional variations are also obvious. In the Diocese of Oslo, the capital of Norway, the largest percentage is to be found. In 2009 38.9 percent of the ministers in Oslo were women, but in the Diocese of Bjørgvin, the area around Bergen on the west coast, only 13.8 percent were women.

The Norwegian dioceses have quite different theological profiles and this depends on the extent to which lay movements influence the regions. The stronger the lay movements, the lower the percentage of women ministers. This corresponds with the observations of Karin Sarja in her chapter on women in Church of Sweden. Traditionally, the southern and western parts of Norway are the most influenced by lay movements and revivalism, while the central areas around Oslo, Mid Norway and Northern Norway, are not influenced to the same extent. The statistics of women ministers follows this pattern clearly.[15] However, the dioceses with the

14. "Mannefall i prestekall."
15. *Etatsstatistikk* 2009.

lowest amount of women ministers are trying to increase the amount by, e.g., encouraging women to apply for jobs. Further, the number of women deans is increasing and in 2010 four of eleven bishops were women. The first woman bishop was elected in 1993, Rose Marie Køhn, to the diocese of Hamar, located in an area where lay movements are weak. The last bishop who refused to ordain women ministers retired from his chair in 1998. In September 2011 a new head of bishops, "preses," was reintroduced in Church of Norway. The first preses is a woman, Helga Haugland Byfuglien.

Liturgy Reform in Church of Norway

In 2004, Church of Norway General Synod initiated a reform of the main liturgy for the Sunday High Mass. The vision for the liturgy reform was manifold and intended to break up the hegemonic tradition of the Norwegian service, which was last reformed 1977. The liturgical tradition in Norway has been hegemonic since 1685 and the liturgy has been approved by the king. The service has been celebrated in the same way all over the country and ministers have been obliged to follow the liturgy in every detail. No one but the minister has acted as liturgical leader and the liturgical texts have been exactly the same every Sunday during the ecclesiastical year. Since the reform of the liturgy in 1887, it is possible to trace certain influences from the first phase of the Liturgical Movement in the middle of the nineteenth century, where the liturgical heritage from the first centuries of Christianity was rediscovered and used to reconstruct a common order for the liturgy. The quest for the reform that was decided in 2004 came originally from the Youth Church Meeting in 2003, which wanted a liturgy that could reflect society in a wider sense than the existing liturgy. The Church Synod adopted the request, but broadened the arguments for why it was necessary.

First, the Church Synod wanted to include the ecumenical liturgical influences that had inspired individuals and parishes over the previous decades. Though Church of Norway for a number of reasons is perceived as low church, the ecumenical impulses have none the less reached certain parts of the church. Secondly, the need for a liturgy that made it possible to celebrate services in ways that reflected the different Norwegian contexts also encouraged the reform. Norway encompasses a large area, with different cultures and traditions in different places, not only according to theology and religious practice, but to nature, climate, population, and ways

PART THREE: Exploring a Heritage—The Role of Women

of living. This is reflected in music, language, and traditional folk culture. The most northern parts in Norway, for instance, include the Sami culture and are quite different from the urban culture in Oslo or the agrarian and fishing culture in the southern and western parts. And thirdly, because of the lay movement, it was argued that it should be possible to celebrate low church services on the basis of a common liturgical order.

The committee for worship and liturgies developed three main visions for the liturgy: contextualization, flexibility, and involvement. They wanted each parish to establish liturgical orders that could reflect their context, to make flexible liturgies that could be varied from time to time, and to ensure that parish members, church musicians, and ministers could get involved in the service, both in the preparation and the celebration of the liturgy. But inclusive language was also an aim for the committee.

Gender-Inclusive Language in Church of Norway

The committee worked from 2005 to 2007 to develop a liturgical order that corresponded with these visions. In 2008, the Church Council of Norway presented a liturgy proposal that used a moderate inclusive language: God was called "Mother" and "Father" in three different liturgical texts and the reference to the Trinity as "Creator, Redeemer and Sustainer" in a couple of texts. About 100 local parishes used the liturgy for about a year as part of a consultative process. In 2009, the parishes and the ordinary consultative bodies wrote their consultative statements that totaled 162. Gender-inclusive language was presented as a critical issue in the consultative statements. After the consultative process, the liturgy proposal was rewritten. Most of the inclusive formulations have been removed. In April 2011, the Church Council adopted the proposition, and the first Sunday of Advent the new liturgy was celebrated in all parishes in Church of Norway

In 2008, I defended my doctoral thesis, *Gender-Inclusive Liturgical Language: An Analysis of Norwegian Services during the Ecumenical Decade 1988-1998*.[16] I analyzed twelve Norwegian services that were developed and celebrated in Church of Norway during the Ecumenical Decade. Fierce debates had been raised in churches, media, and among academic theologians on the subject. The most critical reactions came in 1993, when Church of Norway National Council distributed a liturgy for March 8 to the eleven dioceses in Church of Norway. The liturgy used the formulations "Creator, Redeemer and Sustainer" and "God, Our Mother

16. Thomassen, *Kjønnsinkluderende liturgisk språk*.

and Father." In the Diocese of Stavanger, the liturgy was held back and not distributed. In the Dioceses of Bjørgvin, Agder, Borg, and Møre, it was dissuaded from use by the bishops. These dioceses are located at the western and southern parts of Norway, except Borg, which is located in the east, but covers the area where Hans Nilsen Hauge came from, and where the lay movement is dominant.[17]

The reactions voiced in the debate that carried on in newspapers, TV, and radio, in the democratic councils in the church and in academia, were structured around three main arguments: gender-inclusive language contains an unbiblical and un-Christian, even heathen, theology and anthropology; it is a break with the ecumenical and liturgical consensus; and it constructs a gendered and sexualized image of God. The arguments were strongest against the feminine metaphors where "Mother" and "She" was used in referring to God. Gender-neutral metaphors were considered to be more acceptable, except the gender-neutral formula for the Trinity "Creator, Redeemer, and Sustainer," which was said to break the ecumenical, liturgical consensus on using "Father, Son, and Holy Spirit." This discussion continued during the 1990s and the beginning of the new millennium, and Church of Norway National Council decided to work further with the subject. The discussion became more nuanced and the need for a more varied and metaphorical language on God and human beings was to a large extent accepted. When the liturgy reform was adopted in 2004, gender-inclusive language became a clear aim for the Committee on Liturgy.

The Consultative Process

The liturgical proposition of 2008 has been through an extensive consultative process. Consultative processes in Church of Norway usually comprise 40–50 consultative bodies: the bishops, the theological faculties, the church-employed labor unions, and professional bodies. This time the Church Council decided that also about one hundred parishes were to be consultative bodies, which were included by letting them use the proposed liturgy for their Sunday service over the period of a year. After the consultative period, the statements were written by the parishes and the ordinary consultative bodies. Besides that, everyone who wanted to was welcome to give voluntary consultative statements. At the end of the consultative

---

17. Hauge was one of the leading persons in the revivalist movement. See e.g., Harald Hegstad's chapter in this volume.

period, 162 statements were given, 70–90 from parishes, 40–50 from ordinary consultative bodies, and 30 voluntary statements.[18]

The consultative statements were sent electronically to the National Council secretariat. The consultative questions numbered about 130 and the answers given were both qualitative and quantitative. For some of the questions the consultative bodies were asked to answer "yes," "no," or "do not know." For other question the bodies were to give an appraisal on the extent to which the liturgy proposition reached the intended aims, or succeeded liturgically and theologically. For every question, it was possible to give comments. To summon the statements, Church of Norway National Council used professional expertise on statistics to analyze the answers. When the statements were summoned and analyzed in the autumn 2009 and spring 2010, persons from the National Council and members of the Liturgy Committee suggested changes for a new proposed liturgy based on the consultative hearing. In February 2010, the National Council secretariat presented a new proposal for a Sunday High Mass liturgy. After the consultative process, the liturgy proposition was rewritten. The presentation of the findings was made in autumn 2009 and partially presented on the website of Church of Norway. But an important player in the process of presenting the results was the Christian newspaper *Vårt Land*.[19] The conclusions drawn from the consultative results by *Vårt Land* said that gender-inclusive language was considered as the most critical issue in the consultative statements. The newspaper chose to quote only the most critical statements on inclusive language.[20]

Besides gendered language, the consultative process focused on the two other previously mentioned dichotomies: the proposed liturgy was considered as anthropocentric, not theocentric, and was said to have a creation-theological focus, especially in the new Eucharist prayers, at the cost of a "salvation theology." The new proposal, which was presented to Church of Norway National Council, was motivated by the consultative process in the preparatory paper that followed the proposal.[21] In the preparatory paper, the arguments regarding anthropocentrism versus theocentrism and creation theology versus salvation theology are quoted. On the gender-inclusive liturgical language, the quotations are more

---

18. *Gudstjenestereformen. Oppsummering av høringssvar. Hovedgudstjenesten—forslaget som helhet.*

19. "Our Country."

20. Kallestad, "Vil holde på Gud som 'Far.'"

21. *Gudstjenestereformen—hovedgudstjenesten*, 1.

nuanced in the preparatory papers. None of the most critical statements are mentioned.

The gender-inclusive language is characterized as "unclear." It is maintained as an important principle in the reform. It is said that the process of developing a functional form had not been fulfilled, but the work would continue. It also states that the traditional metaphors will not be changed in the ordinary liturgical texts, but the work will be continued in the collects which had not yet been written.[22] The preparatory paper also claims that the proposal contains a supplied use of gender-inclusive metaphors, not removing the traditional metaphors, but instead adding gender-neutral and feminine metaphor to the traditional masculine metaphors. It says that the proposal avoids combinations of masculine metaphors and dominance, e.g., not using "Almighty Father" but instead "Eternal Father." The gender-neutral formula of the Trinity as "Creator, Redeemer, and Sustainer" is removed from the proposal because "they are not obvious enough" and because "it is unclear whether God means the first person in the Trinity or the full Trinity."

Our Father has recently been translated to a more up to date language. The title of the prayer "Our Father" in Norwegian has until now been said in an old vocative form, "Fader vår." "Fader" is an old term for father, but the modern way of saying "Father" in Norwegian is "Far." The prayer has now been changed to "Vår Far."[23] In the preparatory paper regarding which Norwegian translation to use in the liturgy, it is said that the old form strengthens the metaphorical aspect in the prayer and functions as a gender-inclusive formulation and should therefore be used in the liturgy.[24]

This example from the preparatory paper shows that the notion of "inclusive language" is used quite randomly on all issues concerning metaphors and God-talk. When studying the liturgy proposal, as it stands today, it is impossible to find one single feminine metaphor for God. All the metaphors are masculine and some are gender neutral. "Creator, Redeemer, and Sustainer" has been removed from all texts. After this quite confusing presentation of the consultative statements, both from *Vårt Land* and Church of Norway National Council, and the considerations in

22. The collects has been written and treated by the democratic structures autumn 2011 and spring 2012.

23. The difference between the old and new form will in English correspond with "O thou, Our Father" and "Our Father." Thorkildsen, "Religious Identity and Nordic Identity."

24. *Gudstjenestereformen—hovedgudstjenesten*, 1.

PART THREE: Exploring a Heritage—The Role of Women

the preparatory paper on gender-inclusive language, I decided to read the consultative statements. I read all the consultative statements on questions 109 and 110, which focus on gender-inclusive language, and question 130a, which asked for perspectives on linguistic changes with theological implications. I read the summary made in the secretariat of the total consultative process and the preparatory papers that were used to prepare Church of Norway liturgy proposal. This made for interesting reading.

First of all, the utterances about gender-inclusive language are far more nuanced than the impression that was given. The questions concerning gender-inclusive language are formulated like this: "The proposal uses moderate gender-inclusive language. Do you regard this change as positive, neither positive or negative, or negative?" Besides these three alternative answers, it was possible not to answer. The bodies answered: 40.9 percent were positive, 21.4 percent neither positive or negative, 26.4 percent were negative, and 11.3 percent did not answer. This was presented as a fatal critique, but looking at the figures it is difficult to draw such conclusion simply from the figures. Only 26.4 percent were negative, and 40.9 percent were positive. Almost a third remained silent. On the question "How important do you think it is to work further on this subject until the final liturgy?" 47 percent answered "very important," 31 percent "quite important," 6 percent "not very important," and 9 percent "not important." By reading the comments, it is also interesting to see who has made comments and what they say.

As I said, the consultative bodies are ordinary bodies, consultative parishes, and voluntary bodies. On the language regarding human beings, I cannot find any critical comments from any of the groups. On the language referring to God, the critical arguments arise and not unexpectedly focus on the feminine gender metaphors for God, but also on the Trinity formula. Some of the most critical statements come from the voluntary bodies, individuals, and groups who have given statements on their own initiative.

From ordinary bodies in the Diocese of Bjørgvin, there are four similar statements that claim that changing the Trinity formula is a break with the church's teaching and tradition with classical Christian faith and with historical and actual ecumenical theory and practice. From the most conservative lay organizations with connections to the Charismatic movements, it is said explicitly that God is a man. Some bodies state that feminine metaphors feel strange and unfamiliar. The consultative parishes are less involved on the question than the ordinary bodies, but some parishes, especially on the southern coast, are very critical to feminine metaphors. The theological educational bodies clearly give the most positive evaluations. But also from the parishes come positive evaluations of the gender-inclusive language. The dichotomy "feminist/Christian" is obvious in several of the statements, but other statements gives quite opposite answers to the questions. The critical statements are clear and they were quickly referred to in the presentation in *Vårt Land* in 2009. The positive statements are also clear, and are as numerous as the critical, but there were few or any references to them in the presentation.

When it comes to the questions about creation theology versus salvation theology, it is also possible to see the dichotomies in the consultative answers. The clearest opinion comes from the Charismatic lay movement Oase (Oasis), who means to see "an apokatastasis theology in the Eucharist liturgy." The answers about theocentrism are not dominant at all in the consultative answers. It is difficult to see why the liturgy process has turned out the way it has. What does the silence from the consultative parishes mean? Almost a third of the consultative bodies remained silent. One might ask whether it is a silence of acceptance, indifference, or ignorance. In my opinion it is most likely that the parishes do not know the subject and do not want to express any opinions on it. The impression is that they neither reject nor accept it, but most of the consultative bodies agreed on the importance of a further discussion on the subject.

Feminist Theology: The Extreme Point of Secularization

Church of Norway is influenced by a strong lay movement with roots in pietistic and Lutheran orthodoxy. Feminism and feminist theology appear as an extreme position in this tradition. In the ongoing liturgy reform, Church of Norway is challenged by its own heritage and the challenges from a pluralistic society and the ecumenical church. When feminist theological objectives occur in the church, they are considered as secular, political forces which threaten the church from outside. This becomes evident especially in the discussion on gender-inclusive language, but also in the discussion on reconciliation, creation theology, and liturgical theology. In the consultative process, it seems like the lay movements are given a lot of weight in the process to hold together a church which is threatened by a pluralistic theology. The arguments against the changes are identical with the arguments that were used in the late nineteenth century on women's emancipation and in the 1950s and 1960s on women's ministry.

PART THREE: Exploring a Heritage—The Role of Women

Feminism and feminist theology is still a sign of secularization, a break with the Bible and theological and liturgical traditions. It threatens the foundation of the church.

By letting *Vårt Land* quote the most critical and conservative statements during a period of several weeks in the autumn 2009, without objections from the officials in Church of Norway, the newspaper was allowed to play an important part in shaping the opinion about the liturgy reform. It is worth noting how quoted statements seem to emphasize the connection between the conservative lay movement and the church. The positive statements were not given the same weight and seem to be considered as marginal, and even as an expression of radical feminist forces pressing the church from outside.

Though the need for making women visible is recognized, and the acceptance of women ministers is widespread, the limit is set at feminine God-talk. Though the Strategic Plan adopted by Church of Norway General Synod addresses the topic, it is never referred to. The Strategic Plan is a reality in Church of Norway, but few know of its existence. There has been hardly any attention given to the plan. If one searches the website of Church of Norway thoroughly, it is possible to find it. But it is rarely referred to and never plays an active role in the decisions made on liturgy and theology. At this point, it seems like the status quo is being maintained: women are welcomed in Church of Norway, but feminist theology is not. The consequence is that *some* women are accepted, but not all. Women and men who question and challenge gender dualism and androcentric theology to the extent of speaking about gender equality in God-talk and liturgy are not the desirable ones.

Bibliography

8. mars: Opplegg til 8 mars-gudstjenester og andre gudstjenester med kvinneperspektiv. Oslo: Kirkerådet 1996.

Bjerkås, Ingrid. *Mitt kall.* Oslo: Cappelen, 1966.

Dalen, Anne. *Norsk kvinnelig teologforenings historie 1958–2008.* Oslo: Akademisk Publisering, 2008.

Elstad, Hallgeir. ". . . om der kom kristne Kvinder paa Prækestolen . . . Kvinnelege prestar i Den norske kyrkja. Eit historisk riss." *Tidsskrift for kirke, religion, samfunn.* 1/2000, 355–68.

Etatsstatistikk 2009. Kirkeavdelingen. Fornyings, administrasjons og kirke-departementet, 2010.

Fra kirkens kvinneside: En utredning om kirken og kvinnen ved en komite nedsatt av Kirkerådet. Oslo: Andakstbokselskapet, 1979.

THOMASSEN—Constructions of Gender, Liturgies, and Dichotomies

Friis Eriksen, Gry. *Den automatiske likestillingen: Integreringen av likestillingsperspektiver i Den norske kirke etter Det økumeniske tiåret "Kirker i solidaritet med kvinner."* Oslo: Det praktisk-teologiske seminars skriftserie, 2004.

Gudstjenestereformen—hovedgudstjenesten. 1. behandling. Oslo: Kirkerådet, 2010.

Gudstjenestereformen/hovedgudstjenesten. 2. Språk. 109. Forenklet liturgisk språk. 110a. Inkluderende språk. 110b. Kjønnsinkluderende språk (Høringssvar). Oslo: Kirkerådet, 2010.

Gudstjenestereformen. Oppsummering av høringssvar. Hovedgudstjenesten—forslaget som helhet. Liturgi dok 1. Oslo: Kirkerådet, 2009.

Gudstjenestereformen. Oppsummering av høringssvar. Gudstjenestens hoveddeler. Liturgi dok 2. Oslo: Kirkerådet, 2009.

Hefte med 8. mars-liturgier. Oslo: Kirkerådet, 1995.

Hegdal, Eirin. "Gud må være Far." *Vårt Land*, 6 November 2009, 14.

Hvidsten, Leif Jørn, editor. *Noen må gå foran . . . : Festskrift til Rosemarie Köhn.* Oslo: Pax, 2006.

Kallestad, Jarle. "Vil holde på Gud som 'Far.'" *Vårt Land*, 7 November, 2009, 14.

Kjerneverdier for gudstjenesten. Nemnd for gudstjenesteliv. Oslo: Kirkerådet, 2004. Online: http://www.kirken.no/?event=doLink&famID=9326 (accessed 10/10/2010).

Kjønnsinkluderende språk: 130 språklige endringer med teologiske implikasjoner. Høringssvar. 15 October 2009. Oslo: Kirkerådet.

Lande, Gunvor. *Visjonen om likeverdet: Det økumeniske tiåret 1988-1998: Kyrkjer i solidaritet med kvinner i El Salvador og Noreg, Kenya og Japan.* Lund: Arcus, 2002.

Lein, Bente Nilsen. *Kirken i felttog mot kvinnefrigjøring.* Oslo: Universitetsforlaget, 1981.

Lindekleiv, Heidi Marie. "Hvor er Gud? Hvor radikalt?" *Vårt Land*, 3 November 2009.

———. "Kirkerådet lover mer Gud i gudstjenesten." *Vårt Land*, 2 March 2010.

Liturgi: Forslag til ny ordning for hovedgudstjenesten i Den norske kirke. Bokmål. Kirkerådet. Bergen: Eide forlag, 2008.

Liturgiske ledd til 8. Mars-gudstjeneste. Oslo: Kirkerådet, 1993.

Lov om likestilling mellom kjønnene. LOV-1978-06-09-45, updated LOV-2010-04-09-12.

Lønning, Per. *Kristen tro: Tradisjon og oppbrudd.* Oslo: Universitetsforlaget, 1989.

"Mannefall i prestekall." *Vårt Land*, 13 August 2010, 10.

Norderval, Kristin Molland. *Mot strømmen: Kvinnelige teologer i Norge før og nå.* Oslo: Land og kirke/Gyldendal Norsk Forlag, 1982.

Ordning for hovedgudstjenesten. Oslo: Kirkerådet, 2010.

Reform av kirkens gudstjenesteliv: Orientering om høringsdokumentene. Høringsbrev. Bokmål. Kirkerådet. Bergen: Eide forlag, 2008.

Saksorientering. Oslo: Kirkerådet, 2010.

Stendal, Synnøve Hinnaland. *". . . under forvandlingens lov": En analyse av stortingsdebatten om kvinnelige prester i 1930-årene.* Lund: Arcus, 2003.

Strategiplan for kjønn og likestilling i Den norske kirke 2009-2014. Oslo: Kirkerådet, 2008.

Summary of the Consultative Statements question 130a. Church of Norway National Council. Unpublished working document.

Tekstkritikk/inngangsord/samlingsdeler. Høringssvar. Oslo: Kirkerådet, 2009.

PART THREE: Exploring a Heritage—The Role of Women

Thomassen, Merete. *Kjønnsinkluderende liturgisk språk: En analyse av norske gudstjenester under Det økumeniske tiåret 1988-1998*. Dissertation, University of Oslo, 2008.

———. "Konstruksjoner av liturgier og dikotomier." *Nytt norsk kirkeblad* 5/2010, 11–15.

Thorkildsen, Dag. "Religious Identity and Nordic Identity." In *The Cultural construction of Norden*, edited by Øystein Sørensen and Bo Stråth, 137–60. Oslo: Scandinavian University Press, 1997.

11

Gender Issues and the Status of Women within the Evangelical Lutheran Church of Iceland

ARNFRÍÐUR GUÐMUNDSDÓTTIR

B<small>Y BAPTIZING GIRLS AND</small> boys, the church has made it clear that women and men are equal in the eyes of God. Unfortunately, the practice of the church has not always been in accordance with its practice of baptism. In theory as well as practice, women have frequently been allocated a secondary status to men. For the longest time, women were excluded from educational opportunities, as well as full participation in churchly activities. The Reformation in the sixteenth century affected the lives of women, not only by closing convents, but also by stressing the importance of their education. As has often been the case with movements such as the Reformation in its early stages, women enjoyed more freedom to participate in its activities than they were used to before. Even if their freedom was somewhat restricted later on when the movement had been institutionalized, significant changes still remained.[1]

The aim of this chapter is to explore the status of women within the Evangelical Lutheran Church of Iceland at the beginning of the

---

1. Guðmundsdóttir, "Lúther og konurnar," 15–17; Karant-Nunn and Wiesner-Hanks, *Luther on Women*, 8–14.

PART THREE: Exploring a Heritage—The Role of Women

twenty-first century. The status of women has changed drastically since the first woman became an ordained pastor within the Evangelical Lutheran Church of Iceland. Such changes do not happen in a vacuum. In order to understand the current situation, it is important to trace its theological as well as historical background. So even if the focus will be on the situation as it is today, it will be necessary to pinpoint theological premises that have prepared the ground, but also highlight how the societal changes called for by the women's movement has benefited women within the church.

Icelandic Society and Women's Rights

Women's campaign for equal status and equal rights with men within Icelandic society in the twentieth century affected the status of women within the Evangelical Lutheran Church of Iceland greatly. Thus, in order to understand the current situation, we have to keep in mind what was happening within society at large, but also the developments during the past century when women gradually gained rights (through law, but also through their education and consciousness raising) to become equal to men.

In the end of the nineteenth century and the beginning of the twentieth century, the main goal of the women's movement was set on women's suffrage. Icelandic women over forty years of age gained the parliamentary vote in 1915, as well as eligibility to sit in parliament. The franchise limits on women were lifted in 1920.[2] In 1911, women were granted equal access to scholarships and public office, "presumably making Iceland the first country to grant such legal rights to women. As the University of Iceland was established in 1911, the doors of this institution have always been open to women."[3] From 1880, women had a limited right (depending on their financial status) to vote and become members of parish councils. In 1889, the first woman was elected a member of a parish council (of the cathedral in Reykjavik). However, for reasons still unclear, the moderator of the meeting (who was the parish pastor) decided that the next runner up, a man, would take her seat. It was not until 1907 that women had an unconditional right to vote and to be elected as members of parish councils and in 1908 the first woman was not only elected but actually became a member of the parish council of the cathedral of Reykjavik.

2. "Women's suffrage in Iceland."

3. *Gender Equality in Iceland*, 15. See also Styrkársdóttir, *From Feminism to Class Politics*.

Following the second wave of the women's movement, the first woman pastor of the Evangelical Lutheran Church of Iceland was ordained in 1974. Since the early 1990s women have gradually become more active and more visible within the church, both in ordained ministry but also by shouldering different responsibilities through various offices. In the autumn of 1998, the Church Council of the Evangelical Lutheran Church of Iceland passed a policy on gender equality within the church, which was a clear recognition of the fact that gender equality had not yet been reached within the church.

Before we take a closer look at the gradually improving status of women within the Evangelical Lutheran Church of Iceland, it is important to pay attention to the theological background that made it possible for women to become active participants in daily activities within their church, on par with men.

Luther and the Priesthood of All Believers

The theological premises of Luther's Reformation back in the sixteenth century are significant for the changes related to women's roles within the Lutheran churches that occurred during the twentieth century. An important presupposition is Luther's criticism of the sacramental system of the Roman Catholic Church. By reducing the number of the sacraments from seven to two, granting only baptism and Holy Communion a sacramental status, Luther changed the meaning of ordination. Instead of the sacrament of ordination, Luther maintained that ordination was "nothing else than a certain rite by which the church chooses its preachers."[4] Hence, an ontological understanding of the ordination was replaced by a functional one, with the focus on the role (the function) of the pastor instead of "his" ranking within the ecclesiological hierarchy.

Significant to Luther's understanding of ordained ministry (*ministerium*)[5] was his emphasis on the pastoral standing of all baptized members of the church, what Luther called the "priesthood of all believers" (*sacerdotium*), in tune with the first letter of Peter 2:9, where it is written:

---

4. Luther, *Luther's Works*, vol. 36, 113.

5. In article V of the Augsburg Confession, the office of the ministry is defined as "the ministry of teaching the Gospel and administering the sacraments." See *The Book of Concord*, 31.

> But you are a chosen race, a royal priesthood, a holy nation, God's own people, in order that you may proclaim the mighty acts of him who called you out of darkness into his marvellous light.

Luther's idea of the priesthood of all believers was based on his emphasis on the equality of all in the eyes of God (*coram deo*), and his understanding of baptism being the ordination. In Luther's own words:

> Therefore we are all priests, as many of us are Christians. But the priests, as we call them, are ministers chosen from among us. All that they do is done in our name; the priesthood is nothing but a ministry.[6]

While Luther would argue for the importance of ordained ministry being responsible for the service of the church, he maintained that the role of every Christian, as baptized into the universal priesthood, was no less significant. Rather than implying any privileges, Luther emphasized the responsibility of those who belong to the priesthood of all believers. This is a responsibility towards their neighbors, something Luther amplifies in his treatise on *The Freedom of a Christian*. Christians are called to use their freedom to serve God through their service to their neighbor, what Luther so poignantly called being "Christs to one another."[7]

The radical difference between Luther's understanding of the priesthood of all believers and the ontological distinction between the ordained and the laity, between the spiritual estate and the worldly estate, made by the Roman Catholic Church is clearly represented in the following quotation from Luther's writing on *The Babylonian Captivity of the Church* (1520):

> Therefore I advise no one to enter any religious order or the priesthood, indeed, I advise everyone against it—unless he is forearmed with this knowledge and understands that the works of monks and priests, however holy and arduous they may be, do not differ one whit in the sight of God from the works of the rustic laborer in the field or the woman going about her household tasks, but that all works are measured before God by faith alone... Indeed, the menial housework of a manservant or maidservant is often more acceptable to God than all the fastings and other works of a monk or priest...[8]

---

6. Luther, *Luther's Works*, vol. 36, 113.
7. Luther, *Luther's Works*, vol. 31, 368.
8. Luther, *Luther's Works*, vol. 36, 78.

Behind Luther's notion about the priesthood of all believers is his understanding of *vocation* (*vocatio*). Luther was convinced that God called each individual to faith through his/her occupation, regardless of its nature, since "spiritual" occupations were in no way more valuable than the work of the laborer in the field or the woman in the house. This is how Luther laid the groundwork for a vital reassessment of the value of every occupation, including traditional women's work, which up to his time was considered of much less importance than the work of those who lived inside monasteries.[9]

A strong opponent and critique of Luther named Johannes Cochlaeus (1479–1552) realized what he called the danger of allowing women to become participants of the priesthood of all believers. Luther's translation of the New Testament into German, published in 1522, had made Cochlaeus worried that even "shoemakers and women" would be able to read it and become knowledgeable enough to dialogue with highly educated theologians, which he thought was not feasible.[10] Much less did Cochlaeus like Luther's idea of the priesthood of all believers, which encouraged women to become active participants in churchly practices. The following example of Cochlaeus's criticism of women within the Lutheran Reformation is from his biography of Luther, originally published in Latin in 1549:

> The Lutheran women, with all womanly shame set aside, proceeded to such a point of audacity that they even usurped for themselves the right and office of teaching publicly in the Church, despite the fact that Paul openly speaks against this and prohibits it. Nor were they lacking defenders among the Lutheran men, who said that Paul forbade the right of teaching to women only insofar as there were sufficient men who knew how to teach and were able to do so. But where men were lacking or neglectful, there it was most permissible for women to teach. And Luther himself had long before taught that women too were true Christian priests, and what is more, that whoever crept out of Baptism was truly Pope, Bishop, and Priest,

---

9. Despite the fact that Luther certainly shared the traditional view that women by nature were inferior to men, because of his critique of the current theology he was forced to reconsider some of his previous ideas about women. Much too little attention has been given to Luther and women so far by Lutheran scholars. For an important contribution to future studies of this particular topic, see Karant-Nunn and Wiesner-Hanks, *Luther on Women*.

10. Cochlaeus, "The Deeds and Writings of Martin Luther," 106.

according to this saying of Peter: "Moreover, you are a chosen people, a royal priesthood, a holy nation, etc."[11]

Regardless of Cochlaeus's obvious hostility towards Luther and his Reformation, from his account it is quite clear that, because of Luther's notion of the priesthood of all believers, women were granted, or took for themselves, certain freedom to teach publicly in churches. This was of course against the ancient understanding of the Christian tradition to obstruct women from teaching and preaching, even if certain women had, through the centuries, taken on the role of a teacher or a preacher, regardless of any rules and regulations.

By reiterating women's participation in the universal priesthood of the baptized, Luther acknowledged the true equality of women and men in the eyes of God. A logical conclusion would be to allow women to become participants in ordained ministry. Therefore, one should expect Luther to go all the way and start ordaining women. But he was not willing to go so far. On the contrary, Luther did not have any problem with allowing women to become active participants in the universal priesthood, but at the same time he prevented them from becoming ordained ministers.[12] Eventually, the freedom of the Christian, proclaimed by the reformer and signified by a greater respect of the individual member of the church, was not meant for women to the same extent as men. Thus, to begin with, women's participation in the universal priesthood was restricted to Scripture reading and singing in churches. There was a widespread skepticism toward women's singing and reading in church services, but soon it became a standard practice in both Wittenberg and Strasbourg, cities that both played leading roles in the advancement of the Reformation.[13]

The Evangelical Lutheran Church of Iceland's Policy on Gender Equality

The aim of the Evangelical Lutheran Church of Iceland's Policy Plan on Gender Equality is to enhance the status of women within the church.[14]

11. Ibid, 106–7.
12. Douglass, *Women, Freedom, and Calvin*, 93, 106.
13. Ibid, 87.
14. The Evangelical Lutheran Church of Iceland's Policy Plan on Gender Equality was passed in the autumn of 1998. This policy was a clear recognition of the fact that gender equality had not yet been reached within the Evangelical Lutheran Church of Iceland.

In its beginning the ancient baptismal formula from the third chapter of Paul's letter to the Galatians is quoted as a theological justification for its agenda:

> There is no longer Jew or Greek, there is no longer slave or free, there is no longer male and female; for all of you are one in Christ Jesus. (Gal 3:28)

Two instigations behind the policy plan are given. The first is the Icelandic law on the equal status and equal rights of women and men, originally passed by Althingi, the parliament of Iceland in 1976.[15] The second one comes from international church organizations, including the World Council of Churches and the Lutheran World Federation, and their promoting of member churches to implement gender equality policies within their institutions. By adopting a policy plan, the Church Council signaled its concern but also its interest in creating a true equality between women and men within the church, which should become a role model of true gender equality for the society at large.

The policy on gender equality has been in effect since January 1999. At the same time a commission was established to make sure the policy was realized. The main objectives of the policy were the following:

1. to improve the status of women within the church
2. to enforce gender equality within committees and church administrations
3. to promote equal pay and equal rights
4. to provide training and teaching material regarding gender issues
5. to reconsider language used within the church.

A revised edition of the original policy was passed by the General Synod in the autumn of 2009, with the following objectives:

1. to make sure that women and men within the church benefit from the equality validated by Icelandic law
2. to secure gender mainstreaming in church administration and within the church at large
3. to advocate gender equality as a matter of interest for everybody
4. to promote gender equality wherever it is needed

---

15. The most recent version, *Act on Equal Status and Equal Rights of Women and Men*, was passed by Althingi in 2008.

PART THREE: Exploring a Heritage—The Role of Women

5. to push for equal opportunities for women and men in administrative and authority positions
6. to secure the implementation of these objectives with an execution plan.

Women as Members within the Evangelical Lutheran Church of Iceland

As of January 1, 2010, nearly 80 percent of the Icelandic population belonged to the Evangelical Lutheran Church of Iceland. The difference between the number of women and men was small, 126,257 women and 125,230 men. The membership has been slowly decreasing during the past decade. At the same time a small but very outspoken group of people has been pushing for a clear separation of church and state. The relationship between the church and state will most likely become an important topic at the constitutional assembly taking place during the spring and summer of 2011. Its task is to revise the Icelandic constitution, including Article 62 on the status of the church.[16]

The number of women in parish councils has been gradually increasing and today there are as many female as male members of parish councils within the Evangelical Lutheran Church of Iceland, while women make up 41 percent of the chairpersons. There is, however, a significant difference between the capital area and the rest of the country, as women only make up 20 percent of the chairpersons in parishes in Reykjavik, our capital, and its suburban communities. This is very much in line with the relatively few women serving as parish pastors in the same area, where we have the biggest congregations with the biggest budget. If the church is going to take its policy on gender equality seriously, women need to be recruited and encouraged to take on such duties, as well as offered training if needed.

Women's associations within congregations have been strong supporters of church activities during the twentieth century. Women have raised money to build churches or provide whatever is needed within the church buildings. Recently, it has proved difficult to renew the membership of those associations as younger women have been reluctant to

---

16. Article 62: "The Evangelical Lutheran Church shall be the State Church in Iceland and, as such, it shall be supported and protected by the State. This may be amended by law."

become members. There are, however, a good number of women's associations within the church still going strong. After the economic collapse in the autumn of 2008, a growing number of congregations are opening their churches for knitters who gather together once or twice a month. As knitting is becoming very popular among Icelandic women, it is quite possible that this will become a trend in regular programs within parishes, an interesting opportunity for an "outreach" on behalf of the Evangelical Lutheran Church of Iceland.

An open house for parents with young children has been a part of the regular program of parish churches for at least two decades. Even if women are still the majority of participants, men are also invited. Through those open houses the churches are providing programs for stay-home moms and/or dads, as well as a forum to meet others sharing similar experiences. The program varies, but often parents are offered education of some sort, e.g., regarding childrearing or health-related issues, while the children are busy playing or participating in age appropriate activities. There is usually a time for prayer and reflection at the end of each meeting. Recently some churches have been offering special courses for young children, called "baby songs." The aim is to teach parents to sing for and with their children. The courses are held in church buildings and traditional hymns play a significant role. As women are usually the ones spending more time at home with their young children, women are more likely to participate in activities offered to parents by the church.

Women in Ordained Ministry

From 1886, Icelandic women have had the legal right to study theology in preparation for ordination, even if they were not eligible for public offices, including ordained ministry within the Evangelical Lutheran Church of Iceland, until 1911.[17] Despite the fact that women have had the legal rights to become pastors since the beginning of the twentieth century, it took decades until the first woman was ordained. The first woman finished her *Candidatus Theologie* degree at the University of Iceland in 1945, but she never became an ordained pastor within the church. The second woman to finish her theological training was Auður Eir Vilhjálmsdóttir, who did so in 1962. Twelve years later, she became the first woman to be ordained a pastor within the Evangelical Lutheran Church of Iceland. Pastors were at that time chosen by the entire congregation in general elections and

17. *Gender Equality in Iceland*, 15.

PART THREE: Exploring a Heritage—The Role of Women

candidates had to run their own campaigns, similar to what we know today from campaigns for political offices. Before she was ordained she had made several attempts to become a pastor in Reykjavík and neighboring communities. A widespread opposition against women pastors became obvious during her campaigns. Not until she had been chosen as a pastor by a congregation in a small fishing village in the rural west in the autumn of 1974 was it finally time for the church's administration to take a stand for or against women's ordination.

Given the widespread controversy regarding the ordination of women within other Scandinavian churches, the Bishop of Iceland[18] was concerned about the reaction to female pastors within the Evangelical Lutheran Church of Iceland. Nevertheless, the precedents set in Scandinavian churches became significant for his decision. After consulting with other members of the Church Council, the steering committee of the pastors' association and the two suffragan bishops, Sigurbjörn Einarsson, the current Bishop of Iceland, decided to ordain Auður Eir Vilhjálmsdóttir as the first woman to become a pastor within the church on September 29, 1974. Defending his decision in a pastoral synod meeting in the spring of 1975, Bishop Einarsson maintained that he made up his mind after becoming convinced that there were no theological reasons why women could not be ordained. He had also come to the conclusion that the danger of a split within the Evangelical Lutheran Church of Iceland based on opposition against women's ordination was not real.[19]

The subsequent ordination of women was slow to begin with. The second woman[20] was ordained in 1981, and only six women were ordained from 1974 to 1984. By 2010, 70 women had been ordained altogether. Out of 156 pastors serving within the church, there are 110 men and 46 women. According to a contract between the church and state, the state pays salaries of 138 pastors from taxes collected from members. Out of the 138 pastors paid by the state, there are 100 men and 38 women as of

---

18. There are three ordained bishops within the Evangelical Lutheran Church of Iceland. The Bishop of Iceland is the head of the Evangelical Lutheran Church of Iceland and resides in Reykjavik. Then there are two suffragan bishops, one who serves in the south and the west (residing in Skalholt), the other who serves in the north and the east (residing in Hólar).

19. Einarsson, "Prestastefna 1975," 94–95.

20. Her name is Dalla Thórðardóttir and she is the daughter of Rev. Vilhjálmsdóttir, the first woman to be ordained within the Evangelical Lutheran Church of Iceland. Thórðardóttir later became the first ordained woman to be a member of the General Synod and also the Church Council.

November 2010. 100 out of the 138 serve as parish pastors, 26 women and 74 men. Women are relatively many in specialized ministry, e.g., a woman is a pastor amongst the disabled and another woman is a pastor amongst those who are deaf. Seven pastors serve as hospital chaplains (only one is paid by the church, the others are paid by the hospitals), three women and four men. There are twelve pastors serving as deans, four women and eight men. A woman has never served as a dean in the three largest dioceses, located in Reykjavík and the neighboring communities. Out of the three individuals serving as bishops (the Bishop of Iceland and the two suffragan bishops) all are men. So far, no woman has been ordained as a bishop within the Evangelical Lutheran Church of Iceland.

The association of ordained women within the Evangelical Lutheran Church of Iceland was established in 2009. The intention of those who instigated the formation of the association was to create a forum where ordained women can get together and talk about burning issues, but also to provide stimulating workshops or courses, as well as lectures and talks.

The aim of the association is twofold:

1. to encourage cooperation and sharing of experience amongst ordained women
2. to boost the influence and participation of ordained women within the church

Almost ninety percent (61 out of 70) of the women who have been ordained since 1974 belong to the association.

Deacons

Deacons are a relatively recent addition within the Evangelical Lutheran Church of Iceland. As of now, 45 individuals in total have been ordained as deacons. From 1960 to 1981 four individuals were ordained as deacons, two men and two women. Since 1995, 41 deacons have been ordained, 37 women and four men. Originally people could not be trained as deacons in Iceland, but in 1993 the Faculty of Theology at the University of Iceland began to offer diaconal training. In the autumn of 2010, 22 deacons were serving within the Evangelical Lutheran Church of Iceland or other institutions, 19 women and three men. Given the percentage of women among ordained deacons, this has turned out to be almost exclusively a woman's profession. Most of the deacons work within parishes, hospitals, or nursing homes, thus providing stereotypical "female services" such as

PART THREE: Exploring a Heritage—The Role of Women

caretaking and teaching. The concern has been raised that because of female deacons, the increase of female pastors has not been in line with the number of women who have been eligible for ordination.

The General Synod

The General Synod is the most powerful body within the Evangelical Lutheran Church of Iceland. Members are elected every four years by a limited number of lay people and all working pastors. There are 29 members, 17 lay members and twelve ordained. The president is chosen from the group of lay members. A woman has never served as a president. The members of the General Synod elect four representatives, two lay and two ordained, to be on the Church Council, which is the administrative part of the General Synod. The president of the Church Council and its fifth member is the Bishop of Iceland. The General Synod meets annually for a week, but between the annual meetings, the Church Council is responsible to execute the synod's policies.

From 1964 to 1994, one or two women served as lay members in the General Synod each term. The first ordained woman became a member of the synod 1994. From 1998 to 2001 she was the only female member of the General Synod. She was also a member of the Church Council from 1998 to 2006. There was a significant increase of women in the General Synod serving in 2002–2005 when six women, three ordained and three lay, were elected. Lay women became close to 50 percent of the total number of lay members in 2006–2009, while women were only two out of the twelve ordained members. In the newly elected General Synod for the period 2010–2013, there are three ordained women (25 percent of the ordained members), while lay women continue to be almost half of the group of lay people (or eight out of 17).

During the period from 2002 to 2005 two women and two men together with the Bishop of Iceland (who always serves as the chair) constituted the Church Council. Only one woman, a lay person, was a member of the Church Council that served from 2006 to 2009. A newly elected Church Council for 2010–2013 has exactly the same gender composition. No ordained woman is a member of the Church Council for a second consecutive term.

The Faculty of Theology and Religious Studies, University of Iceland

Future pastors within the Evangelical Lutheran Church of Iceland are all educated at the Faculty of Theology and Religious Studies at the University of Iceland. During the academic year 1994–1995 there was for the first time an equal number of women and men constituting the student body. For the past seven years, women have represented 65–70 percent of the students.

For a long time there was no woman amongst those teaching at the Faculty of Theology and Religious Studies. Two of the seven current full time members of the faculty are women. The first woman was hired as an assistant professor on a temporary basis in 2000. She got a permanent position in 2003, and was promoted to a full professorship in 2008. The second woman joined the faculty as an assistant professor in 2008. In July 2010 the first woman became dean of the Faculty of Theology and Religious Studies.

Religious Language

The Icelandic Bible Association launched a new translation of the Old Testament in 1990.[21] The preceding translation of the entire Bible was published in 1912, but a partially revised translation came out in 1981. No mandate on inclusive language was given by the Icelandic Bible Association regarding the translation of the Old Testament. After the policy of gender equality was implemented by the General Synod in 1998 the commission on gender equality within the church repeatedly called for a gender inclusive translation of the Old Testament. The response was negative and the argument provided was that the translation was too close to being finished and it would be too expensive to revise what was already done.[22]

---

21. Whenever one raises the issue of inclusive language it is important to keep in mind that Icelandic is a very gender-specific language, with a complicated grammar system that includes three gender categories (masculine, feminine, and neutral) and four cases. Given this gender-specific nature, it is not always easy to apply the principle of inclusive language, which, for example, is much easier in languages with less complicated grammar, such as English.

22. This is the very same argument that was used during the 1980s by the Church Synod in Church of Sweden, when the language in the Service Book was discussed.

PART THREE: Exploring a Heritage—The Role of Women

When a new translation of the New Testament was instigated in 2002 the Icelandic Bible Association changed its policy, deciding it should be an inclusive translation. The neutral plural should be used instead of the masculine plural wherever it was seen as being appropriate: e.g., instead of translating "brothers" when women and men were clearly being addressed, the translation should read "brothers and sisters." Important exceptions were made regarding "key liturgical texts," which should continue to be gender exclusive. This is why, for example, the masculine plural is still being used in the Beatitudes, which is a big disappointment to those in favor of inclusive language. While texts frequently used in liturgical settings continue to be gender exclusive, the message is given that when it comes to very important texts, inclusive language is not all that important.

When the new translation of the Bible was finally ready in 2007, a heated debate broke out about the changes being made in favor of inclusive translations. Those who resisted the changes were quite vocal about their disapproval. One who actively opposed to the new translation, a leader of a theologically conservative free church, expressed his objection by buying whatever was left in stock of the old translation. He claimed he did this because the new translation was a falsification of the Word of God. It is not clear if he knew that this very same translation was claimed by those who opposed it to be straight from hell when it was originally published in 1912.

The current Book of Worship, originally intended to be a provisional edition, was approved by the General Synod in 1981. It is still being used almost thirty years later, as a new edition is still in the pipeline. The commission on equal opportunity reiterated, in a letter to the task force which is working on a new edition, the importance of the use of inclusive language in the new Book of Worship. An obvious challenge is posed by the recent Bible translation, as texts most often read in liturgical settings, as mentioned above, are exclusively masculine. Normally the most recent Bible translation is being used when texts are read during church services. Now it is up to those who are working on a new edition of the Book of Worship to provide inclusive translations, otherwise it will be left to those who are preparing church services to come up with their own inclusive versions.

The Evangelical Lutheran Church of Iceland's Hymn Book

The Hymn Book is, like the Book of Worship, currently under revision. Very few hymns in previous Hymn Books were composed by women. Only four women were among the hymn writers in the Hymn Book from 1945. Thirteen hymns out of the 532 hymns in the Hymn Book from 1972 were written by six women. In the current edition, which was published in 1997, only 13 hymns out of 700 belong to eight women. Seven out of those eight women were born before 1920. It is hard to explain why this is the case, but it is clear that women have not really "made it" into the group of recognized Icelandic hymn writers. Nevertheless, women are certainly writing religious songs, as for example in a hymnbook published by the Women's Church in 2003. Maybe it is necessary to redefine our understanding of hymns? At least something needs to be done in order to increase the number of hymns written by women in the forthcoming hymnbook.

The Women's Church

Seven women founded The Women's Church, an independent group within the Evangelical Lutheran Church of Iceland, in 1993.[23] Rev. Auður Eir Vilhjálmsdóttir, the first women to be ordained within the Evangelical Lutheran Church of Iceland in 1974, was a member of the founding group and has served as their pastor from the beginning. She served as a parish pastor in a small farming community on the south coast until 1996, when she joined the staff at the Bishop's office and was in charge of specialized ministry for women. A part of her service was to be a pastor to The Women's Church. After she retired from her job at the Bishop's office in 2007 she has continued to serve as the pastor of The Women's Church.

The Women's Church has its headquarters in a beautiful old house in the center of Reykjavik. The Women's Church receives financial support from the Evangelical Lutheran Church of Iceland and its registered members pay a moderate annual membership fee. The rest of their budget is collected at the coffee hour after worship services, when those who attend pay for their coffee and cakes, prepared by members of The Women's Church.

23. A chapter on The Women's Church figures in a recent book: Berger, *Dissident Daughters: Feminist Liturgies in Global Context*.

PART THREE: Exploring a Heritage—The Role of Women

Registered members of The Women's Church currently number around 200. All the members are invited to attend meetings once a months, where decisions are made and activities planned. The intention is to keep everybody fully informed and provide a forum where everybody can participate in the shaping of the agenda of the Women's Church.

The women hold worship services in various parish churches in Reykjavik and the neighborhood communities once a month. Twice a year they go and visit members of The Women's Church who live outside of Reykjavik, holding worship services and inviting local people. Their worship services are open for everyone, both women and men. The Women's Church has its own choir and choir director. The choir holds weekly rehearsals. Services are usually attended by around 70 people, mainly women.

There is a strong emphasis on participation of those who attend the worship services in The Women's Church.[24] Traditional parts of the Lutheran worship service are mixed with new: old hymns are sung together with new ones from their own hymnbook entitled *Brauð og rósir* (Bread and Roses, 2003). Women are encouraged to compose new music and write new hymns for the services. Communion is celebrated twice a year, in a simplified version.

On Monday evenings from September through May, members of The Women's Church are invited to participate in study groups where they discuss feminist theology and how their theology is affecting their everyday life. Those who choose to do so meet once a month for a Bible study, led by pastors or theologians who are members of The Women's Church. Prayer meetings are held once a month, and workshops dealing with different topics are offered on a regular basis. Groups are formed as needed, for example, a group for women who have been through a divorce and another one focusing on new models of leadership. Pastoral counseling is offered to women in need.

The Women's Church has, from the beginning, emphasized the importance of inclusive language as well as the use of female images for God. Rev. Auður Eir Vilhjálmsdóttir has written two books for her sisters: *Vinátta Guðs: Kvennaguðfræði* (The Friendship of God: Feminist Theology; 1994) and *Gleði Guðs: Sem læknar sektarkennd, kvíða, einsemd og reiði og gefur fyrirgefningu, frelsi, frið og femínisma* (The Joy of God: That Heals Guilt, Anxiety, Loneliness, and Anger, and GivesForgiveness, Freedom, Peace and Feminism; 2004). The women of the Women's Church

---

24. A big inspiration came originally from Konnamon and Gjerding, *No Longer Strangers*.

have also published an inclusive translation of selected texts from the New Testament: *Vinkonur og vinir Jesú: Valdir biblíutextar á máli beggja kynja* (The Friends of Jesus: An Inclusive Version of Selected Texts from the Bible; 1999).[25] In this book, there is a rewriting of Psalm 23 by Rev. Vilhjálmsdóttir, which, I think, summarizes in a nice way the theology characteristic of The Women's Church:

> *Psalm 23*
>
> God is my friend who has never failed me.
> She walks with me downtown and we go into my favorite restaurant.
> We sit by a table next to the window.
> She encourages me
> and helps me to understand
> some of the things I did not understand before.
> She is always like that.
>
> Even if I think everything is hopeless
> She tells me it ain't so.
> It is so great to be in her company
> I am no longer afraid of people I was afraid of before.
> I get a new self-confidence.
> Yes, I become sure of the goodness of life
> And she and I will always be friends.[26]

Conclusion

The status of women within the Evangelical Lutheran Church of Iceland has changed drastically during the second half of the twentieth century, the most dramatic change being the ordination of the first woman in 1974. Since that time women have gradually become more visible, not only as ordained pastors and deacons, but also as active members shouldering various responsibilities in the service to their church. Given its Lutheran theological context, it is my conclusion that Luther's emphasis on the priesthood of all believers has provided an important theological background for the changing status of women within the Evangelical Lutheran Church of Iceland. As baptized members of the universal priesthood women were

---

25. See Bóasdóttir, "Jesu väninnor och vänner."
26. Vilhjálmsdóttir, *Vinkonur og vinir Jesú*, 125. Translated by Arnfríður Guðmundsdóttir.

PART THREE: Exploring a Heritage—The Role of Women

able to break their silence and start singing, teaching, and writing as they did back in the sixteenth century. Even if Luther was not willing to go all the way and allow women to enter into ordained ministry, the notion of the universal priesthood still paved the way for the ordination of women within Lutheran churches all over the world in the twentieth century. The true equality of all, regardless of sex, class, race, etc., that is declared at baptism is still an objective we strive to actualize in the church. In order to help us reach our goal we make strategic plans. There is still a way to go, but the changes we have witnessed over the past decades within the Evangelical Lutheran Church of Iceland give us reasons to believe that we are on the right track.

Bibliography

Act on Equal Status and Equal Rights of Women and Men. No. 10/2008. Iceland Ministry of Welfare. Online: http://eng.velferdarraduneyti.is/acts-of-Parliament/nr/4203 (accessed 05/04/2011).

Berger, Teresa, editor. *Dissident Daughters: Feminist Liturgies in Global Context.* Louisville, KY: Westminster John Knox, 2001.

Bóasdóttir, Sólveig Anna. "Jesu väninnor och vänner: Bibeln på inklusivt språk." *Ad Lucem: Tidskrift för livsåskådning och kultur,* 1-2/2007, 14-17.

The Book of Concord: The Confessions of the Evangelical Lutheran Church, edited by Theodore G. Tappert in collaboration with Jaroslav Pelican, Robert H. Fischer, and Arthur C. Piepkorn. Philadelphia: Fortress Press, 1959.

Cochlaeus, Johannes. "The Deeds and Writings of Martin Luther from the Year of the Lord 1517 to the Year 1546 Related Chronologically to All Posterity by Johannes Cochlaeus." In *Luther's Lives: Two Contemporary Accounts of Martin Luther,* translated and annotated by Elizabeth Vandiver, Ralph Keen, and Thomas D. Frazel, 53-351. Manchester: Manchester University Press, 2002.

Constitution of the Republic of Iceland. No. 33, 17 June 1944, as amended 30 May 1984 and 31 May 1991. Online: http://confinder.richmond.edu/admin/docs/iceland2.pdf (accessed 30/03/2011).

Douglass, E. Jane Dempsey. *Women, Freedom, and Calvin.* Annie Kinkead Warfield Lectures, 1983. Philadelphia: Westminster, 1985.

Einarsson, Sigurbjörn. "Prestastefna 1975: Ávarp og yfirlit." *Kirkjuritið* 2 (1975) 85-99.

Gender Equality in Iceland: National Report to the Fourth United Nations World Conference on Women in Beijing 1995. Reykjavík: Iceland Ministry on Foreign Affairs, 1995.

Guðmundsdóttir, Arnfríður. "Lúther og konurnar." In *Kvennabarátta og kristin trú,* edited by Arnfríður Guðmundsdóttir and Kristín Ástgeirsdóttir, 15-60. Reykjavík: JPV, 2009.

"Jafnréttisstefna þjóðkirkjunnar." Online: http://kirkjan.is/jafnretti/?page_id=3 (accessed 10/11/2010).

Karant-Nunn, Susan C. and Merry E. Wiesner-Hanks, editors and translators. *Luther on Women: A Sourcebook.* Cambridge: Cambridge University Press, 2003.

Konnamon, Katherine and Iben Gjerding, editors. *No Longer Strangers*. Geneva: Lutheran World Federation, World Council of Churches, World Student Christian Federation, World Young Women's Christian Association, 1984.

Lohse, Bernhard. *Martin Luther: An Introduction to His Life and Work*. Translated by Robert C. Schultz. Philadelphia: Fortress, 1986.

Luther, Martin. *Luther's Works*. Vol. 31. Edited by Harold J. Grimm. Philadelphia: Fortress, 1957.

———. *Luther's Works*. Vol. 36, Edited by Abdel Ross Wentz. Philadelphia: Fortress, 1959.

Styrkársdóttir, Auður. *From Feminism to Class Politics: The Rise and Decline of Women's Politics in Reykjavík, 1908-1922*. Umeå: Umeå University, 1998.

Vilhjálmsdóttir, Auður Eir. *Vinkonur og vinir Jesú*. Reykjavík: Kvennakirkjan, 1999.

"The Women's Church." Online: http://www.kvennakirkjan.is/pages.php?idpage=261 (accessed 20/10/2010).

"Women's Suffrage in Iceland." Online: http://kvennasogusafn.is/index.php?page=womens-suffrage (accessed 30/03/2011).

12

The Situation for Women in the Evangelical Lutheran Church in Denmark and Its Theological Underpinning
The Oestrogenic Church?

Else Marie Wiberg Pedersen and Benedicte Præstholm

In this chapter we will highlight the situation for women in the Evangelical Lutheran Church in Denmark (the Danish folk church) from both the pastoral and the lay perspectives. Furthermore, we will bring a historical perspective into the systematic theological perspective on women's roles in the church.

Seen from a first impression, the present situation for women in the Danish folk church is characterized by equality. In 2008, 53 percent of parish council members were women, and in 2009 the proportion of women pastors passed 50 percent. Women's ordination is generally considered an institutional as well as a theological success, and women pastors have become part of the identity and self description of the folk church in the postmodern Danish society. A significant part of the picture, which perhaps distinguishes Denmark from the other Nordic countries, is the fact that feminist theology has had a relatively limited influence on the communication of the folk church. Thus, problems pertaining to gender raised by feminists or themes of feminist theology in a broader sense are not perceived as burning issues for Danish pastors.

On the basis of this description of the present situation, the relevance of the focus on women may be questioned from a Danish perspective. However, there are still issues to study and theology to discuss. Looking at the structural level, it seems to be the case that formerly, women have avoided leadership positions, whereas recent statistics suggest that women have become more interested in Church leadership and organization. Even so, only 29 out of 115 rural deans and only two out of ten bishops are women.

When it comes to theological and sociological areas, it becomes distinctly clear that the question of *women pastors* has not yet left the field of ideological struggle. This can be observed both in the media's preoccupation with women pastors (for example the construction of the problem of "the church's sex change") and in the publications of conservative theological books against women's ordination (for example *Kvinder på Herrens mark*, from 2007).

In this chapter we find it necessary to widen the perspective from the narrow focus on women to a focus that includes gender and sexuality in a broader sense. In 2009, 83 percent of Danish women were members of the folk church, while a little less than 80 percent of Danish men were members. Even though statistics do not explicitly substantiate the assumption that men in large numbers leave the Danish folk church, a growing interest and attention directed towards men and their masculinity can be observed. It is an attention that takes at least two different shapes: a conservative theological and a communicative practical.

Whereas the question of ministry and the female sex has been debated since the second half of the nineteenth century, sometimes vehemently so, the question of ministry and homosexuality curiously enough has never been a separate theme in the Danish context. However, the actual presence of homosexual pastors in the folk church may contribute to a further focusing on the democratization of the church and the humanization of ministry, which the presence of woman pastors already inaugurated. In continuation of this broadened view we will outline the Lutheran theology of ministry that characterizes the Evangelical Lutheran Church in Denmark and constitutes its self-understanding. In short the Evangelical Lutheran Church in Denmark sees itself as shaped around Luther's theology of ministry, which is detached from the minister as person but closely connected with the Word of God. This understanding of ministry goes beyond personal characteristics such as gender, and is based on, or rather anchored in, Luther's concept the priesthood of all believers as well as on his deep incarnation theology.

PART THREE: Exploring a Heritage—The Role of Women

Statistics

The statistical material regarding the active participation of women and the role of women in the Evangelical Lutheran Church in Denmark varies a bit in date and coverage. But it provides us with a good and reliable picture.[1]

Women in Ministry

2009 was a historical year for the Evangelical Lutheran Church in Denmark. Having ordained the first three women pastors in 1948, the proportion of women pastors reached a little above 50 percent of pastors in the country as a whole. Whereas the percentage of women pastors in 2008 was 49.9 percent, in 2009 it rose to 51.1 percent, an average of varying percentages from 41.1 percent in one diocese (as the lowest) to 59.1 percent in another diocese (as the highest).[2] These statistics do not include pastors functioning at hospitals or in electorate and free congregations, nor do they include pastors functioning abroad.

Two points should be accentuated in order to bring these statistics into the right perspective. First of all, it is utterly important to note that among the 51.1 percent pastors who are women, quite a number are only employed part-time, either as constituted full-time pastors for a shorter period or as pastors in a full position with a work load of typically between 20–80 percent. As a matter of fact, women make up the major part of part-time employed pastors, namely about 80 percent, an average of varying percentages from 60 percent to 95 percent in the different dioceses.[3] In contrast, among the 48.9 percent of pastors who are men, the vast majority are full-time employed in full positions, many of which are administratively and structurally higher positions. This becomes glaringly evident when we examine the distribution of positions in the ecclesial hierarchy. Then the percentage of women turns out to be significantly low, and the higher up in the hierarchy the lower the representation of women. In 2002, eleven out of 100 rural deans, i.e., about 10 percent, were women. Today, 29 out of 115 rural deans (about 25 percent) are women. This is a considerably rapid increase that probably has to do with the change of the

---

1. The following statistics are based on a survey of pastors and parish councils during 1996–2004, made for the Danish pastoral organization *Præsteforeningen*.
2. *Statistics on Pastors 2004–2009*.
3. Ibid.

function of rural deans (in 2007, the function of rural deans was reshaped from an administrative function to a leadership function). Of the ten bishops in the Evangelical Lutheran Church in Denmark, two are women (20 percent women and 80 percent men). Secondly, the fact that the share of women now amounts to 51.1 percent of the total of pastors is not the result of a steady development is important to note. Quite to the contrary, like the increase of rural deans it is the result of a rapid development over recent years after a very slow development over more than fifty years. Thus, in 1973, after twenty-five years of ordaining women, the share of women pastors was but about 1 percent. As late as 2002, after about fifty-five years of ordaining women pastors, only a little more than 33 percent of pastors were women. In other words, the recent development has been like a bubble bursting.

However, the fact that men still so univocally hold the majority of full positions as well as the majority of the actual power positions in the church brings some extremely significant nuances to the picture that should not be overlooked. There is still not equality, though numerically women pastors equal male pastors.

Women's Religious Activity in and outside the Church

When it comes to membership, the share of women pastors in many ways could be said to simply mirror the share of members of the Evangelical Lutheran Church in Denmark who are women, i.e., 52 percent. This is on the whole the case. Thus, the share of women in parish councils averaged 54 percent in 2008, having—contrary to the share of women pastors—increased steadily from 35 percent in 1973 and reaching 51 percent as early as 1996.[4] Another survey shows that women are also more active when it comes to seeking practical information about services provided by the folk church such as rituals, contacting pastors, and reading Bible texts.[5]

Nonetheless, the share of women and men is the exact opposite in parishes where election to the council is not by appointment but by vote. According to a survey from 2004 men win more places in councils to which there is an election: 47 percent women and 53 percent men (in comparison with the average of 53 percent women and 47 percent men). The numbers do not reveal why this is so, it could be that: 1) women are more passive than men (that is, women are less liable to candidate when

4. *Menighedsrådsvalgene 1996-2004*, Table 19, 88.
5. Fischer-Nielsen, *Mellem sogne- og cyberkirke*, Tables 1-4.

they have to publicly fight for a place in the church council), or 2) women are less successful than men when actively seeking election (that is, women do worse than men in the votes for the church councils). We do not know the answer. Whatever the explanation, this smaller representation of women at contested elections is interesting and could even be interpreted as alarming when we compare the share of women in church councils with the share of women voting: 56 percent of the voters were women. This means that, as voters women are more active than men in contested elections, but they are not necessarily actively working for a larger representation of women in the parish councils.

83 percent of the women are members in the Evangelical Lutheran Church in Denmark as compared to 79.7 percent of the men. Women are also the most active churchgoers and the survey shows that this activity is irrespective of the degree of traditional Lutheran faith. Many middle aged and older women go to services whether they identify with the traditional Lutheran confession or they are more generally religiously searching.[6] The same observation is made when women's activity on the Internet is measured. A survey on Internet activity shows a tendency that women are more prone to religious activity than to religious argumentation.[7] Women debate their religiosity less than they act it, irrespective of confessional "truth." In contrast, men are more prone to religious argumentation than to religious activity. Men debate religion and religious truth claims more than they act them out. Again, we do not have any concrete answer to why this is so.[8] But transcending the usual stereotypes, we throw the hypothesis that women make an active choice of utilizing existing structures, though not just in order to comply. Thus, if we take the actual changes of the Evangelical Lutheran Church in Denmark into consideration, it might be the case that—in accordance with Foucault's concepts of *discourse* and *governmentality*—women work for change from within by slowly making it act in accordance with their needs and the needs of society at large, instead of standing on the sideline of the church or even outside it debating abstract ideas and principles.[9]

6. *Menighedsrådsvalgene* 1996–2004, Table 16, 84.

7. Fischer-Nielsen, *Mellem sogne- og cyberkirke*, Appendix, Tables A and B.

8. The hypothesis launched by the author of the survey for *Præsteforeningen* (note 1) is that women think more in pictures, while men think more in concepts, referencing Deichsel, "Gemeinschaft und Gesellschaft als analytische Kategorien," 34f.

9. This hypothesis is corroborated by Sjørup, "Diskurser om ligestilling," who exactly, with Foucault's *governmentality* concept as the interpretive key, points to the fact that Danish women have formed the welfare society by working for it on the

PEDERSON *and* PRÆSTHOLM—*The Situation for Women*

But whatever way we interpret the statistics, it clearly shows that numerically women and men are fairly on par. Despite the fact that women, both as pastors and as members of the Evangelical Lutheran Church in Denmark, are more active than men, men are still univocally in power in the church organization and structure by holding the majority of full positions as well as of decidedly power positions.

Media

The news of the numerical equality between women and men pastors was broke by the then Minister of Ecclesiastical Affairs, Birthe Rønn Hornbech, on August 23, 2010, when this new historical situation was highly celebrated in the church ministry as well as in Danish media in general. Though the Minister of Ecclesiastical Affairs stated that her party was not an equal rights arrangement, Danish media celebrated the new situation as a victory of equality for Danish society. Simultaneously, they quoted the concerns of the chairperson of the Danish pastors' organization (*Præsteforeningen*), Per Bucholdt Andreasen, who, instead of expressing joy of the final obtainment of equality, expressed what has become the cliché in Denmark every time women gain terrain in a work area: women will now take over. The notion is that it will be utterly unfortunate to have only women in a sector, in this case to have only women pastors in the church. While it is true of anyone sector, trade, or institution that to be dominated by only one sex is undesirable and unfortunate, this concern is hardly ever verbalized or expressed even when men actually make up the majority in a trade or institution. In view of the impact of discourses,[10] it would have been refreshing if the chairperson for an organization of both men and women welcomed this newly achieved equality, while at the same time expressing heartfelt concerns about the deficit in women's representation in the power hierarchy. This, however, for once was the concern of the Danish media who unanimously welcomed the new situation.

The two very different ways of receiving women pastors reflect the general picture. Ever since the first three women were ordained pastors in

---

professional level, though less obvious on a political level. Sjørup states that while women's impact on a certain form of *governmentality* is less apparent on the political level, it simultaneously permeates the professional discourses for which the political system sets the frames (p. 10).

10. See Sjørup, "Diskurser om ligestilling," 8–9 (cf. note 9); and Dahlerup, "Glasloftlandet," 7–8 (cf. note 16).

PART THREE: Exploring a Heritage—The Role of Women

1948, Danish media in general have been positive towards women pastors. With few exceptions they have treated the slowly increasing presence of women pastors as a positive and right development, thereby voicing the attitude held by the majority of the Danish population. However, while most media has welcomed the growing number of female pastors and the aim of equality in the church, one politically and religiously conservative newspaper, *Kristeligt Dagblad*, has questioned this development. By way of what one could call a discourse of thick construction *Kristeligt Dagblad* has depicted the slowly increasing share of women pastors as a huge problem.

Especially since the share of female students at the theological faculties passed 50 percent in the 1980s, *Kristeligt Dagblad*'s discourse has been that of anxiety, warning its readers against women's take over [*sic!*] of the Evangelical Lutheran Church in Denmark. Later in the 1990s *Kristeligt Dagblad* started a new discourse by propagating the picture of women pastors as representatives of what was pejoratively designated "care theology." Totally ignoring the fact that female pastors have the same thorough university education in theology (six years study for the Masters of Theology) and the same pastoral education (half a year study at the pastoral seminary) as male pastors, *Kristeligt Dagblad* advanced the idea that women pastors presented a care theology rooted in bad education and bad theology of ministry.[11] The advancement of this myth was combined with the invention of a stigmatization: "the church's 'sex change.'"[12] *Kristeligt Dagblad* juxtaposed the two in a warning about "the danger of the pastor's role being defined from motherly values with a special weight put on care and human closeness."[13] Such discourse is built on two strange postulations that one would expect female readers to react against: 1) women will, irrespective of education and profession, always be "motherly"; and 2) a pastor's role should not be defined by such motherly values as care and human closeness.

Apart from the fact that the two postulations imply a dubious understanding of ministry emptied of Christian diaconal elements, the claim that female pastors as a group are different from male pastors has never been evidenced or substantiated, quite to the contrary.[14] It must

11. *Kristeligt Dagblad*, 19 Octoer 1996.
12. *Kristeligt Dagblad*, 14 March 1998.
13. Ibid.
14. Already in 1998, two studies of women pastors showed that women pastors could not be seen as a homogenous group in contrast with men pastors. The first

at best be characterized as a myth. Nevertheless, sometimes using a specific group of pastors or theologians as its mouthpiece, *Kristeligt Dagblad* programmatically advanced the myth and its implied warning during the next ten years: women pastors will take over, theology and service will thereby be in danger of losing quality, and the church will be feminized. It culminated in 2008 when the Evangelical Lutheran Church in Denmark could celebrate sixty years of ordaining women pastors. On that occasion, *Kristeligt Dagblad* two days in a row brought features on the church's sex change, going so far as to calling the folk church "the oestrogenic church."[15] Notwithstanding, this time *Kristeligt Dagblad* was, at least on the surface, more positive to the change. While suggesting that the alleged sex change of the folk church might actually mean its rescue, men apparently were avoiding the pastor's role and vestments and such concerns were mouthed by the Minister of Ecclesiastical Affairs, Birthe Rønn Hornbech. The Minister of Ecclesiastical Affairs was cited for wanting an investigation of the matter, especially pertaining to the reason why men were not attracted to either the study of theology or to function in or for the church. Again it was a reaction to unsubstantiated postulations, which seems to match a typical Danish perception of equality.[16]

It therefore was a historically new situation when *Kristeligt Dagblad* on August 23, 2010 reported the news that the 51.1 percent majority of women pastors was an questionably happy message. After so many years of warning against women pastors and their taking over of the folk church

---

study, a qualitative study by Karen Schousboe, clearly emphasized the professionalism of women pastors: office-wise, they understand themselves as Pastors (with capital P), not as primarily female in sex or gender, and they find their identity in their theology, which of course differs according to their profile. The other study, a text analysis of women's sermons, clearly demonstrates that there are no real substantial differences between women and men as preachers. The difference lies in the listeners' perception of the female pastor as more attached to responsibility and work in the home/family. See Schousboe, "Præsteliv gennem tiden" and Pedersen, "Kvindepræk?"

15. *Kristeligt Dagblad*, "Den østrogene folkekirke," 23 April 2008; and "Kirkens kønsskifte," 24 April 2008.

16. Seen from the perspective of sexual power, a limit of 30 percent representation of women in a group is perceived as equality, while a 50 percent representation of women may be perceived as a domination of women. This distribution of power and representation is corroborated by another model, "saturation without parity," according to which there is a "natural" blockage and stagnation of women's representation in local politics at 30 percent (in Denmark at 27 percent in the political landscape in comparison with 47 percent in Sweden). However, recent research points to the discourse chosen as having an enormous impact on how women's representation is perceived and thus develop. See Dahlerup, "Glasloftlandet," 5–9.

PART THREE: Exploring a Heritage—The Role of Women

with anxiety and fear, when the share of women finally passed 50 percent *Kristeligt Dagblad* surprised and reported the news with pride and joy. Its joy was further underlined by its regret that there is still quite a deficit of female rural deans and its assurance that the development is moving in the right direction towards equality also at that point.[17] The conclusion to draw from *Kristeligt Dagblad*'s features on women pastors and the much higher number of features on homosexual marriages on August 23 and 24, must be that the battle ground had shifted. The explanation for this historically new situation is most likely that *Kristeligt Dagblad* (and its conservative core readers) not only realized that the battle against women's positions within the church hierarchy is lost but also that there is now another threatening phenomenon to fight: marriage ritual for homosexuals.

Examples of Gender-Biased and Gender-Related "Theology" in the Danish Folk Church

In the same way as women's ordination in the Evangelical Lutheran Church in Denmark has been problematized from outside the church by conservative media, it is continuously problematized from the inside by a small group of conservative pastors. Unlike *Kristelig Dagblad*, these conservative theologians maintain the rejection of women pastors also under the pressure from the new threat over the debate on same-sex marriages. They understand the two gender related cases to be part of the same theological decline that allows a drifting away from the word of the Bible.

The conservative right wing has published various books and booklets on the matter of women's ordination, for example a booklet called *Det positive nej til kvindelige præster* ("The positive 'no' to women pastors") published in 1985 and the most recent book *Kvinder på Herrens mark: Essays om kvinder og menighed* ("Women in the field of the Lord: Essays about women and congregation"), published in 2007. This book, however, does not contain contributions from Danish conservatives only but also from other Scandinavian conservatives. The most central means of criticism used in the book is an essentialist and polarized understanding of gender and gender characteristics which are combined with or derived from a theology of orders of creation. This theology is constructed from biblical and historical church texts about creation and gender related social ethics (women are subordinate to men (Gen 3:16; Eph 5:22) and should

17. *Kristeligt Dagblad*, "Flere kvinder gør karriere i folkekirken," 23 August 2010; and "En munter fejring af kvindelige præster," 24 August 2010.

not speak in public (1 Cor 14:34; 1 Tim 2:11–15), for instance). All in all, it provides an ontological and ahistorical parameter for understanding and measuring gender and sexuality. It is claimed that women are born with certain unchangeable gender characteristics (not much unlike the female ideal of the nineteenth century by the way). For example, women are good at caring but incapable of teaching, because they are "more emotional than intellectual."[18] The latter is one of the "natural" and God-given reasons why women are not fit for pastoral ministry. As part of this polarized gender understanding and its claim to be rooted in God "himself" (the claim is to God's maleness) the book presents obedience and submission to the alleged divine order of creation as true liberation for women. In the true church, so the argument goes, women are freed from the pressure of resemblance to men. Women do not have to carry the burdens of men and they can serve God in their own feminine way.[19] Furthermore, the critique of and opposition to women's ordination is underpinned by an "incarnation theology" that stresses that God became a man and that this godly man chose only men, i.e., males, as apostles. In all due reality, it is an understanding of ministry as *vicarious Christi* that is totally in line with the position of papal Catholicism.

The book *Kvinder på Herrens mark* exhibits a gender biased rejection of women's ordination and at the same time expresses a theological focus on gender polarization, thereby demonstrating a positive theological focus on males as normative. Moreover, this polarized understanding not only enables the construction of both "a feminine theology" (very different from a feminist theology) and a "feminized church," but shapes the construction of a theology and church that legitimize, and thus necessitate, the conservatives' rejection of such feminization and the cultivation of a masculine counter theology.

Gender-Related Church Activities

In this chapter we have found it necessary to broaden the perspective from women to gender in general in order to also take into account the initial interest in establishing gender related church activities. We will therefore present a new treatment of gender in the Evangelical Lutheran Church in Denmark that is not linked to right-wing conservative theology.

---

18. Kristensen, *Kvinder på Herrens mark*, 11.
19. Ibid., 19.

PART THREE: Exploring a Heritage—The Role of Women

In recent years, more parish churches have experimented with gender related church activities, primarily activities designed to attract men. These initiatives are rooted in the observation that many church activities are dominated by elderly women, and many experiments seem to share the notion that the dominance by women can be broken if both content and form of church activities are changed. The point of departure is thus the same, but the new activities have taken various shapes. One form is "Service and beer,"[20] a combination of a short service in the church with subsequent tasting of beer from the local brewery. Another form is "Lunch Club for men,"[21] where elderly men gather to lunch together and simultaneously listen to invited guests such as former politicians and businessmen (in the tradition of the Lions Club or Rotary). Both these activities are for men only,[22] but there are also hybrid forms. Thus, one parish church[23] invites both men and women to meetings that, notwithstanding, focus on men with themes such as "Men and Music," "Men and Food," "Men in Literature." This same church also has evening meetings about sports, marketing, and bravery where two or three professionals briefly introduce the theme which is subsequently discussed. The traditional serving of coffee and a Danish pastry, considered feminine, has been exchanged with beer, dark bread, and salami, which are considered more masculine.

When it comes to the evaluations of the activities, pastors report that they have been successful.[24] The activities, both the ones for men only and

20. *Harndrup kirke*, Funen.

21. *Nørremarkskirken*, Vejle.

22. Two other future activities with focus on men should be mentioned. They are activities initiated by young members of conservative organisations (KFS—A Christian movement for students—and Inner Mission). In the autumn of 2011 they invited fathers and sons to what they called "a masculine weekend" in order to encourage the (special) relationship between fathers and sons. A new project in the pipeline is called Be a Man! (*Mand dig op!*), the idea of which is to incite young men to take more responsibility and to engage more in organised children's and youth's activities. In both cases, the understanding of men and women and their gender characteristics is polarized in a traditional way. Gender is not framed or explicitly theologically based, however.

23. *Thomas Kingo*, Odense.

24. Of course, church activities can be evaluated and discussed from various angles. For instance, evaluations can be combined with different theological approaches (from a dialectical "theology of the word" to an activist "theology of practice"), or it can be discussed how the relation between activities (of various kinds) and the preaching of the gospel can or should be defined: Should church activities always concern themes that can be directly related to the gospel? Can a church activity be defined by its ability to create human community or to thematize human life? Is an activity defined by its

the activities open to both sexes, have been very well attended. People who do not usually go to church have participated, as also more young people of both sexes have participated. Thus it seems that the attractiveness of the change of form and content can not only be measured on sex as a parameter but also on age. The attention on men as a focal point and the intention to offer more "masculine themes" within church activities can therefore be apprehended as a more general facelift of the traditional church activity landscape.

From a theoretical point of view, these activities and the focus on men and masculinity are based both on the fact that—of course—biologically men and women are not the same (sex), and on the important fact that gender is continuously constructed through socialization. Certain gender patterns create and recreate men and women and form our understandings and our expectations for doing gender. Since gender plays an important part in social life—as means of identification, as part of the challenges of marriage and family and so on—it makes sense to offer church activities that take masculinity (or femininity) into account. This also enables a more distinct communication and a focused approach to certain groups of people. However, such an attention to masculinity (and/or femininity) involves the risk that men (and women) gather around stereotypes (for men sports and beer, while for women needlework and tea), even though it is an obvious fact that men are not alike simply because they are men. Yet, this risk can also be found in other segment activities to some degree (for instance activities based on age). Moreover, the fact that women attended meetings with "masculine" themes shows that a dominating notion of "masculinity" is not reserved for men, and that socialized gender characteristics cannot be seen as unchangeable gender standards. Men are not only masculine and women not only feminine.

Types of Framing Gender in the Evangelical Lutheran Church in Denmark

As can be seen from the two preceding descriptions, the theme of gender is part of the folk church in two very different ways. The right-wing

---

location in the church or church buildings, and so forth? Answers to these questions are dependent on whether Christianity is primarily a cognitive or a social field, and what we consider to be Christianity's primary service. In this study, we have not been focusing on the various parameters available for evaluation. We have simply been asking if the activities were successful with respect to their initial aim: to attract men to church activities.

conservative theology employs a polarized essentialist understanding of gender, a gender biased anthropology, and a theology of orders of creation to claim that specific unchangeable gender characteristics are created by God and must be obeyed when it comes to church organization and ministry. Hence women's ordination must be rejected, the theologically intolerable feminization of the church must be criticized, and a masculine counter theology must be cultivated in order to lead the church back on track. A gendered anthropology is framed as theology and is closely linked to the understanding of creation, the will of God, sexuality, human relations, ministry, ecclesiology, and incarnation. In this theological tradition, sex and gender have become a core phenomenon.

The "masculine" church activities examined in this chapter show a completely different approach to sex and gender. The most important difference is that sex and gender are not theologically framed. Gender is at work in the socialization of human beings and is part of the lived life. This understanding of gender is seen as a chance to renew the form and content of church activities and as a practical and communicative possibility to approach and invite a group of people who rarely participate in church activities: men. Men and women display differences due to biology and culture, but masculinity and femininity are not seen as identical with man and woman, and none of these considerations are treated as theological themes. Activities for men or activities with "masculine" themes must be seen as part of a general development of diversity, as an extension of the already existing field of communities within the church context which are based on age, life situation (clubs for families or meetings for new parents), interest in literature, or choral singing and so on.[25]

Both of these approaches to gender are represented only by small groups within the Evangelical Lutheran Church in Denmark. While an increasing interest in "masculine" activities and forms can be expected, the exact opposite concern shapes the approach of the conservatives. Based on experience and observations, we anticipate a further decrease in the support for conservative gender theology.

Theology beyond Gender

Most instrumental for the present positive situation of women and for obtaining equality at all levels in the Danish folk church has been the

---

25. A segment-based church activity that we might see in the future is meetings for the so-called *rainbow families* (homosexual partnerships with children).

special relationship between church and state. There is no doubt that the folk church in the aftermath of World War II was forced to change parallel with the Danish society of which it was, and still is, part and parcel. Along with the welfare state grew a welfare church, and part of such a church was that it mirrored the heteronomy of the late modern culture and society.[26] Elements of this change were the in-depth democratization of the church institution and the humanization of ministry, for whom it became imperative to work with the competent lay people. In other words, the Danish folk church understands itself as a church from below and integral to this understanding is the complex conditions of employment of pastors, which is a combination of congregational calling and church ministerial appointment.

When the Danish state [sic] eventually, after some thirty years of hefty debate on the ordination of women in both parliament and church, allowed women to become pastors, only one word in the law text was changed: the "man" (and "he") was replaced with "person" (and "person in concern").[27] Hence, ministry was again made absolutely neutral in the law of June 4, 1947, and thus coherent with the understanding of the folk church as a framework within the Danish state. This neutrality was the result of two factors, the political and the theological, that in a complex blend still play the decisively important part in the Danish folk church. A fact that illustrates how impossible it is to totally discern the political and the theological in the Danish context, where church and state are still not separated.[28]

---

26. See Wiberg Pedersen, "Når præsten er 'køn.'"

27. "Lov om ændringer i Lov Nr. 195 af 16. April 1941 om Adgang til Præsteembeder i Folkekirken" (Act on Changes in Act no. 195 of April 16, 1941 on Access to Pastoral Offices). Paradoxically, not until the question of women pastors was raised in 1918 did politicians realize that there was no law to forbid women from becoming pastors. And when also the theological faculty stated that there were no decisive theological hindrances either—whether in the Bible, Lutheran theology, or ecclesial law—conservative politicians were on their heels. The occasion was that parliament was passing an act allowing women to hold public offices and duties. Now it became imperative to exempt women from holding public offices "to which pastoral ordination is required": "Lov om lige Adgang for kvinder og mænd til Tjenestestillinger og Hverv" (Act on equal Access for Women and Men to public Offices and Duties). See Wiberg Pedersen, *Se min kjole,* Appendix A (225–27), and Rasmussen, "Da mænd blev til personer."

28. Cf. introduction.

PART THREE: Exploring a Heritage—The Role of Women

The Political in Theology

The political factor has been a catalyst for, as well as mediator of, women's equal status in the church, in the everyday life of congregations as well as in the office of ministry. The democratization process in society and church has been coupled to a large extent. But when it comes to the question of equality between men and women, it was clearly the parliamentary democracy that provoked and enabled the democratization process in the Evangelical Lutheran Church in Denmark. It is also important to note that, though the question of equality—closely tied to a modern interpretation of Christianity—was the original and real factor when the question of women pastors was raised politically in 1918, equality after 1948 was generally underestimated and downplayed. Hence in 1978, the Danish folk church was explicitly exempted from the act on equal treatment passed on July 1, 1978, by the then Minister of Ecclesiastical Affairs, Jørgen Peder Hansen (the Social Democratic Party). Since then the shifting Ministers of Ecclesiastical Affairs and bishops have received claims to special treatment, first and foremost a special ordination that upholds the bishop's right to not give a woman the collegial handshake at the ordination ritual. This is supported by the most conservative wing of the folk church, such as Inner Mission and Luther Mission. Paradoxically, the reasons stated for these conservative claims to special treatment are no longer taken from the Bible or tradition but from the postmodern political situation: these conservative pastors and theologians claim to be those discriminated against, arguing that a special ordination will be an expression of equality. However, their claim is consequently ignored by the authorities, despite their inventive shift of arguments, which most recently, in the wake of the Mohammed cartoons, is a claim to their freedom of speech.[29] Nonetheless, from a church political viewpoint, it becomes increasingly clear that the acceptance of the ordination of women, and even the equality of women and men, has become a *status confessionis* in the Evangelical Lutheran Church in Denmark.

Thus, in January 2008, after another wave of harassment of women pastors, the question of harassment of women pastors versus the equality of women and men in the church was addressed theologically and politically. First all the bishops collectively declared that such conduct (not shaking hands) was "quite unacceptable both theologically and collegially"

29. With the exception of one diocese, Viborg, where they were allowed not giving the collegial handshake to a woman at the ordination until December 2007. See Nissen, "Official Statement."

in the spacious folk church, in which "there must be full equality between male and female pastors." This was followed by the Minister of Ecclesiastical Affairs' statement that male pastors who employ such theology to put down female pastors exceed the spaciousness of the folk church and their conduct "may lead to official sanctions."[30] As a result of the heated discussions, Bishop Kjeld Holm, from the diocese of Aarhus, questioned the full exemption from the act of equality of the folk church as a state institution, which must adapt to society and the Danish population. But on International Women's Day, March 8, 2010, the trumpets of victory for women's place in the folk church were sounded without any further discussions of equality. The argument from the head of the bishops, Bishop Kresten Drejersgaard, from the diocese of Funen, was: "one can't imagine the folk church without women pastors at all."[31] The folk church is thus the very argument for why there is equality.

The Theology behind the Politics

The theological factor behind the politics has to do with the recovery of Luther's theology and his understanding of ministry—as opposed to the Roman Catholic understanding of ministry—in the aftermath of the Luther renaissance. Lutheran theology and its particular understanding of ministry as a service of the word (*ministerium verbi*) is central—and is understood as the core of what it means to be church. In line with Luther's desacralization of ministry[32] and his focusing on the fact *that* the word is proclaimed, not on *who* proclaims and administers (i.e., irrespective of sex), pastors and bishops are understood to serve the people by preaching the word of God. Luther's rejection of a sacramental understanding of ordination as well as any special *character indelebilis* attached to such an

---

30. "Vort fælles ansvar," *Kristeligt Dagblad*, 11 January 2008. But previous statements from December 2007 can be found online; see "Folkekirken melder sig ud af kønskampen."

31. "Folkekirken melder sig ud af kønskampen."

32. Key texts are, among others: Luther's *De captivitate babylonica*, on baptism as the true ordination of all believers as pastors; *De instituendis ministris ecclesiae*, that all baptized have priestly obligations "to teach, preach, and proclaim the word of God, baptize, consecrate, and administer the Lord's supper, bind and solve from sins, pray for others, sacrifice oneself and judge all teachers and spirits"; and not least his *In epistolam S. Pauli ad Galatas*, on how pastors are elected from us and how God calls us all to the ministerial call that is also divine, through the human being—"ministri sunt ex nobis electi ... Deus vocat nos omnes ad ministerium vocatione per hominem estque divina vocatio."

PART THREE: Exploring a Heritage—The Role of Women

ordination (of only males) has been stressed in the Evangelical Lutheran Church in Denmark, which along with Luther also stresses that the pastoral office is instituted by God. Coupled with the Lutheran doctrine on the priesthood of all believers and their right calling of the pastor,[33] this Lutheran understanding of ministry has played the central role for the development of the Danish folk church and the overall positive situation for women in it.

The theological awareness of Lutheran theology and ministry was fully developed before World War II when it went hand in hand with a fully developed awareness of women's rights being on par with men, the equality of men and women instituted in the New Testament (Gal 3:27-28). But interestingly enough, the question of equality has been downplayed theologically and politically (in the church) ever since the first three women were ordained. Instead Lutheran Reformation theology has been emphasized.[34] In other words, the arguments adduced for women's equal place in the church and the ordination of women pastors have, rather than being political, been theological. Still, there is no doubt that the postwar folk church needed to change its politics to meet the needs of its members. There was a need for women pastors to meet specific needs of female members of the church, but on the whole there was a need for members to have more influence on the church. In a combination of Lutheran and Grundtvigian theology the freedom of members is accentuated, and especially the congregations' right to call whom they want as pastor among the rightly educated candidates was decisive. This has been a principal idea ever since 1947. Luther underlined the importance of the right public calling for the special ministry of the word several times, not least in his treatise *On the Councils and the Church* from 1539, in which he lists seven marks of the church. Luther stresses how each of the marks is connected with ministry—the word of God, baptism, the Lord's Supper, confession, and ministry itself instituted by God to administer these *dona hominibus*—are independent of who the pastor is and who gives the sacraments or absolves, but instead totally dependent on their being given publicly and on the recipient. Particularly important is the first *nota ecclesiae*, the word of God, by which all the others stand or fall. This word is, as Luther directly articulates it to his reader, "the external word preached orally by human beings, by you and me."[35]

33. The Augsburg Confession XIV: *rite vocatus*.
34. See for example Høgsbro, "Afsluttende replik fra Høgsbro."
35. Luther, *Von den Conziliis und Kirchen*.

It cannot be overstated that Luther, when as here expounding his central theological principles, always employs the generic term *homo*, a human being, not the gender term *vir*, a (male) man. As a continuation of this Lutheran insight, and alongside the central Lutheran teaching on ministry and the priesthood of all believers, a deep incarnation theology has been instrumental in acknowledging women as pastors and an integral part of the church at all levels. It is a deep incarnation theology, which transcends a creation theology in that it accentuates not only that man and woman are created *imago Dei* (Gen 1:26–27), but also that Christ was not incarnated male (*aner/vir*) only. Christ was incarnated truly human (*anthropos/homo*). The latter is corroborated in Scripture, which in each of the formulations emphasize the *humanity* of Jesus the Christ, not his maleness. Christ takes on human flesh (*sarx*) and is sent as a human being (*anthropos*).

It has been a focus of the Evangelical Lutheran Church in Denmark at large that no biblical text connects Christ with the gendered term man (*aner*) but exactly with the generic term human. Likewise, it has been a point of departure and part of the general discourse that in the creeds we confess to Jesus Christ as a human being, not as a male. Hence, the Nicene Creed underlines the humanity of Christ, combining his in-fleshing (*sarxothenta*) with his becoming human (*enanthropesanta*) in contrast (or in tandem) with his divine origin.

Conclusion

The situation for women in the Evangelical Lutheran Church in Denmark has, with few exceptions, improved considerably over the past fifty to seventy years. The church as such has been further democratized and the ministry humanized. The most significant factors are freedom and tolerance. The Evangelical Lutheran Church in Denmark is characterized by some sort of Lutheran "state theology," which determines its spaciousness and openness to all forms of ecclesial "Lutheranism" and leaves room to even those who do not show an equivalent conduct of tolerance as the mainstream. What will be interesting to see is if the folk church will be able to stretch its neutrality to sex and gender so much that tolerance to all believers irrespective of sexuality will be as strong as tolerance to those who are not tolerant. As the situation in Denmark shows, the discourse makes the difference.

PART THREE: Exploring a Heritage—The Role of Women

Bibliography

Dahlerup, Drude. "Glasloftlandet." Dansk kvindehistorie: Valgret 100 år. Copenhagen: Kvinfo, 2009. Online: http://www.kvinfo.dk/side/939/ (accessed 08/10/2010).

Deichsel, Alexander. "Gemeinschaft und Gesellschaft als analytische Kategorien." In *Ankunft bei Tönnies*, edited by Lars Clausen and Franz Urban Pappi, 33–41. Kiel: Mühlau, 1981.

Fischer-Nielsen, Peter. *Mellem sogne- og cyberkirke: En analyse af folkekirkens kommunikation på internettet*. Aarhus: Det teologiske Fakultet, 2011.

"Folkekirken melder sig ud af kønskampen." *Kristeligt Dagblad*, 8 March 2010. Online: http://www.kristeligt-dagblad.dk/artikel/358784:Kirke---tro--Folkekirken-melder-sig-ud-af-koenskampen?article_page=2 (accessed 18/10/2010).

Frøkjær-Jensen, Flemming. *Det positive nej til kvindelige præster*. Århus: Menigheds-fakultetet, 1985.

Høgsbro, Halfdan. "Afsluttende replik fra Høgsbro." In *Kvinden og kirkens embede*, Johs I. Hansen et al., 143–54. Copenhagen: Nyt nordisk forlag—Arnold Busck, 1959.

Kristeligt Dagblad. 19 October 1996; 14 March 1998; 11 January 2008; 23 and 24 April 2008; 08 March 2010; 23 and 24 August 2010. Online: http://www.kristeligt-dagblad.dk/.

Kristensen, Flemming Baatz. *Kvinder på Herrens mark: Essays om kvinder og menighed*. Højbjerg: Forlaget Hovedland, 2007.

Luther, Martin. De captivitate babylonica ecclesia praeludium (1520). WA 6:497–573.

———. De instituendis ministris ecclesiae (1523). WA 12:69–196.

———. In epistolam S. Pauli ad Galatas. Commentarius 1531 (1535). WA 40, 1:33–688.

———. Von den Conziliis und Kirchen (1539). WA 50:624–34.

Menighedsrådsvalgene 1996-2004—med tilbageblik. Copenhagen: Den danske Præsteforening, 2009.

Nissen, Karsten. "Official Statement." Online: http://www.viborgstift.dk/fileadmin/filer/Biskoppen/Pressemeddelelse.pdf (accessed 18/10/2010).

Pedersen, Ingelise. "Kvindepræk?" In *Se min kjole: De første kvindelige præsters historie*, edited by Else Marie Wiberg Pedersen, 32–69. Copenhagen: Samleren, 1998.

Rasmussen, Marianne. "Da mænd blev til personer." In *Se min kjole: De første kvindelige præsters historie*, edited by Else Marie Wiberg Pedersen, 108–43. Copenhagen: Samleren, 1998.

Schousboe, Karen. "Præsteliv gennem tiden." In *Se min kjole: De første kvindelige præsters historie*, edited by Else Marie Wiberg Pedersen, 10–31. Copenhagen: Samleren, 1998.

Sjørup, Karen. "Diskurser om ligestilling, velfærdsstat og kommunal politik i to generationer." Dansk kvindehistorie: Valgret 100 år. Copenhagen: Kvinfo, 2009. Online: http://www.kvinfo.dk/side/1071/ (accessed 08/10/2010).

Statistics on pastors 2004-2009. Copenhagen: Den danske Præsteforening, 2010.

Wiberg Pedersen, Else Marie. "Når præsten er 'køn.'" In *Se min kjole: De første kvindelige præsters historie*, edited by Else Marie Wiberg Pedersen, 189–222. Copenhagen: Samleren, 1998.

———, editor. *Se min kjole: De første kvindelige præsters historie*. Copenhagen: Samleren, 1998.

PART FOUR

Exploring a Heritage
Lutheran Identity

THE FOUR CHURCHES DISCUSSED in this book have all been Lutheran since the time of the Reformation. In other words, each church has a long history of building its Lutheran identity but also a long history of both influencing and being influenced by society in general. Three of the four churches are numerically very large in the family of Lutheran churches, with Church of Sweden as the largest Lutheran church in the world in terms of membership. But despite their long history and many members, all four churches are today concerned about what it means to be a Lutheran church. Up to now, they have been churches with strong ties to the state, a fact that has shaped their identity to an extent that cannot be overestimated. But now that the ties to the state have been questioned or actually cut off, when membership is declining, when immigrants belonging to other religions or denominations are coming in great numbers, and when "secularization" seems to be the catchword of the day, what does it mean to be a Lutheran church—and is such a brand name important? All four chapters in this final part deal with questions like this—but they do so in different ways, from the perspective that makes sense in each country.

In the first chapter of this section, Tomas Ekstrand writes about "The Constructing of Lutheran Identity in the Church of Sweden." Using an analytical tool developed by Johannes van der Ven, Ekstrand discusses Church of Sweden from the perspective of basis and identity. Drawing on a wide range of material, not least journals and Web material, his topics include what he calls the *semper reformanda* type and the confessional type, and how they are visible in the Swedish theological debate. He concludes that Church of Sweden must be understood as an Evangelical Lutheran church, but what that means and how it should be interpreted are debated.

In the next chapter, Steinunn Arnþrúður Björnsdóttir discusses the Lutheran identity of the Icelandic church under the heading "How Lutheran?" She asks whether the Evangelical Lutheran Church of Iceland is a recognizably Lutheran church. To answer that question she uses Luther's marks of the church as a lens when discussing some recent empirical studies of religion in Iceland. She ends by saying that Church of Iceland is a Lutheran church. Luther's marks of the church are to be found, but the church is in many ways in transition and that affects how its identity in a broader sense is to be understood.

"How Is Lutheran Identity Constructed in the Evangelical Lutheran Church of Denmark?" is the title of the third chapter, by Marie Vejrup Nielsen. A major theme is the question of *who* takes part in constructing the identity of the church. Two main issues are considered: how is Lutheran identity presented in communication between church and members, and how is Lutheran identity part of the public cultural, political and social debate? She shows that in church communication with church members, Lutheran identity is a less important concept than "folk church." On the other hand, she holds that Lutheran identity is important, not least, in the cultural and ethnic debate.

Harald Hegstad, finally, presents a picture of Church of Norway in the last chapter in this section, "The Lutheran and Ecumenical Identity of Church of Norway." He discusses what makes up the identity of Church of Norway in the light of the fact that the relationship between church and state in Norway is due to change in 2012. He starts in the past, discusses the formal basis and influences from different traditions in Norway, and ends with future challenges. He asks whether the divisive differences from the past will continue in the future or whether other challenges will replace them. He mentions immigrants from other denominations and their role in Church of Norway as an important factor when it comes to how the future identity will be shaped.

13

The Construction of Lutheran Identity in Church of Sweden

THOMAS EKSTRAND

CHURCH OF SWEDEN IS an Evangelical Lutheran church. It is defined as such both in Church of Sweden Act, which was passed by parliament in connection with the disestablishment of Church of Sweden, and in the church's own Church Ordinance.[1] Church of Sweden Act does not define the meaning of "Evangelical Lutheran" as a description of the confessional identity of Church of Sweden. The Government Committee that prepared the legislation leading to the disestablishment of the church explicitly refrained from giving a theological definition, arguing that it was up to the church to define what should be understood by the term.[2] The Church Ordinance, which is Church of Sweden's statutes, passed by the General Synod, contains a description of what "Evangelical Lutheran" means for the church:

> Church of Sweden belongs to the Evangelical Lutheran tradition with the Augsburg Confession from 1530 as its uniting confessional document. The confessions from the Reformation period

1. *The Church of Sweden Act*, § 1; *Kyrkoordningen*, 1. All references to *Kyrkoordningen* refers to the version published on Church of Sweden website.
2. For a detailed discussion of the arguments of the Government Committee, see Ekstrand, *Folkkyrkans gränser*, 55.

249

PART FOUR: Exploring a Heritage—Lutheran Identity

are guiding testimonies about how the faith was interpreted as an answer to the questions of that time.[3]

In Church of Sweden Act and in the Church Ordinance it is thus stated in no uncertain terms that Church of Sweden is Evangelical Lutheran. These documents do not, however, give a substantial definition of what this means. The Church Ordinance seems to understand it as an expression of historical continuity more than a binding and substantial definition of acceptable doctrine. But as will be shown below, this is not the whole truth, since the Ordinance also points to the Augsburg Confession as a valid summary of the faith, confession and doctrine of Church of Sweden, and to *The Book of Concord* as an explanation and commentary for the doctrine of the church.[4]

The purpose of this chapter is to discuss how Lutheran identity is constructed in the present-day Church of Sweden. The normative statements of Church of Sweden Act and the Church Ordinance make explicit references to Luther, the Reformation in general and the Lutheran Confessions, in particular when trying to define Evangelical Lutheran identity. It is therefore possible to analyze such references in wider material in order to see what is regarded as the central aspects of Lutheran identity in present-day Church of Sweden discourse. For the purpose of this chapter, it is not necessary to make a distinction between "Evangelical Lutheran" and "Lutheran." These concepts will be used synonymously throughout.

Material and Method

The material for my investigation consists primarily of published documents and Web material from Church of Sweden, mainly on a national, and to some extent on diocesan, level during the last decade. In one case I will also refer to a bishop's pastoral letter to his diocese. Another type of material will be articles in journals connected to Church of Sweden, such as *Kyrkans tidning*, *Svensk kyrkotidning*, and *Svensk pastoraltidskrift*. *Kyrkans tidning* is the leading church newspaper, reporting on news relating to Church of Sweden, other churches and religious communities, culture and politics. It is also a forum for debate on issues regarding Church of Sweden. *Svensk kyrkotidning* represents a fairly liberal theological

---

3. *Kyrkoordningen*, 4. All translations from Swedish are my own, if not otherwise stated.

4. *Kyrkoordningen*, chapter 1, § 1.

position,[5] while *Svensk pastoraltidskrift* could be described as the conservative counterpart to *Svensk kyrkotidning* and describes itself as a voice for "classical Christian faith."[6] The reason for choosing articles in these publications is that they together can be seen as representative for a wide range of theological positions and traditions.

I will structure my investigation by using a simplified version of an analytical tool developed by the Dutch theologian Johannes A. van der Ven for studying church identity. Van der Ven argues that it is necessary to make a distinction between the *basis* and the *identity* of a specific church body. The *basis* refers to the "relationship of the church to the Christian tradition." The term basis is thus referring to the specific confessional tradition to which a church connects itself. The basis is formulated when the church in question is founded and it cannot be changed without serious and traumatic conflicts. Being Evangelical Lutheran is thus part of the basis of Church of Sweden.[7]

The *identity* of a church consists, in van der Ven's terminology, of four dimensions: *context, convictions, vision, and mission.*[8] The *context* refers to the wider cultural and political context in which the church exists. The *conviction* dimension is the church's—or the individual church members'—answer to the question "What do we believe?" The *vision* dimension answers the question "Who are we?" and expresses the church's understanding of what it means to be a church. One way of expressing the vision can be to formulate ecclesiological metaphors, such as the metaphor of the church as "the people of God." The last dimension of identity is what van der Ven calls *mission*, which describes how the church understands its main tasks, answering the question "What are we striving for?"

Van der Ven's dimensions of identity are of course intended to structure a complex picture of a church. In this chapter it will be used for a much more limited purpose. I will organize statements about Church of Sweden as an Evangelical Lutheran church in my material with the help of his distinction between basis and identity, thereby making it easier to identify various models of constructing Church of Sweden's Lutheran identity. In discussing identity, however, I will not separate convictions,

---

5. The policy of the journal is available at the journal's website, http://www.svenskkyrkotidning.se.

6. http://www.pastoraltidskrift.nu.

7. van der Ven, *Ecclesiology in Context*, 151.

8. Ibid., 151–52. I have used van der Ven's methodology in my article "Thinking Theologically about Welfare and Religion."

PART FOUR: Exploring a Heritage—Lutheran Identity

vision, and mission. I will limit myself to the use of the overarching concept of identity as an analytical tool for the discussion of how the Lutheran basis of Church of Sweden is understood.

The Basis: Church of Sweden and Its Confessional Tradition

As was said above, both Church of Sweden Act and the Church Ordinance state that Church of Sweden is an Evangelical Lutheran church. According to the Church Ordinance, Church of Sweden belongs to the Lutheran tradition. It also regulates the confessional documents of the church. In the first chapter of the Ordinance, it is stated that

> The Church of Sweden's faith, confession and doctrine, which is shaped through liturgy and life, is grounded in God's holy word, as it is given in the prophetic and apostolic writings of the Old and New testament, is summarized in the Apostolic, Nicene and Athanasian creeds and in the unchanged Augsburg Confession from 1530, is confirmed and acknowledged in the decisions of the Uppsala Synod in 1593, is explained and commented upon in the *Book of Concord*, and in other documents acknowledged by the Church of Sweden.[9]

The Ordinance makes a reference to the decisions of the Uppsala Synod in 1593. This synod was held in order to settle theological and liturgical disputes in the post-Reformation church in Sweden. The synod decided that the Augsburg Confession, along with the patristic creeds, should be the confessional rule of the church. The historical importance of this synod makes it reasonable to say that it was then that the basis of Church of Sweden as an Evangelical Lutheran church was fixed. *The Book of Concord*, on the other hand, was not explicitly included and would not gain official status until it was incorporated in the church's law in 1686.[10]

In van der Ven's terminology, it seems safe to say that the *basis* of Church of Sweden is firmly Lutheran. Both historically and in the present legislation, and in the Church Ordinance, this is stated in no uncertain terms. Church of Sweden also presents itself as Lutheran in various forums—and not least on its own website. Interestingly enough, however,

---

9. *Kyrkoordningen*, chapter 1, § 1. It should be noted that the singular form "is" is also used in Swedish, presumably with the intention of expressing that faith, confession and doctrine should be seen as belonging closely together.

10. Inger, "Kyrkolagstiftningen under 1600-talet," 211.

the website also underlines the fact that the Reformation did not imply the same drastic changes in liturgy and church practice in Sweden as in many other churches. Rather, Church of Sweden is described as a Lutheran church that retained much of the old medieval liturgy.[11] Historically, this is maybe something of an exaggeration—the liturgical changes not least after the Uppsala synod in 1593 were rather substantial, if compared with the medieval Catholic liturgy. But it says something interesting about how Church of Sweden understands its own basis: as a Lutheran church with "a character of its own," which includes an appreciation of liturgy and an Episcopal organization not common in all Lutheran churches.

In my material, it is not easy to find any questioning of the Lutheran basis. Such a questioning would imply a questioning of the formal confessional identity of the church and an argument for a new basis, i.e., more or less a collective conversion to another Christian tradition. There are, however, a lot of views on what the Lutheran character of the church should mean in practice. These will be discussed in the next section on identity.

Identity

There is an ambivalent attitude to Martin Luther in Swedish culture. The popular expression "having Luther on one's shoulder" means having a bad conscience (more or less unjustified), feelings of being inferior to other people, or having an exaggerated work ethic. There are thousands of examples of how Luther is understood in this way. One of them can be found in Swedish artist Niclas Strömstedt's blog post on April 3, 2008, where Luther on the shoulder whispers in Strömstedt's ear that he should do his duty and update his blog regularly.[12] Another blogger argues that it is good to buy oneself away from "boring time" (such as e.g., housecleaning) and concludes—in English: "Fuck Luther."[13]

Describing Church of Sweden as a Lutheran church is thus problematic in a context that perceives "Lutheran" to be synonymous with boredom, bad conscience, a neurotic work ethic, and intolerance. It is therefore not surprising that representatives of the church do their best to change the picture of Luther. Parishes hold seminars on Luther—sometimes using drama. Swedish actor Per Ragnar is, for example, touring Sweden

---

11. "Facts about the Church of Sweden."
12. Strömstedts, "Trötter, Glader, Kloker, Blyger, Butter och Luther. Och jag."
13. Jardenberg, "Hur får du ihop livspusslet?" See also Stolt, *Luther själv*, 26–27.

with a show on Luther and is often giving his performances in churches.[14] Material on Luther is put on church websites, and books and articles try to present a more positive picture of him. Historically, this is of course not so difficult. The negative picture is rather easy to refute. But the need to do so says something of the difficulties for the church presenting itself as an Evangelical Lutheran church in Sweden. In this way, Sweden stands in contrast to another traditionally Lutheran country in Scandinavia, as is shown by Marie Vejrup Nielsen's article on Lutheran identity in Denmark in this volume.

There is a small but notable flow of books on Luther.[15] Some of them are sponsored by Church of Sweden, while others are not. The common themes for most of them are, however, that Luther was not boring, not hostile to joy and happiness, and—if due consideration is taken of the fact that he lived almost five hundred years ago—still continues to be a spiritual resource today. Birgit Stolt, professor of the German language, is one of the leading Luther scholars in Sweden. She has devoted much of her career to Luther studies from a linguistic perspective, but she has also argued that Luther is the "theologian of the heart and of joy," whose message has been misunderstood. She is not least critical of Gustaf Wingren's understanding of Luther's doctrine of vocation.[16]

In the anthology *Luther som utmaning*, which was published by the initiative of Church of Sweden Research Unit, seven academic theologians try to highlight "the liberating aspects of Lutheran theology, without denying what is negative."[17] Even in the editorial section of the Social Democratic newspaper *Aftonbladet* it has been said that "we need Luther's liberating message." Perhaps this is not so surprising, since the author Helle Klein—at the time political chief editor of *Aftonbladet*—is also an ordained minister in Church of Sweden.[18]

It might be argued that the fact that Luther and Lutheranism are often negatively laden concepts in Swedish culture makes it necessary for Church of Sweden to reflect upon its own Lutheran identity and try to present it as attractively as possible. You do not win votes—or members for the church—by describing yourself as Lutheran. But since the Lutheran heritage is a fundamental part of the basis of Church of Sweden, it cannot

---

14. E.g., in Härnösand's cathedral parish, see "Luther—död eller levande."
15. For a survey, see Hidal, "Den svenska lutherbilden."
16. Stolt, *Luther själv*, 37–40. Cf. Wingren, *Luthers lära om kallelsen*.
17. Gerle, *Luther som utmaning*, 7.
18. Klein, "Vi behöver Luthers befriande budskap."

just be given up. This circumstance paves the way for a more or less internal debate on what it really *should* mean to be a Lutheran church today.

What Does "Lutheran" Really Mean?

On Church of Sweden website, there is a link called "Ask the Priest" (Fråga prästen) where people can send in their questions on almost anything. The answers are written by priests and deacons and published on the website. The answers are not officially sanctioned by anyone, but since they are published on the website they contribute to the public image of the church and can therefore be said to represent convictions held in Church of Sweden. Among the thousands of questions and answers on the site, there are of course also some that have to do with the Lutheran identity of the church.[19] The answers given are, however, not easily harmonized into one picture of Lutheran identity.

One person asks if "Luther's teaching remains in our churches today, or if a new Reformation is needed." The answer is quite short and states that since Church of Sweden is Evangelical Lutheran, Luther is a part of its heritage. The most interesting part of the answer is, however, the following: "The church is constantly developing and therefore it is possible to say that we constantly are in a process of reformation."[20] Another person asks if not a new Reformation is needed, since he cannot believe in the Trinity, in a last judgment, or in all the supernatural happenings reported in the Bible. The answer is that the Reformation is an ongoing process in which the church "understands and interprets the Bible, the tradition, doctrine and our experiences of God in ever new ways."[21]

Other questions and answers give a different picture. One person asks whether the church still holds on to what is said in the Lutheran Confessions about unbaptized children as being sinners. The answer begins with declaring that the Augsburg Confession is still a valid norm of doctrine in Church of Sweden. The answer continues by stating that "We hold that baptism is necessary for salvation," even if this is modified by saying that God is not bound by this.[22] Another person asks if there really is anything

---

19. "Fråga prästen." I have not found it necessary to provide the names of the priests giving answers, since my point is that the answers are published on the official website of the church.
20. "Finns Luthers lära kvar i våra kyrkor idag?"
21. "Är det dags för en ny reformation?"
22. "Augsburgska bekännelsen och arvssynden."

PART FOUR: Exploring a Heritage—Lutheran Identity

that Church of Sweden firmly believes in, since the church seems to be so vague. The answer directly refers to the doctrine of salvation by grace alone and justification by faith in the Augsburg Confession as the center of the church's faith. It is followed by a short reflection on the necessity of formulating Christian faith in a way that is relevant in the contemporary context.[23]

These two groups of answers can be described as instances of two examples of relating to the confessional basis of Church of Sweden as ideal types. Ideal types are of course "a one-sided accentuation of certain phenomena found in empirical reality for heuristic and expository purposes."[24] As constructions, they are also in some sense normatively laden. But as long as this is kept in mind, they are useful as models for organizing empirical material. I will use two ideal types, which I will name the *semper reformanda* type and the confessional type, respectively. By constructing these two types I do not claim that they exist in a pure form anywhere in the material, or that either of them should be preferred before the other. They are only used as a way of structuring complex material.

The *semper reformanda* type would argue that being an Evangelical Lutheran church today means being prepared to live in constant reformation according to the Protestant principle demonstrated by the reformers' courage to challenge the authorities of their time, which made it possible to proclaim the gospel in freedom.[25] The confessional type would argue that being an Evangelical Lutheran church today must mean being in some sort of agreement with the central theological convictions of sixteenth-century Lutheran theology and church practice.[26]

An editorial in *Svensk pastoraltidskrift* in 2009 argued that it is the doctrine of justification by faith alone that is and should be at the center of any Lutheran theology worthy of that name. According to *Svensk pastoraltidskrift*, the doctrine of justification by faith alone permeates Luther's teaching "on law and gospel, on worldly and spiritual regiment, on state and church." Further, Luther, according to *Svensk pastoraltidskrift*, found the doctrine of justification in Holy Scripture, "so clearly formulated that, as he thought, every reader of the Bible has to see it." *Svensk pastoraltidskrift*

23. "Håller kyrkan orubbligt fast vid något?"

24. Ekstrand, *Max Weber in a Theological Perspective*, 67f. In formulating these ideal types, I have been inspired by Holte, *Luther och lutherbilden—en kritisk granskning*, 19–21, where he refers to a debate on the interpretation of the Lutheran heritage in Germany in the beginning of the nineteenth century.

25. For the "protestant principle" see, e.g., Tillich, *Dynamics of Faith*, 29.

26. E.g., in Ekstrand, "Luthersk teologi idag," 37.

explicitly argues against the *semper reformanda* type of interpretation of Lutheran identity. *Semper reformanda* should not be taken as "reforms in the word's modern secular meaning." Rather it should be taken literally, as the duty of the church always to return to its roots when it has gone wrong. Church of Sweden, argues *Svensk pastoraltidskrift*, has to take its Lutheran heritage seriously and in fidelity to this heritage define what should be understood by the Church Ordinance's reference to the Lutheran confessional documents.[27]

In his pastoral letter to the diocese of Skara, Bishop Erik Aurelius has stated that the gospel of justification by faith without works has to be at the center of the church's proclamation. Aurelius finds the center of the gospel clearly summarized in St Paul's Epistle to the Romans—God justifies the "ungodly" (Rom 4:5). Aurelius's pastoral letter bears the title *Evangelium för gudlösa* (Gospel for the Ungodly) and is structured as an exegetical analysis of how the gospel is formulated in the teachings of the historical Jesus, by the evangelists, and by St. Paul. Aurelius's argument is exegetical rather than dogmatic or historical, but it is clear that he defends the idea of the doctrine of justification as the necessary center for Lutheran—and indeed Christian—theology.[28] In the typology used here, the argument in Aurelius's book would therefore be an instance of the confessional type.

Philosopher of religion and priest Karin Johannesson, in an article on the need for Lutheran spirituality, also argues for the need for some sort of agreement between the sixteenth-century Reformation theology and contemporary spiritual praxis if the latter should deserve the name Lutheran. A Lutheran spirituality has to start out from the principle of grace alone and it has to acknowledge that there should be no distinction between spiritual gifts of grace and other gifts. Every calling, Johannesson argues, is a gift and a task from God. A Lutheran spirituality also has to live from the means of grace, from the sacraments and from the proclamation of the word present in the church.[29]

Håkan Holmlund in his article "Luther in Vällingby" represents a case where the two ideal types are clearly and consciously combined. Holmlund, who at the time of writing the article was a priest in Vällingby parish, describes a project called *Vuxet växande* (Adult Growing), in

27. *Svensk pastoraltidskrift* 19/2009, 615–16. I have argued similar points in Ekstrand, "Att vara lutheran," 511, and in Ekstrand, "En luthersk kyrkohandbok."
28. Aurelius, *Evangelium för gudlösa*, 9. It should be noted that Aurelius's argument is similar to that put forward by Eberhard Jüngel in *Das Evangelium von der Rechtfertigung*, 13, even if Aurelius does not explicitly refer to Jüngel.
29. Johannesson, "Vi behöver luthersk spiritualitet," 153–55.

which people meet for conversation about faith, pilgrimages, and retreats. Holmlund's point is that the Lutheran tradition provides resources for the work done in *Vuxet växande*. The starting point is the fact that "an Evangelical Lutheran church must, by definition, be a church that is constantly changing." The reason for this is that "the gospel is eternal," while theology always has to be contextual. In the Lutheran tradition, Holmlund finds some components which he finds especially valuable.[30]

The first component is "the personal relation to God," a searching for the God of grace. Any attempt of the church to prescribe how this search for God should be formulated theologically will, according to Holmlund, be fiercely resisted by those participating in *Vuxet växande*. Luther's way of defining the concept of God in the *Large Catechism* could, however, be a common ground: "A god means that from which we are to expect all good and to which we are to take refuge in all distress."[31] The second component that Holmlund highlights is the critique of the church for preaching a joyless faith, which gives people feelings of guilt instead of comforting those in despair experiencing guilt or anxiety. The third component of the Lutheran heritage that Holmlund points to is the liturgy, which often is not perceived as relevant or even understandable by those participating in *Vuxet växande*. The liturgy, argues Holmlund, has to be formed locally in response to the particular context, as was done during the Reformation period. It is also necessary to revive hymn singing, since a "rich musical life ... is to a great extent living Lutheran theology." The fourth component in Holmlund's argument is the Bible, which has to be read in a liberating way. A hermeneutic and poetic reading gives resources for new perspectives, e.g., when it comes to ordination of women or same-sex relationships.

The final point in Holmlund's article is that Church of Sweden should cherish its Lutheran heritage, since it offers resources for Christian faith and life today. But at the same time the church has to be ready to interpret this heritage contextually, focusing on those parts of the Lutheran tradition that are relevant in the particular contexts of today—Lutheran theology has to be dynamic rather than historicizing.

A good example of the *semper reformanda* type is Christer Hugo's article "Det lutherska arvet och en fortsatt reformation" (The Lutheran Heritage and a Continued Reformation). Hugo quotes Luther, "*Creare est semper novum facere*" (To create is to always make new), and argues that for Reformation thinking it is necessary to be "prepared to reconsider,

---

30. Holmlund, "Luther i Vällingby," 494–96.
31. Luther, *Large Catechism*.

reformulate, rethink, and find new paths." A Lutheran approach to contemporary issues should be formed to serve life. Therefore it cannot be bound by traditional problems and answers. According to Hugo, the Lutheran heritage contains a "refreshing relativism." The church is free to serve, to promote hope and liberation for all.[32]

In an interview on Church of Sweden website in May 2009, the newly elected bishop of Stockholm, Eva Brunne, is reported to have expressed a view similar to Hugo's, arguing that Martin Luther "showed that it is possible to change even firm structures." Luther defended every person's right to make a decision for her/himself on faith and therefore he is inspiring for a church that wants to be an open church that welcomes anyone, even those who do not believe in "the right way."[33]

In the words of journalist and priest Kerstin Vinterhed, Luther is seen as the "first modern human being" whose faith was a faith for "the grown up person in an inner dialogue with his/her God." Vinterhed also acknowledges Luther's emphasis on grace alone and thinks that this is an important message for us today. At the same time, however, she concludes that his teachings on predestination and the possibility of eternal damnation are mistakes. An interesting Luther, she argues, has to be "one of us" just as, e.g., Shakespeare has to be read in this light in order to be relevant for today.[34]

Discussion

In his book *Luther i Sverige: Svenska lutherbilder under tre sekler* (Luther in Sweden: Swedish Pictures of Luther During Three Centuries) the Luther scholar and bishop of Gothenburg, Carl Axel Aurelius, polemicizes against the Danish church historian P. G. Lindhardt, who at a conference in 1977 is reported to have said that Luther's importance in the Nordic countries has not been great—rather he was "a name and a symbol."[35] In his book, Aurelius investigates how Luther was presented at three Reformation jubilees in Sweden in 1621, 1721, and 1817 as well as the theological climate

---

32. Hugo, "Det lutherska arvet och en fortsatt reformation," 267–69. The quotation from Luther can be found in *WA* 1:563.
33. "Med blick för de maktlösa."
34. Vinterhed, "Luther—den första moderna människan."
35. Aurelius, *Luther i Sverige*, 7. Aurelius quotes a paper by Lindhardt distributed at the conference, which was held in 1977. The original paper of Lindhardt has not been available to me.

PART FOUR: Exploring a Heritage—Lutheran Identity

at the time of these jubilees.[36] Aurelius concludes that Luther's importance has been great in the history of Church of Sweden in at least three respects. First, his writings contributed to form the confessional culture and the confessional state. Secondly, his writings contributed to the destruction of the confessional state, as they inspired the pietistic movements in their critique of Lutheran orthodoxy and of the Enlightenment theology of the late eighteenth century. Thirdly, they contributed to the formation of modern Swedish society since they were used by the revivalist movements in the nineteenth century in their advocacy of freedom from the state church's monopoly on organized religion.[37]

Ragnar Holte, professor emeritus in ethics at Uppsala University, argued in his book *Luther och lutherbilden—en kritisk granskning* (Luther and the Image of Luther: A Critical Appraisal) that much Luther research has been a mixture of historical and normative studies, often not distinguishing properly between the two. Luther has often been used for purposes alien to the historical Luther. For example, Luther has been understood as a pioneer of bourgeois revolution by German Democratic Republic authorities at the commemoration of Luther's birth in 1983, his appalling support for the suppression of the farmers' revolt and his crude anti-Semitism has been played down in order to present him as a religious genius, and he has been presented as a precursor to the Enlightenment. Holte is not arguing against the use of Luther for constructive theological purposes, but he insists on an intellectually honest distinction between an historical interpretation of Luther and a constructive theological use of Luther.[38]

From the material analyzed in this chapter, I would argue that Luther and the concept of Evangelical Lutheran are often used as "a name and a symbol" in ways that do not always distinguish between historical and constructive interpretations. This is in many ways true of both of the ideal types that I have discussed. The confessional type often highlights some traits in Luther's theology in a one-sided way and risks giving the impression that Luther's theology *only* consisted of an exposition of the doctrine of justification, forensically interpreted. But that is an interpretation of

---

36. The jubilees in 1621 and 1721 were held in commemoration of the accession to the throne by king Gustavus I, who introduced the Reformation in Sweden.

37. Aurelius, *Luther i Sverige*, 167.

38. Holte, *Luther och lutherbilden—en kritisk granskning*.

Luther that is much questioned by the so-called Finnish school of Luther research.[39]

The *semper reformanda* type, on the other hand, often uses Luther in order to argue for a church that is ready to reform itself in order to be relevant in contemporary culture. This is also an exaggeration of some traits in Luther's theological outlook. It is of course true that Luther was in sharp opposition to the ecclesiastical authorities and traditions of his time. But he did not perceive this criticism as the center of his theology. Rather it was a consequence of his deeply conservative theological method—he thought that the church of his time had abandoned the original and true Christian faith, to which it ought to return again and again.

There is a tension between the confessional understanding of Evangelical Lutheran identity and a *semper reformanda* understanding. This tension should not, however, be interpreted as a tension between conservatives and liberals. Even those advocating a confessional understanding of Lutheran identity can be quite liberal in their standpoints on other issues. One example could for example be my own argument that a confessional understanding of the core values implies support for same-sex marriages by the church.[40] This can hardly be seen as a typical conservative standpoint and would of course have been seen as a heresy by Luther himself.

Luther is used as a name and symbol by different theological positions in Church of Sweden today. This does not mean that the Evangelical Lutheran tradition is not important in both of the ideal types that I have used here. By referring to Luther the basis of the church is confirmed. To have some sort of basis is necessary for any church, since it constitutes a connection with Christian history and thereby implicitly to the Christ-event itself. A basis other than Evangelical Lutheran is hardly conceivable in Church of Sweden's case and therefore it is necessary for all those who do not question this basis to present their positions as legitimate variations of the tradition. This process of legitimizing is nothing peculiar to Church of Sweden. Rather, most Christian traditions have some need of presenting their present positions as consistent with tradition.

A specific challenge for Church of Sweden is that Luther and Lutheranism have quite negative connotations in the wider cultural context in Sweden. This creates a need to highlight those aspects of Luther's theology and the Lutheran tradition that can contribute to a change of this negative

---

39. See, e.g., Mannermaa, *Christ Present in Faith*.
40. Ekstrand, "Den lutherska teologins rikedom," 589.

PART FOUR: Exploring a Heritage—Lutheran Identity

understanding of Luther. Whether this is good or not is a normative question that I will not pursue here.

Church of Sweden as an Evangelical Lutheran church is understood in a variety of ways in the material presented in this chapter. It might therefore be appropriate to conclude with a list of the principal ways I have found of interpreting the Evangelical Lutheran character of the church:

- The Church of Sweden is a Lutheran church since the Lutheran confessions are norms for the way the church should interpret the gospel.
- The Church of Sweden is a Lutheran church since being Lutheran is part of its heritage.
- The Church of Sweden is a Lutheran church since it is constantly developing and reforming itself, accepting a "refreshing relativism."
- The Church of Sweden is a Lutheran church since it proclaims justification by faith as a gospel for the ungodly.
- The Church of Sweden is Lutheran because it is an open church that accepts the religious maturity of every human being.

There is of course some truth in all these points. Whether they are—or even have to be—consistent with each other in order for Church of Sweden to be a truly Lutheran church has to be decided by the church itself.

Bibliography

"Augsburgska bekännelsen och arvssynden." Online: http://www.svenskakyrkan.se/default.aspx?id=677401 (accessed 12/09/2010).
Aurelius, Carl Axel. *Luther i Sverige: Svenska lutherbilder under tre sekler.* Skellefteå: Artos, 1994.
Aurelius, Erik. *Evangelium för gudlösa—herdabrev till Skara stift.* Stockholm: Verbum, 2005.
The Church of Sweden Act. SFS 1998:1591. Online: http://www.sweden.gov.se/sb/d/3926/a/27832 (accessed 12/09/2010).
Ekstrand, Thomas. "Att vara lutheran." *Svensk kyrkotidning* 104/43 (2008) 511.
———. "Den lutherska teologins rikedom." *Svensk kyrkotidning* 104/49 (2008) 589.
———. "En luthersk kyrkohandbok," *Kyrkans tidning* 19 (2010) 16.
———. *Folkkyrkans gränser: En teologisk analys av övergången från statskyrka till fri folkkyrka.* Stockholm: Verbum, 2002.
———. "Luthersk teologi idag." In *Religion och existens: Årsskrift för Teologiska föreningen i Uppsala* (2007), 35–47.
———. *Max Weber in a Theological Perspective.* Leuven: Peeters, 2000.
———. "Thinking Theologically about Welfare and Religion." In *Welfare and Religion in 21st Century Europe*, edited by Anders Bäckström et al., 2:107–50. Farnham: Ashgate, 2011.

"Evangeliskt-lutherskt." Unsigned editorial. *Svensk pastoraltidskrift* 51/18–19 (2009) 615–16.
"Facts about the Church of Sweden." Online: http://www.svenskakyrkan.se/default.aspx?di=295603&ptid=0 (accessed 11/08/2010).
"Finns Luthers lära kvar i våra kyrkor idag?" Online: http://www.svenskakyrkan.se/default.aspx?di=68120 (accessed 12/09/2010).
"Fråga prästen." Online: http://www.svenskakyrkan.se/default.aspx?di=263612&ptid=0 (accessed 12/09/2010).
Gerle, Elisabeth, editor. *Luther som utmaning—om frihet och ansvar*. Stockholm: Verbum, 2008.
Hidal, "Den svenska lutherbilden." *Signum* 35/1 (2009) 37–43.
Holmlund, "Luther i Vällingby." *Svensk kyrkotidning* 104/41–42 (2008) 494–96.
Holte, Ragnar. *Luther och lutherbilden—en kritisk granskning*. Stockholm: Proprius, 1984.
Hugo, Christer. "Det lutherska arvet och en fortsatt reformation." *Svensk kyrkotidning* 101/21 (2005) 267–69.
"Håller kyrkan orubbligt fast vid något?" Online: http://www.svenskakyrkan.se/default.aspx?di=62490 (accessed 12/09/2010).
Inger, Göran. "Kyrkolagstiftningen under 1600-talet." In *Sveriges kyrkohistoria— enhetskyrkans tid,* (the main text in the volume is written by Ingun Montgomery), edited by Lennart Tegborg et al., 204–13. Stockholm: Verbum, 2002.
Jardenberg, Joakim. "Hur får du ihop livspusslet?" Mindpark. Online: http://mindpark.se/hur-far-du-ihop-livspusslet/ (accessed 12/08/2010).
Johannesson, Karin. "Vi behöver luthersk spiritualitet." *Svensk kyrkotidning* 105/11–12 (2009) 153–55.
Jüngel, Eberhard. *Das Evangelium von der Rechtfertigung des Gottlosen als Zentrum des christlichen Glaubens.* 5th ed. Tübingen: Mohr/Siebeck, 2006.
Klein, Helle. "Vi behöver Luthers befriande budskap." *Aftonbladet,* 28 April 2008.
Kyrkoordningen. Church of Sweden. Online: http://www.svenskakyrkan.se/default.aspx?id=637938 (accessed 20/03/2011).
Luther, Martin. "Resolutiones disputationum de indulgentiarum virtute." In WA 1:525–628.
"Luther—död eller levande." Online: http://www.svenskakyrkan.se/default.aspx?di=314291 (accessed 12/08/2010).
———. *Large Catechism.* Online: http://bookofconcord.com (accessed 12/08/2010).
Mannermaa, Tuomo. *Christ Present in Faith: Luther's View of Justification.* Minneapolis: Fortress, 2005.
"Med blick för de maktlösa." Online: www.svenskakyrkan.se/default.aspx?id=655265 (accessed 25/08/2011).
Stolt, Birgit. *Luther själv—hjärtats och glädjens teolog.* Skellefteå: Artos, 2004.
Strömstedts, Niklas. "Trötter, Glader, Kloker, Blyger, Butter och Luther. Och jag." Niklas Strömstedts Blogg. Online: http://niklasstromstedt.blogspot.com/2008/04/trtter-glader-kloker-blyger-butter-och.html (accessed 11/08/2010).
"Svensk Kyrkotidning." Online: www.svenskkyrkotidning.se (accessed 12/09/2010).
"Svensk pastoraltidskrift." Online: www.pastoraltidskrift.nu (accessed 10/08/2010).
Tillich, Paul. *Dynamics of Faith.* New York: Harper, 1957.

PART FOUR: Exploring a Heritage—Lutheran Identity

van der Ven, Johannes A. *Ecclesiology in Context*. Grand Rapids: Eerdmans, 1996.
Vinterhed, "Luther—den första moderna människan." *Dagens Nyheter*, 7 April 1996.
Wingren, Gustaf. *Luthers lära om kallelsen*. 2nd ed. Lund: Gleerups, 1948.
"Är det dags för en ny reformation?" Online: http://www.svenskakyrkan.se/default
   .aspx?id=681226 (accessed 12/09/2010).

14

How Lutheran? An Icelandic Perspective

STEINUNN ARNÞRÚÐUR BJÖRNSDÓTTIR

A YOUNG ICELANDER, NEWLY arrived at a large USA university some thirty years ago, applied for a room to share at a dormitory. The first question he got from a potential roommate was, "What church do you belong to?" The surprised Icelander remembered vaguely that the Church of Iceland, *Þjóðkirkjan*, was described as "Evangelical Lutheran." Accordingly he gave the explanation that his religion was "Evangelical Lutheran." The potential roommate hung up. Had he been asked to explain, the Icelandic student would not have been able to do so. The description "Evangelical Lutheran" did not have any meaning for the student. He only knew that the latter part, Lutheran, had something to do with Martin Luther and the Reformation. The word "evangelical" was even less clear. "Evangelical" in Iceland is commonly used only in defining the church, most notably in article 62 of the Icelandic constitution, first written in in 1874. At that time Iceland belonged to the Danish kingdom and the article was a literal translation from the Danish constitution of 1849.[1] The word "evangelical," however, is a foreign word and carries no meaning for those who do not make the connection to the equally foreign word *evangelium*. Icelandic language policy dictates a translation of

---

1. *Constitution of the Republic of Iceland*, art. 62. Cf. the Danish Constitution, *Danmarks Riges Grundlov*, art. 3.

PART FOUR: Exploring a Heritage—Lutheran Identity

most foreign words, including *evangelium*, in Icelandic: *fagnaðarerindi*.[2] The student in question was neither aware of that nor of the implications of the word "evangelical" in the USA.

Iceland is a country where the great majority of the population belongs to the Lutheran tradition. For centuries, "Christian" has been a synonym for "Lutheran." Approximately 85 percent of the population belongs to the Evangelical Lutheran church and even if the nation today is increasingly multicultural there are few efforts made to describe what is meant by "Lutheran." Usually the term "Lutheran" is used only as part of learning church history or in ecumenical contexts, and then only in order to point out that being Lutheran is different than being, e.g., Roman Catholic. There is, however, little doubt that *Þjóðkirkjan*[3] belongs to the Evangelical Lutheran tradition of northern Germany and Scandinavia. It upholds the confessions of Lutheran churches, including the Augsburg Confession. The church model is marked by the connections between church and state, a heritage from the time when the Christian ruler was the protector of the church. Luther's Small Catechism formed a part of the confirmation teaching from the Reformation well into the twentieth century.[4]

The Reformation still forms part of the syllabus in the teaching of religion. Students learn that Martin Luther "protested against selling of indulgence, broke from the authority of the pope, formed a new church, and abolished saints."[5] The Reformation in Iceland is also part of the history curriculum, including the dramatic beheading of the last Catholic bishop in Iceland in 1550 along with two of his sons.[6] But knowing that they are not Roman Catholic does not in itself define Icelanders, neither as Christians nor as Lutherans. If the church model is Lutheran, what can be said about the beliefs? How closely are the beliefs linked with culture? And how does the high membership rate compare to church attendance?

---

2. In accordance with Icelandic language policy that all foreign words are translated or new Icelandic words made for them. Therefore, most international words, such as "telephone" and "television" look completely different in Icelandic. This is also true of theological words such as *diakonia*, "evangelical," and "ecumenical."

3. *Þjóðkirkjan* (literally translated: The National Church) is called the Evangelical Lutheran Church of Iceland in English translations.

4. Hjaltalin, *Ferming í fjórar aldir*, 78.

5. I asked a couple of fifteen-year-old students to tell me what they knew about Martin Luther and the Reformation from class and this was what they remembered.

6. Bishop Jón Arason had six children with his consort Helga Sigurðardóttir. Her father and grandfather were priests. The eleventh-century regulations on celibacy were never completely observed in Iceland.

Þjóðkirkjan, the Evangelical Lutheran Church of Iceland, is today a church in transition. An ongoing debate on questions concerning the relationship between church and state and freedom of religion in Iceland are visible signs that the old Lutheran state church model is changing. So, is the Evangelical Lutheran Church of Iceland still a recognizably Lutheran church? This is the question I want to explore in this chapter. And I will do so first by looking at the development of the church-state relation issue, then I will present some of the findings concerning faith and religious practice that has come to the fore in different surveys over recent decades, and, finally, I will look at these findings against the background of Luther's *marks of the church*. Martin Luther, of course, did not define "a Lutheran church." He was concerned with the true church, a church recognizable as Christian. Such a church should, according to Luther, have certain recognizable features. I have chosen, as an ecclesiological framework for the findings on church and belief on Iceland, Martin Luther's ideas of the marks of the church as it is explained in his writings *On the Council and the Churches*.[7]

Church and State Relations

Some 85 percent of the Icelandic population living in Iceland still belong to Lutheran churches, either the Evangelical Lutheran Church of Iceland or one of the four Lutheran free churches. Of those, the Evangelical Lutheran Church of Iceland is by far the largest, with approximately 80 percent of the population as members, which is a decrease from 90 percent in 1996. The Bishop of Iceland is the head of the church according to law, but the Evangelical Lutheran Church of Iceland enjoys special relations to the state, as is evident in the constitution, which states:

> The Evangelical Lutheran Church shall be the State Church in Iceland and, as such, it shall be supported by the state. This may be amended by law.[8]

The President of Iceland appoints bishops, according to the nominations of the Minister of the Interior[9] who, in his or her turn, is bound by the church's election of a candidate. This is part of the Lutheran heritage of close ties between church and state with the prince or the king as the

---

7. Luther, *On the Council and the Churches*.
8. *The Constitution of the Republic of Iceland*, art. 62.
9. Until 2008 this was the Minister of Ecclesiastical Affairs.

PART FOUR: Exploring a Heritage—Lutheran Identity

head. However, neither the president nor any members of government are acquired by law to belong to the church. According to the present legislation there is therefore the possibility for an Icelandic president, who does not belong to the Evangelical Lutheran Church of Iceland, still to maintain a nominal role as the head of church. And this could be played out by an appointment of a bishop, nominated by a pastor who does not belong to the church either.

Sólveig Anna Bóasdóttir's chapter in this volume has pointed out how the close relationship between church and state has affected, for example, the parliamentary debate on same-sex marriages.[10]

Freedom of religion is also guaranteed in the constitution. A debate about whether the article of the constitution on the state church violates freedom of religion is an occurring theme in public discourse and forms a part of current review of the constitution.[11]

The development from a state church akin to the Danish church model, to a more independent church took place towards the end of the twentieth century. A major change came with new legislation on the Evangelical Lutheran Church of Iceland—the Act on Status, Governance and Operation of the Church (no. 78/1997)—often referred to as the National Church Law.[12] This legislation states in the first article that the Evangelical Lutheran Church of Iceland is an "independent religious association on an Evangelical Lutheran foundation."

- the State should support and protect the Evangelical Lutheran Church of Iceland

- baptism in the name of the holy trinity and registration in the Central Registry gives admission to the church.

The Evangelical Lutheran Church of Iceland defines itself not as a state church but as an independent religious association that enjoys special relations to the state and the nation.[13] Proposed changes to the Evangelical

---

10. See the chapter by Sólveig Anna Bóasdóttir in this book.

11. A Constitutional Assembly was elected in 2010 to review the constitution. Proposals from the assembly include omitting a special clause on the Evangelical Lutheran Church and a new article on the Organisation of the Church. In December 2011 the bill was being reviewed by a parliamentary committee which will give guidelines on response. See also Hafstein, "Setningarræða á 44. kirkjuþingi 13. nóvember 2010."

12. Hugason, "A Case Study of the Evolution of a Nordic Lutheran Majority Church," 112.

13. Article 1 in the legislation concerning the status and administration of the National Church states that the National Church is an independant religious association

BJÖRNSDÓTTIR—*How Lutheran? An Icelandic Perspective*

Lutheran Church of Iceland legislation were adopted by the General Synod in 2008 but have not been passed by parliament. The changes include an assertion of the independence of the Evangelical Lutheran Church of Iceland and strengthen the importance of the General Synod.[14] Another change has to do with the definition of admission and might also be seen as significant. At present, admission is by baptism and being recorded in the Central Registry. The new proposal states admission to the church simply by baptism. There is no mention of the Central Registry.[15] The implication is clear—it is for the church to decide on membership.

Hjalti Hugason discusses this transition in a recent book on *Law and Religion in the 21st Century* and describes the model of church and state relations as a "collaboration model" and not a typical state church model after the changes of 1997. A collaboration model was also established in Finland in 1863 and in Sweden in 2000. This model is summarized thus:

- The Church System is not an integrated part of the fundamental laws of the republic, as it can be changed by law, without conventional constitutional amendment.
- The legislation defines the church as "independent religious organization."
- The legislation grants the Evangelical Lutheran Church of Iceland the status of a legal person, represented as an independent body with independent property rights.
- Administrative links between church and state are insubstantial.[16]

Hugason also predicts further changes in relations between church and state.

---

on an Evangelical Lutheran foundation. See "Lög um stöðu, stjórn og starfshætti þjóðkirkjunnar." See also Hafstein, "Setningarræða á 44. kirkjuþingi 13. nóvember 2010."

14. As the legislation approved in 2008 by the General Synod has not been on the parliament's agenda yet, the General Synod 2010 set up a committee to review that legislation, especially in light of current review of the constitution. See "Tillaga til þingsályktunar um frumvarp til þjóðkirkjulaga" and Hafstein, "Setningarræða á 44. kirkjuþingi 13. nóvember 2010."

15. The Central Registry Office registers religious affiliations of people who belong to any of the registered religious associations. These are the basis for the church tax that the state collects for the religious associations.

16. Hugason, "A Case Study of the Evolution of a Nordic Lutheran Majority Church," 112. Hugason quotes the Norwegian report *Religionsfrihet og Religionspolitikk*, published 2001.

PART FOUR: Exploring a Heritage—Lutheran Identity

In public discussions on church-state relations questions are raised about whether this model is consistent with the idea of religious freedom.[17] The superior status of the Evangelical Lutheran Church of Iceland and the words "support and protect" in the constitution are for many irreconcilable with the idea of religious freedom and equality.[18] The state and the Evangelical Lutheran Church of Iceland have an agreement for church land to be taken over by the state. This guarantees the salaries of a certain number of pastors in the Evangelical Lutheran Church of Iceland and is a bone of contention for many who advocate "total separation" of church and state. These payments are on the basis of ownership of land, not resting on the constitution. However, many see them as the same issue.

There are several organizations that actively support the separation of church and state. One is the humanist organization *Siðmennt*, which says in its introduction of the organization:

> Siðmennt works for separation of church and state in Iceland and does not seek any special privileges from the government. We believe that the state should remain neutral in matters of religion/life stance and that no public institutions should be influenced by one particular religion in a multicultural society. All religions and life stances should be equal with no special privileges to any.[19]

Opinion polls have asked questions on the separation of church and state on regular basis, most recently in October 2010. Then 61 percent supported separation.[20] In August 2010 six out of twelve ministers in the Icelandic government said that in their opinion they should be separated. This included the Prime Minister.[21]

The Lutheran model of the head of state as the protector of the church is therefore much debated in Iceland at present. The link to Luther is occasionally found in this discussion, such as in a recent newspaper by an Icelandic author who argues:

> The countries that have state churches are first and foremost the Lutheran countries of Northern Europe, especially the Nordic

---

17. By "public discussions" I am refering to media online and in print, books, and informal political statements in media.
18. See, e.g., Njardvik, *Spegill þjóðar*, 110.
19. "What is Sidmennt?"
20. "Málefni kirkjunnar."
21. "Sex ráðherrar vilja aðskilnað ríkis og kirkju." The ministers were responding to a question from the media on separation of church and state.

countries. It is probably not a coincidence that precisely in these countries church attendance is among the lowest and most people are not very religious. When the church was brought under the state in the 16th century, the state also took over (the church's) duty, such as assistance to the poor. Nor is it probably a coincidence that precisely in these countries the idea of the welfare system was formed.... In the USA there is no state church. There, welfare is also limited.[22]

A review of the constitution is on the agenda of the government of Iceland. There is public pressure to review simultaneously church and state relations. This was, for example one of the topics of a gathering of one thousand people held to give guidelines for values and emphasis in the new constitution. The gathering stated "that religious groups will not be treated differently and reconciliation will be reached regarding state and the Evangelical Lutheran Church of Iceland."[23]

Within the institutions of the Evangelical Lutheran Church of Iceland opinions are divided on the issue of further separation of church and state. This is also the venue where the Lutheran heritage in "the National Church model" is evident. An example is a debate in the General Synod in 2000. The debate focused on a proposed change in appointing parish pastors, from the Minister of Ecclesiastical Affairs to the Bishop of Iceland. One argument *for* a ministerial appointment was that changing this order implied "a fundamental change in the Evangelical Lutheran Church order" and that the church's relations with the state were based on Lutheran church order and theology:

> Let us not forget that we are a Lutheran church, based on Lutheran church traditions and ecclesiology.... This is what we are and on this we base our Church Order and our interaction and relations with the government.[24]

Hugason argues that further changes in relations between church and state in Iceland are inevitable in the near future but that the Icelandic church system encompasses a great potential for such development. The most important thing to consider is that the state's church system should not violate the current understanding in international human rights dialogue or the international treaties that have articles about freedom of religion, which Iceland is a party to. Additionally, the discrimination made between

22. Gunnarsson, "Til hvers að hata kirkjuna?"
23. "Values for the New Constitution."
24. Transcript from discussion at the General Synod 2000.

PART FOUR: Exploring a Heritage—Lutheran Identity

the Evangelical Lutheran Church of Iceland and other religious organizations on one hand and religious and life stance organizations on the other hand must be decreased.[25]

With further changes in the relationship between church and state a step is taken away from the heritage of Luther with the Christian ruler at the stern. In a secular society with secular authorities the challenge remains for this majority church to find a model of cooperation that is in harmony not only with the concept of religious freedom and equality but also with Christian and Lutheran heritage and identity.

What Do People Believe?

A comprehensive survey on religion in Iceland, including religious ideas and practice, was done in the late 1980s. One of the reasons stated for doing the survey was that "there were indications that religious life of Icelanders was rather unique and translating directly foreign questionnaires would not be helpful if the aim was to find these characteristics."[26] But how unique are Icelanders as Christians? And how does their faith and their religious practice compare with Luther's teachings?

Some answers to the last questions can be gleaned from different surveys on religion in Iceland. Two large surveys on the religious views of Icelanders have been conducted. One was the aforementioned survey published in 1990[27] and another comprehensive survey was done in 2004.[28] Smaller surveys have been conducted on various aspects of church life between the publications of these two and a qualitative survey on religion and church was done in 2005.[29] No questions about Luther have been asked. One can, however, ask if the church that appears in these surveys can be recognized as a Lutheran church when compared with the marks of the church.

I will look at some findings of these surveys, especially the two most recent ones, and measure them against Luther's seven marks of the church[30] to see if their religious ideas can be defined as Lutheran, i.e., if

---

25. Hugason, "A Case Study of the Evolution of a Nordic Lutheran Majority Church," 120.
26. Björnsson and Pétursson, *Trúarlíf Íslendinga*, 5.
27. Ibid.
28. *Trúarlíf Íslendinga*.
29. "Alþingi nýtur enn lítils trausts" and "Traust til Alþingis."
30. I will use Luther's definitions from *On the Council and the Churches*.

the Lutheran heritage is in some way evident in the practice and belief of the people in the church and in society. But before doing that, let us look at what the surveys say about some aspects of religion and practice in Iceland.

Faith

In early 2004, Gallup did a quantitative survey on religion in Iceland for the Evangelical Lutheran Church of Iceland, the Theological Institute, and the Reykjavík cemeteries.[31]

The survey was very comprehensive and covered issues such as religious education and its presence in schools, the media, prayers, religious attitudes, church and state questions and more. It also asked about the liturgical service and the role of the pastor. Some questions were partly or completely comparable to previous surveys.

According to this survey, almost 70 percent of Icelanders are religious. Some 75 percent of those who say that they are religious also claim that they are Christian. Some 22 percent say that they believe in their own way. This means that a total of 51 percent say that they are Christian and religious. A corresponding number from the Nordic hymnology survey in 1994 indicated some 42 percent of Icelanders said they were Christian and 53 percent said they were Christian in their own way. In answers from other Nordic countries less than 20 percent said they were Christian.[32]

A qualitative study in 2005 attempted a clearer understanding of what people meant when they said that they were Christian.[33] Most of the participants said that they were Christian but some defined that as a cultural rather than religious definition. They pointed out that Christian ethics form the basis for Icelandic society; Icelanders are brought up as Christian. It is possible that the word "Christian" has a wider meaning for Icelanders, such as a definition of a religious group to which they belong (e.g., Christian, not Muslim). In this respect it is worth noting that in the survey from 2004, more women than men said that they are religious. However, the same number of men and women say that they are Christian in the survey of 2004.

---

31. This was a phone survey with a random sample of 1,500 people aged 13–75, and the response rate was 60.4 percent.

32. Pétursson, "Nú legg ég augun aftur," 142.

33. See "Trúarlíf Íslendinga og væntingar til Þjóðkirkjunnar."

PART FOUR: Exploring a Heritage—Lutheran Identity

In the European World Value Study of 1990, some 85 percent of Icelanders said that they believe in God. Other surveys from the last two decades show this number to be around 80 percent.[34] But what image of God is it that people believe in? Professor Pétur Pétursson claims that the results of the 1987 survey on religion in Iceland showed that the majority of Icelanders had unclear and incoherent ideas on God, even if the Christian religion formed a backdrop to these ideas.[35]

In Gallup 2004, respondents were asked which statements about God they agreed with. They could respond to more than one statement.[36] Almost 40 percent agreed with the statement "There exists a loving God to whom we can pray"; some 20 percent with "God must exist or life would have no meaning." Similarly, the group was asked about their agreement with statements on Jesus Christ. Some 43 percent agreed with the sentence: Jesus Christ is the son of God and savior of men; almost 30 percent with "Jesus is one of the greatest religious leaders of history"; and approximately 14 percent agreed with "Jesus is a model for perfect life."[37] All of these answers can be considered traditional and in accordance with Lutheran teaching although not exclusive to a Lutheran tradition.

It is also evident that Icelanders are a nation that prays. Some 87 percent of respondents learned prayers at home and 67 percent prayed regularly as children, a slight decline from a previous study of 1987. Some 30 percent of respondents in 2004 said the Lord's Prayer daily and another 30 percent said this prayer several times per week. A closer look at these numbers reveals that 54 percent of those who described themselves as religious and Christian say the Lord's Prayer daily. Even those who do not consider themselves religious say the Lord's Prayer, as almost 12 percent from this group recite the prayer daily. Another surprising answer was that 25 percent of the people that never attend church services pray several times per week.

Almost two-thirds also say that their prayers have been answered and the same number maintain that their religion gives answers to ethical problems in daily life. According to these statistics, Icelanders confess a belief in God that is loving, to whom they can pray, who answers prayers,

34. Pétursson, "Nú legg ég augun aftur," 142.
35. Ibid., 139.
36. This refers to the percentage of the group who agreed with this question.
37. Trúarlíf Íslendinga, 42. It was possible to agree with more than one answer. The percentage is therefore deducted from the number that were decided, not from answers as a whole.

and who gives answers in daily life. It is a God who gives them a feeling of security and peace.

Pétursson has linked the active praying to evening prayers with children, a custom that still seems to be relatively strong in Iceland. He has also pointed out that Icelanders use hymns and verses in their prayers more than their Scandinavian counterparts. Pétursson argues that the religious life of Icelanders is shaped by the faith which directly or indirectly is fostered in them as children, especially with evening prayers. He describes their faith as "childhood faith." This faith is a source of comfort and support in difficulties. Evening prayers link this faith, which in many cases is private, to the Christian tradition in church and culture.[38]

The Service

According to the survey of 2004, 10 percent of Icelanders attend regular Sunday service once a month or more. We need to bear in mind that there is not a service every Sunday in the rural areas. Further, approximately 14 percent claims that they attend church four to eleven times per year, others less. Some 43 percent say that they never go to church. It is, however, noticeable from other questions that this group has good experiences of many aspects of the service.[39] The survey also found that almost 20 percent of Icelanders have been members of a church choir at some point in their life. It should be noted that in addition to the Sunday service there are other services and activities in the church. The survey from 2004 finds that 83 percent attend Sunday school or similar activities or have children that have attended such activities.[40]

The qualitative study from 2005 paints a rather different picture of the service. The general consensus regarding the church service was that it is rather boring—dull and heavy:

> I simply find the liturgy in the Evangelical Lutheran Church of Iceland so incredibly boring, it is the most powerful sleeping drug I know. It needs lighter music. That's what I think.

---

38. Pétursson, "Nú legg ég augun aftur," 156.

39. See, e.g., analyses of the questions "How good or bad is your experience of Sunday Services?" and "Why do you not attend Sunday service?" in *Trúarlíf Íslendinga*, 98, 103.

40. Ibid., 86. The number is similar in all age groups, in the youngest age group, age thirteen to seventeen it is still 82 percent.

PART FOUR: Exploring a Heritage—Lutheran Identity

> The liturgy is so heavy and so long. When I think of the Evangelical Lutheran Church of Iceland I simply see something heavy, like a monster. I completely lose my patience after just one church service.

People that are active churchgoers were more positive, even if they could still criticize the morning Sunday service.

> I have felt that the liturgy is a bit heavy so I started a gospel choir. It sings in gospel services. A lot of people come to those, but not as many attend the ones in the morning, with the heavy setup.

The sermon plays a prominent role in each service and that is recognized by people responding to surveys. There is, however, little criticism of the sermon's content but more of the style:

> It is fun to sit and think about the clothes and the colors and movements and that is in itself a method to survive a service ... But then the preaching is actually the most important thing. That someone speaks to you in normal language and not some elevated Biblical language that no-one understands.
> The preaching is always the most important thing; it is the reason for going to church. Actually, if the music is good then it is easier to survive the service.
> ... sometimes hear a good sermon on the radio ... and think "I should go to church" but I somehow never do. There are many great orators there.

When the message of the pastor is discussed the focus is on society. Pastors should discuss social issues such as poverty, family, vulnerable people, and the pace of society from a religious point of view. But the pastor should not be judgmental and avoid being political.[41] The survey of 2004 asks about the importance of a pastor in the community. On average 66 percent think the pastor is important, but this number is higher outside of the capital area. That is in accordance with previous studies on the status of the pastor in the rural communities, where approximately 80 percent of the parishioners know the pastor.[42]

Icelandic society has experienced a great loss of trust in establishments since the economic crash in 2008. At the bottom of public opinion

---

41. "Trúarlíf Íslendinga og væntingar til Þjóðkirkjunnar," 13.
42. Björnsson and Pétursson, *Þjóðkirkjusöfnuðir í sveit, bæ og borg*, 21.

are the banks; only 5 percent of the population trust banks.[43] The parliament enjoys only a 9 percent trust rating and the media enjoys the trust of 15 percent of the population.[44] In contrast, a survey in October 2010 found that people trust their parish pastors (48 percent).[45] It is especially evident for those who attend church regularly and the trust is generally greater in the rural areas. There is more trust in the local church and the local pastor than in the church as an institution, but trust in the church is still relatively high. It is, however, also an indicator of the importance of the local community and local service in times of transition.

The Evangelical Lutheran Church of Iceland is often described as a church of the clergy. In spite of an ever growing involvement of laypeople in different tasks in the congregation, including the liturgy, the pastor is often the only fulltime member of staff and is very influential in shaping the work of the congregation. The expectations for pastors are significant. They should be

> ... more perfect than the rest of us ... at the same time as pastors should be almost holy and cannot fight for better working conditions and higher salaries, they need to adapt to changing times and have services with popular music and thriving work in the congregation.[46]

Several surveys and analyses have dealt with the role of the pastor and the emphasis on parish work. Pastoral counseling is considered the most important task of pastors, followed by work with children and youth. According to surveys the pastor should be accessible, have a common touch, be a good counselor, engage in social and political discussion, but not be involved in party politics.

In this section I have looked at three aspects of religious life in Iceland: faith and its expression in prayer, the service, and the role of the pastor. Now, let us turn to the question of how this picture of a Nordic Lutheran majority church compares to Martin Luther's vision of the church.

---

43. "Alþingi nýtur enn lítils trausts" and "Traust til Alþingis."
44. Ibid.
45. "Traust til presta og sóknarkirkna," 4.
46. "Um trúarlíf Íslendinga og væntingar til Þjóðkirkjunnar," 15.

PART FOUR: Exploring a Heritage—Lutheran Identity

Defining "Lutheran"

As pointed out already, Martin Luther himself did of course not define "a Lutheran church," but what for him was a true church, a church recognizable as a Christian church. He frequently discusses the marks of the church in his writings, where he is defining his ecclesiology during years of debates, especially with the Roman Catholic Church, but also with others. If the church is not defined by the visible order, like that of the Roman Catholic Church with the pope at its head, how then can it be defined? In his response he stresses that the church is *in* the world but not *of* the world, thereby rejecting "the notion of a completely spiritualized church (it is *in* the flesh) and at the same time refusing a completely politicized version as well (but not *of* the flesh)."[47] "How will or can a poor confused person tell where such Christian holy people are to be found in this world?"[48] It is in response to this question that Luther defines various marks of the Christian assembly, the church. He does not always mention the same factors but in the work *On the Council and the Churches*, written in 1539, he distinguishes seven factors as the marks of the church.

What Luther is claiming is that the true church exists where the *Evangelium* is preached and received and the sacraments of baptism and communion are duly administered.[49] It is a revolutionary new understanding of the credo "I believe in one, holy, catholic church." The pope is not a "mark" of the church, nor are the cardinals, the chasubles, or tonsures of monks—but the Word and the sacrament, the meeting of people who believe. "The Christians, however, are a people with a special call and are therefore called not just ecclesia, 'church' or 'people', but *sancta catholica Christiana*, that is 'a Christian holy people' who believe in Christ."[50]

The seven marks of the church that Luther mentions are:

1. the Word "preached, believed, professed, and lived"
2. the holy sacrament of Baptism
3. the holy sacrament of the altar

---

47. Lathrop and Wengert, *Christian Assembly*, 25.
48. Ibid., 3.
49. Philip Melanchthon also talks about the marks of the church in *The Augsburg Confesson*: "the Marks of the Church occur when the Holy Spirit delivers the Word and Sacraments throught the public office of Ministry." Quoted in Lathrop and Wengert, *Christian Assembly*, 58. For discussion on this and different writings of Luther on the marks of the church see Lathrop and Wengert, *Christian Assembly*.
50. Luther, *On the Council and the Churches*.

4. the Office of the Keys, exercised publicly, i.e., use of absolution or the forgiveness of sins

5. consecration or calling to office bishops, pastors, or preachers who publicly and privately give, administer, and use the other four signs (1-4)

6. prayer, public praise, and thanksgiving to God

7. the holy possession of the sacred Cross, for which the Christians will suffer and by which they are sustained in sorrows.[51]

In addition to these seven principal parts, Luther mentions other outwards signs when people adhere to the ten commandments and faithfully serve their princes and lords, who in turn should love their subjects and protect and guard them.[52]

Luther's aim was to define and preach the gospel of justification by faith. His emphasis was on the *Evangelium* and what it meant for the work and teaching of the church. A renewed ecclesiology follows this new understanding. Unlike many reformers Luther did not see it as his aim to reform existing church order or to reinvent the congregations of the New Testament. His emphasis is on the nature of the church, not a flowchart of the institution.[53] Important for his understanding of the church was also the idea of the priesthood of all believers.

Through the common priesthood of all believers the baptized lay member of the congregation—who is not called to preach—is called to listen to the sermon and judge if it is the *Evangelium*, to listen for "the voice of Christ in the doctrine..."[54] The doctrinal authority is thus moved from the pope and the doctrinal committees to the congregation and the believer.

Furthermore, it is the congregation that calls the pastor. The role of the pastor has therefore changed from a position of power in the medieval church to the position of a servant.[55]

---

51. I am using the list from Lathrop and Wengert, *Christian Assembly*, 40.
52. Luther, *On the Council and the Churches*.
53. Eyjolfsson, *Ríki og kirkja*, 25.
54. Ibid., 55.
55. During the fourth Lateran Council in 1215, priests were "given" the highest authority over salvation in the church and on this earth. See Eyjolfsson, *Ríki og kirkja*, 85.

PART FOUR: Exploring a Heritage—Lutheran Identity

How Lutheran is the Evangelical Lutheran Church of Iceland?

How Lutheran is the church encountered in Iceland through these different surveys and additional information on the church? Would a "poor confused person" recognize the Evangelical Lutheran Church of Iceland, as a Christian assembly? Let us look at the marks of the church and compare them with what we know about the church.

The Word Preached

The Word is always at the centre of Luther's ecclesiology. It is confessed in every service and is present in that everyone attending the service has learned "Our Father" and the Credo.

Preaching the Word belongs to the pastor but the discernment belongs to the common priesthood of all believers. In general there is certainly criticism of services and within it, the sermons, but there is also appreciation of the sermon, as three quarters of those asked in 2004 said that the sermon was important to them, and that appreciation clearly increases with age.

What about the message of the sermon? If the common priesthood of all believers gives the task of discernment to the people, are they listening to hear if it is the word of God that is being preached? Looking at all the surveys it is noticeable how reluctant people are to actually criticize the sermon for its Christian message. It is accepted as the job of the pastor—the pastor should know his/her business in interpreting Scripture. The criticism will be on grounds that people are themselves comfortable—such as with methods of preaching, language, or politics.[56] While there is support for the pastor to speak about issues in society, the call seems to be for politics that are above party politics.[57] Whether the word preached is the *Evangelium* seems to be left to the pastor by the representatives of the priesthood of all believers.

---

56. Björnsdóttir, "Samræða við samtímann," 18–19.
57. Björnsson and Petursson, *Trúarlíf Íslendinga*.

The Holy Sacrament of Baptism

Baptism of infants is a strong tradition in Iceland. Approximately 80 percent of children are baptized in their first year. The only survey that asks about the meaning of baptism is the survey from 1987. The statements that got the biggest response were that baptism is:

> Not a precondition/prerequisite for grace but has a lot of meaning for me. (31 percent)
>
> Is only a church tradition but has nevertheless a certain meaning for me. (39 percent)
>
> Is only an old custom and has no meaning for me personally. (36 percent)[58]

Baptism is an old custom or tradition but has meaning for the majority of people. Exactly what that meaning is might be harder to define, but, seen in the light of the "childhood faith" and expressions of faith linked to culture and tradition, this high rate of child baptism can be seen as part of what Icelanders see as an affirmation of belonging to their faith and tradition.

The Holy Sacrament of the Altar

There is an interesting development with Holy Communion and its place in the service in Iceland. Holy Communion almost disappeared from the service in the mid-twentieth century and has been slowly making a comeback. In 1986, a total of 39,500 people attended communion in the Evangelical Lutheran Church of Iceland. The same survey shows that 6 percent of the population have communion once or more per year, so some are attending many times. In 2007, a total of 111,320 people attended Holy Communion in the Evangelical Lutheran Church of Iceland. Holy Communion is now celebrated in every service in a few parishes and frequently in most other parishes. The trend from the first half of the twentieth century has been reversed. The only survey that asks about the meaning of the Holy Communion is the survey from 1987. People were asked about the meaning of the sacrament for them. One third said that the sacrament was "only a church tradition but has nevertheless a certain meaning for me," and another third said that the sacrament was "only an old custom and has

---

58. Ibid.

no meaning for me personally."⁵⁹ These observations were made in 1987 and, as there has been a distinct increase in the practice of Holy Communion in Iceland since then, it is possible that people's attitude towards this sacrament has also changed.

Office of the Keys, Exercised Publicly

By "Office of the Keys" Luther is speaking of the use of absolution or the forgiveness of sins.

> There are some people with consciences so tender and despairing that even if they have not been publicly condemned, they cannot find comfort until they have been individually absolved by the pastor.[60]

Private confessions and absolutions still occur. Common confession and absolution are part of the liturgy of the table, but private confessions before communion ceased to exist in the Icelandic liturgy in the nineteenth century. Pastoral counseling is, however, a very important part of a pastor's work. All surveys that have been cited above confirm that, and in the survey 2004 it was cited by most people as the most important task of the pastor.

Consecration and Calling to Office

The fifth mark of the church according to the list we set out with is the consecration or calling to office bishops, pastors, or preachers, who publicly and privately give, administer, and use the first four signs. This is present in the Evangelical Lutheran Church of Iceland and the pastor is chosen by representatives of the parish. Any debate about changes in the process of choosing pastors focuses on the right of the congregation to select the pastor. This can in individual cases be in opposition to gender legislation, which the church is subject to. In such cases, the will of the congregation has been considered to have priority, even if the church needs to pay compensation to another candidate.

Expectations of the pastor are high. The pastor needs to be "more perfect than the rest of us,"[61] good at counseling, but also a good preacher,

---

59. Ibid.
60. Luther, *On the Councils and the Churches*.
61. "Trúarlíf Íslendinga og væntingar til þjóðkirkjunnar," 15.

as well as liberal and good with people. Luther wrote about the pastor: "Because he is in office and is tolerated by the Assembly, you put up with him too."[62] The results reflect different times and perhaps different needs and in some respect greater expectations and less tolerance towards representatives of the pastoral profession than in the sixteenth century. On the other hand they reflect much more liberal views on the religious teaching of the church than in Luther's day.

Prayer, Public Praise, and Thanksgiving to God

Iceland was sparsely populated until the mid-twentieth century, when urbanization changed the society. The tradition of going to service every Sunday was never actually realized in rural Iceland as people had to cover considerable distance to go to church. It was common to send one person from each household, often the head of the house. Instead, Christianity thrived in the homes with readings from homiletics and prayers. The practice of praying and teaching children to pray is a continuation of that tradition. Even if there is a slight decrease in the teaching of evening prayers and praying with children, the numbers are still surprisingly high and a significant number of people continue to pray the Lord's Prayer often.

The Holy Possession of the Sacred Cross

This is perhaps the most difficult mark to distinguish and evaluate from surveys on church and religion in Iceland. Does the church suffer for the cross? And what does it mean to "suffer for the cross"? The Evangelical Lutheran Church is a majority church and Christianity has been a majority religion—and for most of the time the only religion—in Iceland since it was adopted in the year 1000. This is changing today as Iceland moves towards a more multicultural society. The church as an institution has been criticized and finds itself in a period of transition. But it can hardly be considered to be a suffering.

But do Christians "suffer" because of their faith? The social media has changed public discussion in Iceland as well as in other countries. Discussion that was previously limited to debates in schools and universities, where religious people were challenged to defend their faith, is now in the public eye. One of the signs that can be distinguished in the discussion

---

62. Luther, *On the Councils and the Churches*.

in the social media is that militant atheism and anti-church attitudes are increasing. It is a timely reminder for the church that it should suffer for the cross, that just as Luther's opponents forced him to work on his ecclesiology so the Evangelical Lutheran Church of Iceland and all Christian people need to be ready to define and defend their religion and stand by what they believe. Given the rather liberal and moderate Christianity that is prevalent in Iceland, this might be difficult to envisage, since it is hard to be passionate about being moderate.

But are the people of Iceland sustained by the cross? As with other nations that often face the forces of nature and their destructive powers, many find comfort and support in the church when disaster strikes. Their faith guides them in ethical problems[63] and many look to their faith for strength.[64] The important role of pastors as counselors, supported by all surveys, is another indication of that. The strong image of God as "a loving God to whom we can pray" and who answers prayers is another indicator that Icelanders are comforted by their faith, "by the cross."

Conclusion

So is the Evangelical Lutheran Church of Iceland a Lutheran church? Would a "poor confused person" be able to recognize it as a Christian assembly?

Surveys only tell a part of the story, but they do give us insight into what people think and how they feel about their faith, about the church, and expectations towards its work, its pastors, and the liturgy. But nevertheless, it can undoubtedly be said that the marks of the church, as put forward by Martin Luther in *On the Councils and the Churches*, are all visible to some extent in the Evangelical Lutheran Church of Iceland, as seen by the members of the church, lay and ordained.

Lay people are active when it comes to choosing the pastor and they participate in the decision making of the parish council, in the church synod, and in the General Assembly. The priesthood of all believers seems, however, not very active in discerning the Word of God and the church is to a great extent considered a clergy-based church.

There might seem to be a contradiction in the relatively high number of people who describe themselves as Christian and religious, who believe in God and in Jesus Christ, on one hand, and the relatively small

---

63. *Trúarlíf Íslendinga*, 122.
64. Björnsson and Pétursson, *Trúarlíf Íslendinga*.

number of people that attend Sunday service. This can partly be explained by history: in sparsely populated areas people had to travel a long way to church. It was therefore not common for everyone to attend. In addition to Sunday worship there are many events in the church during the week and according to statistics Icelanders attend church on average 4.3 times per year.[65] While attendance and participation may always be considered a challenge for the church, there is no indication that church attendance is getting weaker. There is, however, a certain discrepancy in the high percentage of membership (80 percent) and the low rate of active attendance. Similar features can be found in other Scandinavian countries. The British sociologist Grace Davie has described this characteristic of Scandinavian church life as "believing in belonging."

What Pétursson calls "childhood faith" still seems strong in Iceland, visible for example in images and prayers. Many participate to some extent in child and youth work.[66] Christian traditions, such as Christian marking of the crossroads of life in baptism, confirmation, marriage, and funeral, are still very strong in Iceland. It is also evident that some Icelanders see the definition of being Christian mainly as a cultural definition, based on traditions and ethics, and are content to remain in the church and uphold it for that purpose. Hymns and ceremonies link the "childhood faith" to the heritage and tradition of the church and give religious meaning to the cultural Christianity.

The Evangelical Lutheran Church of Iceland is a Lutheran church in transition. The transition is both structural—of the church as institution—and touching the faith of its members. In an increasingly multicultural society, emphasis on passing on the Christian tradition will be left to the homes and the churches, with less emphasis on teaching about Christianity in schools. Parents will need increased support if they are to carry on a slowly eroding tradition of evening prayers. Multireligious society may also increase the need for the church and for the people in the church to define better what it is to be Christian, and even what it means to be Lutheran.

---

65. "Traust til presta og sóknarkirkna."
66. *Trúarlíf Íslendinga*, 86.

PART FOUR: Exploring a Heritage—Lutheran Identity

Bibliography

"Alþingi nýtur enn lítils trausts." Capacent. Online: http://capacent.is/Frettir-og-frodleikur/Thjodarpulsinn/Thjodarpulsinn/2010/03/05/Althingi-nytur-enn-litils-trausts/ (accessed 1/11/2010)

Ásgeirsson, Jón Ma. "Lögmál og Lógos: Ritúal í andstöðu við hinn fórnfærða messías." *Studia Theologica Islandica* 23 (2006) 131–54.

Björnsdóttir, Steinunn. "Samræða við samtímann." In *Um prédikunina*, 16–19. Kjalarness-prófastsdæmi, 2003.

Björnsson, Björn, and Pétur Pétursson. *Trúarlíf Íslendinga: Félagsfræðileg könnun*. Ritröð Guðfræðistofnunnar / Studia Theologica Islandica 3. Reykjavík: Guðfræðistofnun Skálholtsútgáfan, 1990.

———. "Um trúarlíf Íslendinga—frekari úrvinnsla á Hagnvangskönnuninni frá 1984." *Kirkjuritið*, April 1986, 5–30.

———. *Viðhorf kirkjugesta*. Reykjavík: University of Iceland, 1993.

———. *Þjóðkirkjusöfnuðir í sveit, bæ og borg*. Reykjavík: University of Iceland, 1996.

Constitution of the Republic of Iceland. No. 33, June 17, 1944 as amended May 30, 1984, May 31, 1991, June 28, 1995, and June 24, 1999. Online: http://government.is/constitution/ (accessed 1/11/2010).

Constitutional Assembly 2010. Online: http://www.kosning.is/stjornlagathing/english/ (accessed 1/11/2010).

Danmarks Riges Grundlov. 5 June 1849. Online: http://thomasthorsen.dk/dk-co-1849.html (accessed 1/11/2010).

Davie, Grace. *Religion in Modern Europe*. New York: Oxford University Press, 2000.

Eyjólfsson, Sigurjón Árni: *Ríki og kirkja*. Reykjavík: Hið íslenska bókmenntafélag, 2007.

Gunnarsson, Valur. "Til hvers að hata kirkjuna?" *DV-newspaper*, 5 November 2010.

Hafstein, Pétur Kr. "Setningarræða á 44. kirkjuþingi 13. nóvember 2010." Online: http://kirkjuthing.is/files/kirkjuthing-2010-setningaravarp-forseta.pdf (accessed 1/11/2010).

Hjaltalín, Torfi, K. S. *Ferming í fjórar aldir: Saga fermingar á Íslandi eftir siðbót*. Flateyjarútgáfan, 2007.

Hugason, Hjalti. "A Case Study of the Evolution of a Nordic Lutheran Majority Church." In *Law and Religion in the 21st Century: Nordic Perspectives*, edited by Lisbet Christoffersen, Kjell Å. Modéer, and Svend Andersen, 107–22. Copenhagen: Djøf, 2010.

Lathrop, Gordon W., and Timothy J. Wengert. *Christian Assembly: Marks of the Church in a Pluralistic Age*. Minneapolis: Augsburg Fortress, 2004.

Lög um stöðu, stjórn og starfshætti þjóðkirkjunnar. No. 78/1997, 26 May, art. 1. Online: http://www.althingi.is/lagas/nuna/1997078.html (accessed 1/11/2010).

Luther, Martin. *On the Council and the Churches*. In *Luther's Works on CD-ROM*, edited by Jaroslav Pelikan. Minneapolis: Fortress, 2001.

"Málefni kirkjunnar." Capacent. Online: http://www.capacent.is/frettir-og-frodleikur/thjodarpulsinn/thjodarpulsinn/2010/10/06/Malefni-kirkjunnar/ (accessed 22/08/2011).

Njarvík, Njörður P. *Spegill þjóðar*. Akranes: Uppheimar, 2010.

Pétursson, Pétur. "Nú legg ég augun aftur." *Studia Theological Islandica* 21 (2005) 137–57.

BJÖRNSDÓTTIR—*How Lutheran? An Icelandic Perspective*

"Sex ráðherrar vilja aðskilnað ríkis og kirkju." *Fréttablaðið*, 25 August 2010. Online: http://www.visir.is/sex-radherrar-vilja-adskilnad-rikis-og-kirkju/article/ 2010647349930 (accessed 1/11/2010).

"Tillaga til þingsályktunar um frumvarp til þjóðkirkjulaga." Online: http://kirkjuthing .is/mal/2010/6 (accessed 1/11/2010).

Trúarlíf Íslendinga. IMG Gallup. Quantitative survey, unpublished, 2004.

"Trúarlíf Íslendinga og væntingar til Þjóðkirkjunnar." Capacent. Qualitative survey, unpublished, 2007.

"Traust til Alþingis." Capacent. http://capacent.is/Frettir-og-frodleikur/ Thjodarpulsinn/Thjodarpulsinn/2010/10/20/Traust-til-Althingis/ (accessed 1/11/2010).

"Traust til presta og sóknarkirkna." Capacent. September–October 2010.

"Values for the New Constitution." Online: http://thjodfundur2010.is/nidurstodur/tre/ (accessed 1/11/2010).

"What is Sidmennt?" Online: http://sidmennt.is/english/what-is-sidmennt/ (accessed 1/11/2010).

15

How Is Lutheran Identity Constructed in the Evangelical Lutheran Church in Denmark?

MARIE VEJRUP NIELSEN

THE QUESTION OF LUTHERAN identity in the Evangelical Lutheran Church in Denmark is connected to a variety of issues and possible perspectives. In this chapter, specific approaches will be utilized to provide some conclusions on the topic through an analysis of selected domains of the church.

One of the perspectives of this chapter is the question of *who* is behind this identity construction. Therefore, the chapter will take its departure in a discussion of who the relevant representatives or representative domains are. This will also include comments on how the institutional structure of the church influences the study of Lutheran identity, since the lack of an official voice on behalf of the church affects the material available for examination.

This chapter will present material from two different dimensions of how Lutheran identity is present in a Danish context today: first of all, how it is part of the communication of the church to its members; and secondly, how it is part of an overall public debate concerning Danish cultural identity, a debate in which pastors and other representatives of church and theology take part.

What and Who Is the Folk Church/the Evangelical Lutheran Church in Denmark?

As was addressed in the introduction to the Danish context, the issue of the name of this church is in itself an indication of the underlying issues of identity. As can be seen by the contributions concerning the Danish context, there is no agreement on which name is the most appropriate to use and this is often even more clear when it comes to translations of the name.[1] But it can be said that it is a church with at least two names, which indicate two clusters of identity. This will become important in the analysis of how this church presents its identity to its members: as "the folk church," that is, the church for the people of Denmark, and/or as "Evangelical Lutheran," that is as a confessional church and religious community connected to a broader network of churches outside its national context. In the conclusion, the chapter will return to the question of whether one of the two identities is emphasized more than the other in the material analyzed. This chapter will examine the self-representation of Lutheran identity in various domains of the church. The main focus will be on cases that exemplify communication "from above," that is, from the official level of the church to its members. Is Lutheran identity primarily presented in vertical or horizontal communication? In other words, is it something that is strongly emphasized in relation to the members, or is it primarily something the representatives affirm in relation to each other?

The selection of data that can exemplify the communication of the church with its members is connected to the question of who the official representatives of the church are. There are a multitude of levels of official representation; however, it is possible to identify some main representatives. On the political level, the Minister of Ecclesiastical Affairs is the key example. The minister represents the government and the parliamentary system, and thereby the highest political level.[2] On the internal church level, the task is to find communication that can be said to somehow originate from a common official level. This will be done through the analysis of a comparably new resource from the church, the website www.folkekirken.dk.

---

1. See the introduction to the Danish context for more on this, and also the chapter by Peter Lodberg.

2. As was presented in the introduction to the Danish context, the queen and parliament constitute the highest official level of the church.

PART FOUR: Exploring a Heritage—Lutheran Identity

The members of the church feature only as the intended receivers of information, so this chapter will not go further into the various categories of members in the church, e.g., in relation to activity levels and patterns.[3] The view of the members who are intended to receive information on the identity of the church from these sources will be discussed in the analysis of www.folkekirken.dk. Substantial research into the reception of the communication was not possible within the framework of the study.

The first section will include comments on the official church level as such, e.g. the political level (Minister for Ecclesiastical Affairs) and the church level (www.folkekirken.dk). The second section will discuss the phenomenon of church representatives in the public sphere (public debate in newspapers). This again means that two main areas of data are analyzed in this chapter. First, examples of communication from the official level of the church are assessed. Due to the specific institutional structure of this church, it is not possible to analyze official statements from synods or similar official agencies, since there is no synod structure and no official voice of the church. Therefore the cases are taken from the areas of communication available, primarily official church-related websites, which can be said to constitute an official platform of communication from the church to the general public. The other main form of case material will be examples of public debate selected from two Danish national newspapers. This material has been analyzed in relation to a larger study performed as part of my research into how the concept of "Luther/Lutheran" appears in Danish public debates.[4]

To a lesser extent, other forms of case material such as academic publications and church teaching materials will also be drawn into the analysis in order to provide a detailed perspective on the issue.

Church Communication and Lutheran Identity: The Minister for Ecclesiastical Affairs and www.folkekirken.dk

Generally, there is an idea of what constitutes the ideal division of tasks between the political and the internal levels of the church. The political leadership is supposed to deal with certain overall structural and administrative tasks. And the internal church leadership on all levels should deal

---

3. For a presentation and discussion of the main issues, including perspectives on the various types of members, for the Evangelical Lutheran Church in Denmark in relation to a new context of pluralism, see Mortensen, *Kristendommen under forvandling*.

4. See Nielsen, "Claiming Luther as a Religious Resource."

with issues concerning the day-to-day work of the church on its various levels. One example of this division and the connections between the levels is the employment of pastors, which is a process involving both the internal and the political administrative levels of the church. The pastor is selected by the local church council, but has to be approved by the ministry.

Because the boundaries between the two domains are somewhat unclear, the issue of the division between the two levels is often debated.

The research behind this chapter focused on two cases that indicate how the Minister for Ecclesiastical Affairs participates in the construction of Lutheran identity in the church. The first case concerns a meeting called by the minister, Birthe Rønn Hornbech, on November 24–25, 2009. The meeting was by invitation only and the participants were a selection of representatives of church and theology.

The title of the meeting was "Our Lutheran Heritage and Challenge." The event spurred debate: had the minister, by calling a non-public meeting discussing the visions of the church and its confessional identity, moved into the internal domain of church life? The debate will not be reiterated here, but it points to how a specific minister did in this case take an interest in the identity of the church and how at the same time this was seen by some as controversial, because they deemed it to be an interference from the political level into the church level proper. The minister's interest in Lutheran identity can also be confirmed by the series of newspaper feature articles in the *Kristeligt Dagblad* (Christian Daily) written by the current minister. As this was only the actions of one politician, it is necessary to complement this picture with a more general look at the ministry. In the context of this chapter, this has been done through an examination of the official website of the Ministry for Ecclesiastical Affairs, www.km.dk,[5] to see how this contributes to the overall representation of Lutheran identity in the church.

There were thirty-one hits on the website for "Luther" and fifty-one for "Lutheran." The majority of references related to the name of the church and overall half of the links to "Luther" are to Luther as a hymn writer. Fourteen cases of Luther references related to discussions of a more normative kind, that is, Luther is drawn upon as a source of inspiration or identity. All of these fourteen cases are examples of communication between the ministry and other groups, be it through media, public speeches, or seminars. One place where the normative status of Luther

---

5. All translations from websites are by the author.

PART FOUR: Exploring a Heritage—Lutheran Identity

was especially obvious was in various feature articles on the website discussing issues such as how the church should relate to Islam or presenting views on what constitute Danish values. These feature articles are not necessarily written by the Minister for Ecclesiastical Affairs, but are placed on the website in relation to seminars, etc. My analysis of the references on the website gives only an indication of how the ministry presents Lutheran identity. It does not mirror a survey of all the work done by the ministry, that is, a survey of all documents sent out to the church, all cases going through parliament, etc.

The case of the meeting called by the minister seems to indicate that a given minister can have a larger or smaller interest in the issue of Lutheran identity and the website indicates that Luther/Lutheran is called upon in debates concerning certain issues, but that it is not the primary theme of the information given out generally, e.g., to the public using the website. There are no specific sections emphasizing the confessional identity of the church or any other form of systematic presentation of Evangelical Lutheran identity as such.

This could be a small indication of a horizontal communication concerning Lutheran identity, that is, when the minister is communicating with the elite of church and theology, the issue is of interest, if a given minister finds it relevant. But when it comes to the more vertical communication from the official level to users of the website, references which can be linked to Lutheran identity feature to a much lesser degree and primarily in relation to issues of public debate. The website www.km.dk does, however, refer to another relatively new website for further information on the church, www.folkekirken.dk.

As mentioned above, it is very difficult to claim that one has analyzed the official voice of the church seeing that the church has no single official representative or official representative body. But when it comes to finding examples of communication from the church to the members, a new case offers itself to be analyzed. The website www.folkekirken.dk is quite unique in a Danish context because it, to some extent, represents a unified voice of the church presented to the members. The development of the website has its own complex history, which starts with an initiative by a pastor who registered the domain and worked as webmaster of the site. But gradually it changed from the grassroots level to a more official level, ending, after a series of detours and some disagreement, with the current form. Today, it is a website officially owned and registered through the Ministry for Ecclesiastical Affairs and run by a board, which has appointed pastor Ellen

Aagaard Petersen as full-time editor. In the process, a survey was made that pointed to how the potential users of the site were primarily interested in information on the main events such as baptism, confirmation, etc., in line with the activity patterns of the general members of the church. The website today represents a development, where a range of representatives from the church support a common website across the various factions within the church, as a website aimed at informing the members of the issues the church expects them to be interested in. Therefore it is an obvious place to start looking for how the church constructs its identity in relation to its members on an official level.[6]

When surveying the website, which includes introductions to the church calendar, main events such as baptism and weddings, as well as historical background, it is clear that the aim of the site is to be relevant to the members broadly speaking. The layout is addressed to the activity pattern of the majority of the members of the church who have high levels of participation in the major rituals, but are less active in the daily life of the church.[7]

How is Luther and Lutheran identity represented on this primary online platform for meeting the members? The answer to that question gives some indications of the overall pattern of Lutheran identity formation in the communication provided by the church. When Luther does appear on the website, it is often in relation to the historical and theological background for certain events, such as baptism.[8] There are also a few cases where Luther is presented as a normative figure, e.g., in relation to prayer:

> *Do you have to believe in order to pray?*
>
> Many Danes are cautious concerning religious hypocrisy. Some say, that you should not pray, if you do not really believe or if you never go to church. But that is not so. Everyone can pray, no matter how much of a believer you think you are. If you feel the need to pray, then pray. Our church father, Martin Luther, tells us how he would sometimes feel completely empty and cold, and be in great doubt, even about his own faith. But then he would pray anyway, and then it could happen that he felt his heart and body heat up again; faith came again with the words of the prayer. The words of the prayer can come before faith.[9]

6. For a study of the folk church and the Internet, see Fischer-Nielsen, *Mellem sogne- og cyberkirke*.
7. Nielsen, "Transformationer i Folkekirkekristendommen i dag."
8. "Biskoppernes vejledning om dåb i folkekirken."
9. "Bøn."

PART FOUR: Exploring a Heritage—Lutheran Identity

This is a case of a strong normative representation of Luther, not only as church father, but as a model for the personal life of the members of the church. It is formulated in the present tense and it relates to the experience of the reader today. At the same time, it is obviously directed towards the ordinary members in how it takes its departure in the statement on the feelings of "many Danes," and includes the acceptance of a low-activity level, even to the point that it addresses people who "never go to church." This is further confirmed by how the church in other parts of the website is presented as a framework for important events in life with an emphasis on both explaining (historical and theological) events and practical details related to the church and giving advice on how to have a festive celebration with the family.[10] The church thus presents itself as a resource and framework for the important events in life.

Under the section on membership there is another case where Luther/Lutheran is mentioned directly:

As member

As a member of the Danish *Folkekirke* you are member of a Christian church in Denmark. The *Folkekirke* is Evangelical Lutheran. This name comes from the Reformation in the 16th century, where, in relation to Martin Luther's Reformation, the gospel was emphasized over against the tradition of the Roman Catholic Church. The membership fee for the *Folkekirke* is collected through church taxes. This means that no fee is paid for children or young people without a taxable income.[11]

This is a case of a presentation of the two confessional identities over and against each other, but at the same time it is obviously presented in a context of practical information. Another example can be found in the section on the Sunday service, where it is stated in the historical background that Martin Luther reformed the service.[12] These and a few more references are all to be found in relation to historical presentations.

When looking at the website there is one place where one would hypothesize there would be references to Luther and Lutheran identity: namely in the presentation of the church calendar in relation to the Reformation date, October 31. However, the calendar dedicates October 31

10. "Velkommen till dåb i folkekirken."
11. "Medlemsskab." The Danish term *Folkekirke* is a literal translation of the name of this church in Danish. In English it is usually called the Evangelical Lutheran Church in Denmark in the same way as it has been used in this chapter.
12. "Gudstjenstens historie."

to All Hallows Eve. Following the text on All Hallows Eve, it is mentioned that this is also the day where Luther put up his 95 Theses.[13] So, again, the church does not here, at what might be an obvious place, wish to emphasize the Lutheran identity of the church, but does mention the historical circumstances connected to the date.

There are some normative references to Luther/Lutheran on the website in the various texts written by pastors in a more personal form, e.g., in some of the blogs. Here there is more of a reference to Lutheran ideals and concepts than in the rest of the website.

When looking at the website in an overall perspective, there is one feature that might be relevant to the question of Lutheran identity. The key texts on the website often refer to biblical texts in the form of paraphrases of biblical stories as the framework for specific themes. This might point to how the Lutheran identity of the pastors plays a role as a resource for the representatives in the church in the choices they make, even if they do not make this explicit when communicating with the members. Biblical texts are of course central to all church families and traditions, but it might be of special significance in protestant settings due to the emphasis placed on Scripture in Reformation theology, especially connected to the issue of the access to biblical texts as well as the presentation of biblical texts as the access to knowledge on what it means to be Christian.

The analysis of a selected platform for communication of church identity points to two tentative conclusions. 1) The church does not represent Luther/Lutheran as a key point when communicating with its members on the website. Instead, the church primarily presents itself as *Folkekirke*, as a framework for the important events in the life of the people, in line with the survey done in the process of developing the site. 2) The representatives of the church have a practice, which might be seen as connected to the issue of Lutheran identity in that they emphasize Scripture as the main point of contact for the believer, and not the church institution or the pastors.

This second point can perhaps be supported further if one takes a look at the material used in a different setting where the church meets its members, namely the material used for teaching confirmation classes. Again, this is not a detailed survey of all the material used in Denmark today. But a consultation with Lars Nymark, teacher at the Pastoral Seminary in Aarhus, on this issue seems to point to some tendencies in relation to Lutheran identity. First of all, Luther and Lutheran identity is not an

---

13. "Allehelgen."

PART FOUR: Exploring a Heritage—Lutheran Identity

explicit part of the material to any large degree. This does not mean that it is not part of the teaching overall, since this is largely up to the individual pastor, and there is no access to a full overview of what is actually taught in the specific parishes. Luther, the Reformation and Lutheran identity in a broader perspective might be on the agenda. However, the materials that are dominant as the background for teaching confirmation classes do not present the issue of Lutheran identity as a key element. The material instead emphasizes central biblical texts and themes, the main events in the church year, the main liturgical elements such as prayer, ethical issues, as well as some historical background.

The conclusions so far are not that there is an absence of references to Lutheran identity or interest in this identity. Rather the tendency that is found in the material surveyed here seems to be that there is an interest horizontally, so to speak. However, this does not result in an explicit emphasis on the confessional identity of the church in relation to the ordinary members.

Church Representatives in Public Debate

That Lutheran identity should play a role in debates concerning overall issues of national identity, culture, and society is perhaps surprising to many outside a Danish context. But as the following two quotes point out, such links between Lutheran values and Danish values are indeed present, as well as disputed in Denmark today:

> A strange myth haunts Denmark. The myth has spread, just as the interest for the Enlightenment and history are growing. The myth says that the very cause behind the European Enlightenment and freedom of speech is no other than—Martin Luther! By thus placing the Enlightenment in the Reformation and in Protestantism they make it look as if the Enlightenment is both Christian and a "Danish value"—and even more—that it is something that grows directly out of the holy soil of home! This is, however, a coarse and self-satisfied lie![14]

> Euro-Islam—the reformation of Islam: Dear Muslim fellow-Danes: there is an internal fight that you must take concerning the relationship between religion and politics, if you really want us to accept you as future fully-fledged Danes. . . . Here Islam must necessarily arrive at the same distinction that Luther

14. Text from the backcover of the journal *Kritik*, issue 195 (2010).

accomplished almost 500 years ago in the Protestant understanding of Christianity.[15]

How does this debate relate to the church? Pastors are prominent in the material examined here, but the pattern is not exactly as in the other domains surveyed. Instead we find representatives of the church speaking very clearly about the importance of the Lutheran heritage. They do so, not in relation to the life of believers or religious practice, but in relation to issues at stake in Danish society as a whole, such as immigration, the separation of religion and politics, the public school system, etc.

The conclusions presented in the following are based on a detailed study of a selection of debate articles from two major Danish newspapers in 2000–2001, *Jyllandsposten* and *Politiken*. Both newspapers had a significant increase in references to Luther/Lutheran in the debate sections in this period. The study was partially inspired by a now famous feature article by then Prime Minister, Anders Fogh Rasmussen, in which he mentioned Luther and the doctrine of the two kingdoms, as one inspiration for his thoughts on how religion should be kept out of the public sphere.[16] The aim of the study was to identify whether this was a unique occurrence in the Danish debate environment or if the Prime Minister was speaking into an already established discourse. And if so, what this says about Lutheran identity in the Danish context.

The analysis identified certain features of the authors behind the cases. First of all, there is a prominence of people associated with the church and theology. This is very clear in *Jyllandsposten*, where between 40–45 percent have such a background, compared to 15–20 percent in *Politiken*. This makes it relevant to use the material in relation to the issue of Lutheran identity and the church.

Furthermore, the analysis reveals three main discourses in the material: cases that 1) argued for a strong connection between Lutheran and Danish; 2) argued against such a connection in a direct attack on the Lutheran dimension; and 3) argued for a negotiated connection, where the Lutheran heritage is respected but not seen as standing in the way of new dimensions of Danish identity. People related to church and theology feature most prominently in cases one and two.

---

15. Letter to the Editor in *Politiken*, 3 February 2001.

16. The feature article was published in *Politiken*, 20 May 2006, under the title *Hold religionen indendørs* (Keep religion indoor). The full-feature article is printed in Lodberg, *Sammenhængskraften*, along with responses from various researchers, who discuss the views points of the article from various perspectives.

PART FOUR: Exploring a Heritage—Lutheran Identity

The analysis also identified the four key themes of the debates: (a) *Folkekirken*, (b) Islam (addressing both Muslims and immigration), (c) Article 4 of the constitution,[17] and (d) Søren Krarup.[18] The issue of the connection between a Christian/Lutheran history and tradition and Danish society was touched upon in all four themes. And the themes were all related to issues that were on the agenda 2000–2001, an election year. Thus, the election in 2001 meant a change of government from a Social-Democratic to a Liberal-Conservative government, in alliance with the Danish People's Party. Søren Krarup was elected into parliament for this party, and as a pastor in the church represented both the church and the political system. He is also a well-known person in the milieu of theological debate and the editor of *Tidehverv*, a theological journal belonging to a specific church party.[19]

My analysis of the cases leads me to draw the following conclusions. First of all, that there is a debate environment in Denmark where Luther/Lutheran is presented as a normative resource for the development of society in an argument for how the specific combination of Danish history and culture with Lutheran thoughts provides a unique Danish model for the whole of society. There is a group of people in the debate milieu who draw upon such a discourse of a specific Danish cultural inheritance from the Lutheran Reformation and the historical development in Denmark, and they do so especially in relation to debates concerning Muslim immigration and the discussions concerning religion and the public sphere. At the same time, this representation of a Danish Lutheran value system does not stand unopposed; instead it is strongly opposed. And this opposition also focuses heavily on discussing Luther and Lutheran ideas. They argue that Luther and Lutheran values are incompatible with modern society;

---

17. Article 4 of the Danish constitution states that "The Evangelical Lutheran Church in Denmark (Folkekirken) is the established Church of Denmark and, as such, is supported by the State."

18. Søren Krarup is pastor emeritus and former member of the parliament (he retired from parliament in connection with the election of 2011). Both in his theological work and in his involvement in politics, Krarup has been influential in the debate on issues connected to culture and society.

19. For a presentation and discussion of Søren Krarup and *Tidehverv*, see Haugen, "The Evangelical Lutheran Church in Denmark and the Multicultural Challenges." Here Haugen connects the issues of Danish national identity and Christianity in relation to a discussion of the role of the Evangelical Lutheran Church in Denmark. For a study of religion in the public sphere in Denmark, Norway and Sweden, which also includes comments on the involvement of pastors in public debate, see Christensen, *Religion and Authority in the Public Sphere*.

instead they focus on international value systems such as human rights. That is, the debate examined in this research points to how both sides of the conflict agree that Luther/Lutheran is a central topic to disagree upon. The debates concerning the future development of Danish culture in relation to the issue of a negotiation of a form of multicultural society are for these people connected to a debate concerning the status of Luther and Lutheran ideas.[20]

Secondly, the phenomenon of drawing the issue of Lutheran identity into the public debate seems to be unknown in the other Scandinavian countries, as far as discussions with colleagues from those countries point. Of course, it would take similar examinations in the other Scandinavian countries to draw final conclusions on this, but conversations in relation to the work on this volume, as well as the indications found in other research projects, seem to be that the specific reference to a Lutheran identity in connection with national identity, issues of religion and society, and debates concerning the presence of Muslims in the country, is a specifically Danish phenomenon. Norwegian researcher Pål Repstad suspects as much in his question "to what extent can we see attempts at strengthening Christianity as the Nordic civil religion, with a polemic edge towards other religions?" Repstad states:

> My general impression is that this strategy is politically too controversial, both among political leaders and in the church. Maybe this strategy is more accepted in Denmark than in the other Nordic countries, because in Denmark is has more legitimacy among some intellectuals (including a small proportion of the clergy).[21]

And Hans Morten Haugen, associate professor at Diakonhjemmet University College, specifically links the Evangelical Lutheran Church in Denmark to this phenomenon in his research on the Danish situation.[22]

My analysis of the material presented here points to how it is not only Christianity in general, but a specific Lutheran identity, that is brought into play and that there is a number of clergy involved. They may not be

---

20. For a detailed presentation of the research presented here, see Nielsen, "Claiming Luther as a Religious Resource."

21. Repstad, "Civil Religion in an Age of Changing Churches and Society," 212; Haugen, "The Evangelical Lutheran Church in Denmark." In this context organizations such as Islam-Critical Network (*Islam-Kritisk Netværk*) in the *Folkekirken* should also be mentioned.

22. Haugen, "The Evangelical Lutheran Church in Denmark."

PART FOUR: Exploring a Heritage—Lutheran Identity

many in number, but they are prominent in the media, given much space in the debates both in newspapers and in electronic media when it comes to these issues. This may raise the question of whether it is relevant to include these cases as connected to the church, since some people might argue that these pastors are acting simply as individuals in civil society and not as part of their office. But in my view their position as pastors, that is, as official representatives of the church, does play a significant role. They are identified as pastors in the author information given prior to their letters to the editor or feature articles, and often their status as theologians is called upon in the texts, for example in relation to expressing authority on the subject of what constitutes Lutheran thoughts. At the same time, there are also pastors involved who do not agree with the strong connection of Lutheran and Danish values, and therefore point to how there are also many different voices of the church in this domain.

When examining public debate, it is interesting to see how broad a phenomenon the linking of Lutheran/Christian identity with a Danish identity is in the Danish context. This can of course not be examined in detail here. Nevertheless, one indication of how widespread such notions are in a Danish context could be the research performed by Brandt and Böwadt into the final exam papers of students at the teachers colleges in relation to the subject Christianity/Life education/Citizenship. Christianity/Life education/Citizenship provides the background for the teaching of the subject of Christianity in Danish public schools. The conclusion of their analysis was that to a large degree these soon-to-be teachers expressed a viewpoint wherein Christianity was linked to democracy, whereas other religions (e.g., Islam) were presented as being undemocratic. Also, there was a tendency to directly link Luther and Jesus to ideas of democracy.[23] This seems to indicate that there is an environment of debate in Denmark in which such connections are brought forward. This is also something that is a part of the public school system. Of course, it is not possible to conclude that this means that there is a strong tendency everywhere in the school system to present such a view point, as the research focused on the curriculum at the teachers college and not on the actual teaching situation. Yet, it is interesting in relation to the issue of Lutheran identity that such an identity may not necessarily or primarily be presented by the

---

23. Brandt and Böwadt, *Medborgerskab i læreruddannelsen*. In the official goals for the subject taught at the teachers college, it is stated that a key component i "the importance of Evangelical Lutheran Christianity for democracy, the welfare state, and school in Denmark." "Bekendtgørelse om uddannelsen til professionsbachelor som lærer i folkeskolen," 2.3.1, e.

church. Instead it is part of what could be called a cultural Lutheranism linked to the values of a modern secularized and democratic country.

How does this pattern fit with what was concluded in relation to the patterns of the internal church level? Here, in the context of public debate, the pastors involved explicitly refer to Luther and Lutheran identity. For them, as well as for those opposing them, Lutheran identity is no longer a part of a latent resource taken for granted. Instead, it is part of the arsenal utilized in a discursive conflict over what constitutes Danish values today. The context is one where the representatives of the discourse of there being a strong connection see this connection as threatened by changes in society. This situation provides a background for their re-armament of Lutheran/Danish identity.

The context of public debate is interesting in itself, as it has often been stated that many Danes, maybe even most Danes, receive their information concerning religion via the media and not via the information from religious institutions.[24] Therefore, this strong emphasis on Lutheran identity by some partakers in public debate might influence the view of Lutheran identity in the public in general. This may be true, especially since this emphasis on Lutheran identity stands over against an internal church context where Lutheran identity is more or less invisible, as it takes on the form of a given, natural part of the life of the church.

Conclusion—A Cultural Lutheranism?

There are very many areas of the Danish *Folkekirke* that have not been examined here, and with a church with such as complex structure, a membership of approximately 4.5 million, and no official voice, this complexity will remain no matter which kind of approach is taken to a study of the identity of the church. It is, however, possible to draw some conclusions on the basis of the material surveyed. There are two main elements to this conclusion. First of all, when communicating with its members the church primarily represents itself as folk church, perhaps as part of a conscious strategy in relation to the members in light of the expectations at the level of the official church representatives as to what the members want from the church. In this context, the specific confessional identity is not part of the image presented. Second, when surveying the context of public debate, Lutheran identity is a key part of the image presented, not of the church as such, but of Danish society and culture in general. Here, the clergy is

24. See Hjarvard, *En verden af medier* and "The mediatization of religion."

PART FOUR: Exploring a Heritage—Lutheran Identity

not only involved in presenting such an identity, but also in discussing it and modifying it. Again, the clergy and other representatives of church and theology do not speak with one voice. Hence, my study points at how the church, which has no single official voice in presenting its position, on the other hand has many official and unofficial voices when it comes to participation in public debates. Maybe it is even the lack of an official voice that opens the arena for many voices? The floor is wide open for anyone to take on the role of representative of Lutheran identity and this is done in the context of a debate concerning the development of Danish society and culture.

One interesting question which is not answered in this chapter is how these messages are received by the members of the church. A user of www.folkekirken.dk might be excused for not being aware of the confessional identity of the church, as this does not feature prominently. So perhaps this church in its emphasis on being a folk church performs a sort of vicarious Lutheranism, where the pastors are those who take care of the knowledge of what it means to be Lutheran, as the experts?

When it comes to the involvement in the public debate one possible conclusion to this chapter is that the confessional identity marker takes on the form of a more general religio-ethnic identity marker instead of a specific confessional identity. Will this mean an increased focus also within the church, when the issue of Lutheran identity becomes an element in the negotiation of Danish cultural values in a contemporary multireligious setting? If so, the more correct term perhaps is a "cultural Lutheranism" centered on the debate concerning Danish values?

What will the development of the church and state relationship mean for this identity? With an emphasis on folk church, the question becomes how to be a folk church without the state, if church and state should separate. Will this mean that confessional identity will become more relevant in a setting where church and state are separating?

Will the Reformation anniversary in 2017, already selected to be celebrated in various ways in Denmark, be the final countdown for Lutheran identity or a revival? Previous celebrations have been connected to such revivals in the theological environments, but what about the church as such? Will the state fund this event to any larger degree or not? The interest in Lutheran identity seems to be growing within research milieus as well as in the churches, as can be seen by the title of the meeting of Scandinavian bishops in Aarhus during the summer of 2010: "Luther and Post-Secular Scandinavia." Is this sign of how the churches feel a need to strengthen the confessional identity of the church, perhaps through connections to other Lutheran churches? And how does it reflect the Danish situation of a conflict over Lutheran/Danish identity in the public sphere? These are all questions for the future. This chapter has provided some perspectives on the situation in Denmark today, where the church with two names seems to favor the one—folk church—in its communication with the public in the domains analyzed here. At the same time, this does not mean that the issue of Lutheran identity is irrelevant; indeed it seems to be highly relevant in Denmark today in the context of sensitive issues of the development of Danish society in the immediate future.

Bibliography

"Allehelgen." Online: http://www.folkekirken.dk/hoejtider-og-traditioner/allehelgen (accessed 12/08/2010).
"Bekendtgørelse om uddannelsen til professionsbachelor som lærer i folkeskolen." Online: http://www.retsinformation.dk/Forms/R0710.aspx?id=25302#B1 (Accessed 06/09/2011).
"Biskoppernes vejledning om dåb i folkekirken." Online: http://www.folkekirken.dk/livets-begivenheder/daab/biskoppernes-vejledning-om-daab-i-folkekirken (accessed 12/08/2010).
Brandt, Ane Kirstine, and Pia Rose Böwadt. *Medborgerskab i læreruddannelsen: Rapport til Undervisningsministeriet*. Ministry of Education, 2009. Online: http://api.archive.undervisere.dk/binAPI/streamfile.exe?name=FS\Documents\140\59340.pdf&type=application/pdf&path=ArchiveFiles (accessed 06/09/2011).
"Bøn." Online: http://www.folkekirken.dk/tro-og-liv/boen/ (accessed 12/08/2010).
Christensen, Henrik R. *Religion and Authority in the Public Sphere: Representations of Religion in Scandinavian Parliaments and Media*. PhD dissertation, University of Aarhus, 2010.
Fischer-Nielsen, Peter. *Mellem sogne- og cyberkirke: En analyse af folkekirkens kommunikation på internettet*. Aarhus: Det teologiske Fakultet, 2011.
"Gudstjenstens historie." Online: http://www.folkekirken.dk/gudstjeneste/soendagsgudstjeneste/gudstjenstens-historie/?0 (accessed 12/08/2010).
Haugen, Hans Morten. "The Evangelical Lutheran Church in Denmark and the Multicultural Challenges." *Religion and Politics* 4/2011, 476–502.
Hjarvard, Stig. *En verden af medier: Medialiseringen af politik, sprog, religion og leg*. Frederiksberg: Samfundslitteratur, 2008.
———. "The Mediatization of Religion: A Theory of the Media as Agents of Religious Change." *Northern Lights* 6/1 (2008) 9–26.
"Hold religionen indendørs." *Politiken*, 20 May 2006.
Lodberg, Peter, editor. *Sammenhængskraften: Replikker til Fogh*. Højbjerg: Univers, 2007.
"Medlemsskab." Online: http://www.folkekirken.dk/om-folkekirken/medlemsskab/ (accessed 12/08/2010).

PART FOUR: Exploring a Heritage—Lutheran Identity

Mortensen, Viggo. *Kristendommen under forvandling: Pluralismen som udfordring til teologi og kirke i Danmark.* Højberg: Univers, 2005.
Nielsen, Marie Vejrup. "Claiming Luther as a Religious Resource—Civil Religion in Conflict?" *Journal for Religion in Europe* 4 (2011) 300–327.
———. "Transformationer i Folkekirkekristendommen i Danmark i dag." *Religionsvidenskabeligt Tidsskrift* 53 (2009) 63–79.
Repstad, Pål. "Civil Religion in an Age of Changing Churches and Society—A Look at the Nordic Situation." In *Holy Nations and Global Identities: Civil Religion, Nationalism, and Globalisation,* edited by Annika Hvithamar, Margit Warburg, and Brian Arly Jacobsen, 199–214. Leiden: Brill, 2009.
"Velkommen till dåb i folkekirken." Online: http://www.folkekirken.dkmnet.dk/index.php?id=75 (accessed 12/08/2010).

16

The Lutheran and Ecumenical Identity of Church of Norway

HARALD HEGSTAD

CHURCH OF NORWAY IS going through major changes. According to an agreement between all the political parties in the parliament, church and state relations will be changed from 2012 through amendments to the constitution. This process has led the church to rethink and redefine its identity. Even if the official name of the church is Church of Norway (*Den norske kirke*), it is often just referred to as "the state church." After 2012 this nickname will become less fitting and Church of Norway will to a greater extent appear as a church among others, even if its size (79 percent of the population) puts it in a special position. Anyway, the question has been up for discussion: if it is not a privileged relation to the state that constitutes the identity of this church, what is it?

Identity without Confessional Consciousness?

As part of the state church process the General Synod of Church of Norway in 2004 passed a statement on Church of Norway's "identity and mission."[1] The statement covers several aspects of being church in

1. "Den norske kirkes identitet og oppdrag." The translations are mine.

305

contemporary Norwegian society. A striking aspect of the statement is that very little emphasis is put on the confessional character of Church of Norway as a Lutheran church. When the relation to churches from other traditions is mentioned, focus is on the connections and continuities rather than on differences. The statement underlines that "The Church of Norway is part of the worldwide Christian Church" (§ 1), and that it "today is part of a broad community of churches in our country" (§ 2). The Reformation in the sixteenth century is not mentioned at all; the focus is rather the continuity with the medieval Norwegian church: "The Church of Norway is a continuation of the church that was founded by the end of the first millennium" (§ 2). The only place where the Lutheran character of the church is explicitly mentioned is in the description of the doctrinal basis of the church, but also in this context the focus is on this basis as something that connects to a common faith:

> The church sees the confessions from the old church as an expression of the common faith it shares with other churches. The distinct Lutheran confessions are genuine expressions of this common faith (§ 3).

At the end of the document the relation to other churches is mentioned again in relation to the role of Church of Norway's efforts for church unity through participation in ecumenical organizations and bilateral agreements (§ 22).

The missing confessional identification of Church of Norway in the document does not mean that the identity assigned to the church is unclear or without profile. Instead, other categories are used in the formulation of the identity, especially through the understanding of Church of Norway as a folk church. This is for instance expressed through the understanding of Church of Norway as a "confessing, missional, serving and open folk church" (§ 7). Most of what the documents says about the identity and mission of Church of Norway could without difficulties be linked to the Lutheran tradition of the church, but it just does not happen.

In a process leading to the meetings of the General Synod of Church of Norway in 2010 and 2011, the identity of the church has again been up for discussion, this time explicitly related to the Lutheran character of the church. Based on discussions within the Theological Commission of Church of Norway Council on Ecumenical and International Relations, a book on the Lutheran identity of the church was published in early 2011 consisting of articles by several authors discussing the meaning and relevance of different aspects of the Lutheran tradition for today's church.[2] The aim of this process is not to issue a final definition of the Lutheran identity of Church of Norway, but rather to stimulate the awareness of the confessional identity of the church.

A main reason for the low awareness in this matter is mainly a reflection of Church of Norway's majority position in Norwegian society. Even if other churches have been present since the 1840s, Church of Norway has been understood as the main representative of the Christian faith in Norway. When other churches in recent years have become more visible in society, Church of Norway has chosen to stress ecumenical fellowship and openness rather than confessional identity. At the same time this ecumenical profile is an important reason for the recent engagement with its own confessional identity. When approaching other churches with much more distinctive identities, Church of Norway tends to appear rather vague in its profile. In order to engage in ecumenical dialogue, it is necessary to be aware of one's own confessional identity.

Identity Formed by the Past

In order to understand the present situation and be able to navigate for the future, it is necessary to be aware of the past. Church of Norway has been a Lutheran church for almost five hundred years. Engaging with the confessional identity means finding resources for the future, but also acknowledging the limitations of this tradition—and thus seeking mutual enrichment in relationships with churches from other traditions. What it means for a church to have a Lutheran identity may vary according to the given context. A Lutheran identity is not something abstract, but a concrete identity shaped by various factors. What keeps Lutheran churches together is a common reference to the Reformation and the Lutheran confessions. Apart from that they may be very different. In order to understand the Lutheran identity of Church of Norway it is necessary to understand the historical background.

Christianity was introduced in Norway in the tenth century, before the great schism between the Western and Eastern churches. The kings played an important role in this process and the establishment of a Norwegian monarchy and the Christianizing process went to a great extent hand in hand. A formative event, both for the monarchy and the church, was the battle at Stiklestad in the year 1030 where king Olav Haraldsson,

2. Dietrich, Dokka, and Hegstad, *Kirke nå*.

PART FOUR: Exploring a Heritage—Lutheran Identity

later known as St. Olav, was killed. The later canonization of Olav as *Rex Perpetuus Norvegiae* (Norway's Eternal King), the erection of his shrine in Nidaros (Trondheim) and the cult of Olav as a saint contributed to secure the position of the church, as well as the monarchy. In 1152 the pope established the See of the Archbishop of Nidaros. During the middle ages Nidaros became an important pilgrimage destination for pilgrims from all over Europe.[3]

Due to various reasons Norway lost its independence in the fifteenth century and came under Danish rule. The Lutheran Reformation was thus introduced by a decision of the Danish king Christian III in 1536. Most of the Catholic bishops were jailed and the archbishop fled the country in 1537. In contrast to the situation in Germany, the Reformation was not based in any popular movement and this caused resistance in the population. The Reformation also meant an end to the (relative) independence of the church from the state and the beginning of the state church system.[4]

This historical background is important in order to understand the modern revival of medieval traditions, especially connected to Nidaros and St. Olav. In the nineteenth century this revival clearly was connected to the struggle for national independence. When Danish rule ended in 1814, Norway got its own constitution, which prescribed the king to be crowned in Nidaros cathedral. Even if the king was shared with Sweden until 1905, all Norwegian kings have since then been crowned or (from 1958) blessed in St. Olav's church, thus linking the monarchy to *Rex Perpetuus Norvegiae*. A revival of the celebration on July 29 ("Olsok"), the day of St. Olav's death, was inaugurated on the 900th anniversary of the battle at Stiklestad in 1930. In recent years church and state have cooperated to stimulate the "pilgrim tradition" by restoring old walking tracks to Nidaros, employing "pilgrim pastors," and building pilgrim centers. Every year numerous pilgrims make the trip to Nidaros around the time of Olsok, walking at least part of the way.[5] From the point of view of the state the most important motive behind this seems to be of touristic and cultural character, while the church on its part utilizes this newborn interest in pilgrimage for religious purposes.

---

3. Aarflot, *Norsk kirke i tusen år*, 13–35.

4. Ibid., 49–66; Oftestad, Schumacher, and Rasmussen, *Norsk kirkehistorie*, 13–35; Oftestad, *Den norske statsreligionen*, 40–54.

5. For the official information about the National Pilgrim Center see online: http://www.pilegrim.info/en/.

A new chapter in the Nidaros tradition was written when the government—against the will of the General Synod—picked Nidaros as the see for the new leading bishop of Church of Norway. Some advocates for this decision view this as a first move towards a new archbishop in St. Olav's town.

An important question that has been debated in this context is how these "medieval" and "catholic" traditions can be reconciled with the Lutheran tradition of the church. Also the advocates of these traditions are aware of the fact that the traditions have to be reinterpreted to fit in a Lutheran context and also to be meaningful for modern people. However, for some this has led to a relativizing of the importance of the Reformation. In a book on the Reformation, Karl Gervin, a pastor in Oslo Cathedral, primarily pictures the Reformation as a breakaway from positive elements in the ecclesial tradition.[6] Other voices have been arguing for a limitation of the relevance of the St. Olav tradition to the Nidaros diocese, criticizing the attempts to revitalize Nidaros as the geographical centre of the church.

The special background for this discussion is the announced amendments in church-state relations after 2012. These changes will in no way change the Lutheran character of the church. However, the question of how church organization and leadership should be shaped also raises questions that link the church to its pre-Reformation past.

Formal Basis of Confessional Identity

The Lutheran character of Church of Norway is not only a matter of history and tradition, but it also has a legal basis. For a state church this means that the confessional basis is regulated not only in internal church law, but in the laws of the state. In the case of Church of Norway this means that the confessional basis of the church is defined by King Christian V's Norwegian law of 1687. In one of the few paragraphs in this law that is still valid, it is stated that:

> ... in the lands of the king only the religion is allowed that is in accordance with Holy Scripture, the Apostolic, Nicene and Athanasian confessions, the unaltered Augsburg Confession from 1530, and Luther's small catechism.[7]

---

6. Gervin, *Det store bruddet*.

7. *Kong Christian Den Femtis Norske Lov* (1687), Anden Bog, 1 Cap (my translation). Legal texts referred to here and in the following can be found at http://lovdata.no. A recent law reform aimed at replacing all laws older than 1814, however this

PART FOUR: Exploring a Heritage—Lutheran Identity

As can be seen from this law, Church of Norway (together with the Danish church) has a narrower selection of Lutheran confessional documents than most other Lutheran churches (including the Swedish and Finnish) that are bound by the complete *Book of Concord*. The background for this was the attempt of the Danish king to stay away from the theological controversies in Germany at the end of the sixteenth century. It is thus told that King Fredrik II burnt the copies of the *Book of Concord* he received and banned it from his country.[8] A result of this historical circumstance writings such as the Apology and the Formula of Concord have had very little impact on Church of Norway's understanding of the Lutheran identity. Discussions on the implications of the confessional basis have primarily been over the interpretation of selected articles in the Augsburg Confession.

This Lutheran basis was confirmed in the constitution from 1814, which prescribes that "the Evangelical-Lutheran religion shall remain the official religion of the State" (§ 2) and that "the King shall at all times profess the Evangelical-Lutheran religion, and uphold and protect the same" (§ 4).[9] In 1983, the Supreme Court ruled that § 2 is only binding for the state so far as they relate to Church of Norway. According to the court, § 2 does not (at least not today) imply a confessional state, only a confessional church.[10]

In the amended text of the constitution that probably will come into force from 2012 the Norwegian state is no longer understood as Lutheran, even if, according to the amended constitution, "the value basis remains our Christian and Humanistic heritage" (new § 2). A Lutheran confession is no longer attached to the state, only to the church. Thus, "Church of Norway, an Evangelical Lutheran church, remains the folk church of Norway, and is as such supported by the state" (new § 16).[11]

---

paragraph was not replaced due to the unresolved question over how the confessional basis of the church can be regulated by a secular state today. This problem was avoided by keeping the old law.

8. Aarflot, *Norsk kirke i tusen år*, 68.

9. *Kongeriget Norges Grundlov* (1814). English citations from the constitutions from http://www.stortinget.no/en/In-English/About-the-Storting/The-Constitution/The-Constitution/.

10. The ruling was in a case against a pastor that claimed that the abortion law was illegal because it was in conflict with § 2 in the constitution. The court did not decide whether the abortion law was in conflict with the Lutheran confession, as it does not bind the state in any case. Oftestad, *Den norske statsreligionen*, 269–74.

11. The agreement between the political parties may be found in *Staten og Den norske kirke*, 67–68 (my translations). On the church and state process in general, cf. the chapter by Jensen in this volume.

A Pietistic Version of Lutheranism

Even if the Lutheran faith was introduced by a royal decree, without popular support, it gradually was adopted by the Norwegian people. This happened not least through the liturgy, through the singing of hymns, and through sermons. Important books were Bible translations, Luther's *Small Catechism*, various devotional books, and several hymn books. As ministers of the church and of the king local pastors influenced and controlled local communities both in spiritual and worldly matters. An important event was the reintroduction of confirmation in 1736, which made learning Christian fundamentals compulsory for all youth. At the same time the public school was founded, which until recently imparted Lutheran faith to the population. A very important book in this respect was Erik Pontoppidan's explanation of Luther's *Small Catechism* (*Sannhed til gudfryktighed*, 1737), which for generations was learnt by heart by candidates for confirmation. Both Pontoppidan and the confirmation reform were expressions of the *pietistic* movement within Lutheranism in the eighteenth century. As in the case of the Reformation these reforms were the result of royal initiatives, this time the pious Christian VI, who represented the so-called state pietism. Originating in Germany as an internal Lutheran reform movement, pietism stressed the personal relationship to God and the necessity of true faith for bearing fruit in a holy life and the service of others. In addition to an intensification of religious life pietism led to social and missionary initiatives.[12]

While eighteenth-century pietism was a result of initiatives from above, nineteenth-century Norwegian pietism was of a popular, revivalist type. In the early phase of this movement the lay preacher Hans Nielsen Hauge (1771–1824) was the central figure. Later in the century the revivals led to the founding of various organizations for home and foreign missions, which still are important and influential factors in Norwegian church life. In contrast to Sweden, for example, the revival movements mainly kept a Lutheran identity and stayed within the church. An exception to this trend is the Evangelical Lutheran Free Church, founded in 1877, which has become the largest Lutheran church in Norway after Church of Norway.[13]

---

12. Aarflot, *Norsk kirke i tusen år*, 78–85; Oftestad, Schumacher, and Rasmussen, *Norsk kirkehistorie*, 144–66.

13. Aarflot, *Norsk kirke i tusen år*, 91–103; Oftestad, Schumacher, and Rasmussen, *Norsk kirkehistorie*, 171–75, 192–216.

PART FOUR: Exploring a Heritage—Lutheran Identity

As domestic church movements the missionary organizations are formally independent of the official church structure. Their *de facto* relationship to the official church varies considerably among the organizations, as they practice their independence differently. Some organizations employ ordained pastors, some do not. Some see their work as a supplement to the work of Church of Norway, some see their work as something in its own right. At the local level the revivalist movements have traditionally cooperated in the erection of meeting houses (*bedehus*). These meeting houses have been places for voluntary religious meetings, lay preaching, and in many cases also lay-led celebration of Holy Communion. At the same time adherents of the revival movements have in many instances represented an important proportion of the active churchgoers in the local church and often also have had an important influence in parish councils. These movements have also been an important source for recruiting pastors for the church and have thus had an influence in Church of Norway that reaches far beyond their own organizations.[14]

The pietistic influence in the church has since the nineteenth century led to a discussion regarding the relationship between Lutheranism and pietism. From a more orthodox Lutheran position pietism has been criticized for being too subjective and for an insufficient sacramental orientation. Pietism thus has also been charged with being more Reformed than Lutheran. Such charges have been repudiated by the revival movements themselves, which have been eager to prove their Lutheran character.

A big issue in the nineteenth century was whether lay preaching could be accepted in the light of article XIV in the Augsburg Confession, which states that no one should publicly teach, preach, or administer the sacraments without a proper call.[15] To solve this dilemma the leader of the domestic missions movement and professor of theology Gisle Johnson (1822–1894) introduced the so-called principle of necessity, which allowed lay preaching as long as there were not sufficient ordained ministers to do the job. Later this principle was given up and lay preaching became widely accepted in the church. Some strands of the revival movements also applied this to the distribution of Holy Communion.[16] Even if this is not officially accepted by the church, Church of Norway today holds a rather low church attitude regarding this issue. Even if the administering of the sacraments is the main responsibility of ordained pastors, the bish-

14. Hegstad, "Den lavkirkelige vekkelsesbevegelse i Norge."
15. The Augsburg Confession is cited from Kolb and Wengert, *Book of Concord*.
16. Aarflot, *Norsk kirke i tusen år*, 104–8.

ops have the opportunity to license laypeople to take care of this if there is a lack of available pastors.

In the last few decades the relationship between the mission organizations and the church has shifted. There are two basic tendencies in this shift. On the one hand there has been a development towards integrating local groups belonging to such organizations in the work of the local congregations. As the church has taken up tasks that traditionally have been solved by the organizations (e.g., activities for children and youth), the organizations have to some extent been assimilated in the work of the official church. On an architectural level this development has been expressed in the erection of church buildings that not only have room for traditional services and ceremonies, but also for activities that used to be located at meeting houses owned by the organizations.[17]

On the other hand there has been an opposite tendency for local groups to develop into congregations of their own, celebrating full services including baptism and Holy Communion. This has especially taken place in larger cities. There is an ongoing discussion whether these congregations should be understood as a part of Church of Norway, or whether they should form independent free churches. Even if their relationship to Church of Norway is up for debate, the Lutheran identity of these groups seems to be taken for granted.

Other Versions of Norwegian Lutheranism

Even if the revivalist movements have had a strong influence in Church of Norway, they have not been the only version of Norwegian Lutheranism. Another tradition has been a more orthodox, high church expression primarily represented by pastors and theologians. This wing of the church has stressed the sacramental character of the church, the role of liturgy, and the position of ordained ministry in the church. This has sometimes led to controversies with the low church movement, although on other occasions they have been allied to each other, especially in the struggle against the influence of what has been understood as liberal theology. One of the most successful results of such an alliance was the founding of MF Norwegian School of Theology[18] in 1908 as an alternative to the Faculty of Theology at the University of Oslo, which at the time was influenced by German liberalism.

17. For this and the following paragraph, see Hegstad, *Kirke i forandring*, 74–101.
18. *Det teologiske Menighetsfakultet.*

PART FOUR: Exploring a Heritage—Lutheran Identity

Today there is also an ongoing debate between a low church and a high church version of Lutheran theology. The differences especially come to the fore in liturgical questions, related to the way Holy Communion is celebrated. A much-debated issue has been the question over what should be done if there is not sufficient bread or wine on the altar: should bread and wine that is brought in afterwards be consecrated separately or not? The low church position would typically be to say no, arguing against a sort of transubstantiation theory. The high church position would typically be yes, in order to secure the difference between consecrated and non-consecrated elements. Questions like this have again been raised in connection with the ongoing liturgical reform in Church of Norway.[19]

Due to a series of conversions to the Roman Catholic Church and the so-called Nordic Catholic Church, the high church movement within the church has lost much of its influence. The high church organization Ecclesial Renewal (*Kirkelig fornyelse*), which mainly used to be a movement within Church of Norway, is today more of an ecumenical body.

Another important tradition in Church of Norway is the more "liberal" tradition, mainly connected to the Faculty of Theology at the University of Oslo. From holding a rather radical position in doctrinal questions in the first part of the twentieth century this tradition shifted in the 1950s to a more affirming position vis-à-vis church doctrine. In recent years the debate between liberals and conservatives has been on moral rather than doctrinal questions (the position on homosexuality being a main issue). An important aspect of this tradition has been the understanding of Church of Norway as a folk church, thus stressing the necessity of broadness and openness. This position has included a critical approach towards revivalism and revivalist groups. As a consequence of the state church system the university faculty has had a special link to Church of Norway,[20] which also contributes to a focus on the Lutheran identity of its theology. An important aspect of the understanding of Lutheran theology in this tradition has been the stress on the theology of creation. In ecclesiological terms this has contributed to the understanding of Church of Norway as a folk church.[21]

---

19. Cf. Waaler, *Nattverden som offer*.

20. Until recently professors according to the church law normally have to be members of Church of Norway. See *Lov om Den norske kirke* (1996).

21. Myhre-Nielsen, *En hellig og ganske alminnelig kirke*.

Lutheran Identity in an Ecumenical Context

As mentioned in the beginning the understanding of Church of Norway as a Lutheran church has in the recent years been shaped by the understanding of the church in an ecumenical setting. As a signatory of several ecumenical agreements, the confessional identity of Church of Norway is decided not only by its Lutheran tradition, but also by its ecumenical context and relations. These relations have also changed the way Church of Norway understands itself as a Lutheran church. In its ecumenical relations Church of Norway has chosen a rather broad approach. It is thus (together with the Danish church) the only participant both in the Porvoo Agreement between Lutheran and Anglican churches, and the Leuenberg Agreement between Lutheran, Reformed, and United churches.

The oldest of these ecumenical documents is the Leuenberg Agreement from 1973, establishing altar and pulpit fellowship between Lutheran, Reformed, and United churches in Europe.[22] The agreement was not signed by Church of Norway until 1999. There are two main reasons why the agreement was not signed earlier. The first was a more formal one: there are no Reformed or United churches represented in Norway. The other was more substantial theological objections regarding the possibility of altar and pulpit fellowship with Reformed churches.

A fierce critic of the Leuenberg Agreement was Leiv Aalen (1906–1983), professor of systematic theology at MF Norwegian School of Theology. Aalen's contribution is interesting in the context of this article as he was an important representative of a renaissance of Lutheran confessional identity in Church of Norway from the 1930s onwards. Through his writings and teaching he passed on influences from contemporary German confessional theology (represented by Hermann Sasse, Paul Althaus, and Werner Elert).[23] For Aalen Lutheran identity was not primarily established through the study of Luther's writings, but rather in relation to the Lutheran confessions, which for Aalen included the entire *Book of Concord*. Aalen understood the Lutheran confessions as the only legitimate continuation of the confessions from the old church and regarded other churches as deviating from true doctrine. In his exposition of Lutheran theology he often contrasted it to Reformed theology on the one hand, and Catholic on the other. To sign an agreement with Reformed churches was for him trea-

---

22. "Agreement between Reformation Churches in Europe (The Leuenberg Agreement)."

23. Hegstad, *Transcendens og inkarnasjon*.

son against the truth of Lutheran theology. Aalen's position is an example of Lutheran confessionalism that understands the relationship between the Lutheran churches and other churches purely in contradictory and contrasting terms. For him, church unity meant that other churches would have to accept the truth of the Lutheran confessions.[24]

When signing the Leuenberg Agreement in 1999 Church of Norway clearly had distanced itself from this type of confessionalism. Still recognizing theological differences between the different confessional traditions, these differences were understood not as church division, but rather as expressions of "unity in reconciled diversity."[25]

Church of Norway had already in 1994 signed an agreement with another church family, namely the Anglican. In the Porvoo Common Statement the British and Irish Anglican Churches and the Nordic and Baltic Lutheran churches declared mutual recognition. While the difficult question in the Leuenberg process was the understanding of Holy Communion, the central issue in the Porvoo process was the question of ministry, especially of episcopal ministry. In the Porvoo Common Statement the Lutheran churches accept historic episcopal succession as a valuable, but not a necessary sign of the apostolicity of the church. This means on the one hand that the Anglicans recognize the episcopal ministry in the Lutheran churches do not have an unbroken chain of bishops (as in Norway), on the other hand that such churches are free to take up a historical succession without denying its past apostolic continuity.[26]

The understanding of historic episcopal succession as a valuable, but not necessary, sign of apostolic continuity and unity also means that Church of Norway is free to recognize churches that do not have episcopal succession or even an episcopal office. Even if oversight (*episkopé*) is necessary for the church, it can also be carried out in other forms than the personal episcopal office. Based on this interpretation, the signing of the Porvoo agreement has not excluded Church of Norway from also joining the Leuenberg communion. In the Signatory's Protocol for the signing of the Leuenberg agreement this position is explained in the following way:

> In all our churches there are forms of pastoral oversight ("episcope"). Such a function is necessary in all churches. The concrete structure and understanding of such a ministry of oversight may, however, vary. In the Porvoo agreement, the Church of Norway

24. Cf. Hegstad, "Fra konfesjonalisme til differensiert konsensus."
25. Meyer, *That All May Be One*.
26. "The Porvoo Common Statement," par. 50–54.

has stated, together with the other Porvoo signatory churches, that fellowship in word and sacrament is made explicit through the ministry of oversight which is exercised by the pastoral ministry in the church and by the ministry of bishops on whom the ministry of oversight is bestowed in a particular way. . . . This does not for us preclude recognition of other churches which do not have an episcopal ministry, or the possibility of full church fellowship with such churches.[27]

The rationale behind this rather flexible ecumenical approach (which so far only includes the Evangelical Lutheran Church in Denmark) is to be found in a certain interpretation of the Lutheran understanding of church unity. In a reflection on the compatibility of the agreements with the Anglican and Reformed churches Olav Fykse Tveit points to the article VII of the Augsburg Confession, which states that the only necessary condition for church unity is to agree concerning the teaching of the gospel and the administration of the sacraments. As far as this condition is fulfilled, church unity should be possible regardless of divergent ministerial structures.[28]

This way of thinking resulted in 1997 in the signing of an agreement with the Norwegian Methodist Church, which resulted in altar and pulpit fellowship and mutual recognition and exchange of pastors.[29] In 1997 the General Synod of Church of Norway also accepted the "Joint Declaration on the Doctrine of Justification" between the Lutheran World Federation and the Roman Catholic Church. Seen from the point of view of Augsburg Confession VII's view on the necessary conditions for church unity, this declaration can be understood as a breakthrough in the relations with Roman Catholics. Clearly the old understanding of the Lutheran church as the true middle road between Reformed spiritualism and Roman synergism (cf. Aalen) has been seriously weakened. This new situation of course calls for a reconstruction of how to understand the Lutheran identity in this new situation.

The methodological approach of the declaration, which has been characterized as "differentiated consensus," means that it is possible to combine a fundamental agreement on central issues and at the same time recognize differences in the way things are expressed and in less important

---

27. "Signatory's Protocol by the Church of Norway on the Signing of The Agreement between Reformation Churches in Europe (Leuenberg Agreement)," par. 4.

28. Tveit, "Compatibility of Church Agreements."

29. *Nådens fellesskap.*

PART FOUR: Exploring a Heritage—Lutheran Identity

matters. While the ultimate goal of basic unity in faith and doctrine is confirmed, at the same time a certain plurality is accepted as legitimate including certain differences in doctrinal interpretations.

This means that the construction of a Lutheran identity in an ecumenical context should not only be restricted to the central issues that are shared with other churches, but should also include a reflection on what is Lutheran in a more specific sense. The question is not only how Church of Norway is different from other churches, but also how it can contribute to the community of churches through its specific experiences and insights.

At the same time ecumenical recognition and cooperation also represent impulses to change. None of the ecumenical agreements signed by Church of Norway implies any direct demands for changes in church order or practice. This does not mean, however, that the agreements have been without such effects. In particular, the Porvoo Agreement has been an important impetus for certain questions, particularly to the extent that some have been talking about a "Porvoofication" of Church of Norway. The influence from Porvoo has to some extent contributed to a strengthening of the position of the bishops. For example, cathedral deans were no longer allowed to ordain pastors in the absence of the bishops, instead another bishop (even a retired one) has to be summoned for this purpose. The background for this is the clause in the Porvoo Agreement that calls for welcoming "persons episcopally ordained" to serve in each other's churches.[30] Another question that has been discussed with reference to Porvoo is the theological understanding of the diaconate and the service of the deacon. In this discussion some have argued that the service of the deacon should be understood as part of a threefold ministry (bishop-priest-deacon), inspired by the Anglican model. Others see this as difficult to reconcile with a Lutheran understanding of ordained ministry. From a low church perspective the Porvoo Agreement might be understood as an impulse in a high church direction for Norwegian Lutheranism.

At the same time Anglicanism is no uniform entity. As the Porvoo Agreement has opened closer contacts between Lutherans and Anglicans, exchange has increased also with the Evangelical wing, especially within Church of England. Evangelical and Charismatic congregations have been an inspiration for groups in Church of Norway. The same applies to initiatives like "Fresh expressions of church."[31] Whether the Porvoo Agreement

30. "The Porvoo Common Statement," par. 58 (b, v).
31. Hanssen, "Kirke i en ny tid?"

leads to a more high church or low church orientation in Church of Norway remains an open question.

New Challenges

Discussions of the confessional identity of a church often tend to be focused on the past, over how the past should be interpreted and managed in today's situation. An important question has been whether old condemnations and divisions are still valid, or whether they can be overcome. In a changing world confessional identity is increasingly also becoming a question of how to manage present and future challenges. One major challenge that has the potential to change the self-understanding of Church of Norway is immigration. A substantial proportion of the immigrants to Norway from non-Western countries have Christian backgrounds from their home countries. Even if there are some Lutherans among them, from countries like Ethiopia and Eritrea, most of them belong to other denominations. In this situation Church of Norway is challenged to cooperate with immigrant churches (including the Roman Catholic Church) and to integrate immigrants into its own congregations. A question that arises is whether Church of Norway is a church only for Christians with a Lutheran background. Another question is whether the old understanding of Lutheranism as something inherently Norwegian has to be challenged. To be a folk church in this new situation should not be limited to being church for ethnic Norwegians only, but to be a witness of the gospel for persons of different backgrounds.

Bibliography

Aarflot, Andreas. *Norsk kirke i tusen år*. Oslo: Universitetsforlaget, 1978.
"Agreement between Reformation Churches in Europe (The Leuenberg Agreement)." 1973. Online: http://www.leuenberg.net/daten/Image/Konkordie-en.pdf (accessed 11/11/2010).
"Den norske kirkes identitet og oppdrag." Online: http://www.kirken.no/?event= doLink&famID=3197 (accessed 11/11/2010).
Dietrich, Stephanie, Trond Skard Dokka, and Harald Hegstad, editors. *Kirke nå: Den norske kirke som evangelisk-luthersk kirke*. Trondheim: Tapir, 2011.
Gervin, Karl. *Det store bruddet: Reformasjonen i Norge*. Oslo: Andresen and Butenschøn, 1999.
Hanssen, Ove Conrad. "Kirke i en ny tid?: Utfordringer fra 'emerging churches' og 'fresh expressions of church.'" *Halvårsskrift for praktisk teologi* 24/2 (2007) 3–13.

PART FOUR: Exploring a Heritage—Lutheran Identity

Hegstad, Harald. "Den lavkirkelige vekkelsesbevegelse i Norge." In *Nordiske folkekirker i opbrud:National identitet og international nyorientering efter 1945*, edited by Jens Holger Schjørring, 258-68. Århus: Aarhus Universitetsforlaget, 2001.

———. "Fra konfesjonalisme til differensiert konsensus: Refleksjoner om luthersk teologi i en økumenisk kontekst." In *Kirkens bekjennelse i historisk og aktuelt perspektiv: Festskrift til Kjell Olav Sannes*, edited by Lars Østnor, Torleiv Austad, and Tormod Engelsviken, 199-209. Trondheim: Tapir akademisk, 2010.

———. *Kirke i forandring: Fellesskap, tilhørighet og mangfold i Den norske kirke*. Oslo: Luther, 1999.

———. *Transcendens og inkarnasjon: Troserkjennelsens problem i Leiv Aalens teologi*. Oslo: Solum, 1993.

"Joint Declaration on the Doctrine of Justification." 1997. Online: http://www.lutheranworld.org/LWF_Documents/EN/JDDJ_99-jd97e.pdf (accessed 11/11/2010).

Kolb, Robert and Timothy J. Wengert, editors. *The Book of Concord: The confessions of the Evangelical Lutheran Church*. Minneapolis: Fortress, 2000.

Kong Christian Den Femtis Norske Lov. 1687. Online: http://lovdata.no/all/hl-16870415-000.html (accessed 11/11/2010).

Kongeriget Norges Grundlov. 1814. Online: http://lovdata.no/all/nl-18140517-000.html (accessed 11/11/2010).

Lov om Den norske kirke. 1996. Online: http://lovdata.no/all/hl-19960607-031.html (accessed 11/11/2010).

Meyer, Harding. *That All May Be One: Perceptions and Models of Ecumenicity*. Grand Rapids: Eerdmans, 1999.

Myhre-Nielsen, Dag. *En hellig og ganske alminnelig kirke: Teologiske aspekter ved kirkens identitet i samfunnet*. KIFO perspektiv 4. Trondheim: Tapir, 1998.

Nådens fellesskap: Rapport fra samtalen mellom Metodistkirken i Norge og Den norske kirke. 1994. Online: http://www.kirken.no//index.cfm?event=downloadFile&nodeid=5372 (accessed 11/11/2010).

Oftestad, Bernt T. *Den norske statsreligionen: Fra øvrighetskirke til demokratisk statskirke*. Kristiansand: Høyskoleforlaget, 1998.

Oftestad, Bernt T., Jan Schumacher, and Tarald Rasmussen. *Norsk kirkehistorie*. 2nd ed. Oslo: Universitetsforlaget, 1993.

"The Porvoo Common Statement." 1992. Online: http://www.porvoochurches.org/whatis/resources-0201-english.php (accessed 11/11/2010).

"Signatory's Protocol by the Church of Norway on the Signing of The Agreement between Reformation Churches in Europe (Leuenberg Agreement)." 1999. Online: http://kirken.no/english/engelsk.cfm?artid=5895 (accessed 11/11/2010).

Staten og Den norske kirke. St.meld. nr. 17 (2007-2008). Online: http://www.regjeringen.no/pages/2065969/PDFS/STM200720080017000DDDPDFS.pdf (accessed 11/11/2010).

Tveit, Olav Fykse. "Compatibility of Church Agreements." Online: http://kirken.no/english/engelsk.cfm?artid=5897 (accessed 11/11/2010).

Waaler, Gudmund. *Nattverden som offer: En komparativ systematisk analyse av synet på det eukaristiske offer hos Carl Fr. Wisløff, Regin Prenter og Gustaf Aulén*. Dissertation. Oslo: MF Norwegian School of Theology, 2010.

www.ingramcontent.com/pod-product-compliance
Lightning Source LLC
Chambersburg PA
CBHW050617300426
44112CB00012B/1548